Out of Sight

An Art Collector, A Discovery, and Andy Warhol

An Exhibition of Screenprints from the Collection of Gregory McCoy

Goldstein Family Gallery
Kislak Center for Special Collections, Rare Books and Manuscripts

May 19 – July 28, 2022

David McKnight
General Editor

With Contributions by

Hannah Bennett
Kenneth Goldsmith
Maureen McCormick
Gregory McCoy
Reva Wolf

Penn Libraries
University of Pennsylvania
2023

First edition 2023

Published by:

University of Pennsylvania Libraries
3420 Walnut Street
Philadelphia, PA 19104

© 2023 Trustees of the University of Pennsylvania
All rights reserved

ISBN: 978-0-578-53291-2
ISBN: 978-0-578-85091-7

General Editor: David McKnight
Copy Editor: Janice Fisher
Design: Libby Saylor
Photographers: Peter Philbin (Brilliant), Christopher Lippa (Penn Libraries)
Printer: Brilliant, Exton, PA

Printed in the United States of America on acid-free paper.

Cover Image: Detail of AWMM.1968.065 (Plate X, p. 116), two-color screenprint: blue ink on red paper. From the Gregory McCoy Collection. Image used with permission.

Back Cover Image: Detail of AWMM.1968.022 (Plate XXXIX, p. 145), three-color screenprint: metallic gold ink and blue ink on yellow paper. From the Gregory McCoy Collection. Image used with permission.

Frontispiece: AWMM.1968.319 (Plate LXV, p. 172), two-color screenprint: black ink on white paper. From the Gregory McCoy Collection. Image used with permission.

Front Endleaves: Series of assorted McCoy *Marilyns*, arranged in a staggered pattern.

Back Endleaves: Series of assorted McCoy *Marilyns*, arranged in a gridded pattern.

Contents

Part I

Preface | 9
Sean Quimby

Introduction: *Andy Warhol @ Penn Again* | 11
David McKnight

ICA 1965 Revisited | 23
Hannah Bennett

"Filling in Gaps": An Interview with Gregory McCoy | 32
Reva Wolf

Marilyn Mystery | 54
Reva Wolf

Andy Warhol *Marilyn Monroe* Screenprints: A Pedagogical Evaluation | 85
Kenneth Goldsmith

***Out of Sight* Installation Views | 87**

Part II

Notes on an Out of Sight Collection | 93
Maureen McCormick

Catalogue Raisonné of the McCoy *Marilyns* | 105
Including Text Posters and Other Works

Appendix A | 192
Acquisition History and Provenance of the McCoy *Marilyns*

Appendix B: Stories of a Collector | 201
Gregory McCoy

Contributor Biographies | 208

List of Figures and Tables | 210

Permissions | 212

Acknowledgments | 213

"All is pretty."

–Andy Warhol

Part I

Preface

Sean Quimby

As the University of Pennsylvania and the rest of the world continue to open up following a global pandemic, we are reminded of the importance of scholarly pursuits to our institutional identity and cultural events to our humanity. The Penn Libraries is a hub for such activity. With the long-awaited return of on-site activities, our events calendar is filling up with an array of long-delayed programs, like the *Out of Sight: An Art Collector, A Discovery, and Andy Warhol* exhibition of 1960s Marilyn Monroe screenprints.

One of the great pleasures of serving as an associate director of libraries, especially at an institution like the University of Pennsylvania, is that frequently I receive descriptions of unique and compelling research materials. Occasionally, a member of the Penn Libraries curatorial staff will draw to my attention an object that has rarely been seen before. In some cases, the objects are hidden away for years until a family member or a curious collector uncovers them.

The latter is the case with Gregory McCoy. During the past decade, he has assembled a remarkable collection of Marilyn Monroe screenprints that he uncovered in Sweden. McCoy, as I have enjoyed coming to learn, has had a long-standing fascination with Andy Warhol's career and artwork. Since the 1990s, McCoy has acquired a number of Andy Warhol artworks, including a signed dinner roll. (McCoy discusses his Warhol collection in his interview with Reva Wolf elsewhere in this catalogue.) Like Andy Warhol, McCoy is a trained artist who worked in the advertising business in New York City for twenty years.

McCoy acquired his first mystery *Marilyn* screenprint from the Swedish art dealer Börje Bengtsson in 2009. The image of Marilyn in McCoy's possession is based on Warhol's 1962 *Marilyn Monroe in Black and White (Twenty-Five Marilyns)*, which is in the permanent collection of the Moderna Museet, the Swedish contemporary art museum in Stockholm. Intrigued about their origin and possible link to Andy Warhol, McCoy has undertaken extensive research from which he believes that the *Marilyn* screenprints were printed in Sweden in 1968 at the time of Andy Warhol's first international museum exhibition, held in Stockholm.

Since acquiring his first *Marilyn* screenprint in 2009, McCoy has purchased an additional 322 copies of the 1968 *Marilyns*. Warhol created his first iconic screenprint of Marilyn Monroe two weeks after the actor's tragic death on August 5, 1962. Warhol's Marilyn portrait was based on Eugene Korman's publicity photograph that was used on the poster for her feature-length movie *Niagara* (1953). Marilyn Monroe was one of the most photographed actors of her day and has fascinated hundreds of artists ever since. Certainly, Warhol's 1962 screenprint of the actor transformed Monroe into a Pop art icon.

As the title *Out of Sight: An Art Collector, A Discovery, and Andy Warhol* suggests, this is not a simple exhibition. Art historian Reva Wolf has argued that there are many salient factors related to the production of the *Marilyns*; there is as of yet no proof that these were printed with Andy Warhol's knowledge or approval. The *Marilyns* provoke more interesting questions than definitive answers in spite of the quantity of evidence the collector has amassed regarding their authorship. Yet regardless of the uncertainty surrounding the origins of the McCoy *Marilyns*, they are striking and powerful, especially the fluorescent screenprints, which recall the ubiquity of the effects of black light on psychedelic posters that were common in the 1960s.

To some, the McCoy screenprints might be considered period pieces.

Although the origins of the *Marilyns* may be shrouded in mystery, the staff of the Kislak Center, and the Penn Libraries broadly, have risen to the occasion to organize the *Out of Sight* exhibition and publish the beautifully designed catalogue accompanying the exhibition. To complete the exhibition catalogue, the volume editor has included a catalogue raisoneé of the McCoy screenprints, and the University of Pennsylvania Press will distribute it. The exhibition and catalogue are part of a larger Penn Libraries Warhol celebration cleverly entitled *Andy Warhol @ Penn Again*. Complementing the *Marilyns* show will be an exhibition focused on Warhol's seminal 1965 retrospective held at the Institute of Contemporary Art in the former Furness Library and a small exhibition highlighting the career of the actor Marilyn Monroe.

After the official launch of the exhibition on May 19, 2022, the Kislak Center hosted a symposium entitled *Translating Warhol*, on June 23 and 24, during which scholars from around the world discussed the challenges of translating Warhol's written works from English into a variety of roman and non-roman languages. Other events associated with the theme of *Warhol at Penn* include a series of lectures, and films aptly titled Warhol Wednesdays.

I would like to acknowledge the work of the project team, led by David McKnight, Director of the Kislak Center's Rare Book and Manuscript Library; Professor Reva Wolf, Professor of Art History, New Paltz, State University of New York; Brittany Merriam, Director of Exhibits; Sarah Reidell, Margy E. Meyerson Head of Conservation; and Mary Ellen Burd, Director of Strategic Communications. In addition to the core project team, I would like to thank David Nerenberg, Chief Financial Officer and Senior Director for Organizational Effectiveness; Sam Duplessis, Director of Advancement; and Sal Caputo, Director of Facilities Management, all of whom have been integral in providing support for *Out of Sight*.

Finally, I would like to thank Gregory McCoy for his important role in collaborating with Penn Libraries staff to make the *Out of Sight* exhibition and celebration of *Andy Warhol @ Penn Again* an enormous success.

Among the many fascinating pieces in the exhibition are the "text posters" that would have adorned kiosks in Stockholm to advertise the Moderna Museet's Warhol exhibition in 1968. Among the posters is one that reprints Warhol's best-known quip: "In the future everyone will be world famous for fifteen minutes." Thus it was in 1965 when Andy was King of Pop at the ICA and again in 1968 at the Moderna Museet. Penn has stretched the fifteen minutes into a three-month exhibition, and to quote the artist, "All is Pretty." If I may add, mysteriously so.

Introduction: *Andy Warhol @ Penn Again*

David McKnight

Out of Sight: An Art Collector, A Discovery, and Andy Warhol is an exhibition of late sixties Marilyn Monroe screenprints created in Malmö, Sweden, at the time of Warhol's first international exhibition at the Moderna Museet in Stockholm and now exhibited for the first time anywhere since their production. At the University of Pennsylvania, interest in Warhol dates to his historic exhibition that was on view at the ICA in Philadelphia in 1965. The *Out of Sight* exhibition focuses on his first international retrospective held in Stockholm in 1968. The newly discovered Swedish *Marilyn* screenprints serve as a case study in which Penn faculty, students, and the public can engage with these unique screenprints to understand their design, production, curation, aesthetics, copyright, and authorship, and the wiles of the art market.

"All is pretty."

–Andy Warhol

On October 7, 1965, an estimated 2,000 University of Pennsylvania students gathered in the historic Horace Howard Furness Library, anticipating the arrival of Andy Warhol and his entourage, which included his Silver Factory acolytes Edie Sedgwick, Gerard Malanga, and Chuck Guiliano, among others.[1] The occasion was Warhol's first institutional retrospective exhibition, organized by Sam Adams Green (1940–2011), the recently hired Pop art–savvy director of Penn's Institute of Contemporary Art (ICA). Founded in 1962, the ICA was a new cultural venture conceived by Professor G. Holmes Perkins (1904–2004), the distinguished dean of the University's School of Design. Holmes believed that Penn students, as part of their college education, should be exposed to contemporary trends in art.[2]

One witness described the scene as Beatles-like, with Warhol mobbed by his sobbing, screaming fans.[3] The comparison with the Beatles is apt. Although Warhol was a decade older than the members of the Liverpool group, their careers were on a parallel track from 1962 to universal stardom by the end of the decade. As one recent commentator observed, "It was the Beatles' admixture of pop and art, commerce and experiment, which now seems to prefigure so much of mass culture to come."[4] The same might be true of Warhol's enduring impact on today's networked-soaked world of social media. In spite of the large crowds that attended the preview, and to many of the gatherers' dismay, Warhol and company arrived over two hours late for the much-anticipated exhibition preview, which included an invitation-only VIP cocktail party.

ICA director Sam Green was so concerned about the size of the crowd inside the gallery that he had had many of the artworks removed from the walls for fear they might be damaged. Expecting several hundred students at the preview, Warhol was delighted with the large turnout, and the mob seemingly crowned Warhol the "King of Pop Art" on this wet October evening. The Warhol ICA exhibition is legendary and has led to Warhol's celebrated place in the cultural history of Penn and the ICA.[5]

The interior of the famous Frank Furness building has long since been restored, mostly, to its former grandeur as Penn's Art and Architecture Library. The full extent of the decorative late 19th-century railing is obscured by a painted drywall ceiling. However, one can still observe traces of the iron wrought stair landing from which Andy and Edie escaped the swarming crowd through a hole, chopped in the ceiling by Philadelphia firefighters, and then scrambled down a fire escape. Upon Warhol's return to New York City after the event, the ICA exhibition was declared a great success. Since that first show, the ICA has held several Warhol exhibitions and celebrations. Fifty-seven years later, Warhol returns to Penn in the guise of a new exhibition showcasing a group of mysterious Marilyn Monroe screenprints attributed to him and a rearview mirror exhibition of the 1965 ICA show, the publication of a comprehensive catalogue documenting the newly discovered screenprints, and other celebratory public lectures under the banner of *Andy Warhol @ Penn Again*.

Of the three exhibitions organized by the staff of the Kislak Center, the main event is the exhibition of 18 never-before-seen Marilyn Monroe screenprints inspired by Andy Warhol's 1963 *Marilyn Monroe in Black and White (Twenty-Five Marilyns)*, a large painting in the permanent collection of the Moderna Museet in Stockholm. Out of sight for five decades, the new screenprints were unearthed by Börje Bengtsson, a Swedish rare book and art dealer who sold his first copy of the previously unknown *Marilyns* to Gregory McCoy in 2009. An enthusiastic, deeply committed Warhol collector, McCoy might be described, in the case of the *Marilyn* screenprints, as obsessive. But this quality is surely one of the characteristics of a true collector.[6] To date, McCoy has acquired 323 examples (or "impressions") of the undated[7] *Marilyns*, representing 73 different ink and paper color combinations. The Kislak exhibition is dedicated to unveiling for the first time anywhere a selection of the *Marilyn* screenprints.

Out of Sight: An Art Collector, A Discovery, and Andy Warhol features the newly discovered "Warhol" *Marilyns* that were printed, it is believed, at the time of Warhol's first international retrospective held at the Moderna Museet in February and March 1968 in Stockholm.[8] Indeed, the legacy of the Stockholm exhibition endures. In 2018, the Museet commemorated the 50th anniversary of the Warhol exhibition with a retrospective exhibition and catalogue.[9] In addition to the screenprints, McCoy has acquired an equally impressive number of related exhibition objects and ephemera.[10]

But I return to the collector. I was introduced to McCoy in the fall of 2016. In search of an exhibition venue, he was eager to meet me and show me samples of the mysterious Marilyn Monroe screenprints, carefully removing them from a large poster tube at

Kelly Writers House, the undergraduate creative writing center on the Penn campus. Once they were unfurled, I was overwhelmed with their multicolored brilliance. Immediately, I peppered the collector with questions: What are these? When and where were they printed? Who owned these copies of the screenprints? Who is the artist? Warhol? After my initial reactions and reflections, it was obvious that the screenprints were either by Andy Warhol or inspired by the artist's iconic 1962 portrait of the movie star, or possibly fakes. As I would soon learn, McCoy has devoted almost a decade and considerable resources to solve the riddle of this mysterious collection of Marilyn Monroe screenprints. The mystery remains unsolved.

At the same time as I met Gregory McCoy, I was introduced to art historian Reva Wolf and poet Kenneth Goldsmith. They had been contracted by Eric Allan Weinstein, a Penn lecturer, to evaluate the unknown *Marilyns* on behalf of the collector. Their reports were shared with the collector, and I reviewed the documents as well.[11] The screenprints were stored in an art storage facility in Philadelphia. Wolf and Goldsmith are experts on Pop art, and both have written extensively on Andy Warhol. In 2010, Goldsmith organized a year-long undergraduate seminar focused on the 1965 ICA exhibition.[12]

After Wolf and Goldsmith had analyzed the Swedish *Marilyns*, McCoy asked me whether the University of Pennsylvania might be interested in mounting an exhibition of them. Authorship aside, Wolf and Goldsmith produced encouraging reports on the cultural significance and pedagogical value of the *Marilyns*: as objects for the study of Warhol's art production techniques, aesthetic, and overall artistic value. With their reports in hand, I felt encouraged to pursue the possibility of Penn Libraries hosting an exhibition of the McCoy collection.

After several exploratory conversations with the staff of various Penn arts organizations, including the Institute of Contemporary Art, I proposed that the Penn Libraries take on the exhibit on of the McCoy screenprints and with their collaboration contribute to the broader programming objectives related to the exhibition. Circumstances did not permit the ICA to become involved in the project, and other Penn groups' interest faded. COVID-19 has derailed the project for over two years. The McCoy *Out of Sight* exhibition is wholly the responsibility of the Kislak Center for Special Collections, Rare Books and Manuscripts, and I am indebted to Constantia Constantinou, the H. Carton Rogers III Director of Libraries, for her continued support for this exhibition project.

In August 2017, William Noel, then the director of the Kislak Center, and I met Gregory for a productive discussion in Princeton, New Jersey. At that meeting, we expressed our interest in mounting an ambitious exhibition of the *Marilyns* in the Penn Libraries' Goldstein Family Gallery. The date of the exhibition was set for the last quarter of 2020. (Because of the COVID-19 outbreak, the exhibition was postponed and rescheduled for May 19 to July 28, 2022.)

Why Penn? Gregory McCoy is not an alumnus of the University of Pennsylvania. During our many exhibition planning meetings, McCoy often mentioned that Warhol was born in Pittsburgh, was celebrated at the 1965 ICA exhibition, and frequently visited Philadelphia; but most importantly for McCoy, he feels indebted to Penn Medicine for saving his father's life in the early 1990s.[13] Given the number of *Marilyn* prints and the enigma of their origins, it seemed from an institutional perspective to be a wonderful opportunity for the Penn Libraries to serve as a laboratory for scrutinizing these recently uncovered screenprints in an academic library exhibition setting. Furthermore, it was an opportunity to create a dynamic exhibition team that included the collector, scholars, curators, and exhibition designers to organize a probing presentation of the *Marilyn* screenprints.[14]

In the winter of 2018, McCoy and the Library exhibition project team began planning. After some discussion, the project expanded to include a separate retrospective exhibition focused on Warhol's 1965 ICA exhibit and a tribute to the actor Marilyn Monroe. Furthermore, it was my hope to involve Penn's Common Press and the Fine Arts Department to engage undergraduates to create artistic responses to the *Marilyns*; the student reactions were intended to be exhibited in the Van Pelt–Dietrich Library's Kamin Gallery. Because of COVID-19 and the change in the *Out of Sight* dates, the Fisher Fine Arts Library was not available in the spring of 2022. Thus, the Kamin Gallery is now dedicated to celebrating the 1965 ICA Warhol show and the visual legacy of Marilyn

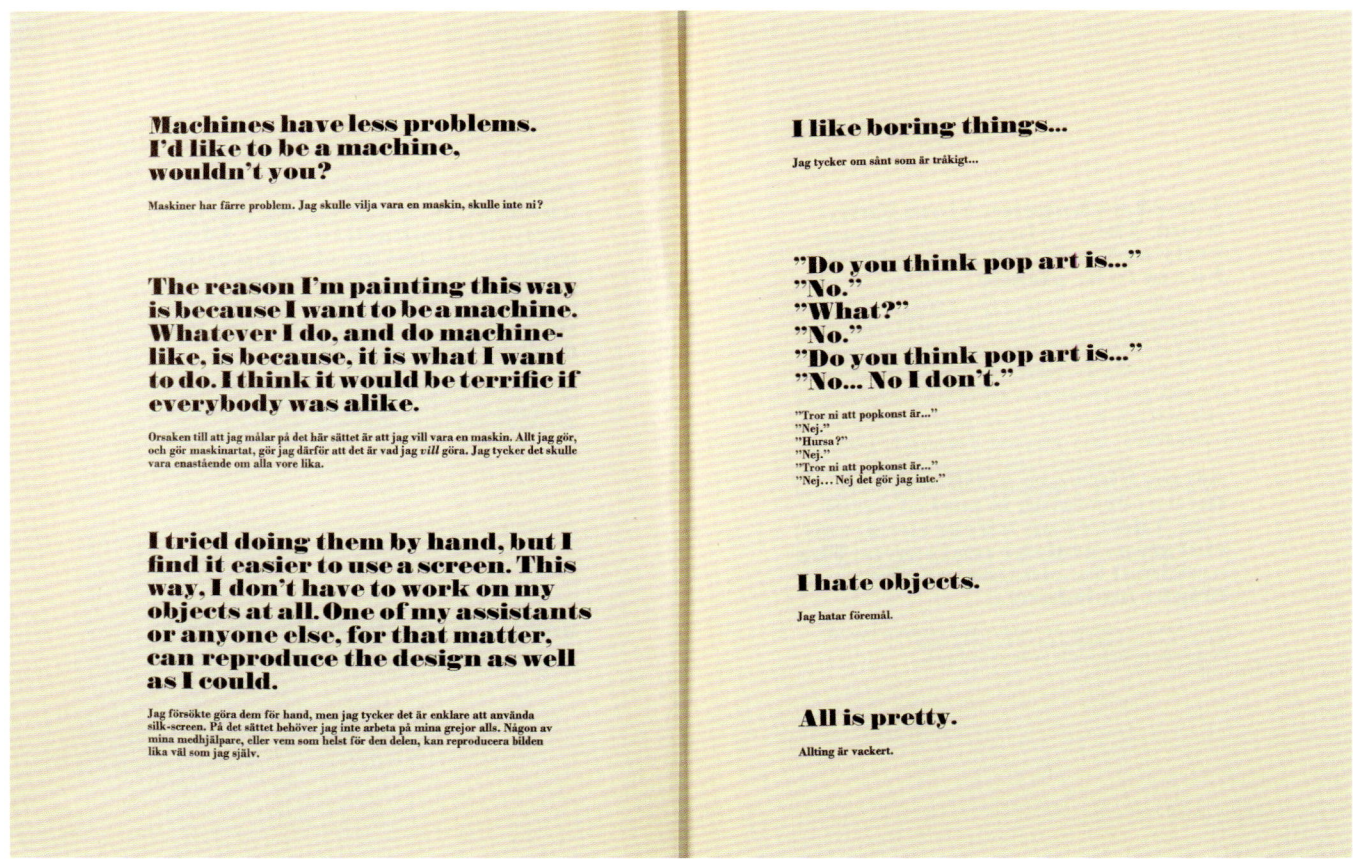

Figure 1.1   Andy Warhol's aphorisms printed in English with Swedish subtitles. Reproduced in the exhibition catalogue (n.p.). Image used with permission.

Monroe. In addition to the exhibitions and the catalogue of record for the *Out of Sight* show, Reva Wolf and I have co-organized a related symposium entitled *Translating Warhol*, the first conference of its kind to examine Andy Warhol's written works in translation, funded in large part by the Terra Foundation.[15] Indeed, the inspiration for the symposium can be traced back to the 1968 Moderna Museet Warhol retrospective. In the front matter of that exhibition's catalogue, Warhol's aphorisms appear in English and are translated into Swedish *(Fig. 1.1)*.

"I never read, I just look at pictures."

–Andy Warhol

Among the first decisions that the project team made was to create a catalogue of record for the exhibition that would document the McCoy *Marilyn* screenprint collection and other objects acquired by the collector related to Warhol's Moderna Museet 1968 exhibition. In your hands is the result of four years of planning, research, and composition. In addition to Hannah Bennett's essay on Warhol's 1965 ICA exhibition,[16] another key editorial decision was the inclusion of a catalogue raisonné of the McCoy collection. Maureen McCormick, former Chief Registrar and Manager of Collections Services at the Princeton University Art Museum, has contributed a technical essay preceding the description of the 73 unique *Marilyn* screenprints and other items in McCoy's 1968 Warhol Moderna Museet collection.

Given the uniqueness of the *Out of Sight* exhibition, it is important to note that the *Marilyns* exhibition might have concluded an important year for the celebration of avant-garde art in Philadelphia during the 1960s. Sid Sachs, chief curator at the University of the Arts, curated an encyclopedic three-venue show entitled

Invisible City: Philadelphia and the Vernacular Avant-Garde—short-lived because of COVID-19.[17] The Philadelphia exhibition that has achieved mythic status and continues to arouse interest is Warhol's 1965 ICA retrospective.[18] Five years ago, independent curator and artist Cheryl Harper curated a fiftieth anniversary show celebrating the appearance of Warhol's *Exploding Plastic Inevitable Happening* that was performed at the Gershman YMHA in Philadelphia in December, 1966.[19]

From a historical perspective, Warhol's 1965 and 1968 retrospective exhibitions fall into the middle of the sixties.[20] On the one hand, in 1965 the United States had declared war against North Vietnam, and the anti-war movement was gaining traction internationally; the use of psychedelic drugs was on the rise; the counterculture was growing in terms of size and reaction against establishment norms. One of the most remarkable aspects of the sixties was an explosion in all the arts. In the field of fine art, Abstract Expressionism, the reigning stylistic paradigm since the forties, was rapidly in decline during the fifties, with new trends emerging in Great Britain, Europe, and the United States: Nouveau Réalisme, Machine art, neo-Dadaism, Conceptual art, and Pop art were all competing for aesthetic dominance during the turbulent, experimental sixties.

In 1967, John Lennon and the Beatles recorded "All You Need Is Love," and a year later Lennon, one of the most iconic cultural figures of the 1960s, posed the question: "You say you want a revolution?" Lennon seemed to suggest, disappointingly, no; but the response from millions of students around the world was yes. Although Warhol was not overtly political, he transformed our concept of what is art and who is an artist. This was enacted and symbolized with the creation of the Factory, a communal model for producing works of art in all mediums. (From 1965 to 1968, Warhol claimed that he had ceased painting, arguing that he had grown bored and had shifted much of his creative energy to live music, photography, filmmaking, and audio recording. But in truth, he painted almost every day of his career.)

In many respects, the ICA and Moderna Museet exhibitions complement one another. The ICA exhibition was the artist's first American retrospective, while the 1968 Moderna Museet show was Warhol's first European institutional show.[21] The Swedish show ran from February 10 through March 17, 1968.

"I like boring things."

–Andy Warhol

In *Popism*, Warhol records that in July 1967[22] he was working on six new large versions of his *Electric Chair* silkscreens intended for his much-anticipated exhibition in Stockholm.[23] The exhibition team consisted of museum director Pontus Hultén, Swedish expatriate Billy Klüver, German-born exhibition curator Kasper König, and Moderna Museet curator Olle Granath.[24] According to Warhol biographer Blake Gopnik, Hultén had first met Warhol in 1959 and had remained in contact with the American artist during the 1960s *(Fig.1.2)*.[25] Hultén did not include Warhol in his 1962 Moderna Museet show of American Pop artists, the first major public show of its kind in Europe, but he did include Warhol in his 1964 survey of American Pop artists.[26]

Pontus Hultén (1924–2006), an artist, philosopher, curator, and museum administrator, was an avant-gardist in spirit and deed. He admired Marcel Duchamp and his aesthetic of disruption and shared both Duchamp's rejection of "retinal art" in favor of art as a concept framed in the mind of the observer and Duchamp's fascination with the machine's role in creating "art." Under Hultén's direction, Sweden and the Moderna Museet emerged during the 1960s as *the* European center for the exhibition of artists associated with the nascent international avant-garde. And, perhaps subversively, Hultén openly welcomed American Pop art to Sweden and Europe in the 1960s.[27]

Unlike many of his contemporaries, Hultén articulated a curatorial vision embracing New Realist/European Pop artists who were rebelling against the Abstract Expressionism wave that had dominated the art world during the post–World II period. Hultén, like expatriate Swede Billy Klüver (1927–2004), embraced American Pop artists at a time when Europeans generally were very critical of the United States from both a political and cultural perspective. Throughout his career, Hultén was and remains a controversial figure.[28]

Like the Penn ICA show, the Moderna Museet's theme was repetition. The exterior of the museum was adorned with *Cow Wallpaper* screenprints *(Fig. 1.3)*. On view in the gallery were ten large *Flowers* paintings, twelve large *Electric Chairs*, and twenty *Marilyn Monroe* screenprints.[29] It was too expensive to ship the silver pillows that were intended to be filled with helium and float freely in the gallery. Instead, König substituted the original helium *Clouds* with large plastic bags filled with oxygen that sat obliquely on the museum's floor.[30]

Included in the exhibition were 500 Brillo boxes. At the same time as Warhol was preparing the large *Electric Chair* screenprints during the summer of 1967, Kasper König, the curator of the Warhol show, ordered 500 unfolded Brillo boxes from the Brillo Company because it was too expensive to ship Warhol's wooden originals. Once the pallet of flattened boxes arrived, König and another museum employee spent several days making the boxes for the Warhol installation. Was this expediency or a joke?

Excerpts from Warhol's films were intended to be projected onto the museum walls, but the Warhol films *Eat, Sleep,* and *Bike Boy* were never shipped. König found an out-of-copyright film of a circus troupe in performance, and a loop was projected onto large screens attached to the gallery's walls. There was a small cinema in which Warhol's film *Chelsea Girls* was screened twice a week. (A set of small steps led up to the cinema, and a small number of framed *Marilyn* screenprints decorated the hallway. It is difficult to determine if these were in fact copies of the screenprints later acquired by Gregory McCoy.)

Perhaps Hulten's most radical decision was to produce a book of still photographs depicting life in Warhol's Silver Factory, rather than create a traditional exhibition catalogue. Instead, Hultén asked Olle Granath to oversee the production of the book conceived as an extension of the exhibition. The book featured over 450 photographs taken by Warhol's assistant Billy Linich (aka Billy Name) and Factory acolyte Stephen Eric Shore. Through the lens of the camera, the volume provided a monochrome glimpse into life at the Silver Factory. Selling for one dollar, the first edition was inexpensively printed on newsprint in an edition of 100,000. *(Fig. 4.17)*. Hultén had promised Warhol that he would produce a deluxe edition of the book, which he did in 1969. One hundred copies were printed and bound in a Plexiglas slipcase, but Warhol did not sign them until seven years later.[31] The catalogue appeared in three editions, and a total of 200,000 copies were printed.

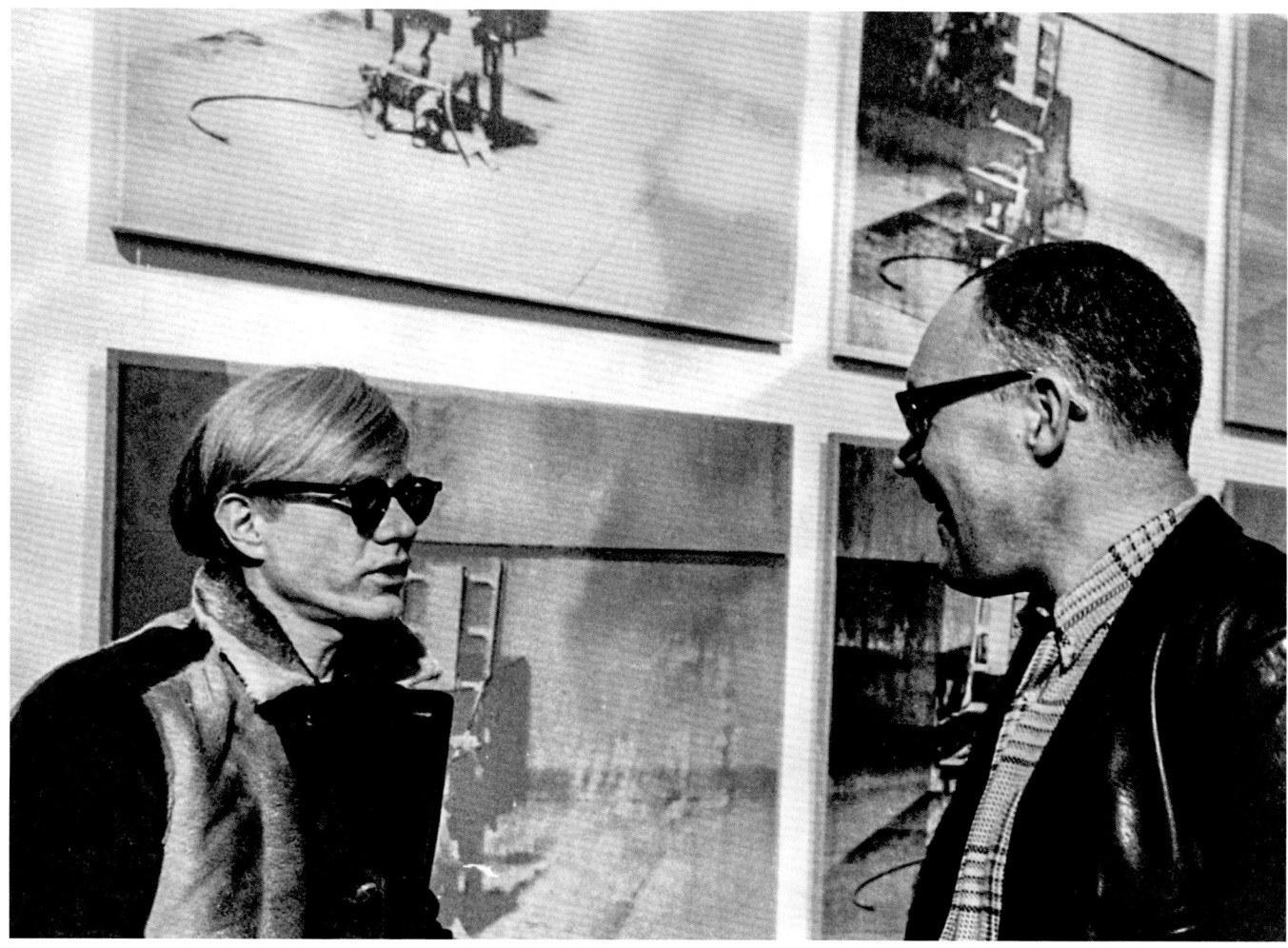

Figure 1.2   Andy Warhol and Pontus Hultén in the Moderna
Museet, 1968. Source: Moderna Museet. Image used
with permission from the Moderna Museet.

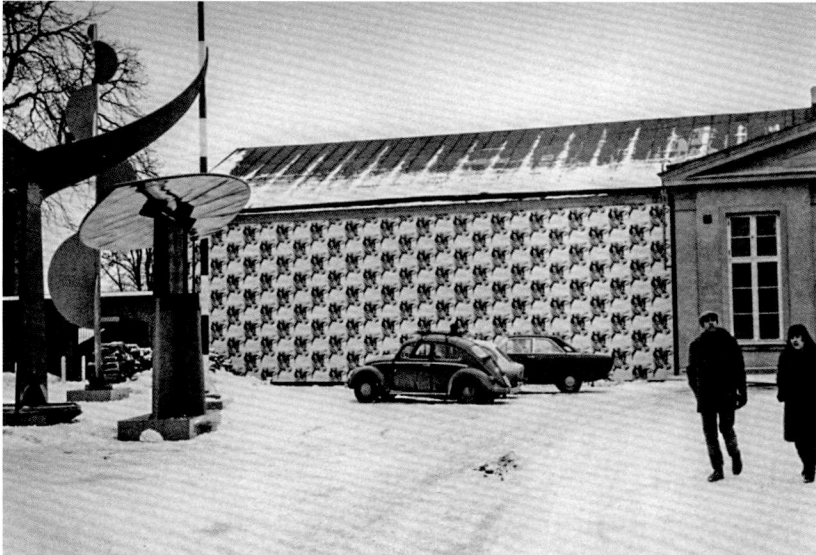

Figure 1.3   Photograph of the exterior of the Moderna Museet
covered in *Cow Wallpaper*. Source: Moderna
Museet, 1968. Image used with permission from the
Moderna Museet.

As for the exhibition poster, it appears that the image of Warhol's portrait of Marilyn Monroe was a possible candidate. (In her essay in this volume, Professor Reva Wolf examines in detail the question of whether the *Marilyn* screenprints are in fact posters, and she discusses the poster fetish of the 1960s at length.) However, to save money, it was decided to produce large promotional text posters on inexpensive paper. Each poster featured a short quip by Andy Warhol, including this: "In the future, everyone will be world-famous for 15 minutes."[32]

According to art critic Willem de Rooij, the Warhol exhibit was poorly attended; 1968 was one of the coldest Swedish winters on record.[33] Anti-American sentiments in Europe and elsewhere were intense and violent, in part because of the Vietnam War, the rise of the counterculture, student uprisings, and the explosion of Marxist-Leninist political views and violent reactions to the old-world order, as European countries abandoned their colonial possessions in the face of violent revolutions. Welcome to the post-colonial world! Still, Warhol was the most recognizable name in the American Pop art world. On June 3, three months after his European triumph, Warhol was lying in a New York hospital bed in critical condition after being shot by his nemesis Valerie Solanas.

Without doubt, the *Out of Sight* exhibition will cause a great stir in the art world and within the Andy Warhol universe, which is riddled with periodic controversy—for example, the recent brouhaha over Warhol's use of Lynn Goldsmith's photograph of Prince for the artist's screenprint portrait of the musician.[34] Warhol faced similar copyright infringement cases in the 1960s including, famously, Eugene Korman's suit against Warhol for his use of his 1952 publicity photograph he took of Marilyn Monroe that adorned the 1953 *Niagara* movie poster and served as the source for Warhol's 1962 portrait of the actor.[35] In the case of the Malmö *Marilyns*, doubt remains as to who is responsible for the production of the 323 *Marilyns*. The evidence suggests that the posters were printed by master printer Arne Wahlqvist at Reklamteknik Screen Printing, a business that operated in Malmö, Sweden (it is now defunct). According to one source, all the Warhol-related materials for the 1968 exhibition were printed in Malmö.[36]

But in the case of Andy Warhol, authorship and authenticity are confounding terms, dependent upon an understanding of the role of the fine art market and the factors that come into play in ascertaining the monetary value of an art object—which, until recently, were dependent upon a fixed notion of what is art and the behavior of the art market. It is not a coincidence that the fine art market exploded in the 1960s in part because of the rise of the Pop art movement itself during the decade and, at the same time, Warhol's own contempt for the art market (although entrepreneurial, he always emphasized the need to earn money to run his various enterprises). With the dissolution of the Andy Warhol Authentication Board in 2011, controversies aside, the basic question of what is an authentic Andy Warhol work, signed or unsigned, seems moot. It is the "concept," not the image itself that expresses the artwork's value and it transcends the social/economic construct of its perceived value, especially given the history of fakes and forgeries that co-exist in the world of Warhol's art. Most famous are the production in the early seventies of the "Sunday B. Morning" *Marilyns* that flooded the art market and in their own way are inexpensive and collectible.

As for the McCoy *Marilyns*, it may be the case that future researchers can prove beyond reasonable doubt that Warhol was aware of the run (or not) of the 1968 Malmö *Marilyn* screenprints. Consider Warhol's views on the antiquated notion of the "artist" in a 1963 interview in which he stated, about his use of the silkscreen print technique, that

> I think somebody should be able to do all my paintings for me. I haven't been able to make every image clear and simple and the same as the first one. I think it would be so great if more people took up silk screens *so that no one would know whether my picture was mine or somebody else's* (emphasis added).[37]

Warhol's statement may be cheeky. He was at the beginning of his career as a Pop artist, and he is uttering his classic "I am a machine" authorial pronouncement; a decade later he was obsessed with making money yet he turned out screenprint celebrity portraits in an industrial fashion, ironically. Like Duchamp and Hultén, Warhol was fascinated by the role of the machine in the production of works of art. Sixty years later, Warhol would be delighted, no doubt, with recent developments in the field of robotic art.[38] His dream of machine dominance in the production of artworks masked by anonymity and neutrality has arrived. Does the appearance of artificial intelligence and robotics signal the end of art and death of the artist, akin to Roland Barthes' pronouncement of the death of the author? Perhaps, as we marvel at robotically produced works of "art."

To my mind, Warhol's wish to remain anonymous reveals much of the story of the production of the McCoy *Marilyns*. Thus, the central thesis of the Penn exhibition returns to three W's: why, when, who? The *Out of Sight* exhibition should be viewed as an intellectual/aesthetic project that will present McCoy's vivid and unique screenprints of Marilyn Monroe to a captivated audience who will examine the prints in the context of the 1968 Moderna Museet exhibition, and it will provide the evidence enabling the viewers to draw their own conclusions regarding the question of who produced them and their meaning and value today.

In his effort to document the origins, provenance, and production of the McCoy *Marilyns*, the collector has created a meticulous archive[39] of technical data, correspondence, and other documents that he has assembled in his efforts to

a) date the printing of the *Marilyns*;
b) determine who designed and printed the screenprints;
c) determine where they were printed;
d) if possible, determine Andy Warhol's involvement in their production; and
e) identify and document the provenance of the 323 screenprints.

In the case of these 1968 *Marilyns*, it is the nagging, conventional question of authorship upon which we seem to stumble in the hope of resolution. In many respects, Warhol and the other exponents of Pop art exploded the myth of the original artist and the idea of the original work of art, and yet, paradoxically, we admire Warhol for his genius. The epistemological question of what a copy is and who is the artist seems moot when you stare at a framed soup can or Brillo box. Famously and notoriously as noted earlier, in 1968, the curator of the Warhol Moderna Museet show decided it was cheaper to order 500 Brillo boxes from the Brillo factory in the United States rather than ship Warhol's originals to Stockholm. For the curator, the sleight of hand was a brilliant joke on the intelligence of the audience who admired the 500 Brillo factory-made boxes presuming they were the Warhol "originals."[40]

Nevertheless, in retrospect the juxtaposition of the original Brillo box presented as a Warhol work of art works conceptually, but it invites the question of whether the viewer can interpret and judge the Brillo box as a "work of art" attributed to an artist with an audience in mind. Perhaps it's the concept, not the work itself, that creates value and meaning in the eye of the beholder.[41] With the *Marilyns*, admittedly, we celebrate McCoy's discovery, and we are confronted with the nagging questions regarding their origins.

As I have delved deeper into the history of the Warhol 1968 Moderna Museet exhibition, as I have learned more about Pontus Hultén, and as I consider and weigh the evidence, I see the production of the Malmö *Marilyns* in the context of the collaborative ethos of the sixties, partially exemplified by Warhol himself, the Silver Factory, and Hultén's curatorial Duchampian vision, and, most importantly, the subversive nature of Pop art itself.

Ultimately, *Andy Warhol @ Penn Again* is a tribute to the importance of the archive in multiple senses. Thankfully, the ICA has been very diligent in retaining all of their exhibition files for almost sixty years.[42] The archive is housed in the Kislak Center for Special Collections and accessible to the public. Other Penn archives, for example the Architectural Archives and the University Archives, have relevant documents and photographs documenting the 1965 Warhol show. For their part, the Moderna Museet is very active in documenting and celebrating its defining role as the leader in promoting the avant-garde during the 1960s. What has not survived, unfortunately, are the business records of Reklamteknik, the Malmö screenprinting business where the *Marilyns* were printed.

Considering the potential controversy surrounding the McCoy *Marilyns*, the purpose of the *Out of Sight* exhibition is and remains a challenging case study focused on the production of "art" in the age of mechanical reproduction, a concept that has endured since Walter Benjamin published his seminal essay seventy years ago. What better place than the University of Pennsylvania to scrutinize and question the origins and and materiality of the McCoy Marilyn Monroe posters.

As Professor Reva Wolf notes in her essay in this volume, "Whatever the origin and status of the intriguing McCoy collection of *Marilyn* works, it is hoped that bringing them to light, exhibiting them, and laying out the available information will lead to further study so that their story can be fully told." With the launch of the *Out of Sight* exhibition, and with this catalogue in hand, the collector and the curatorial team are providing Warhol admirers with an opportunity to acknowledge McCoy's discovery and engage in solving the mystery of the *Marilyns* for posterity's sake.

1. Victor Bockris, *The Life and Death of Andy Warhol* (New York: Bantam Books, 1989), 176. See also Blake Gopnik's recent biography *Warhol* (New York: Ecco Press, 2020), 464.

2. In the early sixties, according to Bill Whitaker, Director of the University of Pennsylvania Architectural Archives, "Perkins had been involved in university-wide discussions about establishing an art museum. Unlike others, he could see that going for a traditional university museum didn't make sense. For one thing, what chance would an institution like that, established in the 1960s, have of catching up with its Ivy League peers? Instead, the forward-thinking Perkins pushed for a contemporary institute that would expose the students to what was 'new and happening' in the art world." Rachel Pastan, "Opening the Box: Holmes Perkins and the Founding of ICA44" (blog), April 30, 2014, https://icaphila.org/miranda_posts/opening-the-box-holmes-perkins-and-the-founding-of-ica/.

3. Bockris, *Life and Death of Andy Warhol*, 176.

4. Ian Penman, "Four Mop Top Yobos," *London Review of Books* 43 (no. 12), June 17, 2021, 3.

5. For more information on the ICA 1965 exhibition, see Hannah Bennett's essay in this volume. With the arrival of Pop art at Penn, the Warhol show inspired both critical contempt and praise.

6. For a recent discussion on collecting art, see Mari Shaw, *Words, Books, and the Spaces They Inhabit: The Noble Art of Collecting, Book One* (Berlin: Sternberg Press, 2017). Marilyn Karp in her In *Flagrante Collecto (Caught in the Art of Collecting)* (New York: Abrams, 2006), writes of collectors, "Sometimes it's personally important and meaningful to compose a collection to which you are able to add consistently" (338). McCoy has been persistent and consistent in his search for the *Marilyn* screenprints.

7. The exact date of the screenprints is unknown, but all the evidence suggests that they were printed in either 1968 or 1969

8. Reva Wolf, in her essay "Marilyn Mystery" in this volume, has suggested that the screenprints might have been printed in 1969.

9. See Berit Jonsvik, *Vernissage 68 Andy Warhol På Museet Stockholm 1968* (Stockholm: Knostepedenim, 2018).

10. McCoy has acquired four copies of the 1968 catalogue/book: the purported proof copy, a trade copy, one of the deluxe editions, and a presentation copy signed by Warhol and dedicated to Olle Granath, the original compiler of the 1968 catalogue. He has also acquired copies of the invitations in English and Swedish, a signed copy of the Andy Warhol SAS airline ticket, and a set of the seven original text posters created to advertise the Warhol retrospective.

11. Weinstein had asked Goldsmith and Wolf to determine whether the McCoy *Marilyns* might make for a worthwhile exhibition at the University of Pennsylvania, accompanied by academic and creative programming, scholarship (ideally in the form of an exhibition catalogue), and course offerings.

12. See Reva Wolf, *Andy Warhol, Poetry and Gossip* (Chicago: University of Chicago Press, 1997); *Andy Warhol: Private and Public in 151 Photographs* (New Paltz, NY: Samuel Dorsky Museum of Art, 2010); Kenneth Goldsmith, ed., *I'll Be Your Mirror: Selected Andy Warhol Interviews* (New York: De Capo Press, 2004).

13. See Reva Wolf's interview with Gregory McCoy in this volume. His father's medical emergency occurred in the early 1990s.

14. In December 2019, three key members of the exhibition team either resigned or retired from Penn Libraries. Happily, their positions were filled.

15. The Terra Foundation in Chicago has provided a significant grant to support the symposium.

16. Hannah Bennett, the former head of Penn's Fisher Fine Arts Library, selected the objects for the Warhol 1965 exhibition. See her essay in this volume.

17. *The Invisible City* exhibition fell victim to the pandemic and was on view for only a matter of weeks. However, Sachs succeeded in publishing the catalogue, and it is highly recommended.

18. Of historical interest, Allan Kaprow's Chicken Happening at the Gershman Y in 1962 anticipates Warhol's Exploding Plastic Inevitable Happening event, which was held in December 1967, two years after Warhol's ICA exhibition.

19. *Underground Nights: When Warhol's Exploding Plastic Inevitable Met the Y*, December 1, 2016–January 4, 2017.

20. In 1966, Warhol was the subject of his second ICA show in Boston.

21. Warhol's first commercial exhibition in Europe was held in Paris in 1964 at the Ileana Sonnabend Gallery, where *Thirteen Most Wanted* silkscreens were on view.

22. Andy Warhol and Pat Hackett, *Popism: The Warhol '60s* (London: Hutchinson, 1981), 217.

23. To reduce costs, Hultén agreed to print the *Electric Chair* screenprints in Sweden.

24. Olle Granath, "With Andy Warhol 1968," Moderna Museet website, https://www.modernamuseet.se/stockholm/en/exhibitions/andy-warhol-other-voices-other-rooms/with-andy-warhol-1968-text-ol/.

25. Gopnik, *Warhol*, 603.

26. Curated by Hultén, the 1962 show was entitled *Four Americans* and was on view from March 17 to May 6. It included the work of Jasper Johns, Alfred Leslie, Robert Rauschenberg, and Richard Stankiewicz. In 1964, Hultén organized his second show on American Pop art: *American Pop Art: 106 Forms of Love and Despair*. Hultén included Warhol in this exhibition; Warhol's films were screened in a follow-up exhibition on new American cinema immediately following the American Pop art exhibition.

27. See Patrik Lars Andersson, "Euro-Pop: The Mechanical Bride Stripped Bare in Stockholm, Even," Ph.D. diss., University of British Columbia, 2001. In 2017, the Moderna Museet published a collection of essays honoring Hultén entitled *Pontus Hultén and Moderna Museet: The Formative Years* (London: Koenig Books, 2017). Andersson contributed an essay to the volume.

28. In her essay on the "Marilyn Mystery" in this volume, Reva Wolf examines Hultén's role in the 1968 Warhol exhibition in more detail.

29. The 12 *Electric Chair* silkscreens were printed at the Museum's expense.

30. There were other challenges in mounting the Warhol show, including the fact that Stockholm had no source for helium gas to fill the silver pillows.

31. Olle Granath recalls that when Warhol visited Stockholm in 1976, the artist agreed to sign the deluxe copies. See also Gopnik (*Warhol*, 147), who notes that Name's photographs were "an extraordinary document of life at the Silver Factory that would be collected for Warhol's first European retrospective. . . "

32. Granath explains that he collated a number of Warhol's utterances and selected seven of what he thought were the most appropriate for the exhibition. While six of the statements are innocuous, the origins of the "fifteen minutes of fame" quote remain the subject of controversy. See Rachel Nuwer, "Andy Warhol Probably Never Said His Celebrated 'Fifteen Minutes of Fame' Line," *The Smithsonian Magazine*, April 8, 2014, https://www.smithsonianmag.com/smart-news/andy-warhol-probably-never-said-his-celebrated-fame-line-180950456/.

33. Willem de Rooij, "On Andy Warhol," https://www.modernamuseet.se/stockholm/en/exhibitions/andy-warhol-other-voices-other-rooms/willem-de-rooij-on-the-andy-wa/.

34. Alex Greenberger, "Court Delivers Blow to Warhol Foundation in Fair Use Appeal Over Prince Portraits," *ARTnews*, March 26, 2021, https://www.artnews.com/art-news/news/andy-warhol-prince-lynn-goldsmith-appeal-decision-1234587961/.

35. Richard Chused, "The Legal Culture of Appropriation Art: The Future of Copyright in the Remix Age," *Tulane Journal of Technology & Intellectual Property* 17 (Fall 2014), 169.

36. Letter from Mattias Swinge to Börge Bengtsson, August 10, 2012. See the discussion by Reva Wolf in this catalogue, p. 60.

37. Goldsmith, *I'll Be Your Mirror*, 17.

38. See Suyin Haynes, "This Robot Artist Just Became the First to Stage a Solo Exhibition. What Does That Say About Creativity?," *Time Magazine*, June 17, 2019, https://time.com/5607191/robot-artist-ai-da-artificial-intelligence-creativity/.

39. Gregory McCoy, "Andy Warhol: Marilyn Monroe Screenprints—Traditional, Reversal and Black Light," white three-ring binder with documents, 2016.

40. In her essay in this volume, Reva Wolf describes the *Marilyns* as interpretations rather than fakes. Interestingly, in February 1968, Warhol, it was revealed, had sent a stand-in for himself on his U.S. college lecture tour, which caused a great scandal. He had considered sending an impersonator to the opening in Stockholm.

41. Notoriously, after the Warhol exhibition closed in March 1968, Hultén instructed a museum carpenter to produce a number of fake Brillo boxes. The unauthorized copies were discovered in 1994.

42. See Institute of Contemporary Art Records, Ms Coll. 777, Kislak Center for Special Collections, Rare Books and Manuscripts, University of Pennsylvania.

ICA 1965 Revisited

Hannah Bennett

Penn Before Warhol

As he did for a number of Philadelphia institutions, with the 1751 founding of the University of Pennsylvania, Benjamin Franklin established a set of guiding principles that would meld traditional liberal arts disciplines with the worlds of business and commerce. Franklin, drawing from his *Proposals for the Education of Youth in Pensilvania*, established a nondenominational curriculum, in stark contrast to that of most other colonial academies, which remained unapologetically sectarian.[1] Innovative subjects and pioneering programs would flow from this unique amalgam of venerable educational values and a modernizing society. We can imagine him approving, at least after some tutoring in twentieth-century mores, the launch of the Institute of Contemporary Art (ICA), in 1963, by G. Holmes Perkins.

Perkins, a professor of architecture at Harvard University, came to Penn in 1951 to serve as Dean of the School of Fine Arts (today's Weitzman School of Design). Whether or not Perkins knew of Franklin's synthetic ambitions for Penn, he worked from the start to adapt the School's traditional approach to architectural practice, based on the model of the École des Beaux-Arts, with tenets of modernism, which embraced new materials and methods of construction and focused on a visibly functionalist formal aesthetic. In this, Perkins was part of a transformational wave of educators and practitioners who, by taking on leadership positions at prominent design programs—Paul Rudolph at Yale University, Jean Labatut at Princeton University, and José Luis Sert at Harvard—effectively institutionalized modernism as the architectural style of the postwar era. His early faculty hires were nothing less than inspired, and included Ian McHarg, a landscape architect and early leader in the

environmental movement; Louis I. Kahn, one of the most original and influential architects of the postwar era; and Robert Venturi, arguably the most important architect and theorist of postmodernism. All shared Perkins's drive to keep design education relevant to the changing world they lived in.

In 1958, Perkins established a graduate program in fine arts, which was the likely spur to his advocacy for a university art museum or gallery. Many of Penn's Ivy League peers housed encyclopedic teaching collections to introduce students to the long history of art. But Perkins wanted something "new and happening," a space that would reflect the rapidly changing world of contemporary art.[2] Consequently, the ICA was established in 1963 as a kunsthalle, an art facility forgoing a permanent collection in favor of a series of varying exhibitions, much like a commercial art gallery. With this mission, the ICA was poised not only to accommodate new directions in art. By fostering novel or even *outré* works, it could also help carve the contours of cutting-edge art. In keeping with its educational mission, it could instill in Penn students a simultaneous respect for artistic methods and an experimental ethos tied to contemporary society. Shades of Benjamin Franklin.

At first glance, the ICA's earliest home was incongruous. One of the most forward-looking new institutions on campus, the ICA was situated in one of the most derided relics of Victorian excess, the former University Library (today the Fisher Fine Arts Library), built in 1893 by the Philadelphia architect Frank Furness. Even the books fled the building, once the modern-styled Van Pelt Library was completed in 1962, designed by the firm of Harbeson, Hough, Livingston & Larson, heirs of the firm of the primary Philadelphia-based proponent of the Beaux Arts style, Paul Philippe Cret, who taught design at Penn for nearly the entire first half of the twentieth century. With the books gone, the Furness Building's central space, today regarded as one of the city's greatest interiors, needed a program to house; the ICA needed a space. No document records whether the irony was appreciated at the time: the ICA, with its future entirely before it, is cradled in a building just then teetering on the brink of demolition. Gimlet-eyed modernists saw it as an embarrassment, possibly even an impediment for students unwittingly muddled by its Victorian vapors, and were pushing it toward oblivion.[3]

In another twist, the Furness Building itself would turn out to be a leading actor in what only in retrospect can be understood as a fledgling movement to restrain modernism's own excesses and trampling, utopian spirit. Denise Scott Brown, who married Venturi and partnered with him both in practice and writings, vigorously protested the building's proposed demise, as early as 1960, years before the destruction of New York City's Pennsylvania Railroad Station would galvanize activists and spark new state legislation that would be validated by the US Supreme Court in 1978. Years later, Venturi acknowledged his admiration for Scott Brown's strong voice and, in hindsight, recoiled at his own reticence on the matter.[4]

Perkins appointed 25-year-old American art curator Samuel Adams Green as the ICA's first director, bringing an inveterate New York art scene sensibility and a curatorial fierceness. Green's presence set the ICA far apart from many contemporaneous, more middle-of-the-road exhibition spaces in Philadelphia, leading one critic to praise the appointment as filling "a long existing void" in the city's art outlook.[5] While in New York working at Richard Bellamy's Green Gallery on 57th Street, Green met Andy Warhol and quickly became both a proponent and a friend. Green was buoyed in his role by an advisory board open to exhibitions of current and vital art. It included the likes of Thomas Baer Hess, who had worked with Alfred Barr at New York's Museum of Modern Art and later went on to become the chief editor of *ARTnews*, and Clement Greenberg, possibly the most important art critic of the postwar period and a champion of Abstract Expressionism, whose reign as a leading style would only be eclipsed by 1960s Pop art figures such as Warhol. The combination of experience and prescience was seen even then as defining an exhibition program to "foster thinking of the visual arts

with respect to the community and to the University."[6] Perhaps most influential of all was the board's chair, Mrs. Horatio Gates Lloyd, Jr., a.k.a. "Lallie," who would work closely with Green to secure Warhol's first retrospective.[7]

The ICA quickly defined itself in relation to the Philadelphia art scene with its inaugural exhibition in 1963, dedicated to Clyfford Still and organized by Ti-Grace Sharpless (a.k.a. Ti-Grace Atkinson). Still was well known at the time as a progenitor of Abstract Expressionism and Color Field painting. But, by his own choice, he had not exhibited for years, only returning to the gallery world a few years before, thus kindling a great deal of interest in the ICA exhibition.[8] Sharpless, who was instrumental in organizing the ICA and would soon become a leading feminist theorist and educator, spent several weeks in Baltimore with the artist, courting and cajoling him to commit to a novel program for the ICA.[9] With Sharpless's steady curatorial vision and Green's leadership, three stimulating exhibitions followed in 1964: *David Smith: Sculptures and Drawings, The Atmosphere of '64,* and *Group Zero.*[10] Given Green's close ties to the Pop art movement and his friendship with Warhol, the idea for a retrospective must surely have occurred to him early in his ICA tenure.

Was the campus ready for such a show? To be sure, Warhol and his contemporaries were touched on in history of art classes and occasional invited lectures, and the spirit of much contemporary art aligned with protest movements in the 1960s that swept college campuses and similarly inveighed against repressive cultural norms and structural racism. But student responses to Pop art in particular were mixed, as documented in the student-run newspaper, *The Daily Pennsylvanian*, and, to some extent, they would remain so even after the retrospective.[11] What is undeniable, however, is that the episodic commentary on art found in the *"DP"* ballooned with the ICA's program and clearly led to further forays into contemporary art, including student-run film screenings and subsequent ICA exhibitions of Warhol's work.

Warhol Comes to Penn

Though not the paramount figure he is today, Warhol was acknowledged as one of the more inventive and

"Pop" Comes to Penn

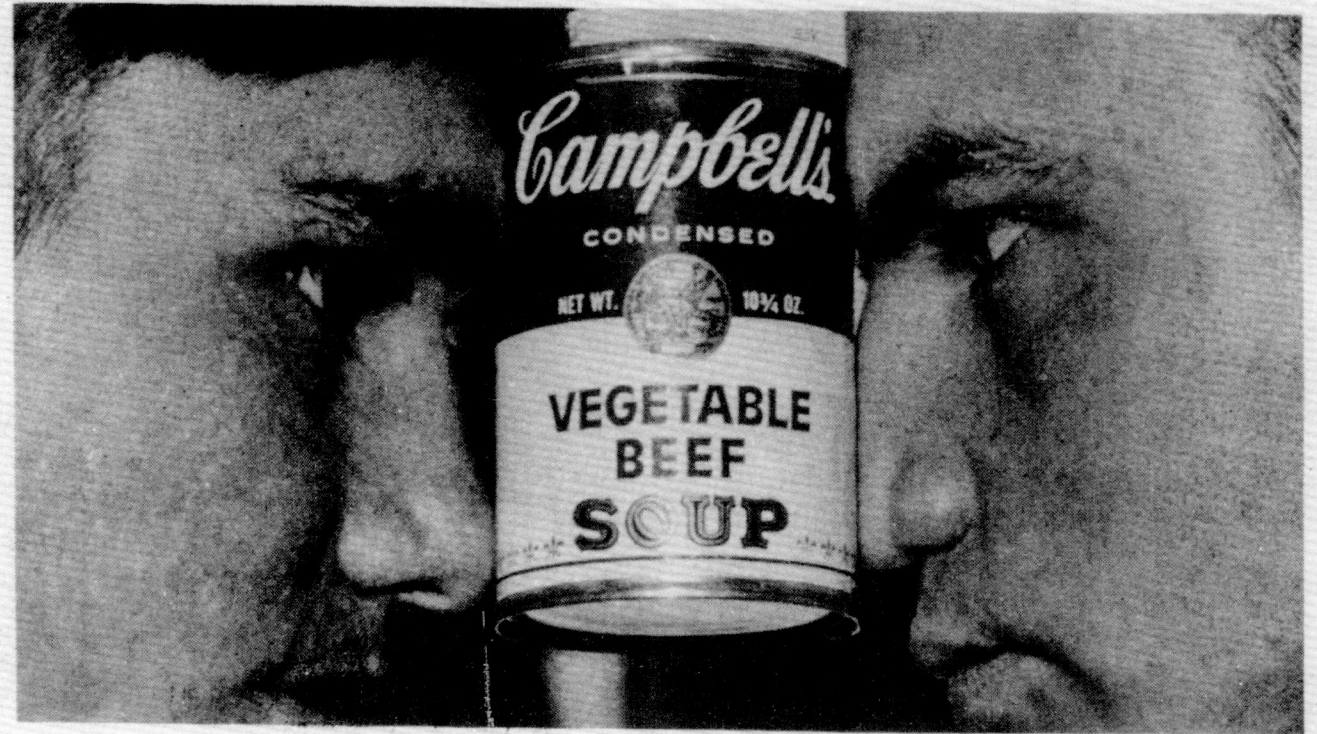

The Daily Pennsylvanian (by Bob Kosiba)

Pop artist Andy Warhol, who immortalizes Brillo soap boxes in paintings on silk screen, will personally open an exhibit of his work tonight at 8:00 at the Institute of Contemporary Art in the Furness Building.

The public opening will "evoke Mr. Warhol's working atmosphere—music, dancing, people, films." The artist's socialite girlfriend, Miss Edith Sedgwick will accompany him.

The exhibit, continuous until Nov. 21, will contain Warhol's series of repeated Campbell soup cans, Marilyn Monroes and Elizabeth Tay-

lors, as well as many sculptural works and paintings not publicly displayed before.

One of the most controversial figures in contemporary art, Warhol generally uses as his subject matter the most vulgar and banal images of American society.

Although he has been exhibiting his work for three and a half years, this is the first museum exhibition of his work.

The institute will be open form 10 a.m. to 5 p.m. on weekdays and from noon to 5 p.m. on Sundays.

Figure 2.1   Penn's student-run *Daily Pennsylvanian* readies campus
                   for Warhol. Courtesy of the *Daily Pennsylvanian*,
                   Volume LXXXI, Number 48, 8 October 1965.
                   University of Pennsylvania Libraries.

even disruptive artists of the time. In the years leading up to the ICA show, his art—Brillo Boxes from 1964; 1965 S&H Green Stamps lithographs; Campbell's Soup Can canvases from 1961 and '62; silkscreen paintings of Marilyn Monroe, starting in 1962, and Jackie Kennedy, from 1964—thrilled the art world then based in New York City, and resonated, or at least was recognizable, around the world. Increasingly, though, and certainly by the mid-1960s, Warhol was discussed as much for his eccentric lifestyle and entourage as for his ground-breaking art.[12] His studio was both a workplace and a party venue, attracting innovators in everything from musical composition to sex working. He called it "The Factory," a reference to his experiments with mechanical processes of art-making and, no doubt, a self-deprecating gesture toward the serial production of cheap goods for commercial society, a fusion that might have given Franklin pause. In a further transgression, so to speak, Warhol announced, during an exhibition of his work at the Sonnabend Gallery in Paris in May 1965, that he was giving up the paintings that established his fame in order to pursue filmmaking.[13] Green, thanks to his close relation with Warhol, possibly knew of Warhol's imminent pivot in terms of medium. Regardless, he arranged for the artist's first retrospective in 1965, which, almost by definition, would center on a stage of Warhol's work that was, at least to the artist, already behind him.

In these circumstances, no venue could have been more appropriate than the Furness Building, with its departed library and echoing main hall. As noted above, though celebrated in its time, it had itself become irrelevant, even ignominious. It was in this way as compromised a venue as would be an exhibition of painting and sculpture by an artist interested in film. Green made it even more of an enigma by costuming the space in the regalia of industrial production, with the floors painted a metallic silver and with clamorous rock music blasting in the background.[14] The building, whose ornament was inspired in part by mechanical imagery, was transformed into a simulacrum of an art-scene social club that was itself modeled on the architectural embodiment of industrialization, the factory.

Green's transformation proved a wild success or, at least, completely wild. As a precaution, Green removed a number of pieces before the opening to the general public, set for October 11 following a special preview on October 8 for members of the ICA, Penn trustees,

etc. It was an astute decision. The flood of advance publicity, including invitations printed up as Campbell's soup can labels and as S&H Green Stamps, guaranteed what Henry Geldzahler, an eminent critic and curator of contemporary art at New York's Metropolitan Museum of Art, as well as a good friend of Warhol's, remembered of the moment as a "peak of media insanity about pop art."[15] At the opening, the space Furness had designed to hold 700 people was crammed with nearly three times that number, most of them students. According to the *Daily Pennsylvanian*, visitors were "packed into the three rooms like the beans in a Campbell soup can. Mostly blank walls, television microphones, blasting stereophonic discotheque music greet the guests."[16]

When Andy arrived with his entourage, including Edie Sedgwick, Chuck Guiliano, and Gerard Malanga, the crowd exploded in a frenzy. Two students had to be rushed to a nearby hospital. Andy, dressed head to toe in black, with yellow-lensed ski glasses and safety pins on the collar of his turtleneck, was overwhelmed by the swaying crowd. As shared with the *Daily Pennsylvanian* reporter, Samuel Green remarked that "Everybody here thought they were going to get killed."[17]

Art curator Walter Hopps had been to other openings of the artist's work, but this one was special:

> That Philadelphia exhibition of Andy's was one of the most bizarre mob scenes I've ever witnessed . . . It was the first survey of all his work. . . It was crazy. It was the first time I saw a young avant-garde artist have a show mobbed as if it were a movie premiere. . . all kinds of people clamoring to get at Andy as if he were a star.[18]

Sam Green remembered it in similar terms:

> Andy was mobbed. We were pretty scared because we arrived late from drinks and thousands were jammed into the museum. It was a mob scene and they were all out for blood. Somehow, once inside we managed to get to an old iron staircase that led up to the ceiling. . . an architectural student was trying to break through the fake ceiling above us so we could get out through the library private stacks, over the roof, and down the fire escape and out where the police could protect us. . . That's how we escaped.[19]

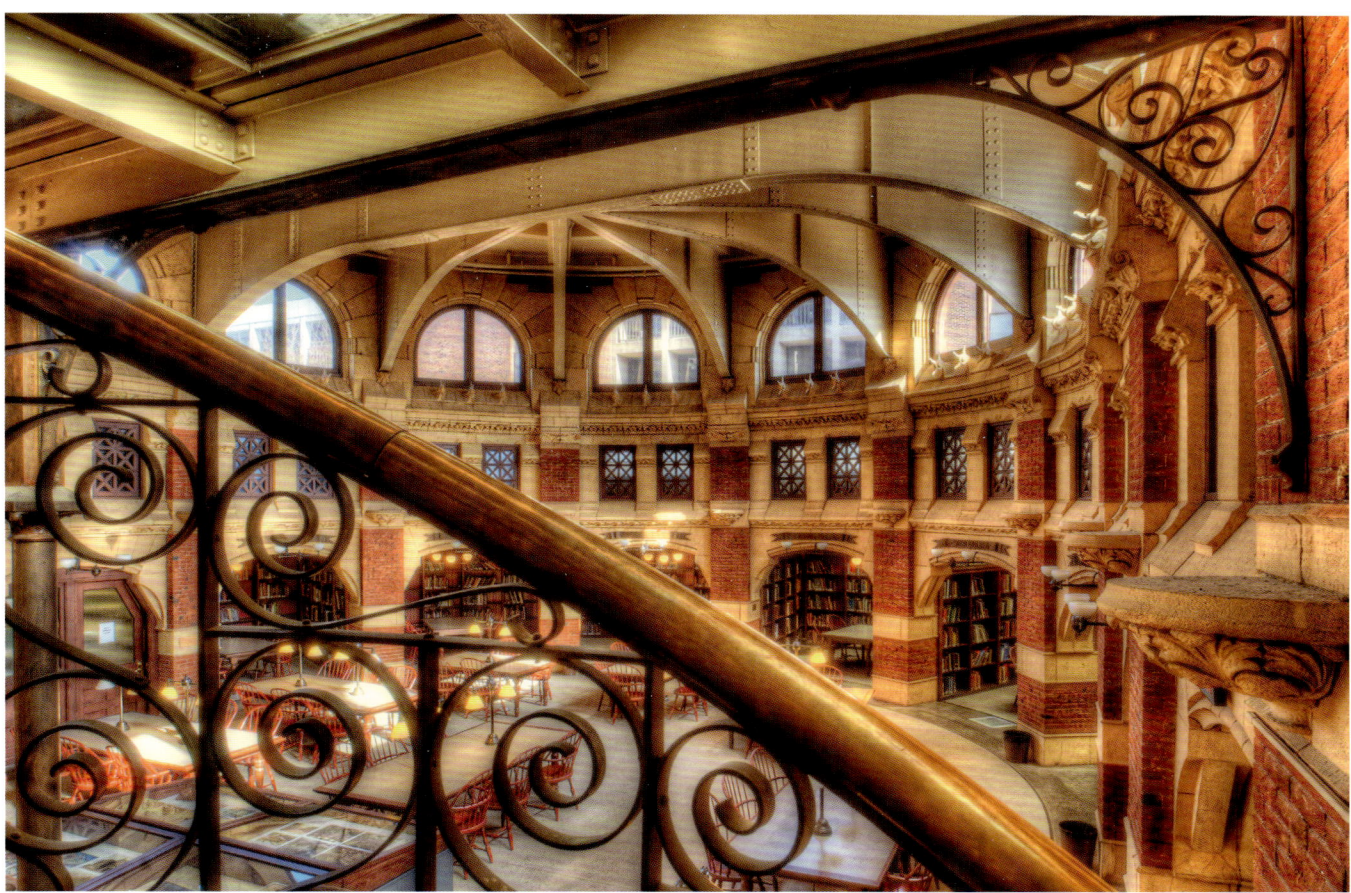

Figure 2.2   Interior of Fisher Fine Arts Library taken in 2010. Courtesy of the University of Pennsylvania.

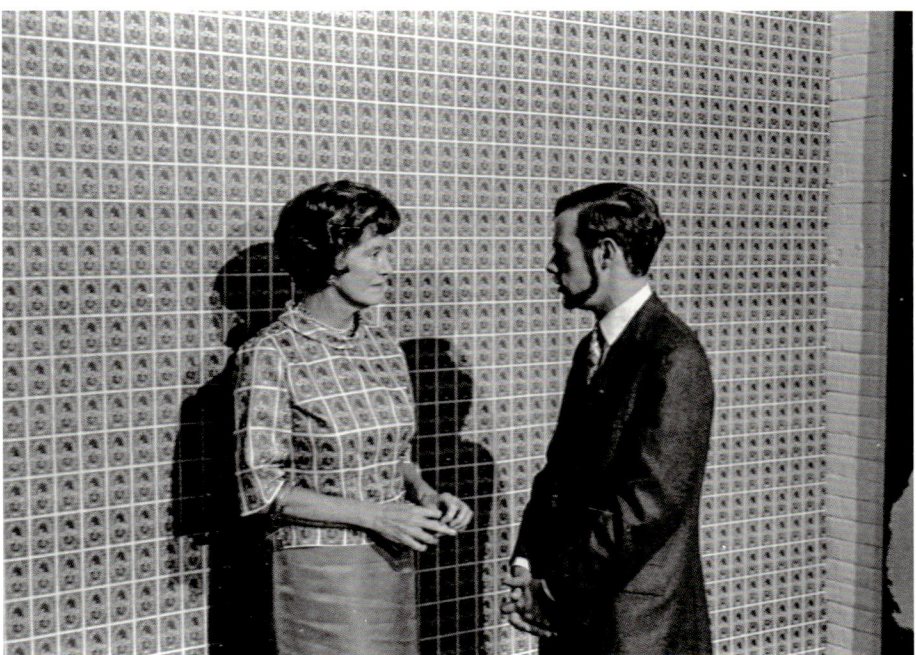

Figure 2.3   Lallie Lloyd adorned in her custom-made S&H Stamps blouse speaking with Samuel Green at the VIP preview on October 8th, 1965. Image courtesy of the Weitzman School of Design's Architectural Archives' George Pohl photography collection.

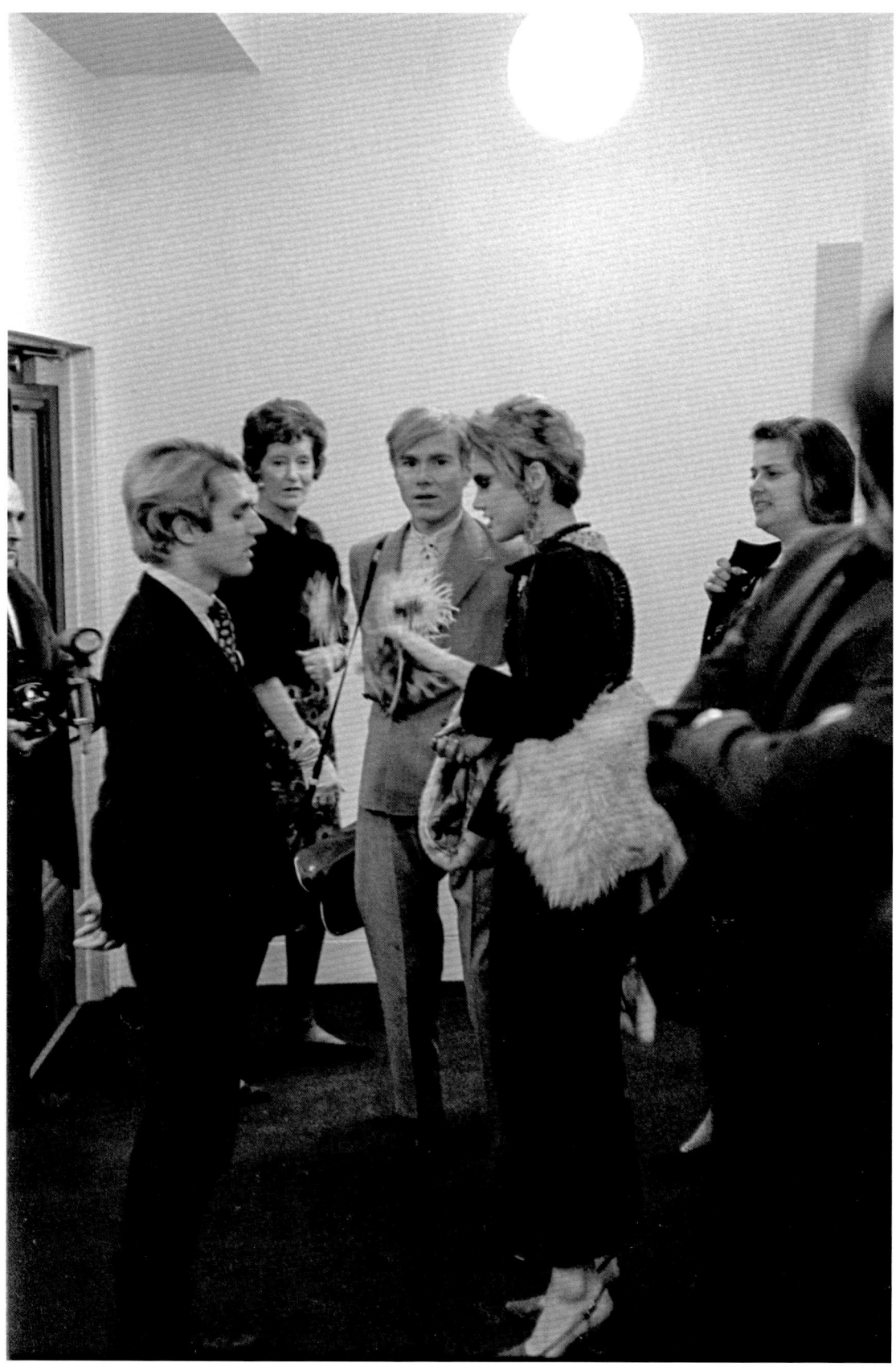

Figure 2.4   A much milder preview night at the ICA with Andy
Warhol and Edie Sedgwick socializing with VIP
guests. Image courtesy of the Weitzman School
of Design's Architectural Archives' George Pohl
photography collection.

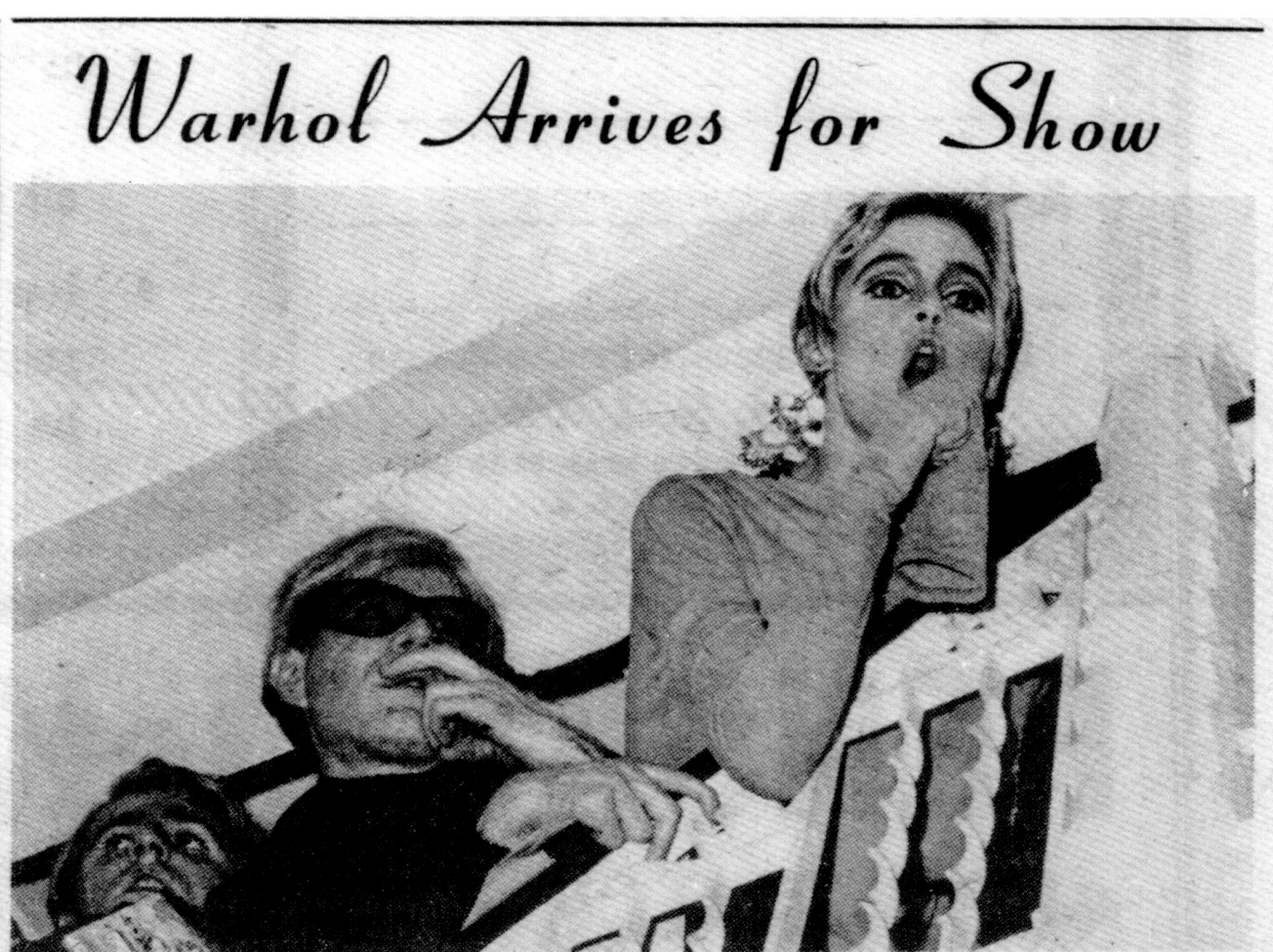

Warhol Arrives for Show

The Daily Pennsylvanian (By Bob Kosiba)

Andy Warhol looks on as playmate Edie is dismayed at the absence of FooFoo", one of the members of the elite group who arrived for the opening of Pop Art Exhibit at the Furness Building on Friday night.

Figure 2.5   Andy and his entourage seeking safety from clamoring crowds on a small iron staircase in the Furness Library, on top of missing FooFoo. *Daily Pennsylvanian*, Volume LXXXI, Number 42, 11 October 1965. University of Pennsylvania Libraries. Image courtesy of the *Daily Pennsylvanian*.

Most of the coverage of that night focused not on the little Warhol art that might be seen but on the crazed crowds that had come to see Warhol. While it might seem ironic to have an exhibition with much of its art removed, nevertheless generating such enthusiasm, the ICA opening night was a milestone in cementing Warhol's reputation as a cultural phenomenon as much as a leading contemporary artist.

It was a formative moment as well for the other key figures of the show. The opening's swollen attendance, with art-lovers crawling over one another to get inside the space, contributed powerfully to the ICA's cutting-edge reputation in contemporary art circles. At the same time, the visual and acoustic cacophony of the opening further darkened its disrepute among more conservative sets. As one Philadelphia critic, possibly recalling Franklin's mandate or, equally possible, misunderstanding it, put it: "If ever it is necessary to document the fact that the artist and not the art is of primary concern to the public, surely this sorry episode makes it clear. The cult of personality can have no further flowering."[20] Sam Green remained as director of the ICA for just two more years, but then, perhaps inspired by his brush with stardom at the opening, went on to become a personal assistant to a string of celebrities, such as Greta Garbo, Cecil Beaton, and Yoko Ono, among others. Years later, he also became active in the preservation movement. The Furness Building, as discussed above, was an early icon of preservation efforts. By 1985, it was deemed a National Historic Landmark and is today the most widely revered building on Penn's campus.[21] For Warhol, perhaps, it was just another opening, although Green reports that Andy was frightened and grew ashen. Certainly, his work appeared increasingly in art history classes and in more general discussions of contemporary art, whether at Penn or beyond. And readers nationwide could ponder reviews of an art exhibition opening like no other, accounts that told of Andy and the crowds and had little to say of the art that was nowhere to be seen. To whatever extent he may have entertained the notion before the opening, the press of the mob that night, reaching out, possibly, to touch the hem of his turtleneck, made Andy realize he was a star.

2. "Death: G. Holmes Perkins," *University of Pennsylvania Almanac* 51, no. 2 (September 4, 2004), https://doi.org/https://almanac.upenn.edu/archive/volumes/v51/n02/death_ghp.html.
3. Michael Lewis, "Building Power," *Wall Street Journal*, November 8, 2012.
4. Robert Venturi, "Introduction: Furness and Taste," in *Frank Furness: The Complete Works*, ed. George E. Thomas (New York: Princeton Architectural Press, 1991), 5-6.
5. Eunice Leopold, *Pennsylvania Guardian*, November 2, 1962.
6. Dorothy Grafly, *Art in Focus* 15, no. 1 (October 1963).
7. Blake Gopnik recounts an amusing dinner introduction in Philadelphia's Rittenhouse Square between Warhol and Lallie Lloyd in his *Warhol* (New York: Allen Lane, 2020), 465.
8. See Beatrice K. Reynolds entry for Atkinson in *David De Leon's Leaders from the 1960s: A Bio-bibliographical Sourcebook of American Activism* (Westport, CT: Greenwood Press, 1994).
9. See Ti-Grace Atkinson's typewritten preface, located in the Clyfford Still Archives, to the exhibition catalogue "Clyfford Still," Institute of Contemporary Art, University of Pennsylvania, Philadelphia, October 18–December 15, 1963 (Record ID: CPSA.SB007.B003.F028.001).
10. For a detailed description of the ICA's exhibitions during the 1960s, see its exhibition history website, https://icaphila.org/exhibitions/?decade=1963.
11. Beyond the student-run *Daily Pennsylvanian*, the ICA exhibitions received sometimes skeptical, other times enthusiastic attention from local papers such as the *Main Line Times, Evening Bulletin, Pennsylvania Guardian*, and *Jewish Exponent*.
12. In 1964, Jonas Mekas, an avant-garde filmmaker and advisor to Warhol, referred to the artist as the "orchestra conductor of extreme possibilities." See Victor Bockris, *Warhol* (London: Muller, 1989), 204.
13. Bockris, *Warhol*, 223.
14. Bockris, *Warhol*, 233.
15. Bockris, *Warhol*, 234.
16. Sam Green removed all but the Jackie Kennedy paintings, flower paintings, and the Brillo Boxes. See Tina H. Laver, "Pop Art and the Masses," *Daily Pennsylvanian* 81, no. 49, October 11, 1965, 2.
17. Laver, "Pop Art."
18. Jean Stein and George Plimpton, *Edie: An American Biography* (New York: Knopf, 1982), 252.
19. Stein and Plimpton, *Edie*, 254.
20. In Blake Gopnik, *Warhol* (New York: Allen Lane, 2020), 263.
21. The author's personal observation, after having directed the Fisher Fine Arts Library and negotiated numerous requests to use the building for the widest range of events. Louis Kahn's 1965 Richards Medical Research Laboratories is equally, if not even more revered, albeit by a far narrower and specialized constituency, few of whom, if any, ever actually worked in the building.

1. *Proposals Relating to the Education of Youth in Pensilvania* (Philadelphia: Benjamin Franklin, 1749). Accessible at https://archives. upenn.edu/digitized-resources/docs-pubs/franklin-proposals.

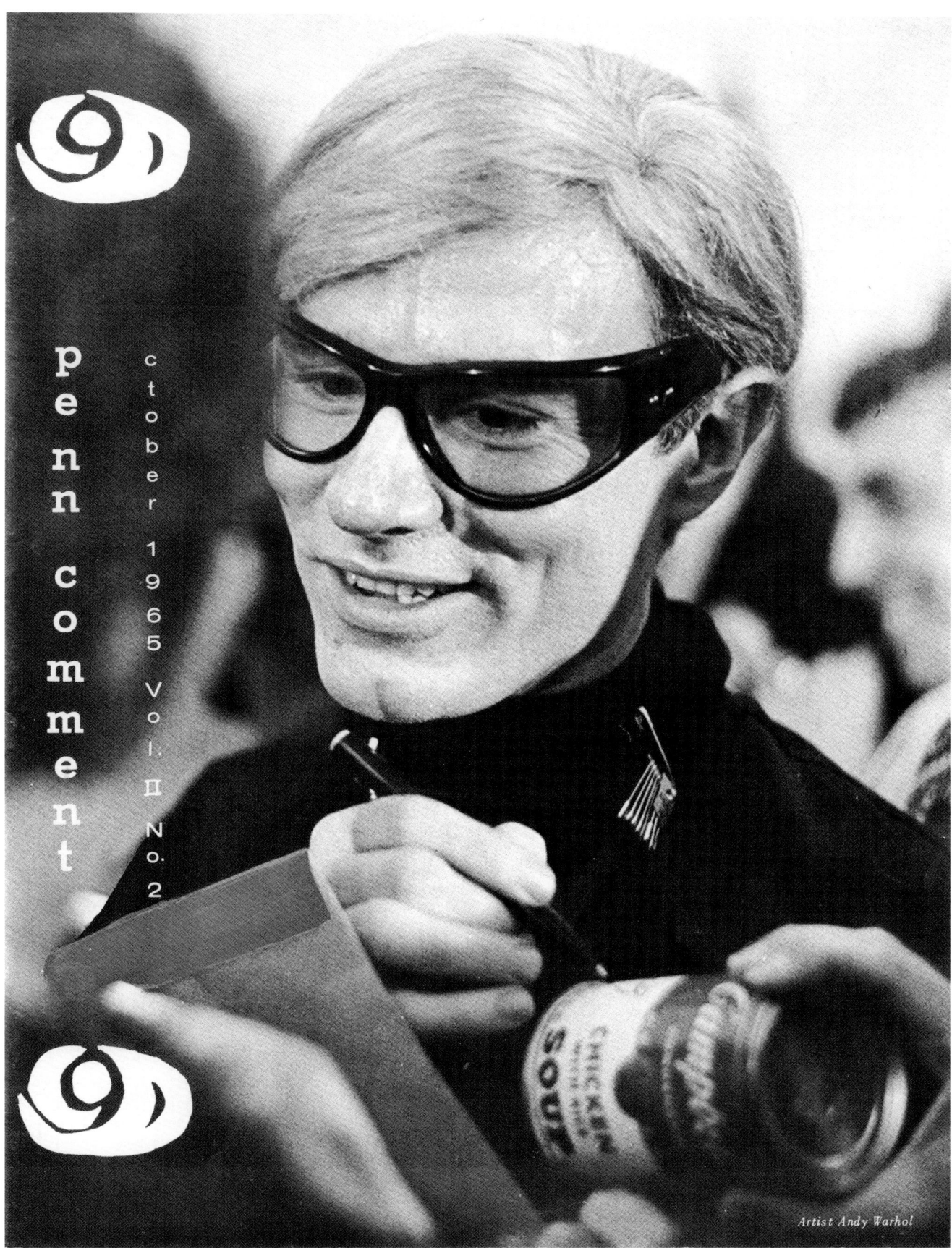

penn comment

october 1965 Vol. II No. 2

Artist Andy Warhol

Figure 2.6   A small Penn student magazine captures Andy in top form, outfitted in
what would become his iconic black turtleneck, safety pins, and ski goggles,
from the opening night, for its cover. *Penn Comment*, 1965. Image courtesy
of the University of Pennsylvania Archives.

"Filling in Gaps": An Interview with Gregory McCoy

Reva Wolf

This interview is edited and revised by Reva Wolf in consultation with Gregory McCoy from a video recording made at Van Pelt–Dietrich Library Center, the University of Pennsylvania, on June 27, 2019. Information not in the recorded interview was added occasionally to provide useful context and typically appears within brackets. Updated information also appears in brackets.

Reva Wolf: How did you first become interested in the art of Andy Warhol?

Gregory McCoy: The first time I saw Andy Warhol's work was at a small art gallery in Lambertville, New Jersey, Avanti Galleries, Inc., that had a wonderful print exhibition. Lambertville is near New Hope, Pennsylvania [where Warhol's assistant Rupert Jasen Smith had a studio and produced a number of Warhol's paintings and prints]. I was there on a weekend daytrip and was walking down the street with a friend and we took note of the exhibition. I think the moment I walked in, my life changed.

RW: When was this?

GM: Around 1989 or 1990. I started collecting in 1990.

RW: This was just shortly after Warhol died [in 1987].

GM: Yes.

RW: What works in the Lambertville exhibition attracted you?

GM: One of the first things that caught my eye was one of Warhol's *Dollar Sign* prints [of 1982].[1] I remember my first reaction to that was, "Boy, I wish I had done that!" I thought it was absolutely spectacular.

RW: Why?

GM: Well, I thought it was interesting, having been familiar with Jasper Johns' work using numerals [dating from the mid-1950s onward].[2] As time went on, I became aware of Warhol's *Dollar Bills* paintings [of 1962], from a few years prior to his *Dollar Sign* images.[3] But when I first saw the *Dollar Sign* works, I thought the subject matter was interesting; at the time, having enough money to own a Warhol seemed impossible! But I then realized that if I saved, at some point I could own a *Dollar Sign*, and I did ultimately buy one, but only after several years of saving *(Fig. 3.1)*. I had to save for approximately three years to be able to buy one print. I ended up eventually also purchasing a small canvas—a 10 × 8-inch *Dollar Sign* painting *(Fig. 3.2)*. I love both of them.

As a collector, I always try to go back and fill the spots in between pieces. For example, I acquired a signed invitation from the Leo Castelli Gallery on which Warhol drew a dollar sign—a quick illustration—and then signed it at the base *(Fig. 3.3)*. One of the reasons I love it is because of the way Warhol drew the dollar sign. It almost looks like a race car going between the printed type. You can see from this casual drawing how great an illustrator Warhol was. The dollar sign was perfectly positioned between the type; it wasn't just randomly drawn over it.

RW: Was the *Dollar Sign* print the first work by Warhol that you acquired?

GM: The first piece that I acquired was a sheet of wallpaper. A bright pink cow with a yellow background.

RW: Where did you find it?

GM: It was at a gallery in Philadelphia, I. Brewster & Company Gallery. There were many great pieces available at the time. Now there is much less to pick from.

RW: Over time, you amassed a fairly large Warhol collection. Some of it would conventionally be classified as "art" and some as "ephemera." I'm fascinated by your interest in ephemera. Could you talk a little bit about your collecting of Warhol-related ephemera? What attracts you to it?

GM: Ephemera was more affordable when I first started collecting. In the case of Andy Warhol, you could get a self-portrait or *Flowers* exhibition invitation that Castelli Gallery had done. I have two of those, and they are very sentimental to me [because a dedicated dealer of art ephemera, Jean-Noel Herlin, offered to get them directly from Leo Castelli for me] *(Figs. 3.4 and 3.5)*. Needless to say, they were priced a lot lower than signed edition prints. When I acquired them, I was satisfied with having something nearly identical to those prints. Later, as my career progressed, I was able to buy the signed edition prints.

Another reason I am drawn to ephemera is that, having a print production background and having worked at an advertising agency, as an art buyer I was interested in the marketing side of collecting art.

RW: How art is marketed to be sold?

GM: Yes. It tied in to the commercial side of the fine arts.

RW: This point brings us back to the *Dollar Sign* works! You mentioned that your career was in advertising, and of course Warhol worked in advertising for the first decade or so of his life in New York City. Do you think

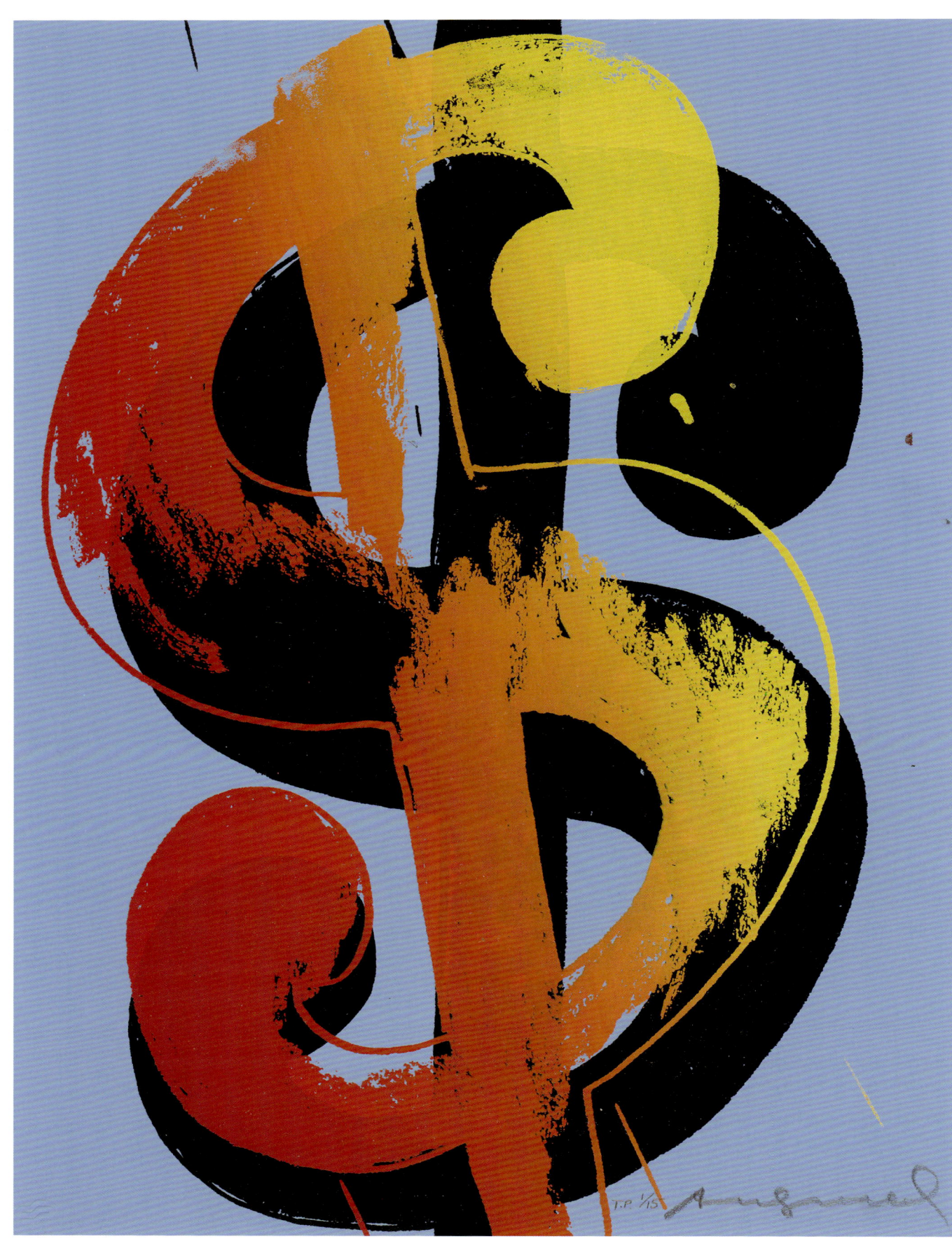

Figure 3.1   Andy Warhol, *Dollar Sign*, 1981, screenprint, 19 ¾ x 15 ⅝ in.
Trial proof, T.P 1/15. Gregory McCoy Collection. Image used
with permission.

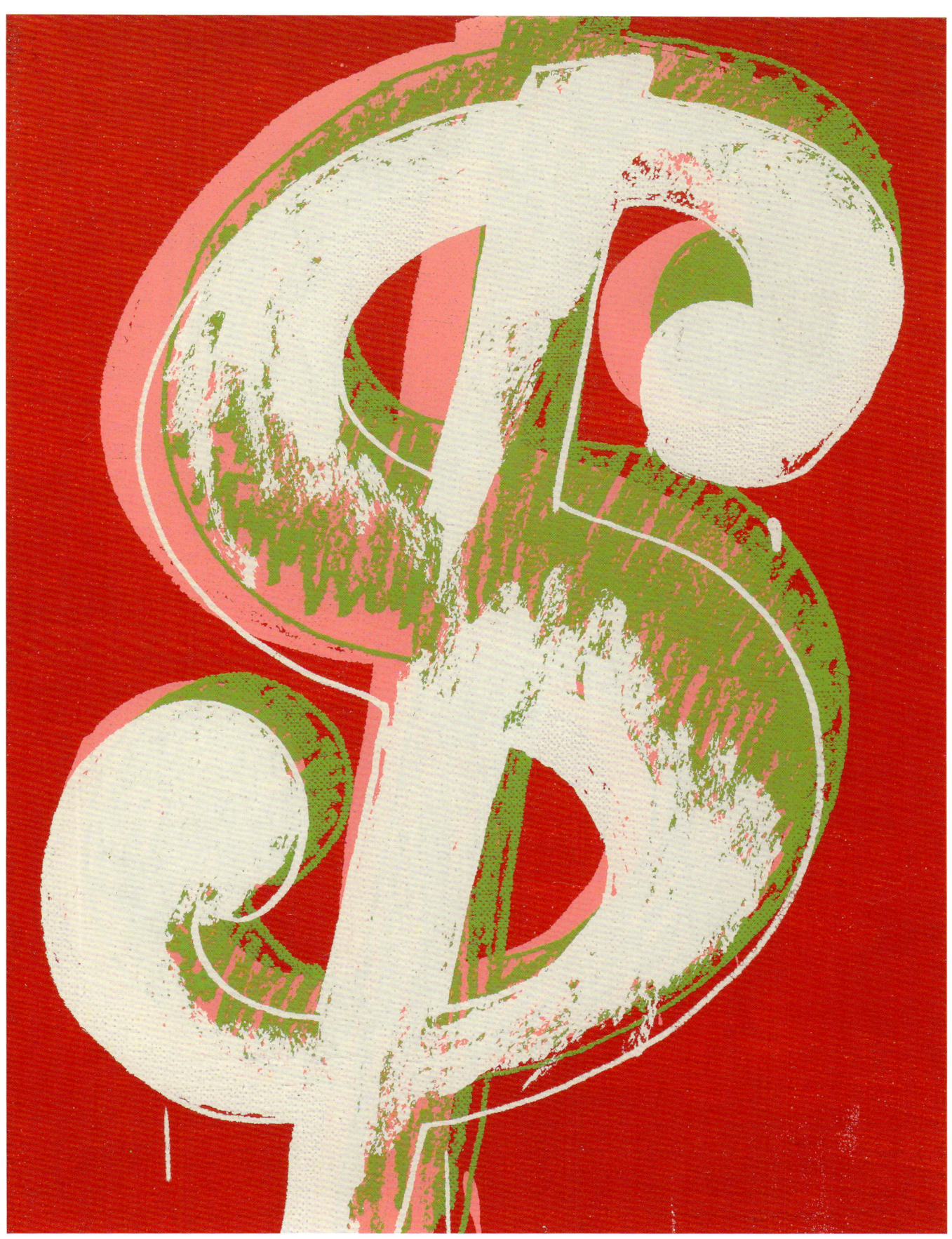

Figure 3.2   Andy Warhol, *Dollar Sign*, 1982, screenprint ink on
acrylic on canvas, 10 ¼ x 7 ⅞ in. Gregory
McCoy Collection. Image used with permission.

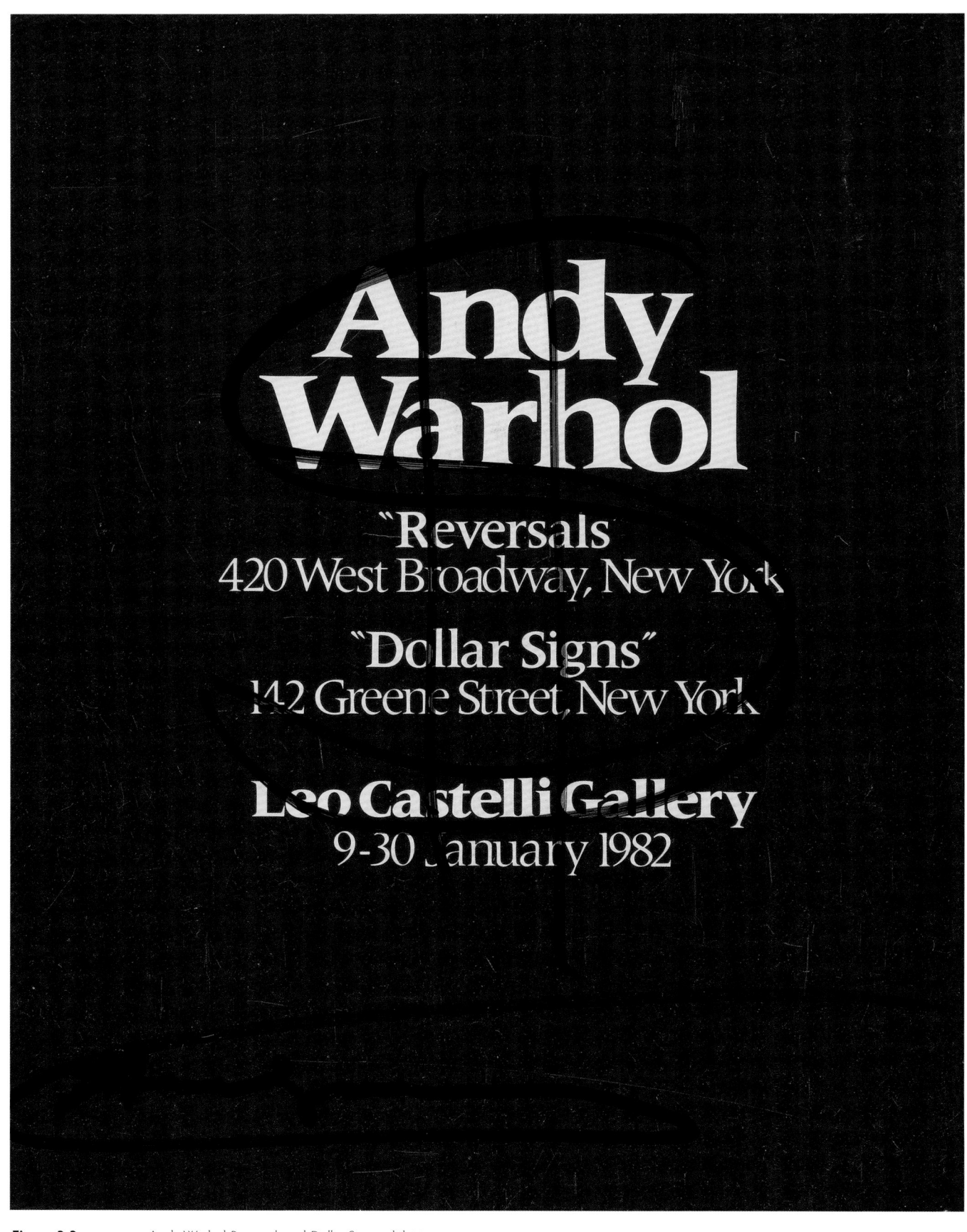

Figure 3.3   Andy Warhol *Reversals* and *Dollar Signs* exhibition announcement with Andy Warhol's hand-drawn dollar sign and signature, 1982, 10 ⅞ x 9 ⅞ in. (sight). Leo Castelli Gallery. Gregory McCoy Collection. Image courtesy of the Leo Castelli Gallery.

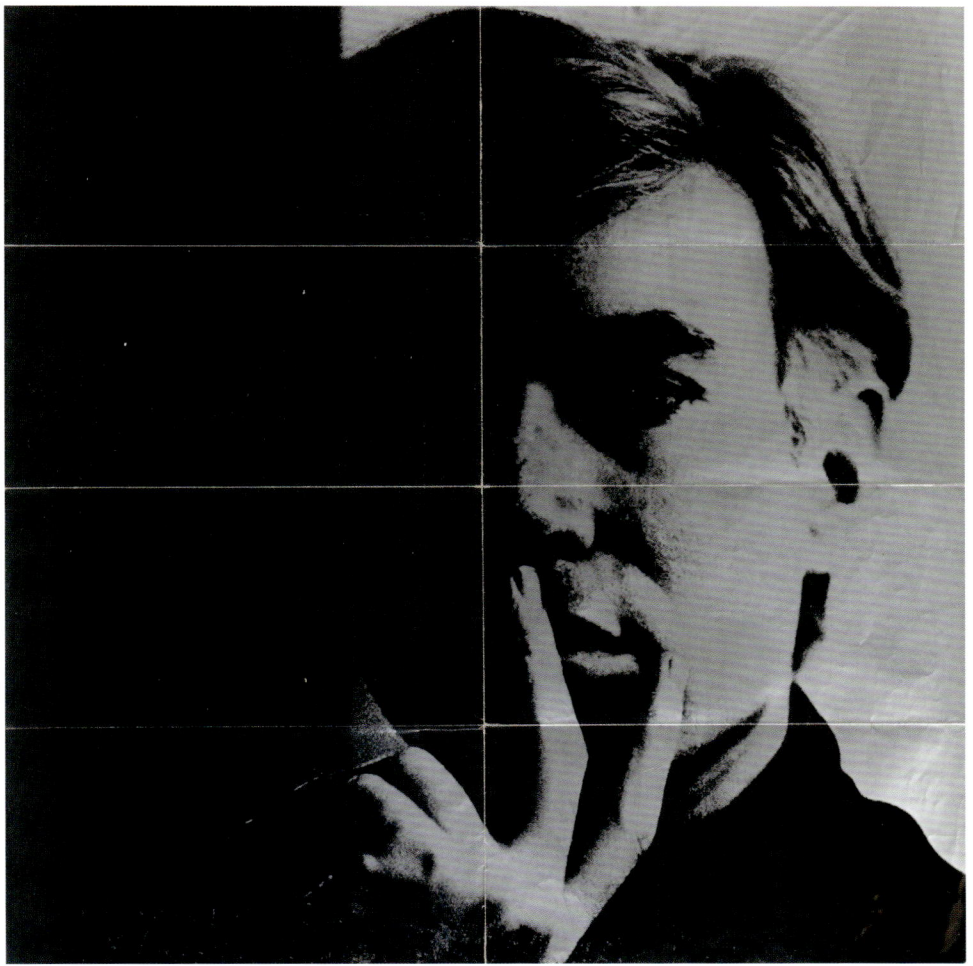

Figure 3.4   Andy Warhol exhibition announcement, 1966, offset lithograph on silver coated paper, 22 x 22 in. Leo Castelli Gallery. Gregory McCoy Collection. Image courtesy of the Leo Castelli Gallery.

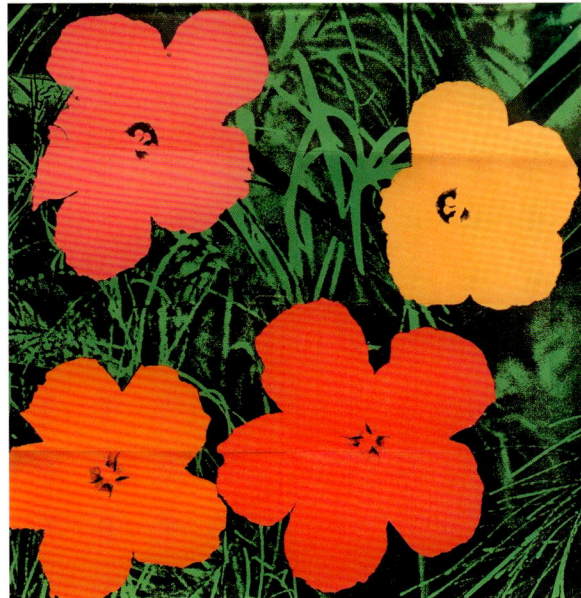

Figure 3.5   Andy Warhol exhibition announcement, 1964, offset lithograph, 21 ¾ x 21 ¾ in. Leo Castelli Gallery, 1964. Gregory McCoy Collection. Image courtesy of the Leo Castelli Gallery.

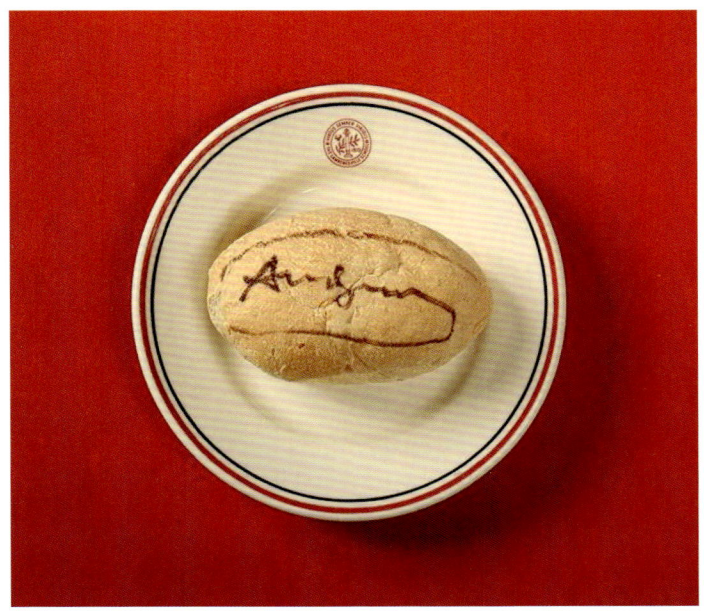

Figure 3.6   Invitation to The Lawrenceville School's 2011 exhibition: dinner roll signed by Andy Warhol, ca. 1971, 4 ¼ x 5 ⅝ in. Gregory McCoy Collection. Image used with permission.

one of the reasons you ended up fascinated by Warhol is this similarity in background?

GM: Absolutely. I really admired the fact that Warhol had had an extremely successful career as an illustrator. He was challenged to cross the bridge into the world of fine art and was able to do that. I found my own way to cross that bridge, not only by collecting. After working twenty years for an advertising agency, I did an internship at the Violette de Mazia Foundation as a way to make a contribution to the field of fine arts, because of my fondness for art.

Back to ephemera. I think my initial interest in it had something to do with Andy Warhol's celebrity. In my collection, I have objects such as a signed soup can, a signed box of Brillo soap pads, and even a dinner roll that was signed by Warhol *(Fig. 3.6)*, and some photographs.

RW: The dinner roll is my favorite!

GM: I purchased it to use on the postcard announcing an exhibition of my collection that was held in 2011 at The Lawrenceville School. I wanted something that would be especially interesting. I had spotted it many years earlier on eBay, and it had worked its way up the ladder. To me, such items were like miniature works of art. In that way, I envisioned the pieces as having a Duchampian angle.[4] I collected vintage clippings of Warhol that I loved, such as a picture of him signing a soup can *(Fig. 3.7)*.

RW: All this gets into some really interesting questions regarding art and ideas about social class. We might associate the Campbell's Soup can with the lower classes. But in making it a subject of art, Warhol elevates it. It becomes symbolic of Warhol's own move from one world to the other. He grew up in modest circumstances. What was your own background like, and how do you see it as fitting into your interests as a collector?

GM: I had an—I'll use the word "epiphany"—at one moment: my father had worked for U.S. Steel, and he had made cans for a living, and how funny that I collected cans!

RW: Where did you grow up?

GM: In Moorestown, New Jersey, in South Jersey, close to Philadelphia. In fact, I lived close to the Campbell's

Soup corporate headquarters. Campbell's Soup was a big part of my life. I enjoyed the product and was raised almost in the shadow of the company. As a graphic artist, I appreciated the graphic quality of the can's design.

RW: Where did you study graphic art?

GM: I went to the School of Visual Arts in New York City, which was a great experience. I had wonderful teachers. It was a blessing that I found this art school—and then a career that allowed me to make enough money to go buy Warhol.

RW: Is there anything in Warhol's identity as a gay man who contributed to the rise of gay liberation that spoke to you?

GM: I always admired Warhol's independent nature. And I like the fact that the design world is inclusive . . . a very open and accepting world.

RW: The *Out of Sight* exhibition at the University of Pennsylvania that has occasioned this interview features several prints of Warhol's Marilyn Monroe image that in one way or another, directly or indirectly, are connected to a well-known 1968 exhibition of Warhol's work held in Stockholm. How did you discover these works, and when did you first acquire one?

GM: The first piece I acquired was in 2009 *(Fig. 3.8)*. Since then, I've collected a total of 305 [now 323] of these prints.

RW: How did you come across the first one? How did that happen?

GM: I found it through a dealer I work with in Sweden, Börje Bengtsson.[5]

RW: Did you already know him at the time? Had you acquired other works from him before that?

GM: My connection to him ties right into the rare book world. I found through experience that one of the best sources for finding art and ephemera is bookdealers. Many of the people who collect rare books also have art. So I reached out to Bengtsson to find what he might have. One of the first things he offered me was a balloon that had been signed by Damien Hirst *(Fig. 3.9)*.

RW: Did you take it?

GM: I did. I bought it really to start a relationship with Bengtsson.

RW: How much did he sell it for? Do you mind if I ask?

GM: $400. It was the skull. It was a wonderful little piece. Hirst had signed a little [printed] tag that was clipped onto the balloon. Once again, it was ephemera, made for an exhibition. I have found that people who have rare, cool, odd little things like that either have one of them, or they have hundreds of them. In this case, it was hundreds. And over the years, I bought many different things from Bengtsson—a signed *Campbell's Soup Can* mug *(Fig. 3.10)* and many interesting odds and ends. He would send me lists of items that were available. On one of these lists was a *Marilyn* screenprint said to be from the 1968 exhibition of Warhol's work at the Moderna Museet in Stockholm *(Fig. 3.8)*. For a collector of Warhol's work, the Marilyn Monroe image is at the top. Bengtsson sent me a digital image of the work, and as soon as I saw it, I was excited, and then, when the piece arrived, I was blown away by the quality of the printing. There was a distinctive shimmer to the piece. It had a blue background with the image in black—or almost like a shimmering gray—and I knew that a master printer had made it.

RW: Due to your background.

GM: Exactly. As a print production person, I realized what had just come into my life and how special it was.

RW: Warhol himself did not print this work, but someone with great skill did.

GM: After many years of research, I feel confident we know who that printer was: Arne Wahlqvist. But at the time I could see how talented the person was. The execution was perfect. The works seem to have been printed in Malmö, based on my findings.

RW: The mystery is, what was the purpose of these images? Why were they made? Were they all made at the same time? Hopefully, by exhibiting these works, scholars will try to seek answers, and we'll learn more about this unique collection.

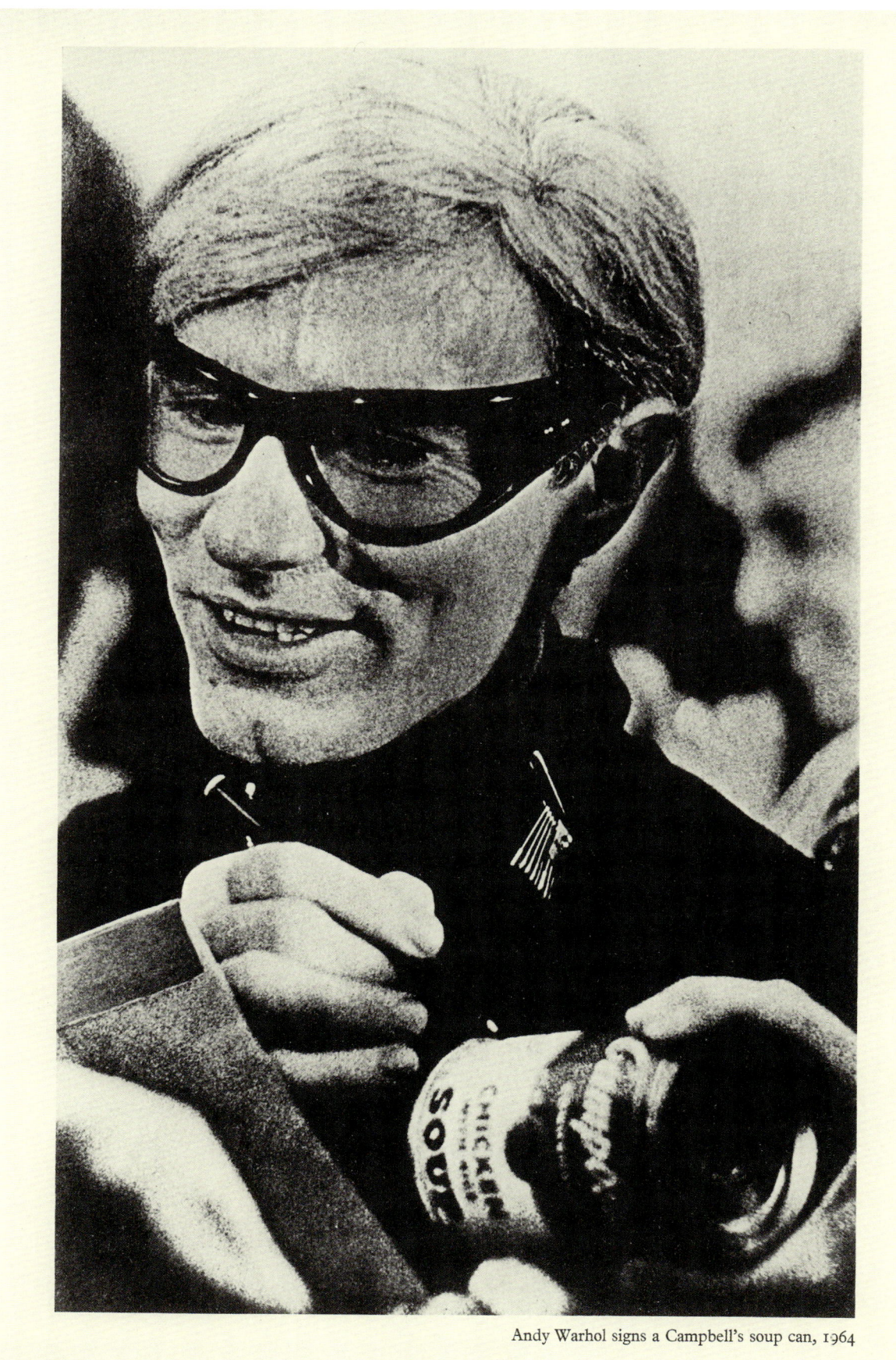

Andy Warhol signs a Campbell's soup can, 1964

Figure 3.7   Image from *Penn Comment* article, 1965. Source: University of Pennsylvania Archives. Image used with permission.

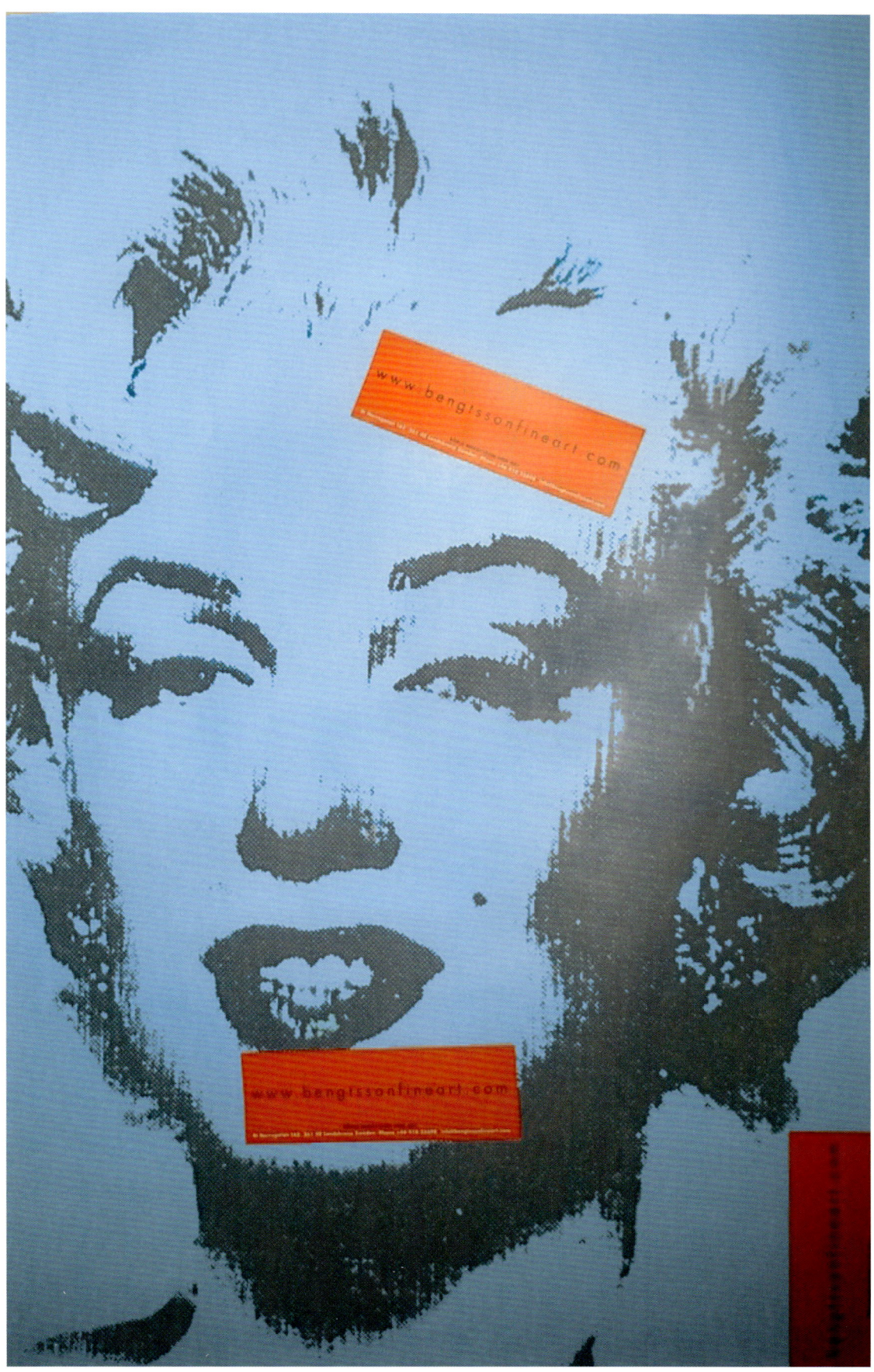

Figure 3.8   The first screenprint in the collection (AWMM.1968.001, Plate I). Photo taken
by Borje Bengtsson and sent to Gregory McCoy to gauge his interest.
Bengtsson's business cards were laid on top to identify it as offered by him.

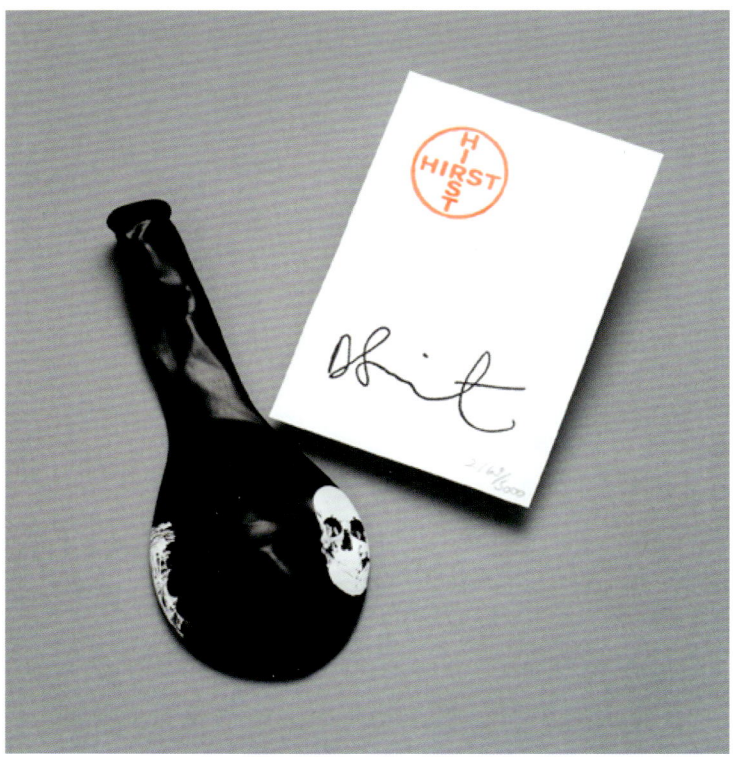

Figure 3.9   Damien Hirst, *Untitled* [skull balloon], 2009.
Gregory McCoy Collection. Image used with
permission from the Artists Rights Society.

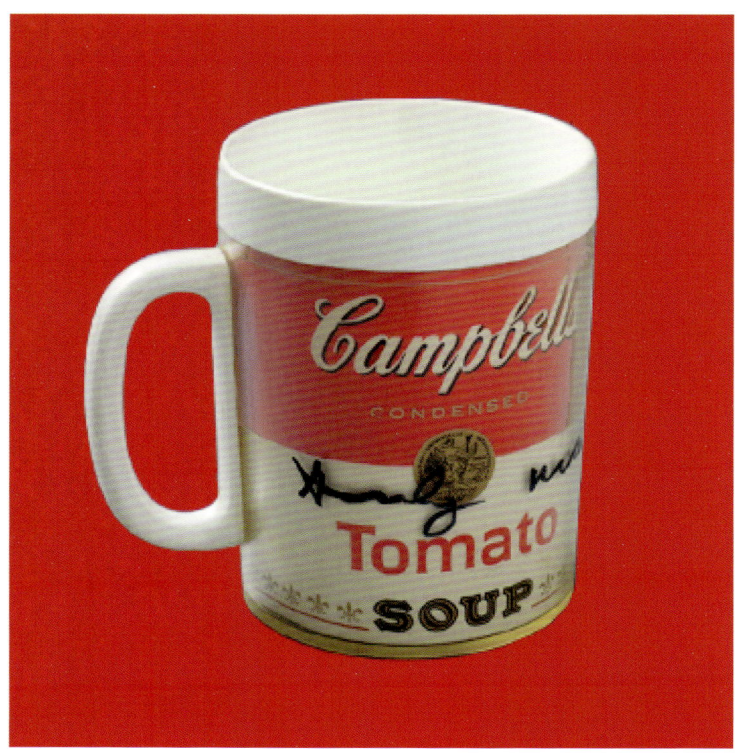

Figure 3.10   *Campbell's Soup Can* mug, signed by Andy Warhol,
date unknown. Gregory McCoy Collection. Image
used with permission.

GM: Of the 305 [now 323] prints that I currently have, I acquired them from approximately nineteen distinct sources ["approximately," because in one or two instances the prints were purchased in groups and it was unclear from how many sources they came]. I have spent years collecting all these prints—reuniting them—and to me that's one of the most exciting parts of all this.

RW: Were all the previous owners of the prints in Sweden?

GM: Yes. All in Sweden. The advertising agency Stig Arbman AB had worked for the Moderna Museet, and worked with Reklamteknik, the printer. That seems to have been the chain of command. The prints ended up being distributed to various parties after they were never displayed or sold after they were made. They were virtually unknown. Word got out that I was interested in purchasing them, and over time I was able to bring a large number of them together.

RW: Do you know who the owner was of the first print in the collection that you acquired?

GM: John Melin. He was the graphic designer who was responsible for the text posters that were made to advertise the 1968 Moderna Museet Warhol exhibition (*Plates LXXVI–LXXXII*).

RW: These were the posters made of things Warhol either said or was said to have said. The same statements also were included [and several others] in the exhibition catalogue, along with Swedish translations. The most famous of these statements, which also is probably Warhol's best-known quip, is: "In the future everybody will be world famous for fifteen minutes."[6]

GM: John Melin not only worked on the text posters but also on the exhibition catalogue (*Figs. 4.15–4.17, 4.19–4.22*). Regarding the posters, it's interesting to try to ascertain why they ended up using posters with words on them to promote an art exhibition. Again, the marketing.

RW: Did they sell those posters?

GM: They did. There are seven distinct posters. My understanding is that they sold one hundred of each.

Some also ended up being sold in Los Angeles—by the art dealer Irving Blum—and were advertised as being in sets of six *(Fig. 3.11)*. I purchased one of the sets of six *(Plates LXXVI–LXXVIII and LXXX–LXXXII)*. I also recently acquired a copy of the *Flowers* poster for the Moderna Museet exhibition, which connects directly with the cover of both the invitation and the catalogue.

RW: You seem to be endeavoring to collect each and every item that you can connect to this exhibition.

GM: Absolutely. I have three copies of the catalogue. Two are signed. I also have the original mock-up copy that Warhol okayed. He apparently was given this copy at the opening of the exhibition and asked to sign off on it. I also have a copy that was owned by Kasper König, who helped with the 1968 exhibition from New York, under the curator, Pontus Hultén's, direction. I also have a copy of a special edition that came with a Plexiglas case and that Warhol was to have signed; the attempt on his life in June 1968 prevented him from signing copies of this special edition. But when he returned to Sweden in 1976, he signed them.[7]

RW: It's a fascinating catalogue.

GM: In many ways, it's a collection unto itself. The photographs of Andy Warhol and his studio, the Factory. The quotes.

RW: And it begins with the quotes. They fill the first twelve pages of the catalogue *(Fig. 4.19)*. These are followed by page after page of reproductions of paintings by Warhol, some repeated in a sequence of several pages *(Figs. 4.15, 4.16, and 4.20–4.22)*. After this come the photographs.

GM: One large group of photographs by Billy Name, and another by Stephen Shore. One of the photographs in the book shows Warhol's *White Painting* [1964] *(Fig. 3.12)*.[8] It is an "invisible" painting—the image is visible only in black light. Some of my *Marilyn* prints are similar; they are made with fluorescent inks. And many of the color combinations in these *Marilyn* prints are identical to the ones Warhol used. In an interview, Matt Wrbican [former archivist at the Andy Warhol Museum in Pittsburgh] stated that every Warhol is a collaboration. And these pieces are absolutely a collaboration.

RW: I agree that it's important to appreciate Warhol as a collaborator, and that collaboration is central to his work. It always was and it continued to be central throughout his career, in various ways. One question that arises out of his multifaceted collaborative approach is: how much was he involved in the collaboration? Sometimes more. Sometimes less. Sometimes the collaboration can be in the imagination of the person making the work.

GM: With my *Marilyn* prints, I think it's important to consider the fact that, years ago, the distance between New York City and Malmö or Stockholm would also have played a role in the artist's involvement.

RW: The prints are based on a detail of one of Warhol's *Marilyn* paintings. The Moderna Museet owns *Marilyn Monroe in Black and White (Twenty-Five Marilyns)*, of 1962 *(Fig. 4.11)*. Several of the prints contain small type running vertically upward along the edge from the viewer's right corner identifying the source of the image as being this painting *(Fig. 4.12)*. Yet these prints are not really posters of the painting, because a poster typically reproduces the entire painting, or maybe a detail, but not so transformed as we see in these prints, with various color combinations added. And part of what's fascinating is that these works are not easily categorizable.

GM: I think that's exactly it. And it's interesting, too, not only to consider the distance between the two locations, but also how terminology has changed through time. For example, the *SAS Passenger Ticket* print for the 1968 Stockholm exhibition is described as a poster in the original advertising for it *(Figs. 3.13 and 3.14)*. But in the catalogue raisonné of Warhol's prints, it is listed as a signed edition print with a run of 250.[9] Over the course of some fifty years, then, the definition of this work has changed.

RW: You are getting into really interesting questions about how things are classified, and about what classification means in terms of the value that we put on things. And these questions bring us back to the *Dollar Sign* with which we started this interview.

GM: Another point is that although I have 305 [now 323] of the prints, they can be perceived as one large work. You can divide it up into sub-categories: pieces that are printed using traditional printer's ink, fluorescent ink, and lacquer ("Lac") prints.

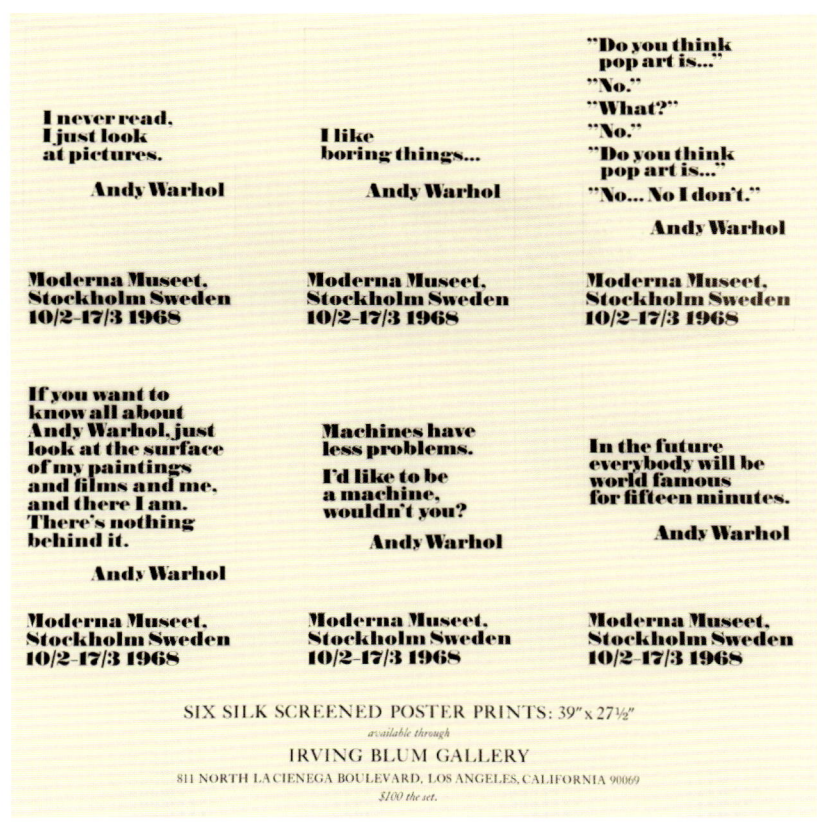

Figure 3.11   Advertisement for set of six Moderna Museet silkscreen text posters (n.d.), Irving Blum Gallery. Source: Gregory McCoy Collection. Image in the public domain.

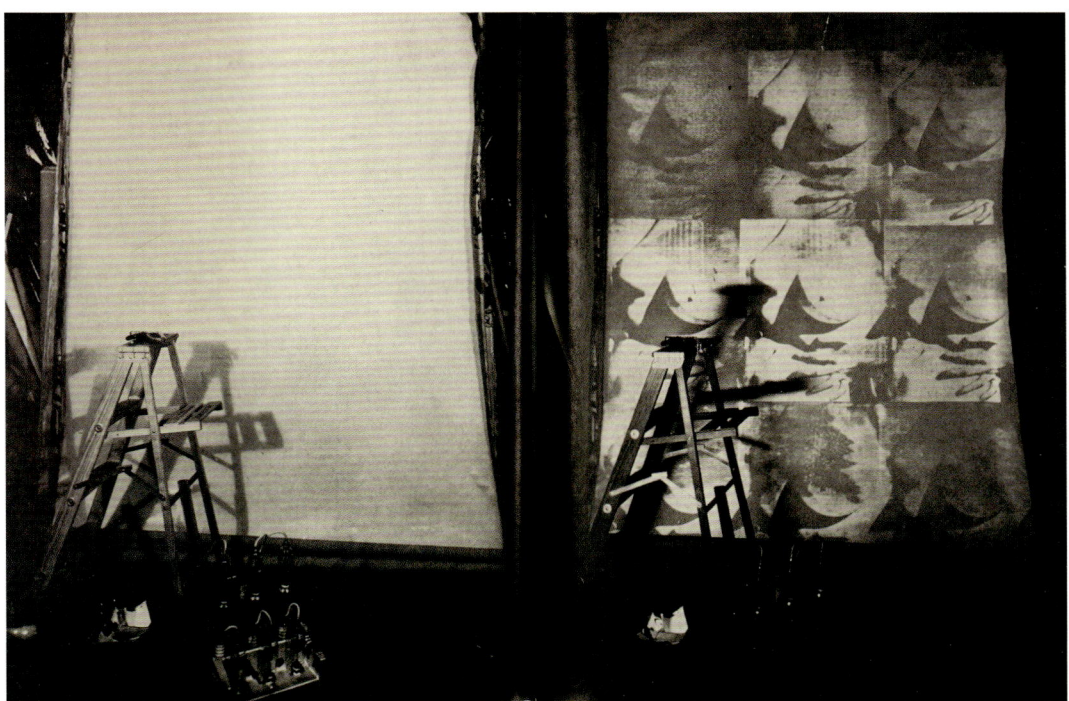

Figure 3.12   Andy Warhol, Moderna Museet exhibition catalogue, 1968. Two-page spread showing Andy Warhol's *White Painting* without and with fluorescent light (n.p.). Gregory McCoy Collection. Image used with permission from the Moderna Museet.

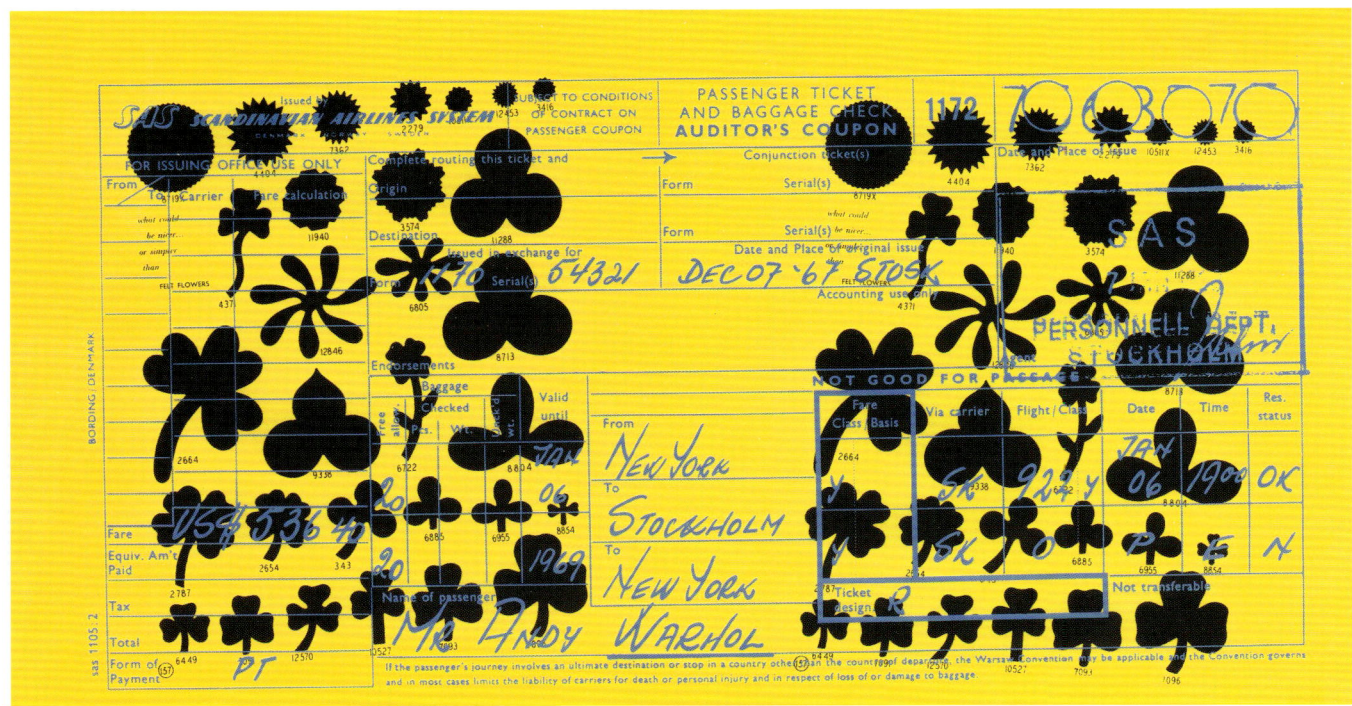

Figure 3.13   Andy Warhol, *SAS Passenger Ticket*, 1968, screenprint, 26 ¾ x 48 ¾ in. Gregory McCoy Collection. Image used with permission.

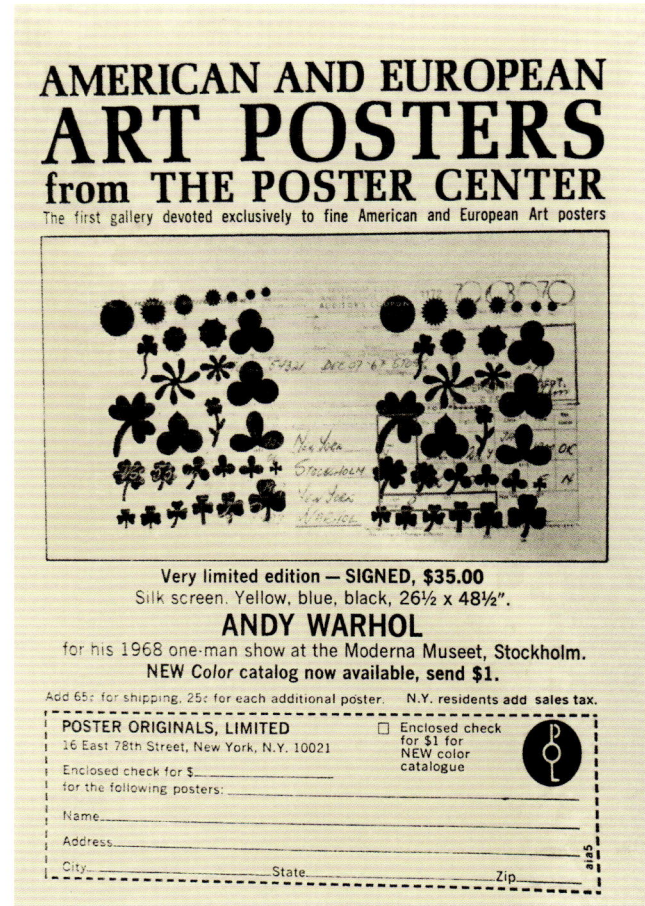

Figure 3.14   The Poster Center advertisement for Andy Warhol, *SAS Passenger Ticket* screenprint, ca. 1968. Gregory McCoy Collection. Image in the public domain.

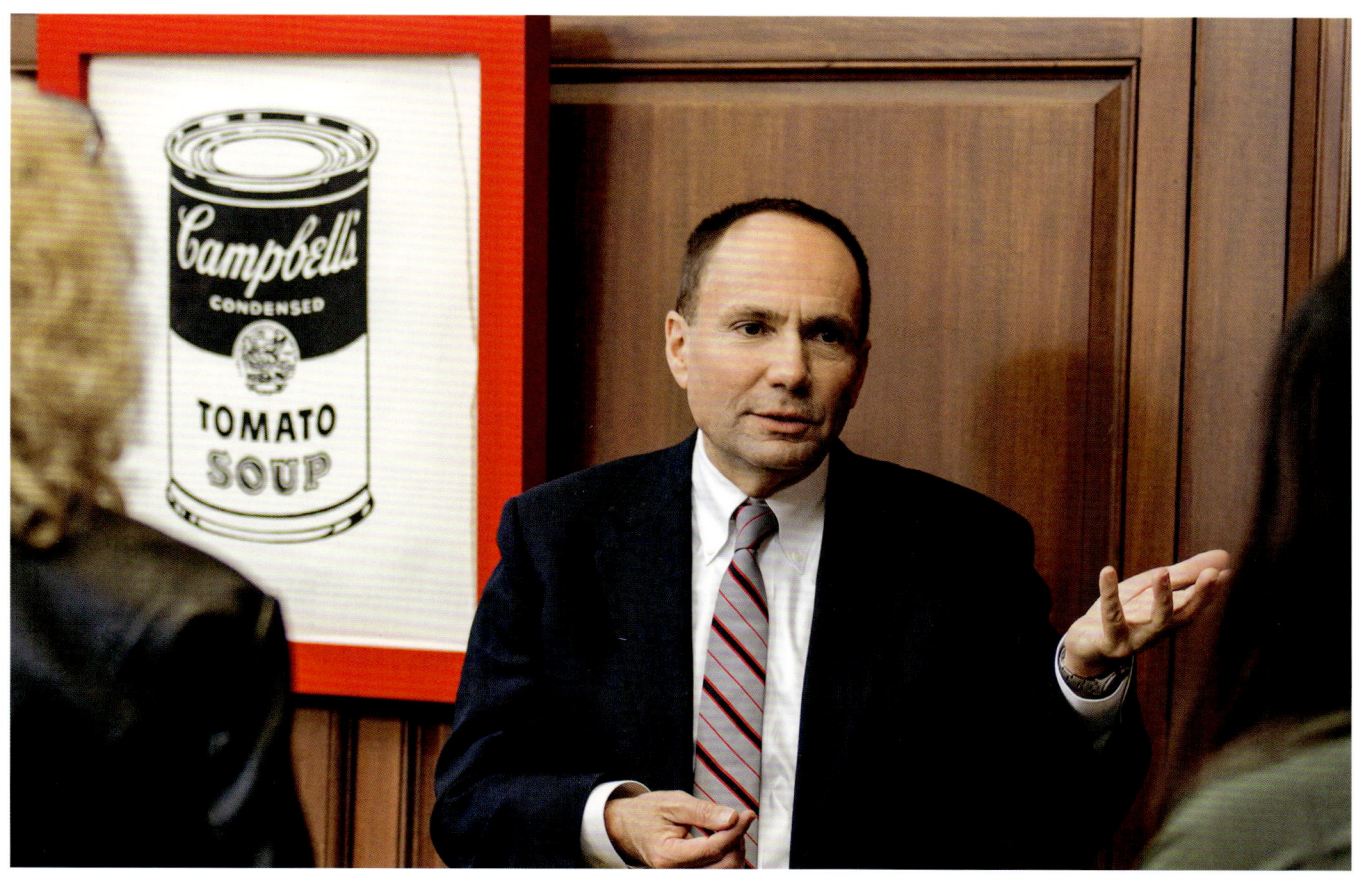

Figure 3.15   Gregory McCoy with a *Campbell's Soup Can* screenprint from
his collection in the background, The Lawrenceville School,
2011. Gregory McCoy Collection. Image used with permission.
Photographer Paloma Torres. Copyright © Paloma Torres.

RW: The range of experimentation in how these works were printed is noteworthy. It shows an attention to detail, and care, which you noticed immediately when you observed the quality of the first print that you acquired.

GM: In terms of experimentation, I also have many "reversal" pieces within the collection. I think these may be considered Warhol's first "reversal" pieces.

RW: Yet we don't know absolutely for sure when the prints were made, or whether Warhol in any way authorized them. So we need to leave the possibility of "firsts" a little open.

GM: I do have multiple sources dating the prints to 1968. The dating also can be determined by the way many of the prints were rediscovered. It's almost like rings in a tree. They were found with other prints from that time, within large stacks.

RW: Yes. Yet there are still a lot of open questions.

GM: There are. That's kind of the fun of it, too, working on trying to solve the mystery. And there *is* some mystery. I have my own theory about what my collection of *Marilyn* prints is. For the 1968 Stockholm exhibition, the façade of the Moderna Museet was covered with Warhol's *Cow Wallpaper*, five rows high and twenty-seven wide. It was placed on Masonite that was attached to the façade. There were some wallpaper fragments used, and the image was staggered, with multiple sheets used to fill in space.

RW: Do you think they were considering using the *Marilyn* prints for the façade?

GM: There's a possibility. Other works in the exhibition also came from what one might call secondary sources. There are the *Brillo Box* works.

RW: The *Brillo Box* objects exhibited in Stockholm were not made by Warhol, the way his first ones, of 1964, were; instead, they were ordered directly from the Brillo company.[10]

GM: Yes, because of the cost. And there was talk that Warhol said, go ahead and print them in Sweden, but

it would have been far too expensive. The Moderna Museet was working with a very limited budget.[11]

Another theory I have about the *Marilyns*, after many years of thinking about it, is that it's possible they were a plan B. The exhibition was organized on short notice, and in the event that Warhol's work didn't arrive, these *Marilyns* would be available to put on display. A backup plan.

RW: That makes sense as a possibility. Warhol ended up making works specifically for the exhibition, large *Electric Chair* and *Flowers* paintings, and these were sent to Stockholm along with two sets of his 1967 *Marilyn* print portfolio.[12]

GM: When I first started buying the made-in-Sweden *Marilyn* prints, there were around twenty examples known. I acquired one and dreamed of having two, and then as time went on, more and more became available. They found them in cold storage and they had sat in rooms for forty-eight years. Through research, and by looking for them, people discovered them, along with some of the text posters for the exhibition. They had been sitting there buried.

RW: It sounds a bit like archaeology.

GM: Exactly. And we also have located two or three people who were around back in 1968 and remember seeing these prints.

RW: I'm just curious, to change the subject, whether you have any other collections in addition to your collections related to Warhol.

GM: My first collection was of heart-shaped stones. I collected them to give to my mother. And we still have a little box of these rocks. I was a little boy walking around collecting rocks. And I was famous in the family for coming home at night with leaves and sticks. You know, the beautiful leaves from the change in the season. My mother always had me empty my pockets out.

Also, I collected empty Coca-Cola bottles, so that I could redeem them to get a new bottle. I think a bottle of Coke was eleven cents. I remember one time having eight cents and needing to find two empty bottles at two cents each so that I could go buy a bottle of Coke.

RW: It's interesting how collecting can turn into money in that way, even on this really modest level.

GM: Exactly. I was always interested in filling in gaps. I needed to fill in the gap of four cents so I could go buy a Coca-Cola. I think the approach I developed had to do with the fact that I had limited funds. I used to buy what I called "studio scraps." I have an original black-and-white *Campbell's Soup Can* on Curtis rag paper that had been ripped in half *(Fig. 3.15)*. I have one side of the sheet of paper, and I believe the Andy Warhol Museum in Pittsburgh has the other half—whether it was Warhol or his assistant Rupert Jasen Smith, someone ripped it in half. The rip was intentional, not accidental. It is a "good" rip, in other words, not the rip of a work in poor condition.

But back to my other collections. When I was young, like many people, I collected stamps and coins, and in many ways, my stamp collection was like the beginning of my first art collection. As time went on and I visited museums, whether the Philadelphia Museum of Art or the Barnes Foundation or the Museum of Modern Art, I saw some of the paintings that were reproduced on stamps that I had collected. My stamp collection was like a small print collection. My grandmother had relatives in Europe, and when they corresponded with her, she saved the stamps for me.

And then I graduated to other kinds of collecting. I collected Keith Haring's work. And, locally, I acquired some Andrew Wyeth pieces, and work by different artists. Warhol was somebody I ended up focusing on. At the time I started collecting, prices were relatively reasonable. Today, I could never do what I did thirty years ago. I used to walk into Ivan Karp's or Leo Castelli's gallery and buy a small piece for a thousand dollars. Today, some of those same works are tens or hundreds of thousands of dollars. Ivan was wonderful. He and Leo Castelli recognized that I was a sincere collector working with very little money, and they would make pieces available to me—items in their offices that weren't on display.

The first work that I bought from Ivan Karp [owner of O.K. Harris Gallery, established in 1969, and an early supporter of Warhol, and Pop art generally, as an employee of Leo Castelli Gallery earlier in the 1960s] was my first signed piece—a piece of *Mao Wallpaper* *(Fig. 3.16).*

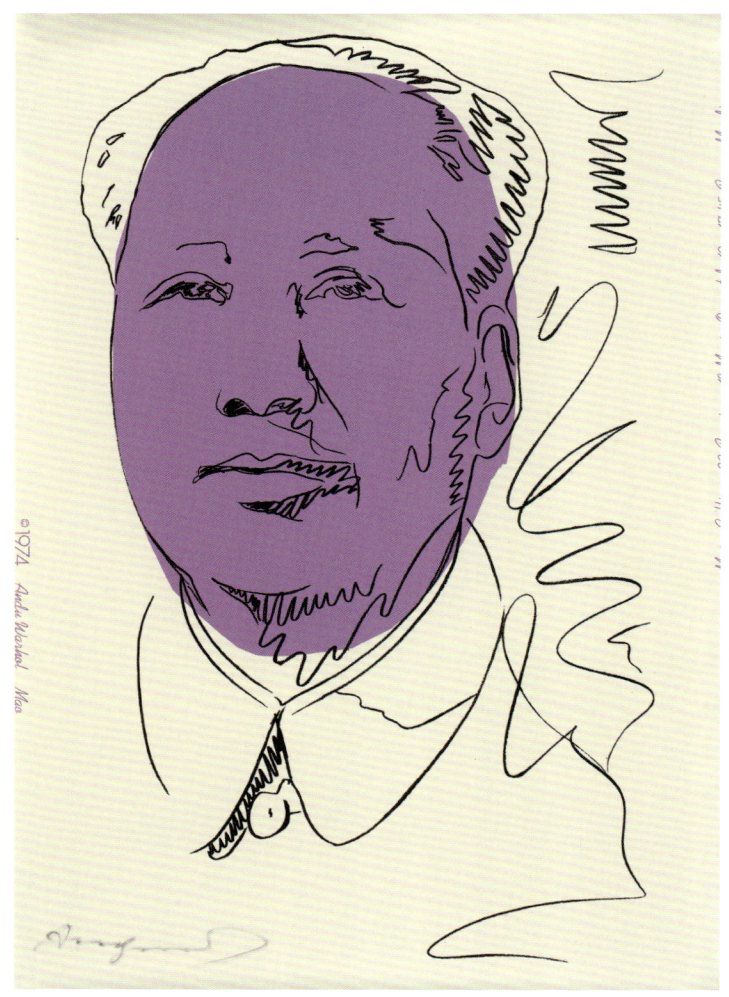

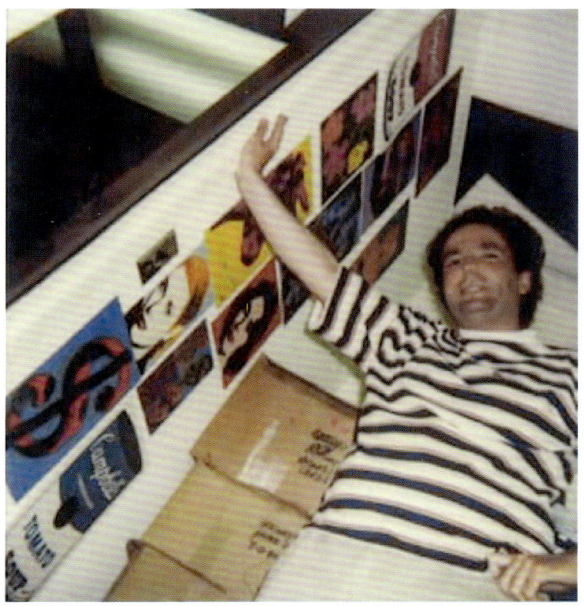

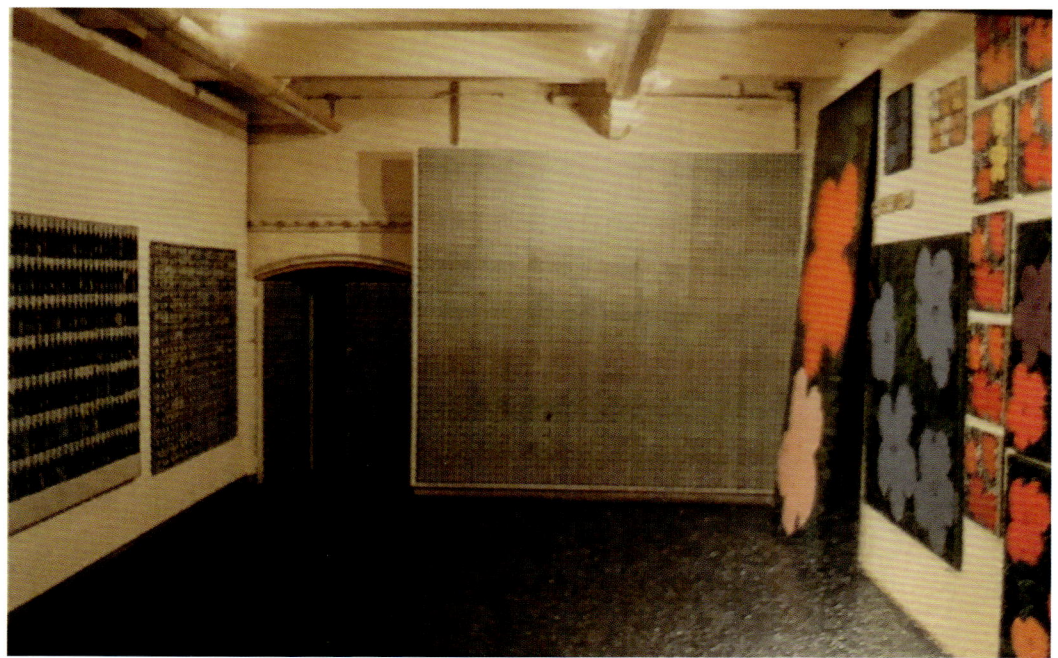

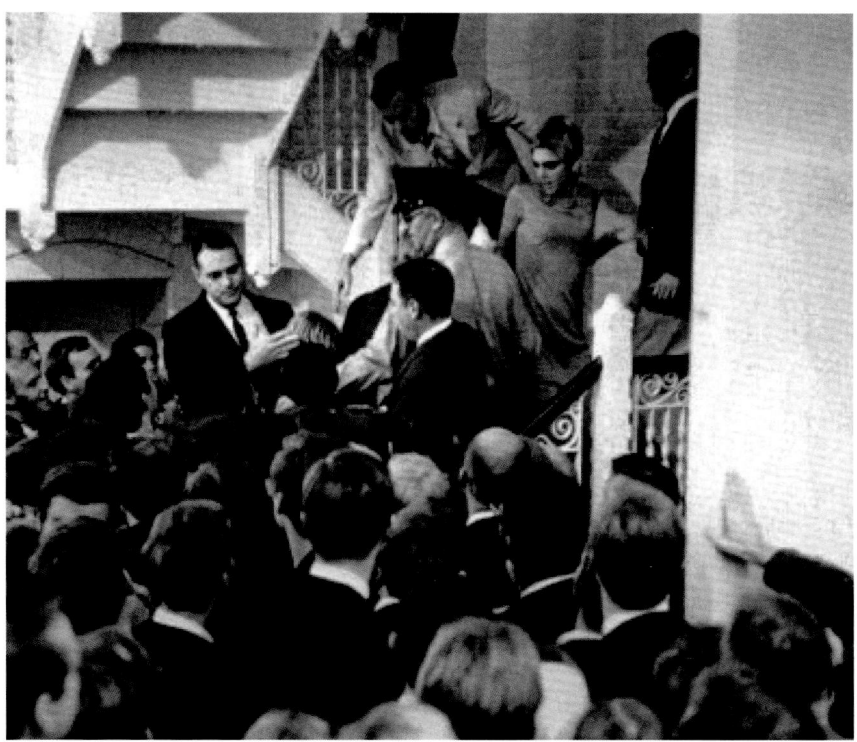

Figure 3.19   Photograph depicting the crowd scene at the opening of
the 1965 Andy Warhol ICA exhibition. Source: Institute of
Contemporary Art Archives. Image used with permission.

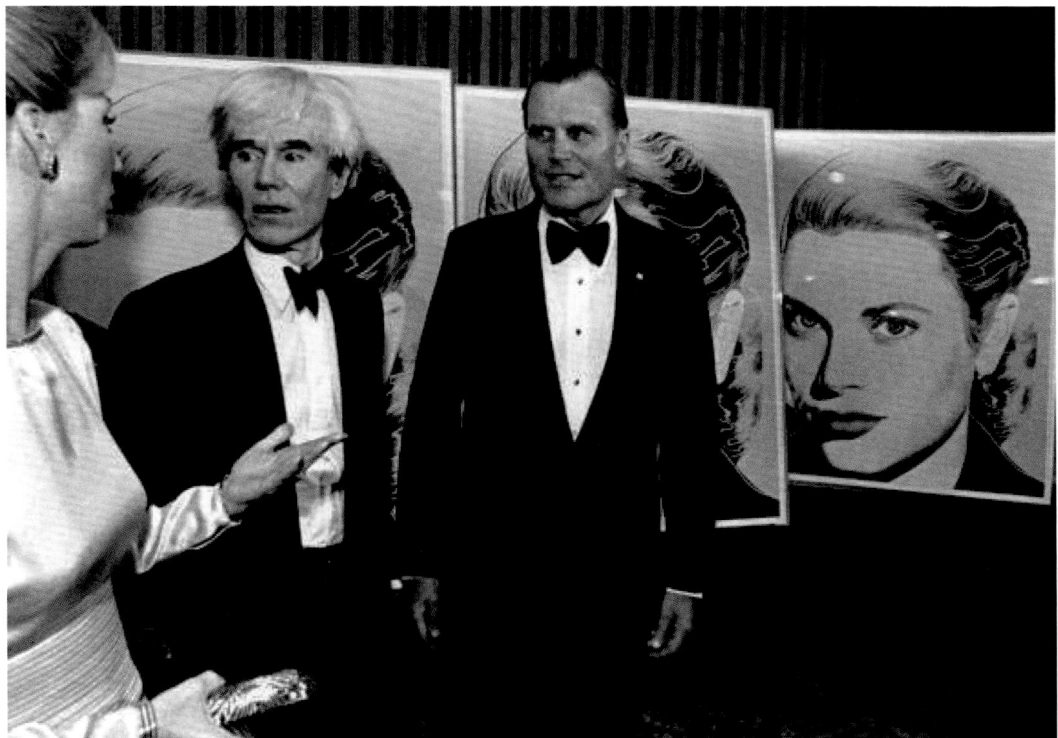

Figure 3.20   Andy Warhol stands in front of a limited edition serigraph
of Princess Grace of Monaco to benefit the Institute of
Contemporary Art in Philadelphia on June 1, 1984. Jack
Kelly (R) and his wife Sandra (L) join Warhol at the Institute.
The ICA is celebrating its 20th anniversary. Source: Institute
of Contemporary Art Archives. Image used with permission.

I had received a thousand-dollar bonus that year, and that's what I had to work with. In those days, it went a long way.

RW: Do you have a favorite piece in your collection?

GM: I have a sentimental attachment to some of the earliest works that I collected. It's been like a journey through time for me. I have long been aware of the importance of Warhol's Marilyn Monroe works. The first Warhol *Marilyn* image that I hoped to acquire was an exhibition invitation. A 1960s piece. I loved the color. I dreamed of owning something like that, but never did I dream that I would amass a collection of over 300 *Marilyn* images. Having *one* of those works would have been remarkable.

I started my Warhol collection by making color copies and mounting them on foamcore. Then I positioned them throughout my office. As the years went on, I slowly was able to purchase actual works and ephemera, one at a time. I still have my original little color copy of the *Dollar Sign*. It was on a piece of 8½ × 11 copier paper, mounted on board. I taped half of a paper clip to the back and hung it on the wall and that was my collection *(Fig. 3.17)*. As I mentioned before, eventually I acquired a *Dollar Sign* painting. Just to give a feel for Warhol's market, with the amount that I paid for that painting, I could have purchased a much larger painting, a ninety-inch work, at the time when I first started collecting. By the time I was able to afford a painting by Warhol, I could afford only a ten-inch painting. So you can see the trajectory of Warhol's market. It's really quite remarkable.

RW: You wanted the show focusing on your *Marilyn* prints to be at the University of Pennsylvania. Why at Penn?

GM: Well, first of all, I was aware of Warhol's history with the University of Pennsylvania. There was an important exhibition of his work at the ICA [Institute of Contemporary Art] here in 1965 *(Fig. 3.18)*. It was his first one-person exhibition at a museum. There are well-known photographs of the extremely crowded opening, which Warhol attended *(Fig. 3.19)*.

Also, I was aware of the print he made in 1984 of Grace Kelly as a fundraiser for the ICA on its twentieth anniversary.[13] Warhol made an appearance at the ICA

with Mr. Kelly [Grace Kelly's brother, John B. ("Jack")] *(Fig. 3.20)*.[14] So that was something.

I had a friend who introduced me to a couple of people at Penn, moving the project along.

And also, I will share with you a personal story connected to my choice of Penn. My father had been ill many years ago, when he was in his late forties, and having discussed the situation with his doctors, he ended up being rushed to the University of Pennsylvania's hospital, thinking that he might have to lose both his legs, and the doctors at Penn saved him. So I have a special place in my heart for the University of Pennsylvania. It helped me to keep my father for a long time, and I'm very grateful for that.

RW: That's quite a moving story.

GM: Oh, it is. It was dramatic. Obviously, my father and mother were very important to me. My mother was creative, and perhaps I had a similar relationship to my mother to the one Warhol had with his mother. He was very close to his mother. My mother was the type who was always producing a little something. For example, as a little boy, one night I remember coming home to discover my mother with rolls of contact paper. She was cutting out the shapes in the contact paper. I asked, "Mom, why are you cutting out all these little shapes?" She said, because those were the elements of the design that she liked. She would edit the design in that way and use the parts she liked on the wall. I think most people would have accepted the design of the paper as it was and put it on the wall intact. I know Warhol's mother made objects and pictures.

1. Frayda Feldman and Jörg Schellmann, *Andy Warhol Prints: A Catalogue Raisonné 1962–1987*, 4th ed., rev. and expanded by Frayda Feldman and Claudia Defendi (New York: D.A.P./Distributed Art Publishers, Inc., in association with Ronald Feldman Fine Arts, Inc., Edition Schellmann, and the Andy Warhol Foundation for the Visual Arts, Inc., 2003), 126–27, cat. nos. II.274–86.
2. On these works, see Roberta Bernstein and Carter E. Foster, *Jasper Johns: Numbers* (Cleveland: Cleveland Museum of Art, 2003).
3. Georg Frei and Neil Printz, eds., *The Andy Warhol Catalogue Raisonné, Paintings and Sculpture 1961–1963*, vol. 1 (London: Phaidon Press, 2002), 131–50, cat. nos. 125–68.
4. Several writers have noted connections, of various types, between Warhol's work and that of Marcel Duchamp, as well as Duchamp's influence on Warhol. A 2010 exhibition, *Twisted Pair: Marcel Duchamp/Andy Warhol*, devoted to the subject, was organized by Matt Wrbican for the Andy Warhol Museum, Pittsburgh. See also "Marilyn Mystery" in the present volume.

5. See http://www.bengtssonfineart.com/.

6. This quip was not actually Warhol's, but the invention of Pontus Hultén, according to Olle Granath, who worked on the catalogue; see Granath, "With Andy Warhol 1968," in *Andy Warhol, A Guide to 706 Items in 2 Hours 56 Minutes*, ed. Eva Meyer-Hermann (Rotterdam: NAi Publishers, 2007), 00:13:00.

7. See Granath, "With Andy Warhol 1968," 00:13:00.

8. See Georg Frei and Neil Printz, eds., *The Andy Warhol Catalogue Raisonné, Paintings and Sculpture 1964–1969*, vol. 2B (London: Phaidon Press, 2004), 266 and 275–77, cat. no. 135.1.

9. Feldman and Schellmann, *Andy Warhol Prints*, 67, cat. no. II.20.

10. Granath, "With Andy Warhol 1968," 00:12:00. The Brillo box cartons used for the Stockholm exhibition are described, in a (perhaps unintended) conceptual twist, as "cardboard facsimiles of the *Brillo* box sculptures" of 1964 in Frei and Printz, *Andy Warhol Catalogue Raisonné*, vol. 2B, 345. See also "Marilyn Mystery" in this volume.

11. Granath, "With Andy Warhol 1968," 00:12:00.

12. Frei and Printz, *Andy Warhol Catalogue Raisonné*, vol. 2B, 344–65.

13. Feldman and Schellmann, *Andy Warhol Prints*, 133, cat. no. II.305; 193, cat. no. IIB.305; 218.

14. See Ruth Seltzer, "By Contrast, This Warhol Visit Was Tame," *Philadelphia Inquirer*, June 5, 1984, 3-E. The Kellys were from Philadelphia, and Grace and Jack's mother had taught physical education at the University of Pennsylvania, while Jack received his undergraduate degree there; https://archives.upenn.edu/exhibits/penn-people/biography/john-brenden-kelly-jr.

Marilyn Mystery

Reva Wolf

In October 2009, Gregory McCoy, an avid collector of work by and about Andy Warhol, purchased the first in an unusual and interesting group of prints based on one of Warhol's renowned Marilyn Monroe paintings.[1] Over the course of twelve years, McCoy has amassed 323 of these prints. They come in a wide range of color variations, with backgrounds in yellow, blue, green, light blue, silver, reflective silver ("Lac" prints), orange, red, tan, and white. Seventy-four examples are fluorescent (transforming in appearance when viewed in black light), with backgrounds in either green, orange, or white. Around half the prints are "reversals" (made using negatives of the *Marilyn* composition). Most are two-color prints, and ten are three-color.[2] The prints were acquired through an art and book dealer in Sweden, Börje Bengtsson, from around sixteen distinct sources.[3] Bengtsson associated them with a well-known exhibition about Warhol held at the Moderna Museet in Stockholm in early 1968. The circumstances surrounding the history of these prints are murky. The purpose of this essay is to explore why the prints have been associated with the 1968 Stockholm show, to present the distinct theories that have emerged about what functions they served, to consider their relationship to other *Marilyn* imagery based on Warhol's composition—not all authorized—made during the 1960s, and to look at how they connect to the exhibition practices and artistic vision of the curator of the 1968 show, Pontus Hultén. The aim is not so much to draw a conclusion regarding what these prints are as to present a range of possibilities, opening a door to future work that could ascertain how they came to be made, and why.

The 1968 Moderna Museet Exhibition

The screenprints in Gregory McCoy's collection appear to have been created at a press in Malmö, Sweden,

called Reklamteknik, where several were discovered in storage, according to materials in a binder that McCoy compiled documenting the collection.[4] Reklamteknik was the firm the Moderna Museet typically used for printing posters to advertise its exhibitions, including the seven posters created for the 1968 Warhol exhibition containing statements by Warhol *(Plates LXXVI–LXXXII)* and another of an SAS airplane ticket showing Warhol as the passenger for a round trip to Stockholm *(Fig. 3.13).*[5] Reklamteknik was also where several *Brillo Box* sculptures, based on Warhol's 1960s *Brillo Box* projects, were made in 1990, three years after the artist's death. More on these objects later in this story.

The 1968 Moderna Museet exhibition, entitled *Warhol: Screens, Films, Boxes, Clouds and a Book*, is significant as the first one-person exhibition of Warhol's work at an art museum in Europe.[6] Organized by the then director of the Moderna Museet, Pontus Hultén, together with the electrical engineer Billy Klüver (who was deeply involved in projects connecting art with technology) and the curator Kasper König (then at the outset of his career), and with the assistance of the art historian Olle Granath (who later, in the 1980s, served as director of the Moderna Museet), it was anything but a conventional retrospective covering the trajectory of the artist's career. Apparently, the museum was short on both time and funding, requiring creative problem-solving in order to fill in when desired materials were not forthcoming.[7] Instead of an overview of his career, the show featured new versions, with significant revisions, of previous works by Warhol. In a sense, these works—many produced expressly for the exhibition—were Warhol's own retrospective on, or retrospective interpretations of, his previous accomplishments.

The existing descriptions and documentary photographs of the exhibition provide a good sense of its content and unique qualities. In looking back at the exhibition from the vantage point of the early twenty-first century, Olle

Granath called it "one of the perhaps strangest exhibition productions I have ever been part of."[8] Among its many unusual features was the *Cow Wallpaper* produced to cover the façade of the Moderna Museet building *(Fig. 4.1)*. Two sets of paintings were created for the exhibition: ten *Ten-Foot Flowers*, in a new, large-format version of paintings first made in 1964; and twelve *Big Electric Chair* pictures, in enlarged and slightly transformed renditions of the *Electric Chair* works Warhol had produced in 1964–65, the composition now cropped more closely so that there is a greater focus on the chair and an elimination altogether of the "silence" sign in the viewer's upper right that had been an important detail of the first version *(Figs. 4.2–4.5)*.[9] The use of wallpaper and *Flowers* paintings in combination with the "disaster" imagery of the *Big Electric Chair* pictures has led to a comparison of the Moderna Museet show with the 1965 exhibition of Warhol's work at the Institute of Contemporary Art (ICA) at the University of Pennsylvania *(see Figs. 3.18 and 3.19)*.[10] Furthermore, just as the Moderna Museet show was a first in Europe, so the ICA show was a first in the United States, as Warhol's earliest one-person exhibition in a space other than a commercial art gallery.

At the Moderna Museet, film footage was shown on screens interspersed between the *Flowers* paintings; the plan was to show several Warhol films, but apparently it was not possible to obtain them, and footage of a circus was substituted *(Fig. 4.6)*.[11] On the floor were enormous translucent "clouds" *(Fig. 4.6)*, enlarged variations on the silver helium *Clouds* Warhol had exhibited two years earlier at Leo Castelli Gallery in New York together with the first version of his *Cow Wallpaper*.[12]

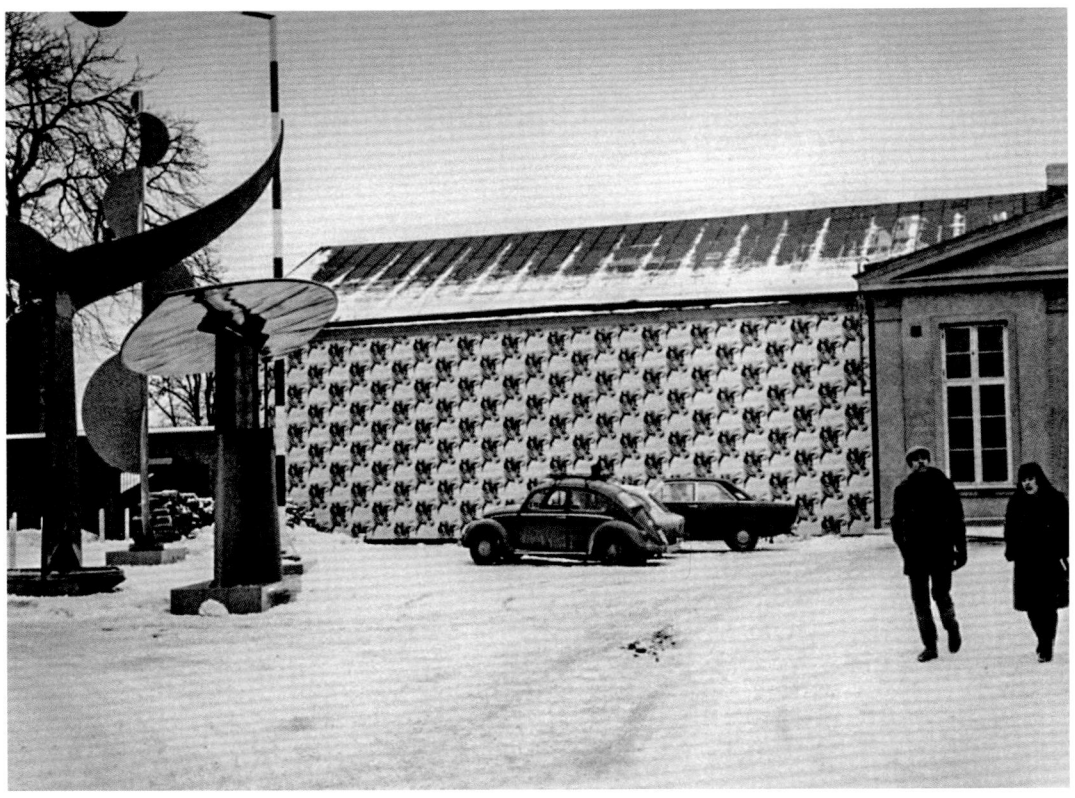

Figure 4.1   Photograph of the exterior of the Moderna
                   Museet covered in *Cow Wallpaper*. Source:
                   Moderna Museet, 1968. Image used with permission
                   from the Moderna Museet.

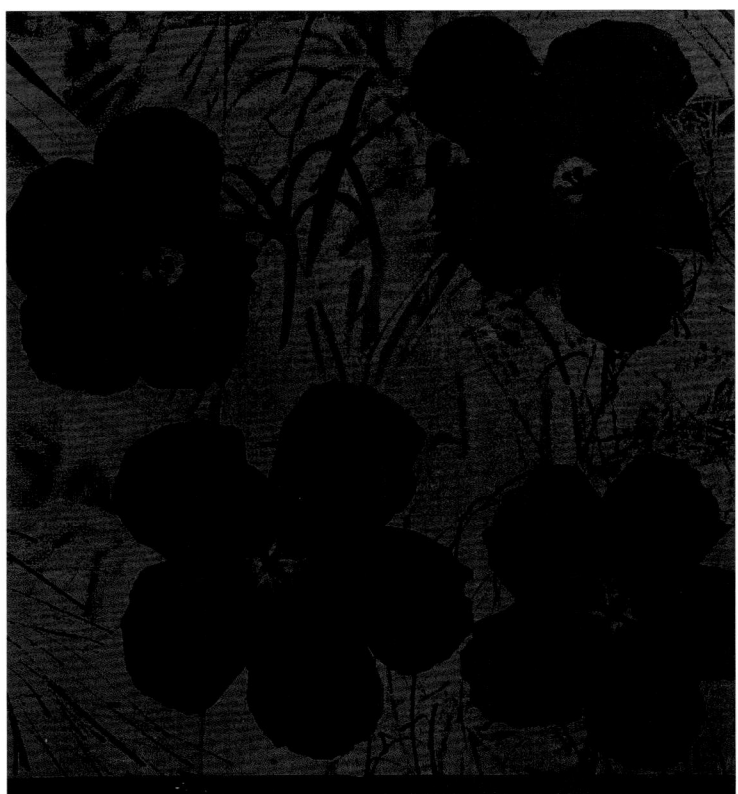

Figure 4.2   Andy Warhol, *Ten-Foot Flowers*, 1967, silkscreen ink on synthetic
                   polymer paint on canvas, 116 x 116 in. Moderna Museet,
                   Stockholm. Donation 1976 from the artist.

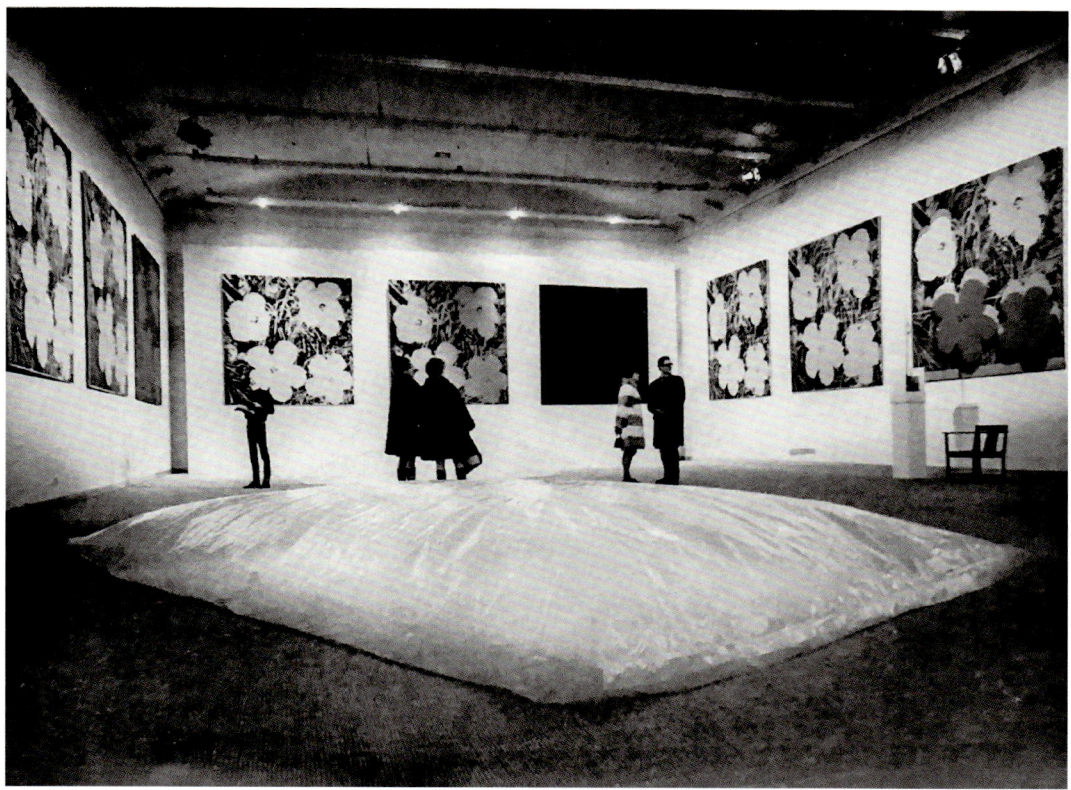

Figure 4.3   Installation view of the 1968 Warhol exhibition at the
Moderna Museet, Stockholm, showing the *Ten-Foot
Flowers*, from *Andy Warhol*, 3rd ed. (Stockholm:
Moderna Museet, 1970), unpaged.

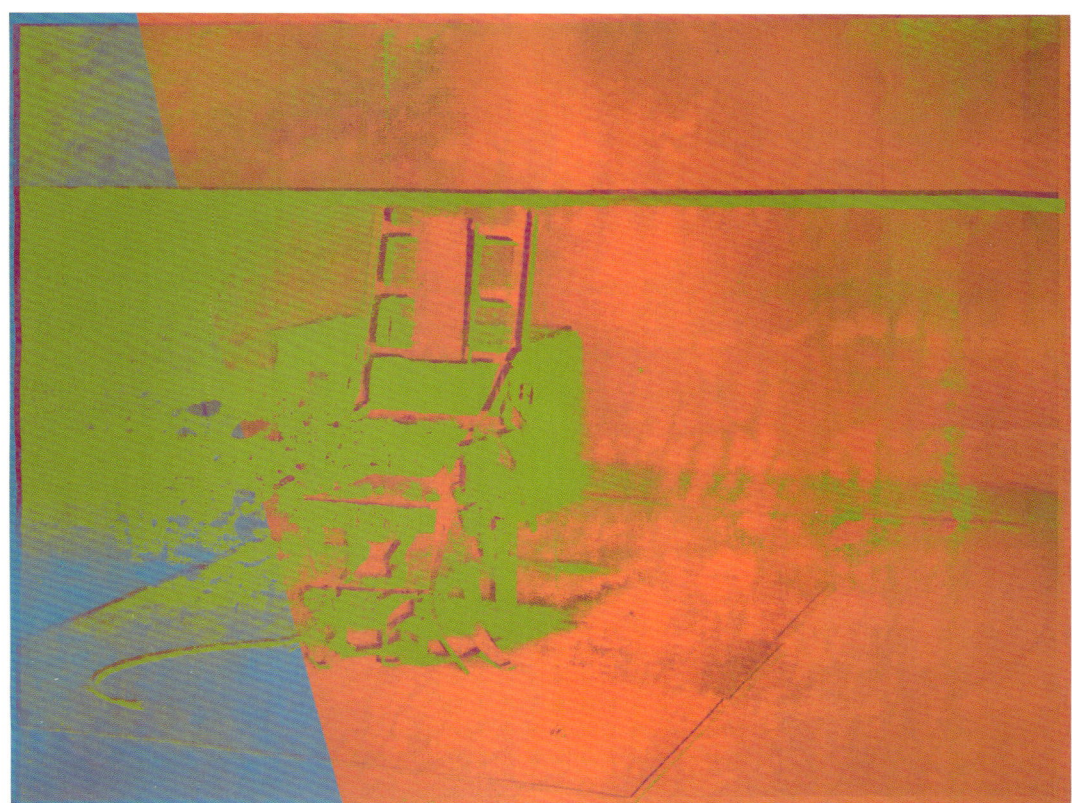

Figure 4.4   Andy Warhol, *Electric Chair*, 1967, silkscreen ink on synthetic polymer
paint on canvas, 54 x 73 in. Moderna Museet, Stockholm. Donation
1976 from Kasper König.

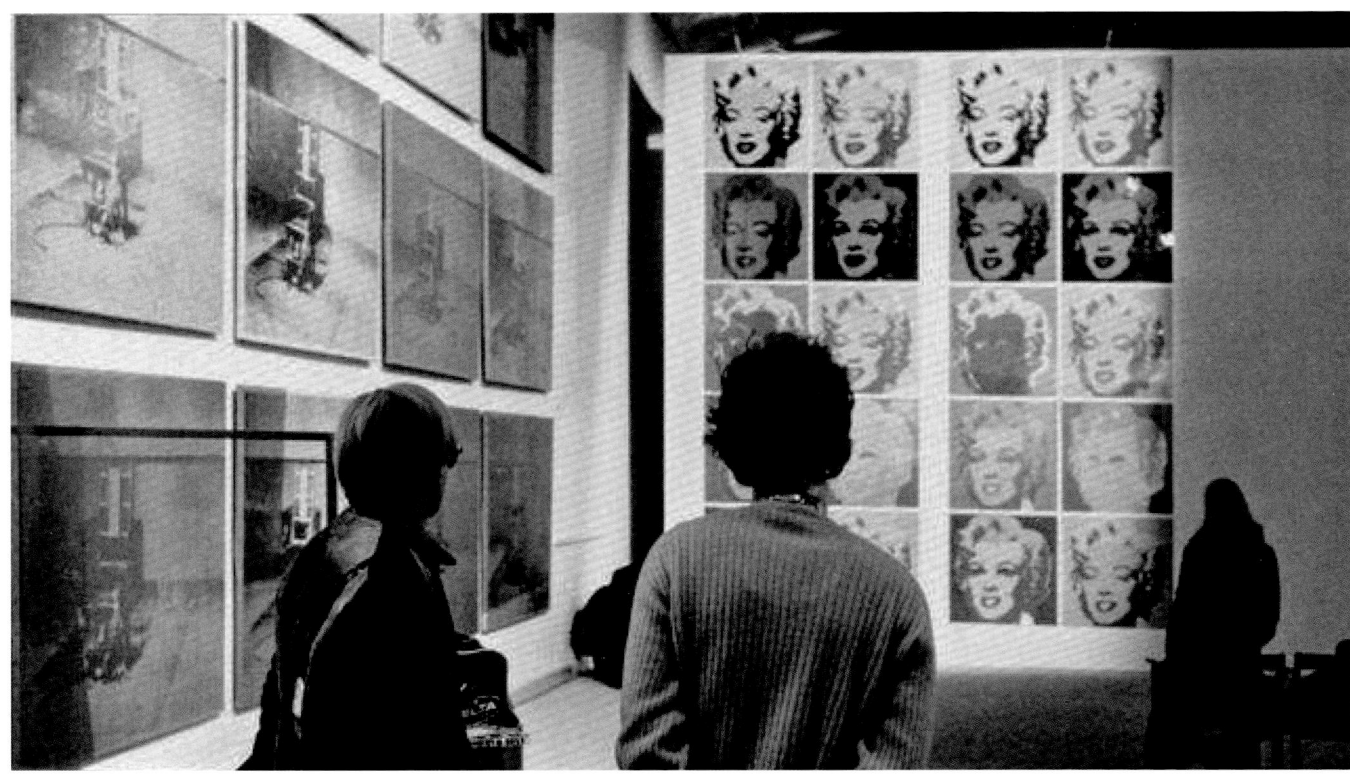

Figure 4.5   Installation view of the 1968 Warhol exhibition at the
Moderna Museet, Stockholm, showing the *Big Electric
Chair* paintings. Image used with permission from the
Moderna Museet.

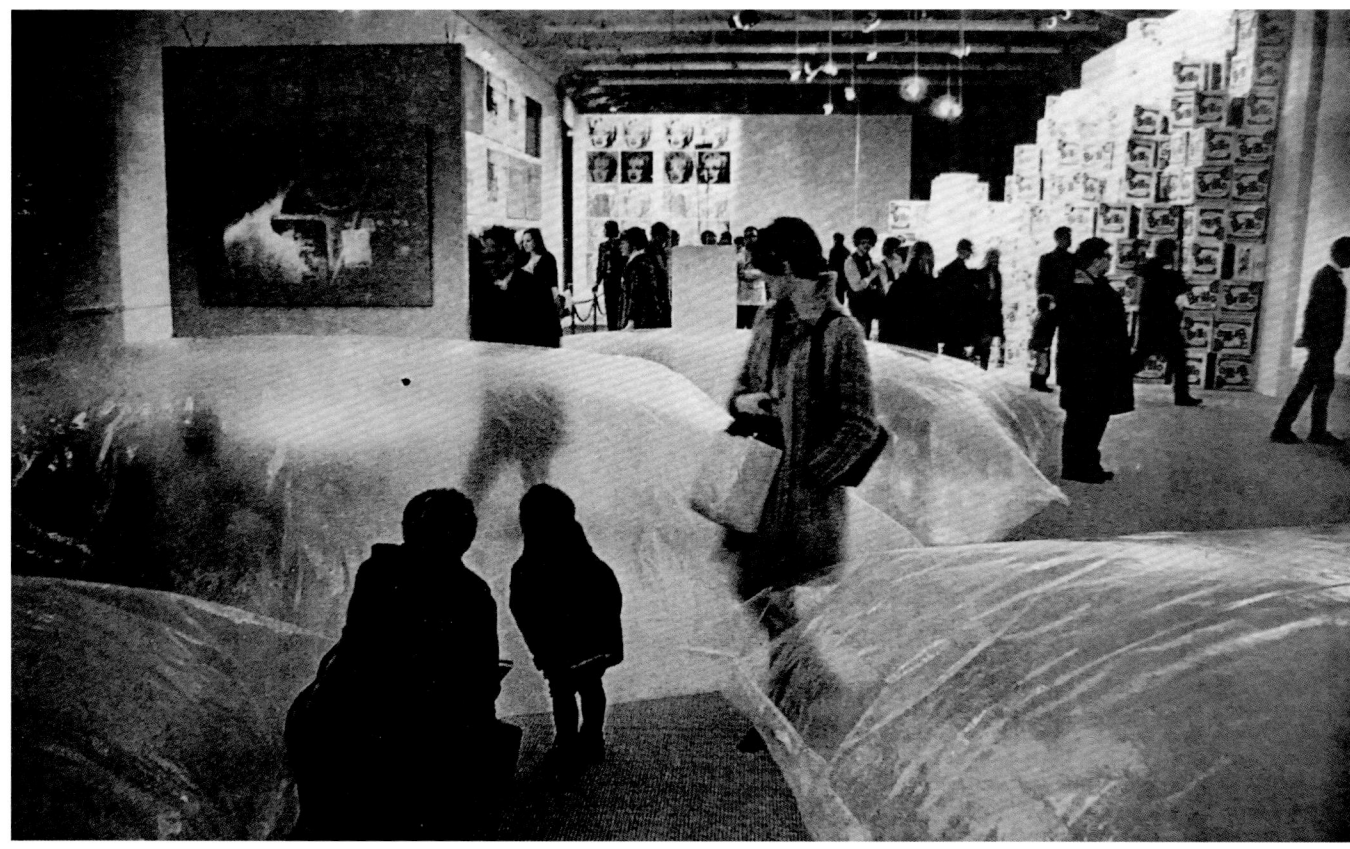

Figure 4.6   Installation view of the 1968 Warhol exhibition at the Moderna Museet, Stockholm, showing the Brillo
soap pad cartons, from *Andy Warhol,* 3rd ed. (Stockholm: Moderna Museet, 1970), unpaged.

The organizers of the exhibition were also keen to include examples of Warhol's *Brillo Box* sculptures, a large number of which he had made and exhibited together at the Stable Gallery in New York in 1964. However, as the art critic and friend of Warhol David Bourdon noted, the "exhibition contained about five hundred *actual* Brillo boxes—not Andy's facsimile sculptures, but real cardboard containers" *(Fig. 4.6)*.[13] In the catalogue raisonné of Warhol's work, these objects were described as "cardboard facsimiles of the *Brillo Box* sculptures."[14] Life imitates art. Olle Granath later recollected:

> Displaying the number of Brillo boxes required by the theme of repetition involved an expensive production as well as an enormous shipping volume. Warhol suggested that the boxes should be made in Sweden, but that wasn't cheap either and we were running out of time. At this point someone came up with the brilliant idea of buying five hundred cardboard boxes from Brillo. They were shipped in flat packs across the Atlantic and folded at the museum. The museum attendant and I became real wizards at folding boxes. The result was a magnificent mountain of boxes which accentuated the repetition theme of the exhibition.[15]

A letter of July 7, 1967, from the Brillo Manufacturing Company to Kasper König shows that a plan to acquire 300 cardboard Brillo cartons was already in place some six months prior to the opening of the exhibition in Stockholm *(Fig. 4.7)*.[16]

Along with these objects, within the central interior space of the exhibition were two sets of ten *Marilyn* prints, produced the previous year *(Fig. 4.6)*. As with other items in the exhibition, these works on paper—among the earliest of Warhol's prints based on paintings—are revisions of his previous works. In the case of the prints, the remake of paintings constituted Warhol's third version of his *Marilyn* imagery. The distinctions between these versions are important to keep in mind when considering the *McCoy Marilyn* works, and will be discussed in further depth later in this essay. For now, it is helpful to highlight the choice to use *two* sets of the prints, and their role within the exhibition. One set of the prints already signifies, but two accentuate, what Olle Granath noted as among the "basic themes" of the exhibition: repetition.[17]

Granath connected these prints to another element of the exhibition: "on the divider wall at the staircase leading to the small cinema, one could find a number of *Marilyn* portraits which continued the wallpaper theme of the exterior."[18] This parallel of the interior with the exterior echoes a subject that Pontus Hultén had explored in a previous exhibition at the Moderna Museet, *Inner and Outer Space: An Exhibition on Universal Art*, of 1965, a point that will be picked up below in the discussion of Hultén's practices as a curator.

Granath's description of the location of the prints, in a spot leading to the museum's cinema, makes a connection between the images and Marilyn Monroe's profession as an actor and her status as a movie star. In the catalogue raisonné of Warhol's paintings and sculptures, it is proposed that the main point of the Stockholm exhibition was to show the relationship between Warhol's work in film and in painting, with the large size of the *Flowers* paintings coinciding with the size of a film screen, while the *Marilyn* prints were the only works referring to film directly.[19] The key position of Warhol's *Marilyn* images within the exhibition suggests a link to the McCoy *Marilyn* prints. But what kind of link?

Why and When?

What could have been the purpose of printing over 300 *Marilyn* prints in a variety of color combinations? Over the years since Gregory McCoy started collecting them, distinct ideas have been proposed, and these are documented in an extensive email correspondence between him and Börje Bengtsson. Throughout this correspondence, Bengtsson was keen to establish a direct connection between the prints and the 1968 Warhol exhibition at the Moderna Museet. Early in this process, in October 2010, Bengtsson prepared a "Letter of Authenticity and Provenance," issued to McCoy for *Marilyn* prints that he stated had been owned by the graphic designer John Melin (1921–92). These prints were described as "proof copies," and it was noted that "John Melin got a request fr[om] the director Pontus Hulten to produce a serie[s] of unique prints for the staircase inside the Museum."[20] The letter noted that "copyright and economy" made this plan unworkable, and that Pontus Hultén instead suggested making the seven posters with statements by Warhol that ultimately

were used to advertise the exhibition; these posters were designed by Melin and printed in black ink on cheap white poster paper (*Plates LXXVI–LXXXII*). Bengtsson claimed his account came from information in books (this author has found no books mentioning the McCoy *Marilyn* prints) and from interviews he had conducted with Hultén (who had died in 2006), Olle Granath, John Melin (he died in 1992), Signe Melin, and Matthias Swinge (the assistant to Signe Melin and a representative of the estate of John Melin).

Two years after Bengtsson issued this letter, he sent McCoy a letter in Swedish written by Matthias Swinge, along with his translation of it, dated August 10, 2012. This letter states that in 2009 Swinge helped the Melin family go through and clean out a storage unit and that, in the process, they found around twenty *Marilyn* prints in unique colors. He asked Melin's son what they were. "He told me that they were prints that probably where [*sic*] done for the Stockholm Exhibition in 1968 w Andy Warhol cause John did everything else for that show, catalog, posters, SAS Passenger Ticket and more."[21]

Bengtsson sent a similar statement to McCoy the following year, dated July 16, 2013, signed by Nils Erik Balcke of the Stig Arbman Advertising Agency, where John Melin had worked: "These Marilyn posters/ screenprints were done at Reklamteknik in Malmö January-February 1968 for the Stockholm exhibition." According to this account,

> Arbman was working for free for Moderna Museet, Pontus Hulten. John Melin & Pontus Hultén agreed that these prints [*sic*] to Moderna Museet. John started to print these with Arne Wahlqvist and the prints were done on the side. To my knowledge there were never any written invoices from Arbmans to Moderna Museet.[22]

The idea that the McCoy *Marilyn* prints were made for the 1968 exhibition but then not used was also suggested in a handwritten statement of January 22, 2014, from the widow of a partner in the Arbman Advertising Agency.[23] This account is second-hand—a kind of hearsay, perhaps. According to the widow, who wished to remain anonymous, "What we have heard about these screenprints of Marilyn is that they were done for an exhibition in Stockholm. It says they were

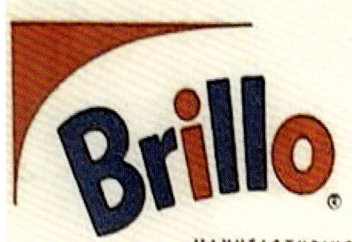

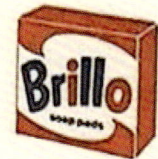

MANUFACTURING COMPANY BRILLO BUILDING. 60 JOHN ST.. BROOKLYN 1. N. Y.·UL 2·4700
(Division of Purex Corporation, Ltd.)

July 7, 1967

Mr. Kasper Konig
65 East Broadway
New York, N. Y. 10002

Dear Mr. Konig:

It was interesting to receive your call, and to learn that you
represent a museum in Stockholm, Sweden, and that a major show
is being planned on pop art and Andy Warhol.

You have asked whether we can supply you with 300 empty Brillo
Soap Pad corrugated shipping cartons, and this we will be very
pleased to do.

The cost which we quoted you on the phone is correct, at 20¢
per carton, F.O.B. our plant. The cartons would be supplied
flat.

We understand that you will arrange to have the merchandise
picked up after sending us your check to cover the quantity
you will require. Please contact our Mr. Ernst Hirsch, advising
him when the pick-up will be made.

Thank you for your interest in Brillo.

We look forward to the opportunity of being of assistance to you.

Yours very truly,

John H. Loeb

JOHN H. LOEB
Executive Vice President

JHL:cbb

GUARANTEE · A NEW UTENSIL FREE IF BRILLO FAILS TO CLEAN

Figure 4.7   Letter from John H. Loeb, Brillo Company, to Kasper
König, July 7, 1967. Image used with permission from the
Moderna Museet.

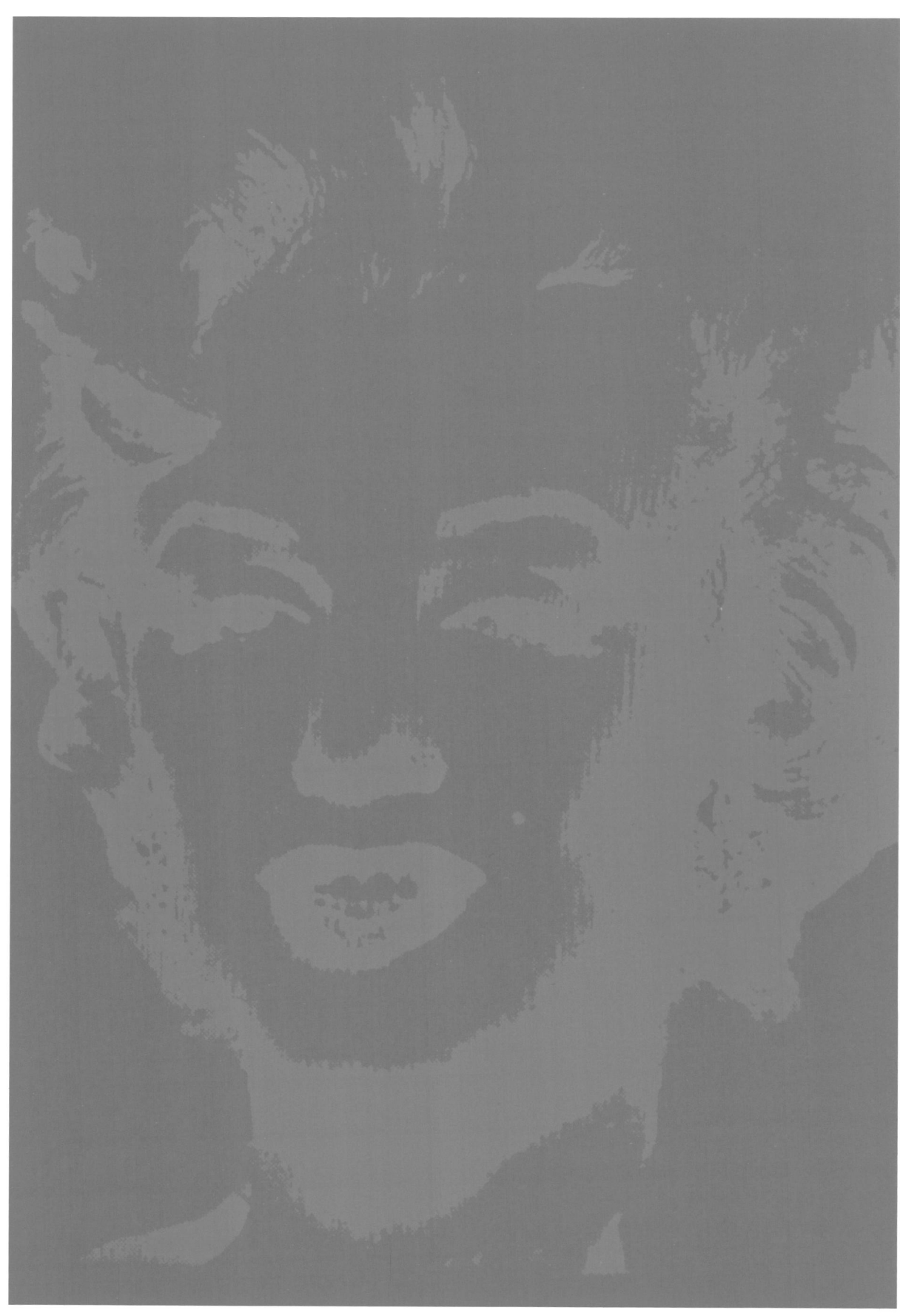

Figure 4.8   AWMM.1968.058 (Plate L.B, p. 156), two-color reversal screenprint: clear ink base on paperboard that has been laminated on both sides with silver foil (Lac-print). Gregory McCoy Collection. Image used with permission.

Figure 4.9   John Melin and Anders Österlin, *Inner and Outer Space* exhibition poster, 1965, 39 x 27 in. Museum of Modern Art, New York.

Seeking to determine the date of his *Marilyn* prints in whatever way possible, and with care, in 2012 Gregory McCoy submitted a sampling of three of his prints to a technical study at the highly regarded firm of Orion Analytical, LLC, in Williamstown, Massachusetts. The conclusion of this study was that "the generic pigments and other materials detected in three inks were available as early as the 1960s (and also in subsequent decades, including the 1980s)."[34] It was recommended to examine prints with red or yellow inks "for possible anachronistic materials to help you date the prints."[35] Some years later, McCoy followed up on this recommendation, submitting two prints with a red and two with a yellow background to Williamstown Art Conservation Center, Inc. for similar tests (see Appendix, *Fig. A.7*). In a report of March 24, 2017, from this center, Christine Puza indicated that both the red and the yellow pigments began to be used commercially in the 1950s and that both pigments are still in use; thus, the prints could have been made any time from the late 1960s forward. The study did reveal that certain types of red and yellow pigments that were first manufactured in the mid-1980s were not present in the prints, leaving open the possibility that they could have been made around the time of the 1968 Warhol show in Stockholm.[36]

Warhol's 1960s *Marilyns* and the McCoy Collection

The two sets of ten *Marilyn* prints by Warhol that were included in the 1968 Moderna Museet exhibition are among the first screenprint editions that Warhol made based on compositions he had previously explored in painted works *(Figs. 4.5 and 4.6)*. These works followed the composition of his 1964 *Marilyn* photo-silkscreen paintings *(Figs. 4.14–4.16)*. They are square, with the neck largely cropped, unlike the first *Marilyn* photo-silkscreen paintings, of 1962, which are rectangular compositions of around 20 × 16 inches, showing more of the neck *(Figs. 4.11 and 4.13)*. As is well known, both versions are based on a c. 1952 publicity photograph *(Fig. 4.10)*—in each version, the focus is progressively closer in on the face than in the source photograph. Among the 1962 works is *Marilyn Monroe in Black and White*, also known as *Twenty-Five Marilyns*, owned by the Moderna

Museet *(Fig. 4.11)*.[37] The McCoy *Marilyn* prints appear to be based on one of the twenty-five images within this painting, slightly cropped—notably, on the viewer's right, where the edge of the hair, present in the painting, is not visible. Nearly two thirds of these prints include a vertically oriented inscription in the bottom right corner indicating this identification *(Fig. 4.12)*.[38]

This identification of the source of the McCoy *Marilyn* image as coming from the Moderna Museet's painting raises a fascinating question of classification. Typically, a print made after a painting and identified as such would be classified as a poster. But one expects that posters after paintings—a common product sold in museum shops—show the paintings as they appear, with the same color schemes. In the case of the McCoy collection, however, the prints come in a wide assortment of colors, and in various color combinations; only eight of the over 300 prints are, like the painting, in black ink on a white ground (*Plates LXV and LXXI*).[39] Furthermore, several of the prints are in three colors and use off-register printing so that the details of the face (lips, eyes, eyebrows, nose) are not aligned, an effect seen in Warhol's *Marilyn* print portfolio of 1967 included in the Moderna Museet's 1968 exhibition much more than in his *Marilyn* paintings of 1962 and 1964. The McCoy *Marilyn* prints do not attempt to copy Warhol's work. In this respect, they are not like the unauthorized copies of his 1967 *Marilyn* prints issued around 1970 with "Sunday B. Morning" printed on the back.[40] It is possible they have some connection to the silkscreened *Marilyn* images included in a catalogue that was made for the Moderna Museet's show (along with silkscreened "Bären Export" beer labels) when it traveled to Berlin, about which little seems to be known.[41] They are not posters in the conventional sense. And the fact that they include inscriptions shows that they are in no way forgeries and do not present themselves as original works of art. Instead, they could be labeled interpretations of a work by Warhol. But why these interpretations were made, and when, is a mystery.

If the prints were made in the late 1960s, around the time of the Moderna Museet exhibition, it could be enlightening to understand them as products of the "cult of the poster" that reached its zenith exactly at this time.[42] Design historian Elizabeth C. Guffey observes that posters "mimicked the modes of fine art, though often

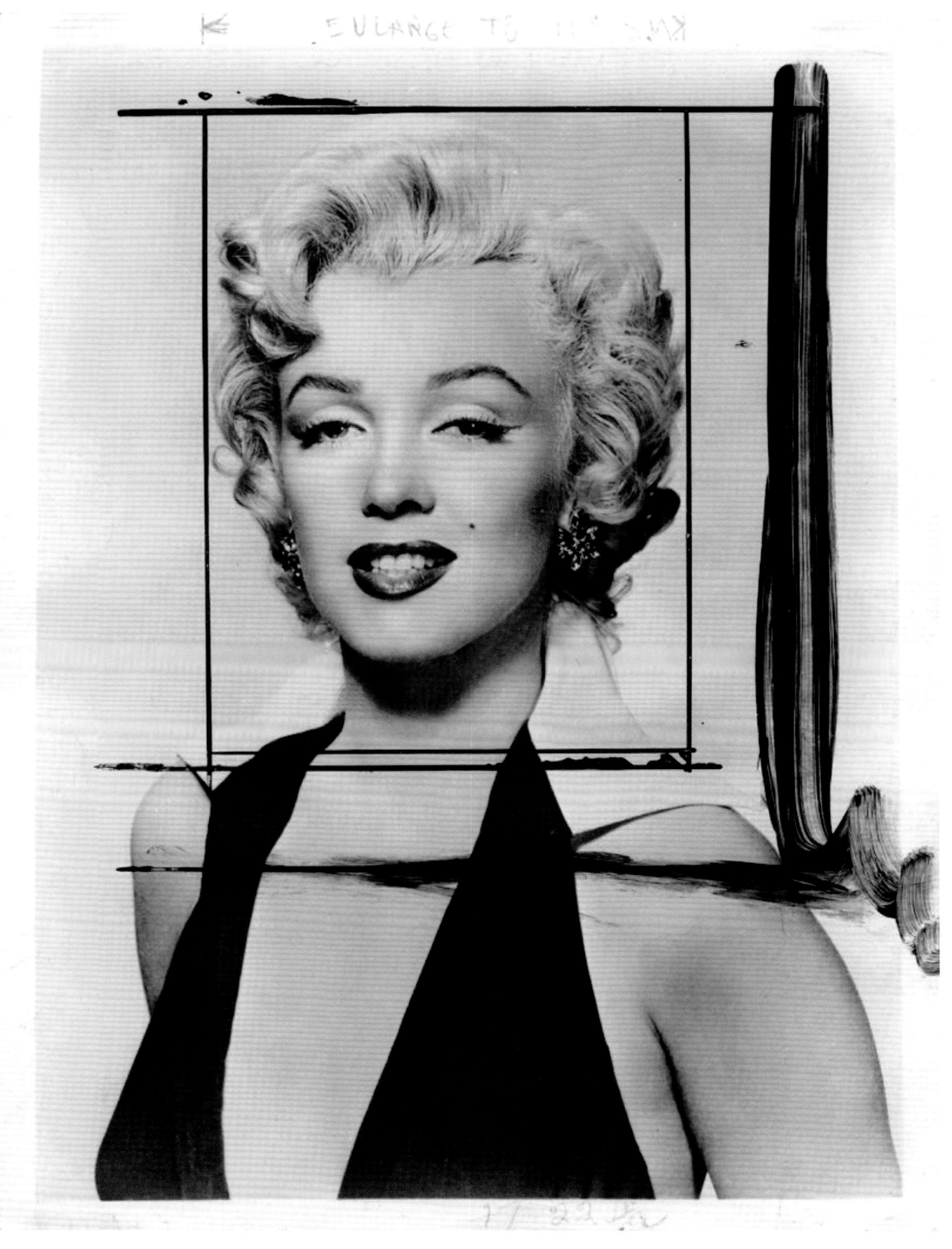

Figure 4.10   Gene Korman, publicity photograph of Marilyn Monroe, c. 1952,
marked by Warhol for cropping. The Andy Warhol Museum,
Pittsburgh; Founding Collection.

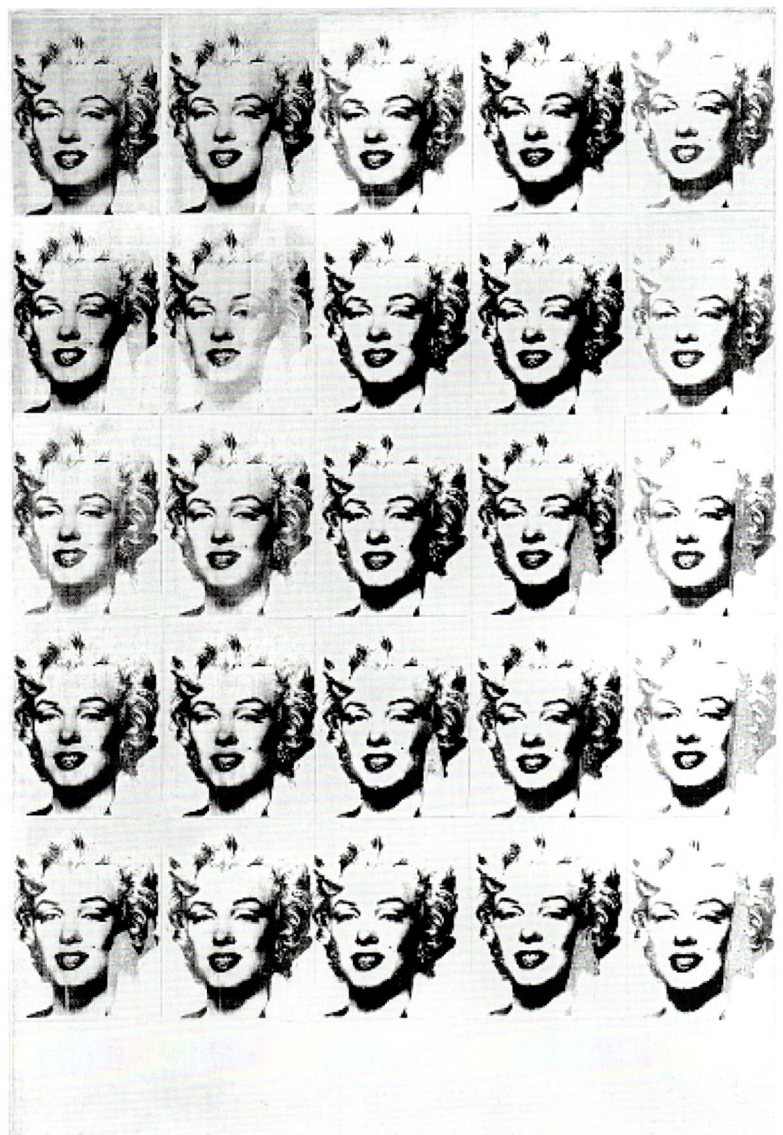

Figure 4.11   Andy Warhol, *Marilyn Monroe in Black and White (Twenty-Five Marilyns)*, 1962, silkscreen ink, graphite and acrylic paint on canvas, 82 x 55 in. Moderna Museet, Stockholm.

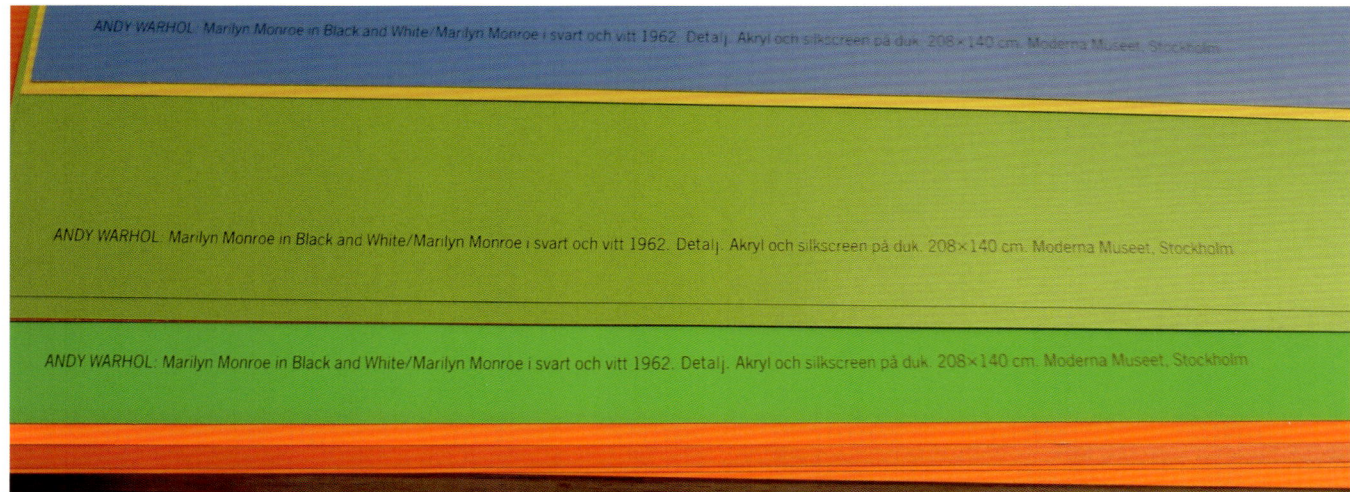

Figure 4.12   Details of three *Marilyn* prints in the McCoy collection showing the inscriptions.

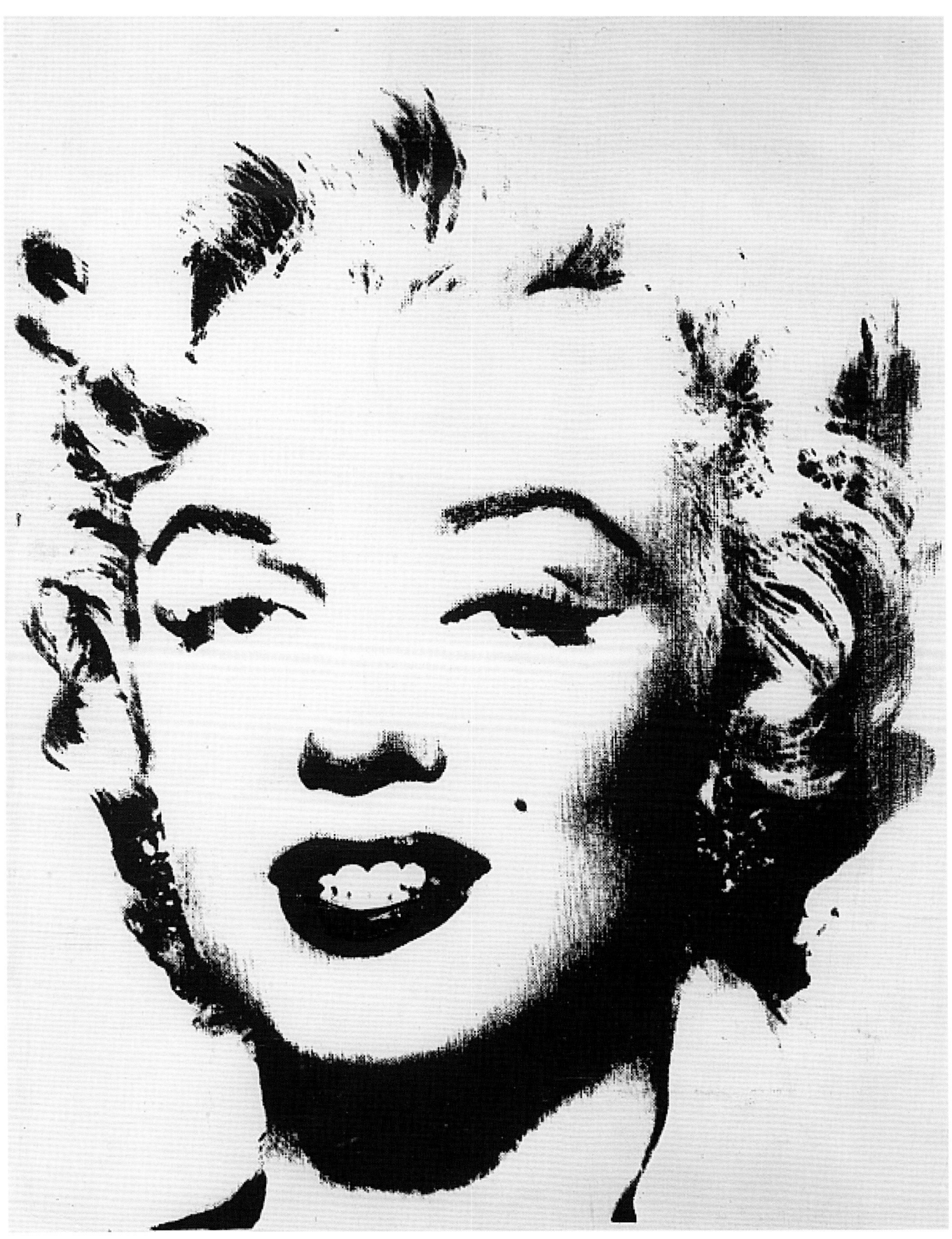

Figure 4.13   Andy Warhol, *Marilyn*, 1962, reproduction in Andy
Warhol, Photo Album, volume 1, 1968. Moderna Museet,
Stockholm, FM 1968 004 001.

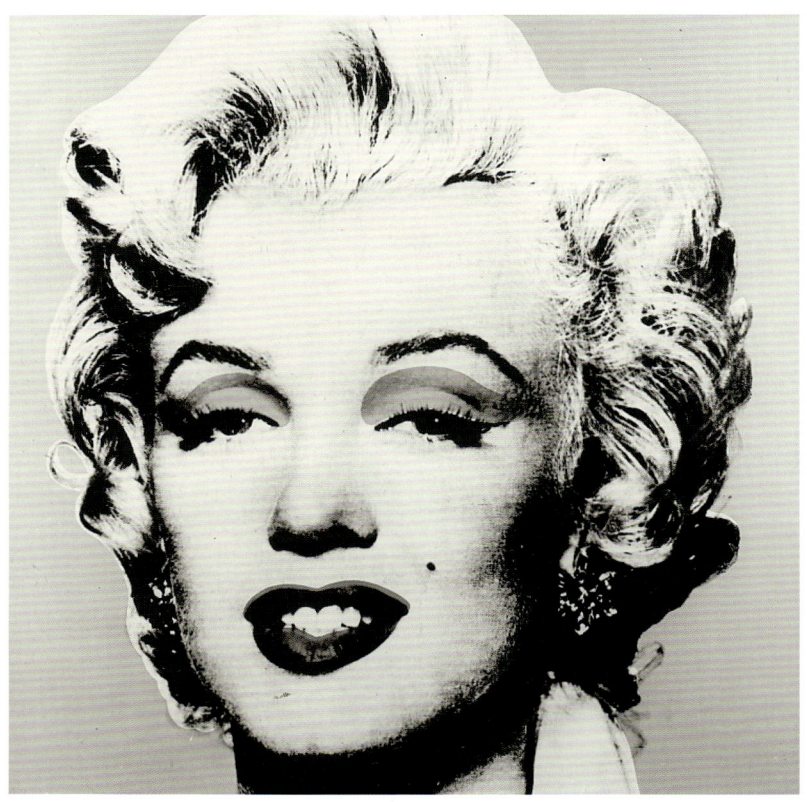

Figure 4.14   Andy Warhol, *Marilyn*, 1964, reproduction in Andy
Warhol, Photo Album, volume 1, 1968. Moderna Museet,
Stockholm, FM 1968 004 001.

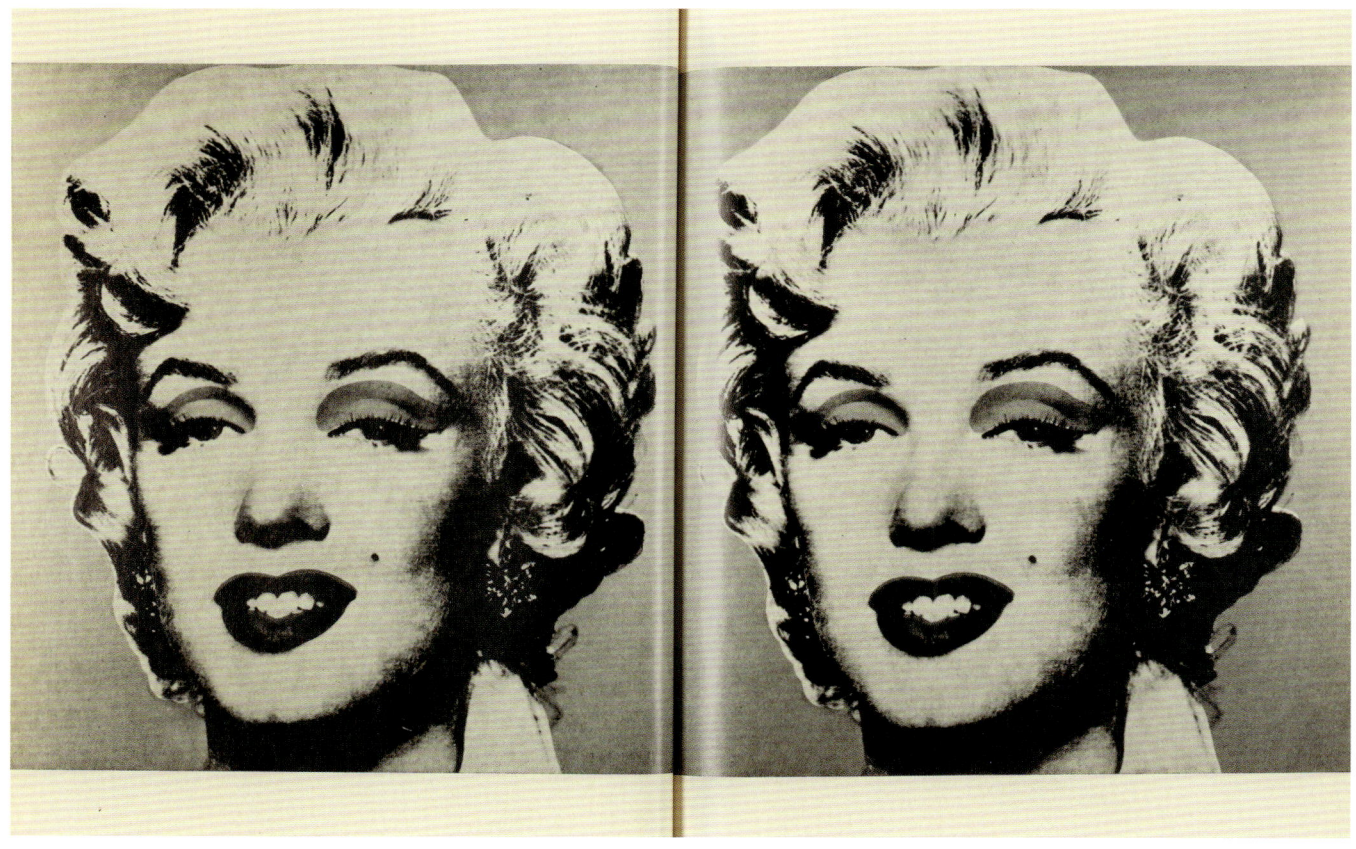

Figure 4.15   Andy Warhol, *Marilyn*, 1964, reproductions in *Andy
Warhol* (Stockholm: Moderna Museet, 1968), unpaged.

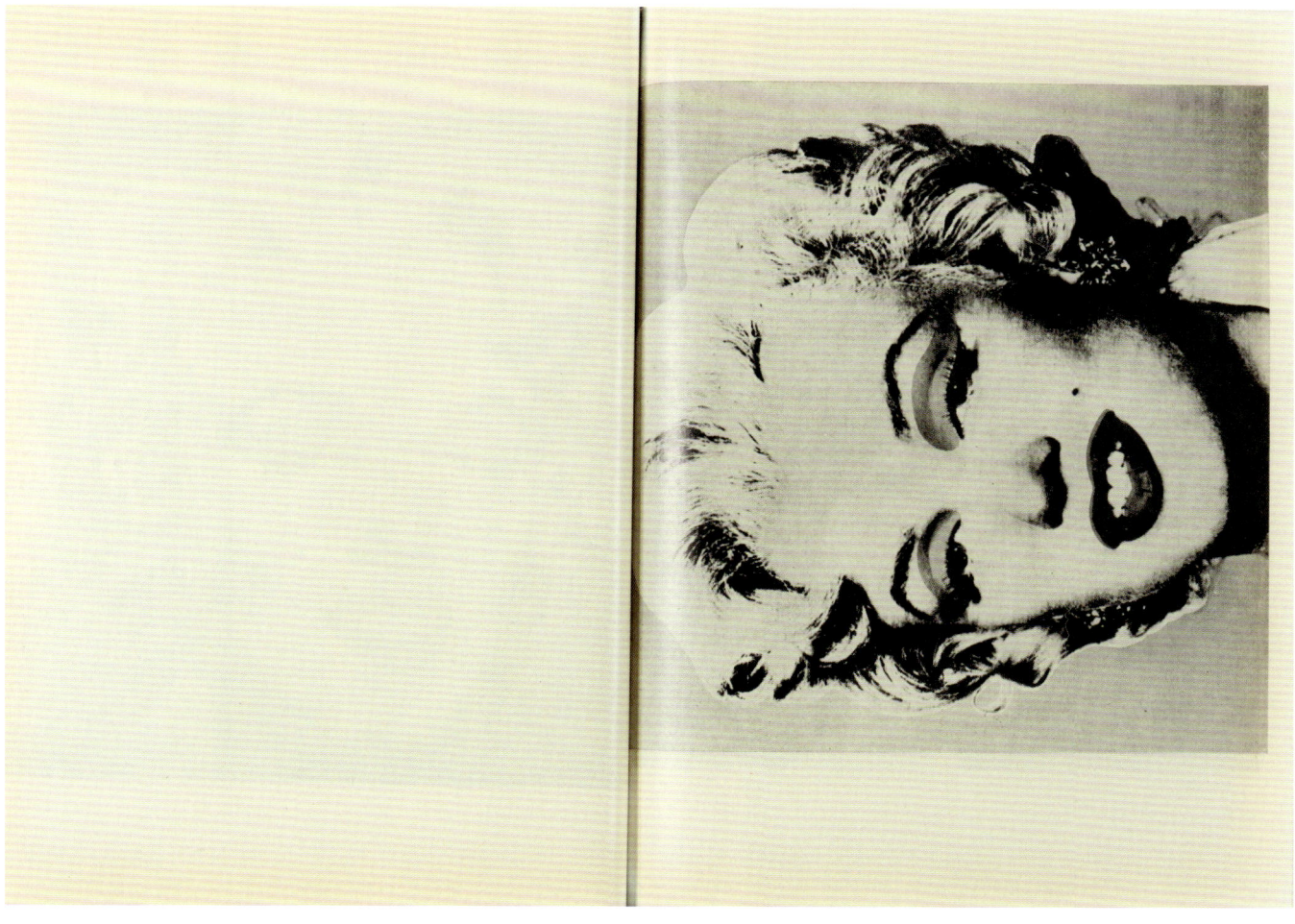

Figure 4.16   Andy Warhol, *Marilyn*, 1964, reproduction in *Andy Warhol*
(Stockholm: Moderna Museet, 1968), unpaged.

with fantastic exaggeration. They were shown in museums and lauded in prestigious biennials," and the "history of posters in this period is a complicated thing . . . since it straddles several different worlds."[43] The popular press in the United States covered the poster craze with zeal. High-circulation magazines such as *Life*, *Newsweek*, and *Time* ran stories about it; so did art and culture magazines, including *ARTnews* and *Horizon*, commercial-oriented graphic design journals such as *Graphis*, and the *New York Times* and other major newspapers. A story from 1967 in *Life* magazine declared that "suddenly posters are the national hang-up" (using what must have been an irresistible if embarrassingly silly pun) and that they "serve as low-cost paintings, do-it-yourself wallpaper, comic Valentines or propaganda for . . . Batman and rye bread."[44] The wallpaper effect (interesting to consider in connection to Warhol's *Cow Wallpaper*!) is borne out in several photographs from the period showing entire walls in cafés, bedrooms, shops, and other places covered with posters.[45]

Returning now to the inscription on the McCoy *Marilyn* prints, the information in it is relevant, if inconclusive, for the nagging question of when the *Marilyn* prints were made. It is helpful to know, first, whether the painting named in the inscription, *Marilyn Monroe in Black and White*, was already in the collection of the Moderna Museet by the time of the 1968 exhibition. According to the museum's website listing on *Marilyn Monroe in Black and White*, the painting was included in a show of 1964 at the Moderna Museet, *American Pop Art*.[46] The museum records it as having been acquired as a purchase in 1965.[47] Why, then, was this painting apparently not included in the 1968 Warhol show? One possible reason is that *Marilyn Monroe in Black and White* is an example of Warhol's early, 1962 rectangular *Marilyn* compositions, while all the works in the 1968 Stockholm exhibition, including the 1967 *Marilyn* prints, are of the later, square version, just as the *Flowers* and *Electric Chairs* in the exhibition are subsequent versions of earlier works.

Archival materials housed in the Moderna Museet about the 1968 exhibition include a few interesting items pertaining to Warhol's *Marilyn* pictures. An item labeled "Photo Album Volume 1" (one of two such volumes) contains photographs to be used in the book accompanying the 1968 show. One photograph is of a 1962 *Marilyn* painting, and another is of a 1964 *Marilyn*

painting *(Figs. 4.13 and 4.14)*.[48] Curiously, only the 1964 version ended up being reproduced in the book *(Figs. 4.15 and 4.16)*. The existence of a 1962 version in the photo album (though not the exact source of the McCoy collection prints), but its omission from the book, perhaps is a clue that can help solve the mystery of the McCoy *Marilyn* prints.[49] It is worth noting that one other photograph in the album, showing the SAS ticket issued to Andy Warhol—the image that was used to make a poster/print advertising the exhibition *(Fig. 3.13)*—also was not included in the book.[50] Could it be that the decision to omit a 1962 *Marilyn* from the book led to an idea for it, too, to be used for a poster/print?

The "Book"

The publication accompanying the 1968 exhibition, which features the 1964 version of Warhol's *Marilyn* composition, is an intriguing artifact in its own right, as several authors have noted *(Fig. 4.17)*. Like so much that surrounded this exhibition, it is not easily classifiable. In the invitation for the exhibition, instead of being called a catalogue, it is called a "book" (a label that is honored in the present discussion): "Andy Warhol: Screens, Films, Boxes, Clouds and a Book, 1968" *(Fig. 4.18)*. This being the title of the exhibition, it seems the book was envisioned as *part of* the exhibition, not an accompanying document as conventionally would have been the case. This elevated status of the publication is echoed in a news story appearing in the Swedish press at the time:

> A brilliant catalogue has been made for the Warhol exhibition, the most comprehensive in the museum's history. 644 pages and 619 pictures for a fairly cheap amount of money. The catalogue was part of the exhibition says Pontus Hultén.[51]

Several writers have noted the various ways in which this book departs from the conventional exhibition catalogue. "Unlike most museum publications," David Bourdon observed in 1989, "the catalogue contained not a single work of critical commentary on the art."[52] Andreas Strobl, writing in 1991, declared that "it breaks conventions: it is no longer a catalogue of the exhibition but a parallel event, and it mocked all the aesthetic conventions of the well-made book or catalogue."[53]

It was printed on newsprint and lacked the typical scholarly apparatus of a catalogue. Instead of discussions of the works in the exhibition, it contained, first, a series of statements by Warhol, in both English and Swedish (Fig. 4.19), followed by reproductions of his art and two sequences of photographs—one by Billy Name and another by Stephen Shore—sometimes arranged in loosely thematic groupings (for example, a cluster picturing cigarette smoking by Name, and a set of portraits by Shore). A later edition of the book, from 1970, includes a coda with installation photographs of the Moderna Museet exhibition (Figs. 4.3 and 4.6).[54]

In recent years, as interest in Warhol's books has grown, writers have reconsidered the significance of the publication that was created for the 1968 Stockholm exhibition. Nina Schleif has noted that while Warhol's contribution was limited, it is often treated as an artist's book.[55] If so, who is the artist? Could it not be Hultén and his assistants together with Warhol? In her recent study, Andy Warhol, Publisher, Lucy Mulroney considers this object as indicative of Warhol's practice of functioning as the publisher: "Warhol did not make a book; he appropriated the entire publication process. He created something beautiful and unusual by letting everyone else do the creating."[56] However one chooses to conceptualize it, the volume was, like much of Warhol's work, a collaborative enterprise.

In their history of Warhol and Pop art, Tony Scherman and David Dalton describe the Moderna Museet publication as the "most enduring legacy" of the Stockholm exhibition, "a photographic and graphic masterpiece," adding that "Warhol's artwork was not even featured."[57] His art was featured—just not the same art that was in the exhibition. In fact, there are 174 pages containing reproductions of Warhol's works. These reproductions are arranged in a loose and imprecise chronological order, beginning with 1962, the year Warhol started to make paintings using photo-silkscreen, and they include filmstrips as well as paintings, concluding with examples of a 1966–67 Self-Portrait. Several of the exact same works appear on consecutive pages, producing the effect of repetition that Olle Granath had pointed out as a key theme of the exhibition.

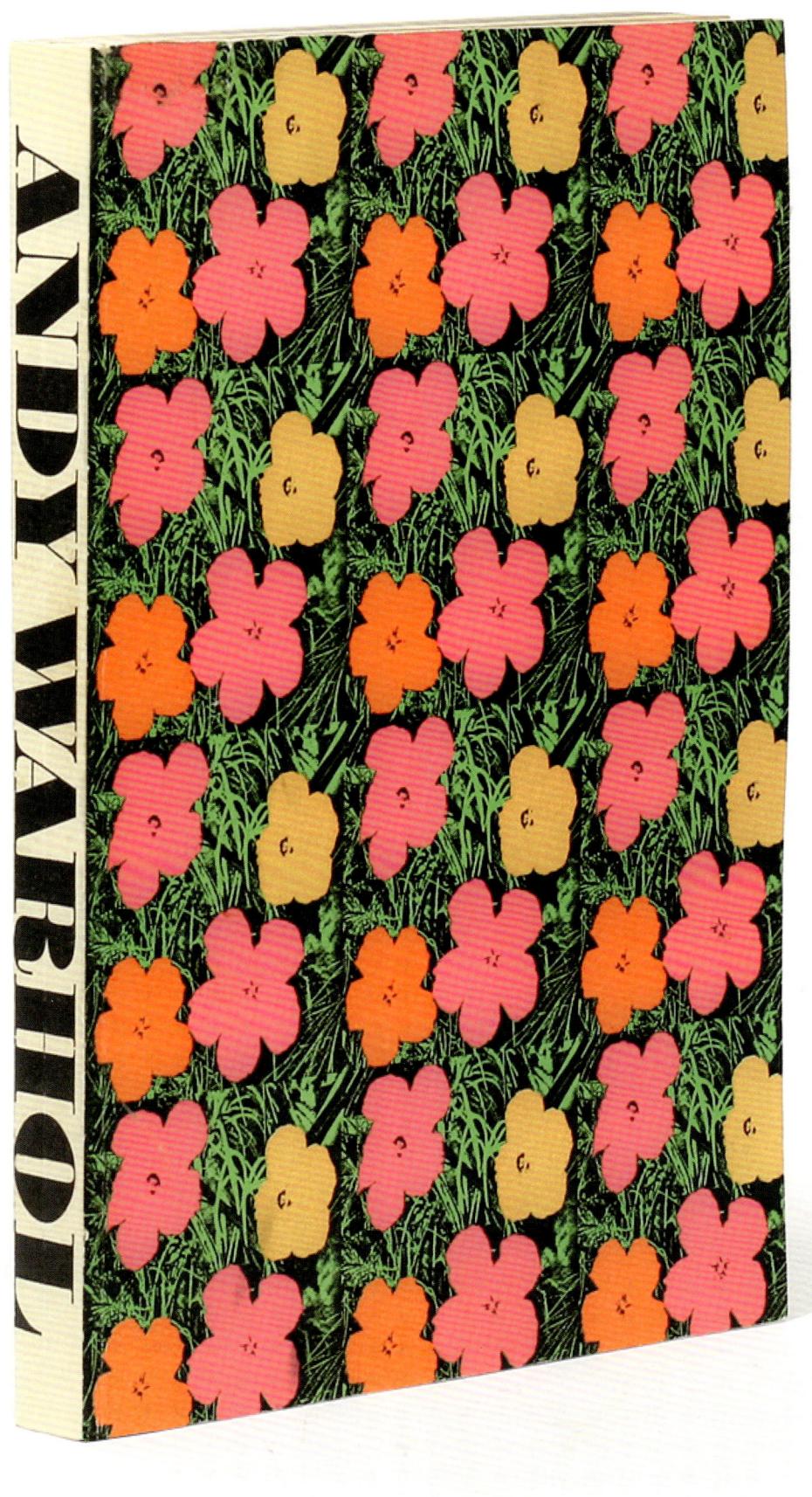

Figure 4.17   *Andy Warhol* (Stockholm: Moderna Museet, 1968), front
cover and spine, 11 ¼ x 8 ¾ x 1 ⅜ in.

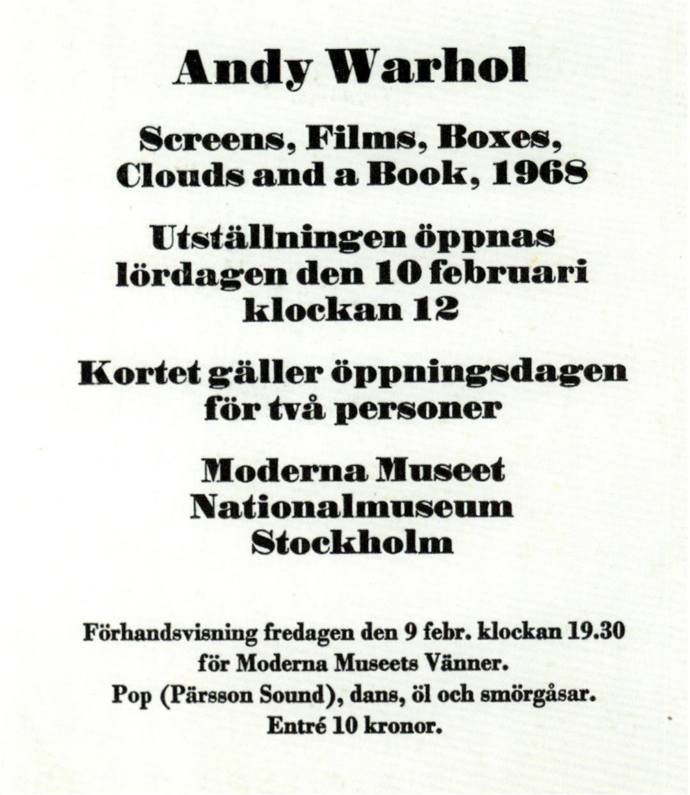

Andy Warhol

Screens, Films, Boxes, Clouds and a Book, 1968

Utställningen öppnas lördagen den 10 februari klockan 12

Kortet gäller öppningsdagen för två personer

Moderna Museet Nationalmuseum Stockholm

Förhandsvisning fredagen den 9 febr. klockan 19.30 för Moderna Museets Vänner.
Pop (Pärsson Sound), dans, öl och smörgåsar.
Entré 10 kronor.

Figure 4.18   Exhibition opening invitation for *Andy Warhol: Screens, Films, Boxes, Clouds and a Book, 1968.* Gregory McCoy Collection.

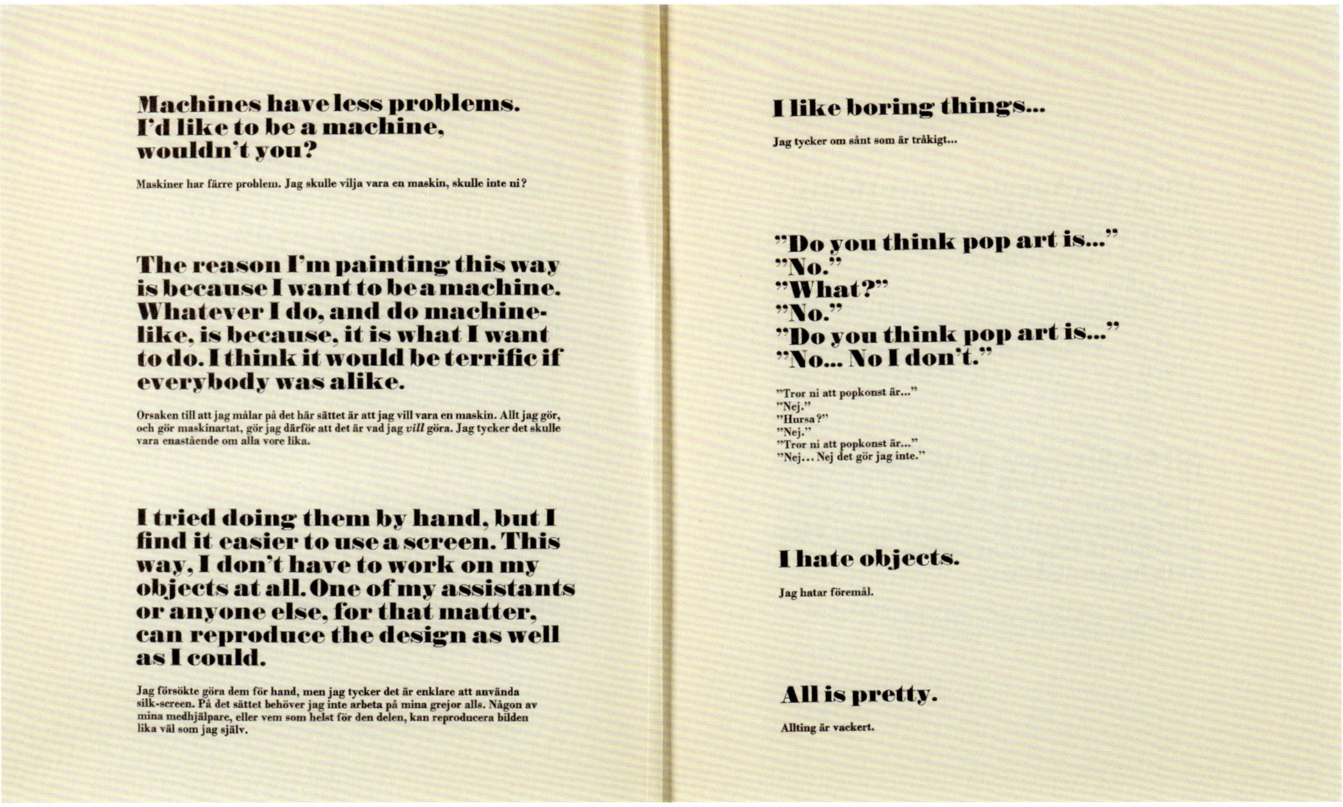

Machines have less problems. I'd like to be a machine, wouldn't you?

Maskiner har färre problem. Jag skulle vilja vara en maskin, skulle inte ni?

The reason I'm painting this way is because I want to be a machine. Whatever I do, and do machine-like, is because, it is what I want to do. I think it would be terrific if everybody was alike.

Orsaken till att jag målar på det här sättet är att jag vill vara en maskin. Allt jag gör, och gör maskinartat, gör jag därför att det är vad jag *vill* göra. Jag tycker det skulle vara enastående om alla vore lika.

I tried doing them by hand, but I find it easier to use a screen. This way, I don't have to work on my objects at all. One of my assistants or anyone else, for that matter, can reproduce the design as well as I could.

Jag försökte göra dem för hand, men jag tycker det är enklare att använda silk-screen. På det sättet behöver jag inte arbeta på mina grejor alls. Någon av mina medhjälpare, eller vem som helst för den delen, kan reproducera bilden lika väl som jag själv.

I like boring things...

Jag tycker om sånt som är tråkigt...

"Do you think pop art is..."
"No."
"What?"
"No."
"Do you think pop art is..."
"No... No I don't."

"Tror ni att popkonst är..."
"Nej."
"Hursa?"
"Nej."
"Tror ni att popkonst är..."
"Nej... Nej det gör jag inte."

I hate objects.

Jag hatar föremål.

All is pretty.

Allting är vackert.

Figure 4.19   Statements by Andy Warhol as quoted in *Andy Warhol* (Stockholm: Moderna Museet, 1968), unpaged.

Granath explained, regarding the book, that the "images of Warhol's works were to comprise the theme of repetition as well as the retrospective element that was not present in the exhibition."[58] But it did include earlier versions of all the works included in the Stockholm exhibition (*Marilyn* pictures, *Brillo Box* objects, *Flowers*, *Electric Chair* paintings, *Cow Wallpaper*, and inflated balloon *Clouds*). As Bourdon put it, the book "relentlessly promoted the Warholian concept of repetition, offering two reproductions of each painting on facing pages and repeating some of the pictures, such as *210 Coca-Cola Bottles*, for sixteen consecutive pages."[59]

Of particular interest to the focus of this study is the repetition on nineteen pages of the same 1964 *Marilyn* painting, the nineteenth of which is positioned sideways (*Figs. 4.15 and 4.16*).[60] Flipping through the pages of the book and discovering this unusual repetition of the exact same image, page after page, results in an almost eerie effect, in particular in the case of the *Marilyn* pictures. The repetition of an inanimate object, such as Coca-Cola bottles, somehow seems less disturbing: we expect Coca-Cola bottles to all look the same, but not human faces. In any event, through their extended repetition, the *Marilyn* works are featured prominently in the book, just as they are in the exhibition.

In thinking about the conceptual aspects of the book, it is worth pausing to consider the fact that the section of it containing Warhol's art begins, on the first six pages, with *Dollar Bill* paintings, two each of three distinct compositions (*Figs. 4.20–4.22*). It is tempting to understand this ordering—putting money first—in relation to, and even perhaps as a reflection of, Pontus Hultén's complex ideas about Pop art. Hultén's 1964 exhibition *American Pop Art* apparently was not meant as a positive endorsement of the art, but rather to expose a negative impulse in society at the time.[61] Hultén noted in the preface to his catalogue for the 1964 show that the work in it was the product of a generation that "feels powerless to transform the world . . . and in order to survive is forced to accept it."[62] He also observed that the Pop artists achieved success rapidly and that "economic success is what they strive for."[63] Some forty years later, Hultén praised his artistic hero, Marcel Duchamp, for condemning "the violence in the use of money" that surrounds us.[64]

Pontus Hultén: Curator, Artist, Instigator

In fact, Hultén's interpretation of Warhol seems to have been very much through the lens of Marcel Duchamp, who was probably the artist he most admired and a central figure of his curatorial endeavors. One of Hultén's first major shows after he became director of the Moderna Museet in 1959 (just one year after its founding) was *Movement in Art* of 1961, organized in collaboration with the Stedelijk Museum, Amsterdam, and giving a central place to Duchamp's *Rotoreliefs* (1935/1959) (*Fig. 4.24*).[65] In the 1970s, after he had left the Moderna Museet for the Centre Pompidou in Paris, Hultén's first exhibition in this new position was on Duchamp.[66]

In Hultén's essay on Duchamp for the catalogue of a 2004 exhibition at the Moderna Museet of Hultén's collection, he explained his long-standing admiration for the artist. He proclaimed that Duchamp "has now emerged as the most influential visual artist of our century" and, on a personal note, that "Duchamp had ever since my first reading about modern art interested me especially—."[67] He particularly appreciated what he considered to be Duchamp's probing of the nature of the art market (as noted above) and his "total unwillingness to exploit his ideas for a production, a unique decision in the history of art."[68] For Hultén, Duchamp was a great artist-philosopher: "We have probably not yet seen the most important consequences of the contributions that Duchamp's work have given and are still giving to art and philosophy," and looking at his work is "an incitement to reflect and contemplate on the great questions."[69]

Hultén, who was a visual artist and filmmaker in addition to museum curator and director, also found ways to incorporate some of Duchamp's work into his own artistic creations. In an early work, a collage of 1954 for the cover of a student magazine, *Blandaren*, he included a reproduction of one of Duchamp's *Rotoreliefs* (*Fig. 4.23*).[70] Another of these *Rotoreliefs* had pride of place in the front of the 2004 catalogue of Hultén's collection (*Fig. 4.24*); just as with the Warhol catalogue of some three decades earlier, this one was designed with careful choices in the ordering of the images for the purpose of making a statement.

Hultén's appropriation of Duchamp was not limited to his early artistic explorations. A notable example is his reproduction, in Murano glass, of Duchamp's readymade, of 1914, *Bottle Rack* (the "original" of which Duchamp did not preserve).[71] In addition, several replicas of Duchamp's works were made expressly for the Moderna Museet under Hultén's leadership, many by Ulf Linde (Duchamp had authorized numerous replicas of earlier works during the 1950s and 1960s, as is well known).[72] It is tempting to link the McCoy *Marilyn* prints to Hultén's general enterprise, based on Duchamp's practices, of rejecting conventional ideas about artistic value and ownership. Hultén himself compared Warhol to Duchamp, noting that the idea of the readymade was "pursued even further here."[73]

It has long been recognized that Hultén did not clearly separate out his identity as an artist from that of curator and museum director. As the recent Moderna Museet director Daniel Birnbaum put it, "it was clear that Hultén was quite willing to privilege the creative side of his institutional role and that he . . . had the soul of an artist."[74] Not only the installations of his exhibitions, but the accompanying posters and catalogues—or the "book," in the case of Warhol—were distinctive objects.

For the late 1965–66 exhibition *Inner and Outer Space: An Exhibition on Universal Art*, the catalogue included handmade pieces and came in a square box, and, Patrik Andersson observed,

> Hultén followed [the Dutch typographer and museum director] Willem Sandberg's footsteps in seeing the catalogue and poster design *[Fig. 4.9]* not only as a document of the exhibition but also as a creative outlet for his own artistic impulses.[75]

(It is worth mentioning, as an aside, that *Inner and Outer Space* takes its title from the name of a film made by Robert Breer in 1960, which Warhol also likely alluded to in titling one of his films *Outer and Inner Space* [1965], inverting inside and outside, just as the *Cow Wallpaper* was placed on the façade of the Moderna Museet instead of indoors *[Fig. 4.1]*, or just as posters, formerly understood as for exterior use, were now commonly being used indoors.[76]) Perhaps the McCoy *Marilyn* prints were in some way inspired by Hultén's "artistic impulses."

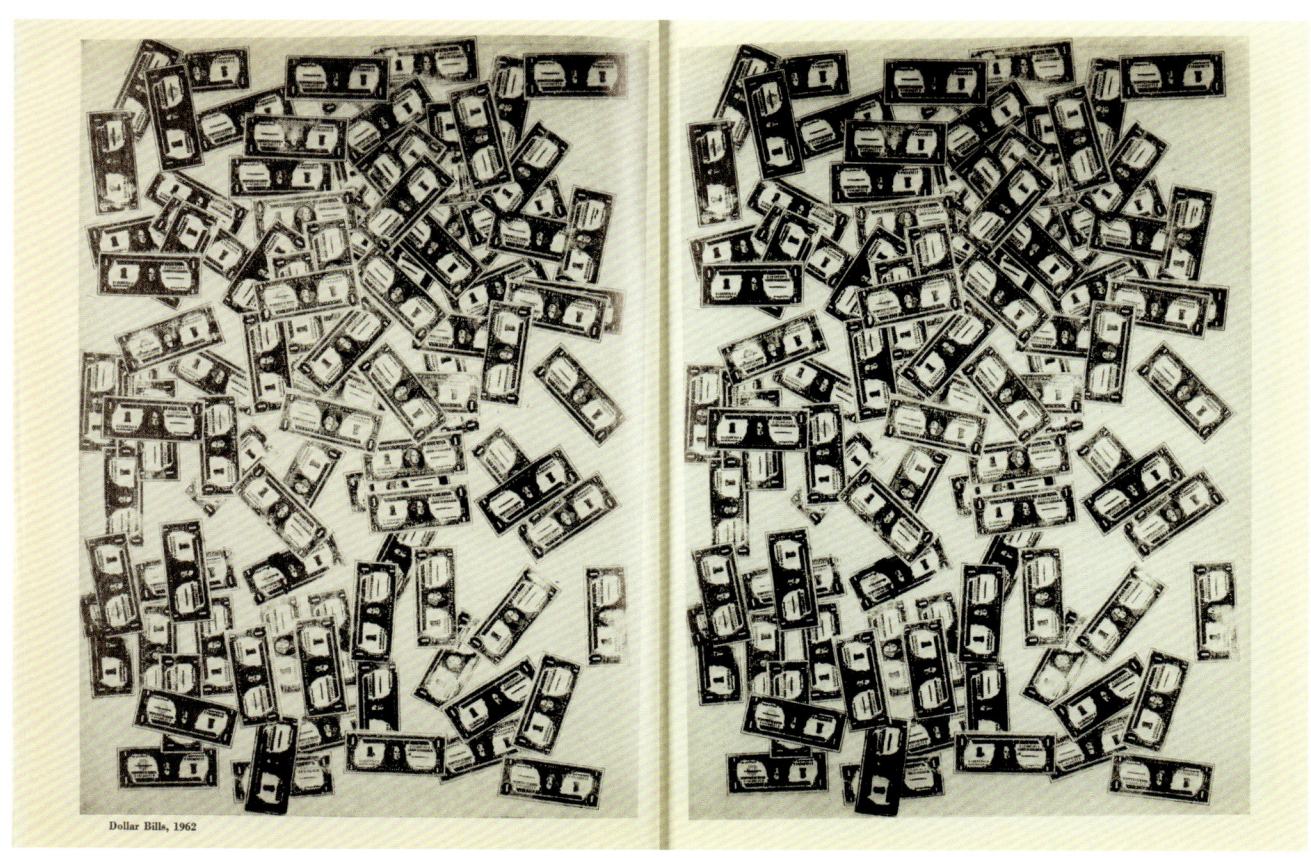

Figure 4.20   Andy Warhol, *Dollar Bills*, as reproduced in *Andy Warhol* (Stockholm: Moderna Museet, 1968), unpaged.

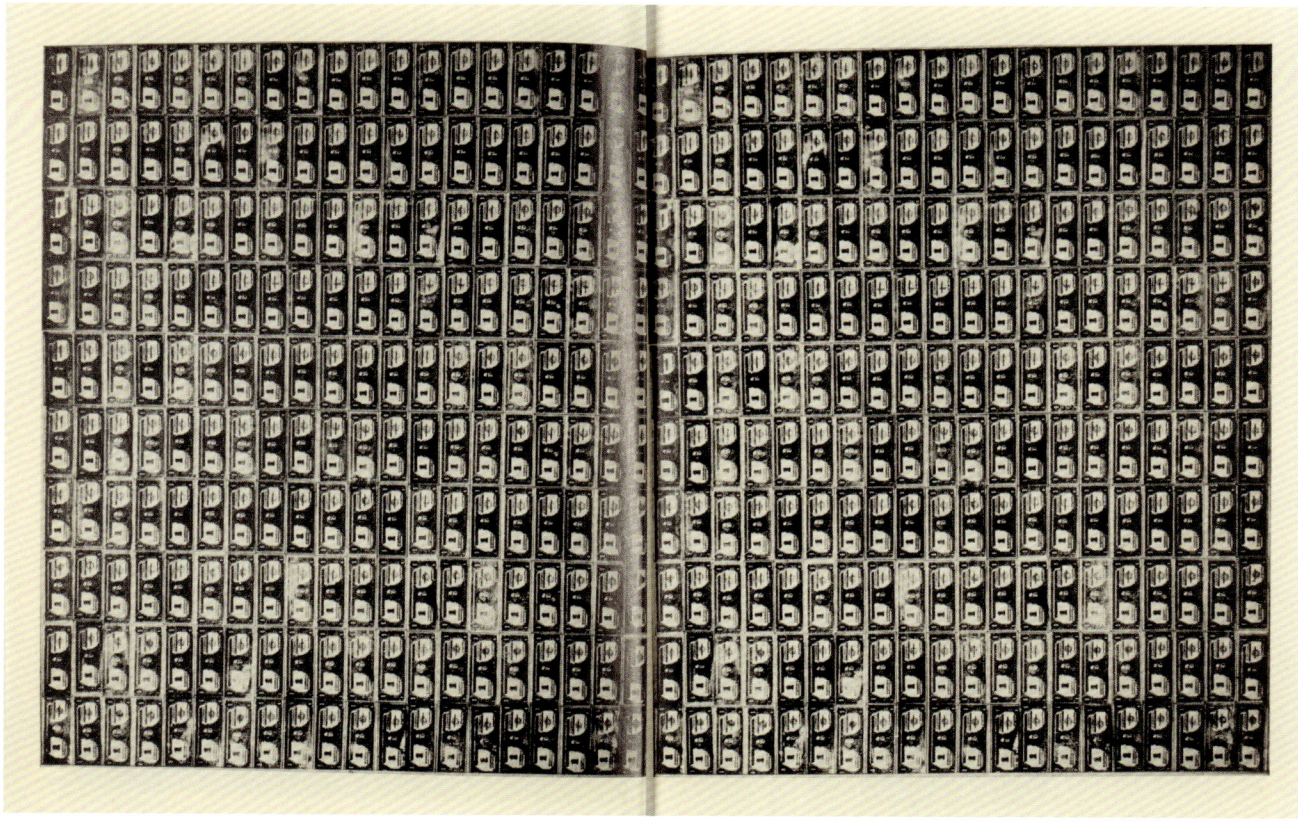

Figure 4.21   Andy Warhol, *Dollar Bills*, as reproduced in *Andy Warhol* (Stockholm: Moderna Museet, 1968), unpaged.

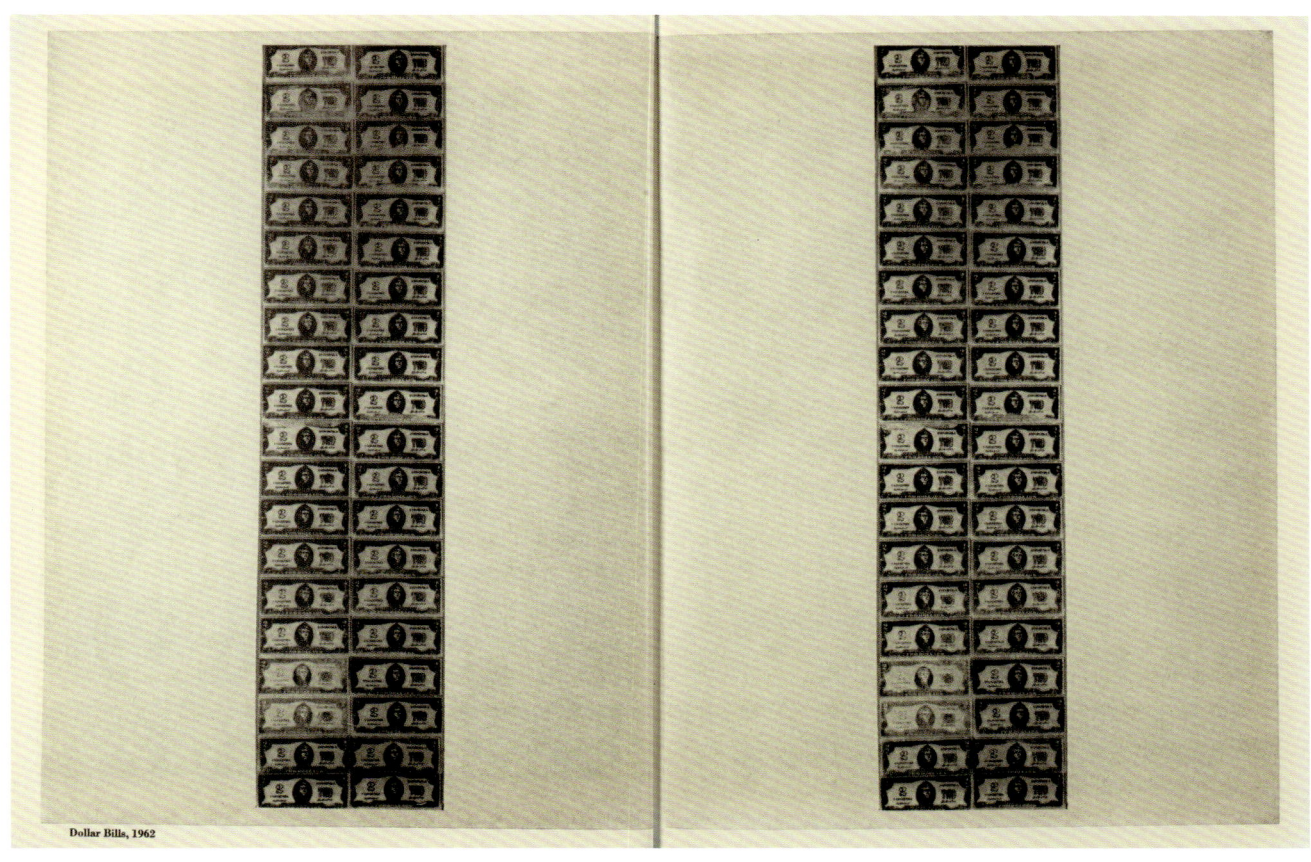

Figure 4.22   Andy Warhol, *Dollar Bills*, as reproduced in *Andy Warhol*
(Stockholm: Moderna Museet, 1968), unpaged.

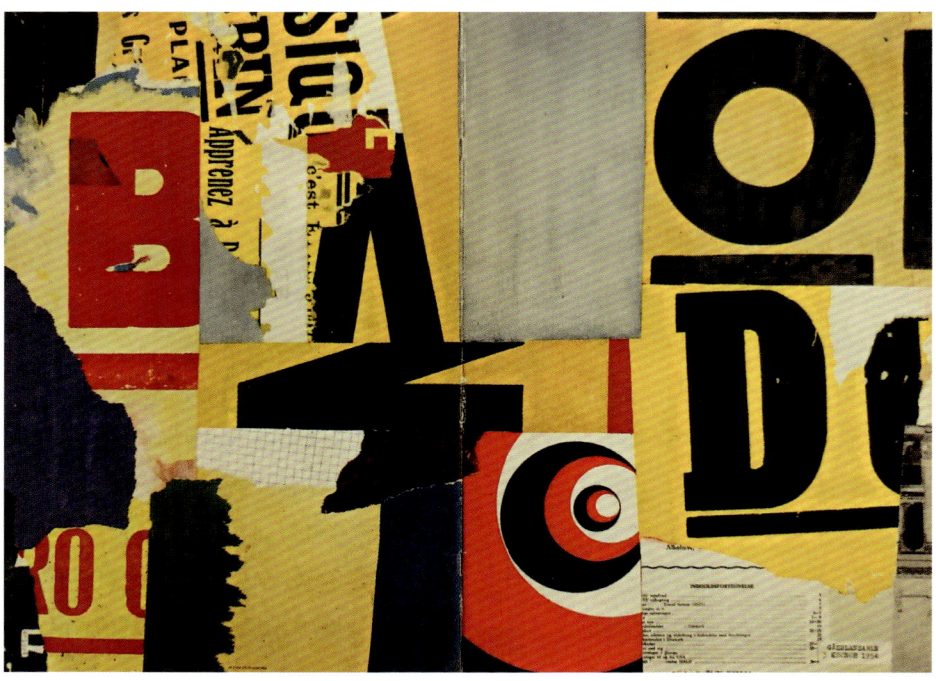

Figure 4.23   Pontus Hultén, design for the cover of the publication *Blandaren* (aka *Gåsblandaren*), as printed, 1954. Moderna Museet, Stockholm. Image used with permission.

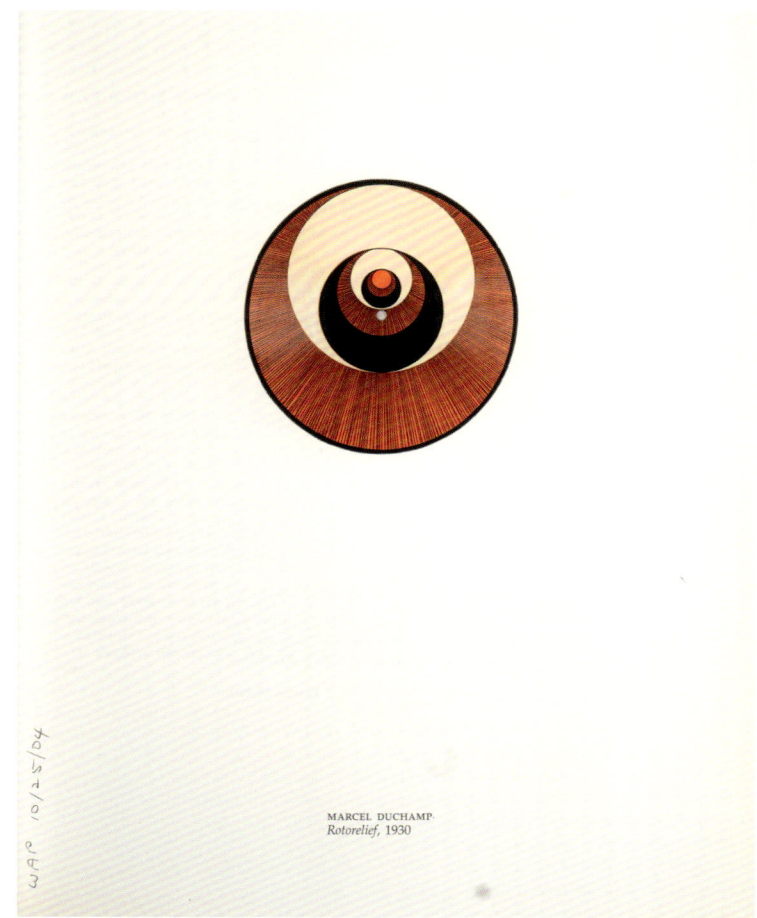

MARCEL DUCHAMP
Rotorelief, 1930

Figure 4.24   Marcel Duchamp, *Rotorelief* (1935/1959), as featured within the front matter of *The Pontus Hultén Collection...*, ed. Iris Müller-Westermann, Nathalie Meneau, Teresa Hahr, and Margareta Helleberg (Stockholm: Moderna Museet, 2004). Image used with permission from the Artists Rights Society.

Another possibility for how these prints came into existence relates to Hultén's decision, on several occasions, to improvise when work he needed for an exhibition was not forthcoming. He reminisced about calling upon the Icelandic artist Erró, whom he had known for a long time, to help out when he was curator of the Venice Bienniale for Sweden in 1966, represented by the artist Öyvind Fahlström, who apparently was unavailable to assist.[77] In the case of an exhibition of Russian constructivist artist Vladimir Tatlin, held at the Moderna Museet the very same year as the Warhol exhibition, it was impossible to borrow any of his work from the Soviet Union, and so Hultén relied on reconstructions of Tatlin's famous model for the *Monument to the Third International* (1920) and other works by Tatlin, custom-made for the occasion.[78]

Hultén also was involved in a more notorious form of reconstruction when, in 1990, he ordered the production of one hundred *Brillo Box* sculptures, which were produced at Reklamteknik in Malmö, apparently intended as "props" for the exhibition *Territoire de l'Art* in Leningrad, Russia, but later "authenticating" and selling some as works made for the 1968 exhibition in Stockholm.[79] Why Hultén made such a move is an open question. Did he conceive it as a way to extend the ideas of Duchamp?[80] Was it a radical method of attacking from within the ways economic value is placed on art?[81] The person who did the printing work on these *Brillo Box* objects was, as noted earlier, the same Bengt Andersson through whom Börje Bengtsson acquired numerous *Marilyn* prints that are now in the McCoy collection. This fact may be one reason Andersson (who had helped the Warhol Foundation sort out the Brillo Box "scandal") told Bengtsson he had some anxiety in deciding whether to sell these prints.

Whatever the origin and status of the intriguing McCoy collection of *Marilyn* works, it is hoped that bringing them to light, exhibiting them, and laying out the available information will lead to further study so that their story can be fully told.

This essay was completed in January 2020, in anticipation of a September 2020 exhibition catalogue publication date. Since then, a study has been published that discusses the 1968 Warhol exhibition in Stockholm, covering some of the same ground, and while it does not lead me to any new conclusions, I would like to acknowledge it here: Natalie Musteata, "Odd Walls, Even Pages: Andy Warhol as Curator and Editor," in *Andy Warhol Exhibits: A Glittering Alternative*, ed. Marianne Dobner (Vienna: Museum moderner Kunst; and Cologne: Walther König, 2020), 109–24 (see especially 109–16). Also appearing since the completion of this essay is the discussion of the 1968 Stockholm exhibition in Blake Gopnik's expansive biography *Warhol* (New York: HarperCollins, 2020), 602–7. For including me in this project, and for their generous assistance throughout, I thank Hannah Bennett, Maureen McCormick, Gregory McCoy, David McKnight, William Noel, and the entire team of collaborators at the University of Pennsylvania Kislak Center for Special Collections, Rare Books and Manuscripts. I am deeply grateful to Eugene Heath for making possible numerous road trips to Philadelphia and for his unflagging support from start to finish.

1. See Reva Wolf, "'Filling in Gaps': An Interview with Gregory McCoy," June 27, 2019, in the present publication.
2. This overview of the range of prints in the McCoy collection is based on the cataloguing work of Maureen McCormick at Atelier Fine Art Services in Philadelphia.
3. These sources are identified in Maureen McCormick's catalogue of the McCoy collection; see also McCoy, "'Filling in Gaps.'"
4. Gregory McCoy, "Andy Warhol: Marilyn Monroe Screenprints—Traditional, Reversal and Black Light," white three-ring binder with documents, 2016 (hereafter cited as McCoy, 2016 binder).
5. The *SAS Passenger Ticket* print was made in a signed edition of 250; see Frayda Feldman and Jörg Schellmann, *Andy Warhol Prints: A Catalogue Raisonné 1962–1987*, 4th ed., rev. and expanded by Frayda Feldman and Claudia Defendi (New York: D.A.P./Distributed Art Publishers, Inc., in association with Ronald Feldman Fine Arts, Inc., Edition Schellmann, and the Andy Warhol Foundation for the Visual Arts, Inc., 2003), 67, cat. no. II–20.
6. Georg Frei and Neil Printz, eds., *The Andy Warhol Catalogue Raisonné, Paintings and Sculpture 1964–1969*, vol. 2B (London: Phaidon Press, 2004), 345. For a detailed history and description of the Moderna Museet exhibition, and a listing of the works in it, see Frei and Printz, *Andy Warhol Catalogue Raisonné*, vol. 2B, 344–65, cat. nos. 2030–2055.
7. On this aspect of the exhibition, see Olle Granath, "With Andy Warhol 1968," in *Andy Warhol, A Guide to 706 Items in 2 Hours 56 Minutes*, ed. Eva Meyer-Hermann (Rotterdam: NAi Publishers, 2007), 00:10:00–00:13:00.
8. Granath, "With Andy Warhol 1968," 00:13:00.
9. On the *Flowers* and *Electric Chair* paintings produced specifically for the Stockholm exhibition, see David Bourdon, *Warhol* (New York: Harry N. Abrams, 1989), 280–81; Frei and Printz, *Andy Warhol Catalogue Raisonné*, vol. 2B, 345; and Granath, "With Andy Warhol 1968," 00:12:00. Bourdon stated there were ten *Electric Chair* and twelve *Flowers* paintings, but Frei and Printz pointed out that a typed inventory for the exhibition lists twelve *Electric Chairs* and ten *Flowers* paintings sent to Stockholm on four rolls (to be trimmed and stretched upon arrival) and that the works were recorded by the Castelli Gallery, which represented Warhol at the time.
10. In the catalogue raisonné of Warhol's paintings and sculpture, Warhol's *Cow Wallpaper*, as first exhibited in 1966, is compared to the posters based on an *S&H Stamp* painting that were used to paper the walls at the ICA in 1965; see Frei and Printz, *Andy Warhol Catalogue Raisonné*, vol. 2B, 209; see also Frei and Printz, *Andy Warhol Catalogue Raisonné, Paintings and Sculpture 1961–1963*, vol. 1 (London: Phaidon Press, 2002), 117. For the observation that the combination of *Disaster* paintings and *Flowers* at the ICA show is echoed in the subject matter of the paintings at the Moderna Museet exhibition, see Frei and Printz, *Andy Warhol Catalogue Raisonné*, vol. 2B, 347.
11. Granath, "With Andy Warhol 1968," 00:12:00.
12. See Frei and Printz, *Andy Warhol Catalogue Raisonné*, vol. 2B, 209.
13. Bourdon, *Warhol*, 281.
14. Frei and Printz, *Andy Warhol Catalogue Raisonné*, vol. 2B, 345.
15. Granath, "With Andy Warhol 1968," 00:12:00.
16. A reproduction of this letter was included in the 2018–19 Moderna Museet exhibition, *Warhol 1968*.
17. Granath, "With Andy Warhol 1968," 00:11:00.
18. Granath, "With Andy Warhol 1968," 00:12:00.
19. Frei and Printz, *Andy Warhol Catalogue Raisonné*, vol. 2B, 345.
20. McCoy, 2016 binder.
21. McCoy, 2016 binder. Letters and emails quoted in this essay that were submitted by Bengtsson to McCoy were written in Swedish, with translations into English provided by Bengtsson unless otherwise noted.

22. McCoy, 2016 binder. Included with his translation of this statement, Bengtsson gave McCoy a note indicating that he asked Balcke what he meant by "on the side" and that Balcke responded by stating that everything for the Moderna Museet was without any invoices documenting the work. In a message of July 17, 2013, Bengtsson stated that he wrote the letter of the 16th, but that Balcke signed it, and he reported that Balcke had stated the *Marilyns* were done in early 1968 and that it was Pontus Hultén's idea and that they were done on the side, after hours; he also reported that Balcke thought Hultén would not have done something illegal, without permission of the artist; he further noted that there was no invoice for the *Cow Wallpaper* either.
23. McCoy, 2016 binder. All the quotations in this paragraph come from this same letter of January 22, 2014, as translated by Börje Bengtsson.
24. McCoy, 2016 binder. This last sentence is alternately given as "Father received them as payment for a variety of paint work he did" in a translation by Nicola Knipe of June 2021; my thanks to Maureen McCormick for sharing this translation with me. In an undated note, Bengtsson wrote to McCoy (2016 binder):

> Re some other posters bought yesterday like the one w BOTERO without text he told me that John Melins [*sic*] idea was to print some copies for the people involved in the project without the museum/exhibition text and give them away sometimes as part payment for work, the people in the ad agencies didnt [*sic*] want regular exhibition posters in their homes and offices so John came up w the idea of this.

25. Granath, "With Andy Warhol in 1968," 00:12:00–00:13:00. This statement is identical to one that Bengtsson sent to McCoy, dated September 28, 2010, identifying it as coming from Anna Lena Wibom, the ex-wife of Hultén.
26. According to the online catalogue of the Moderna Museet, *Ten-Foot Flowers* (cat. no. MOM58) and *Big Electric Chair* (cat. no. MOM57) both entered the museum's collection in 1976, the former donated by the artist and the latter by Kasper König. See also Frei and Printz, *Andy Warhol Catalogue Raisonné*, vol. 2B, 360 and 365, cat. no. 2052; and 353 and 364, cat. no. 2042. Perhaps 1976 represents the official date of an acquisition that had occurred earlier, or some kind of swap took place, or there was some confusion over time concerning the provenance of these works. One example of each was listed as being in the collection of the Moderna Museet already in 1970 in the first catalogue of Warhol's works, but in this catalogue, the *Ten-Foot Flowers* seems to be the painting that belonged to Leo Castelli Gallery at that time (corresponding to the provenance in Frei and Printz) and not the one listed as belonging to the Moderna Museet; see Rainer Crone, *Andy Warhol*, trans. John William Gabriel (New York: Praeger Publishers, 1970), 309, cat. nos. 594 and 577, respectively (the *Big Electric Chair* painting in the Moderna Museet's collection is in Crone, *Andy Warhol*, 301, cat. no. 384, which Frei and Printz identify as the same one that is currently in the museum's collection).
27. McCoy, 2016 binder.
28. All the emails described in this paragraph are contained in McCoy, 2016 binder.
29. McCoy, 2016 binder. Accompanying the letter is a translation that Bengtsson sent to McCoy in an email of April 29, 2015. All the quotations in this paragraph are from this April 26, 2015, message from Bengt Andersson to Börje Bengtsson.
30. A retranslation of the letter, made by Nicola Knipe and completed June 7, 2021, renders this same sentence as follows: "You should know that my decision anxiety regarding the Marilyn-posters has been HUGE!" Knipe notes that the Swedish word Bengtsson translated as "anxiety" but Knipe as "decision anxiety"—*beslutsånger*—suggests a particular type of anxiety for which there is no equivalent in English. This decision-making anxiety, it has been proposed, "is not so much about the prints themselves, but about whether or not to sell them"; email message from Maureen McCormick to David McKnight, June 8, 2021. I thank Maureen McCormick for acquiring the new translation and analysis.
31. In an email of April 24, 2015, to Gregory McCoy from Börje Bengtsson, Bengtsson reported that he met Andersson at the screen factory in Malmö and they went through a stack of prints and found several *Marilyns*. Some were Lac prints, and Andersson recalled that Melin used this paper in the 1960s. He did not know when the prints were made—the 1960s was before his time at Reklamteknik. Bengtsson wrote in this email, regarding Andersson, "he knows I want to connect the prints to the 1968 show and that several people have told me so or that they were probably produced for that show"; McCoy, 2016 binder.

32. McCoy, 2016 binder.

33. McCoy, 2016 binder.

34. Letter from James Martin of Orion Analytical, March 27, 2012; in McCoy, 2016 binder. Martin noted that the three inks tested were fluorescent orange, orange, and green, "using Fourier transform infrared microspectroscopy (FTIR) and dispersive confocal Raman microspectroscopy (Raman)."

35. Letter from James Martin of Orion Analytical, March 27, 2012; in McCoy, 2016 binder.

36. C. Puza, "Analytical Services Report," March 24, 2017; in McCoy, 2016 binder.

37. Frei and Printz, *Andy Warhol Catalogue Raisonné*, vol. 1, 246, cat. no. 265, lists several exhibitions of the 1960s at which the painting was shown, beginning with 1963 at the Galerie Sonnabend in Paris, and including *Pop Art Américain*, but does not state when the Moderna Museet acquired it; for further information, and an updated exhibition history, see the Moderna Museet's website collection entry for Andy Warhol, *Marilyn Monroe in Black and White (Twenty-Five Marilyns)*, NM 5885, at https://sis.modernamuseet.se/.

38. On this inscription, see Maureen McCormick's essay, "Notes on an Out of Sight Collection," in the present publication. After a careful study of the prints, McCormick concluded that in the cases when the inscription was not visible, it was because too much ink went through the screen, covering it up (conversation with the author, University of Pennsylvania, November 8, 2019).

39. "Andy Warhol: Marilyn Monroe Screenprints—Moderna Museet—1968—Collection Statistic Totals," document prepared by Maureen McCormick, June 19, 2018, 5, cat. no. AWMM.1968.260 and Plates LXV and LXXI in the present volume.

40. On the "Sunday B. Morning" prints, first made in 1970, see Feldman and Schellmann, *Andy Warhol Prints*, 213, and Gary Comenas, "Sunday B. Morning, anyone," at https://warholstars.org/andy_warhol_0511.html.

41. There is virtually no information about these silkscreen prints, and in one instance in this author's recent experience, when a reproduction of it surfaced online, in a sale listing for the 1969 catalogue that Harper's Books circulated by email on August 22, 2019, it soon disappeared from internet view. A similar *Marilyn* print was owned by Hultén; see *The Pontus Hultén Collection . . .* , ed. Iris Müller-Westermann, Nathalie Meneau, Teresa Hahr, and Margareta Helleberg (Stockholm: Moderna Museet, 2004), 363.

42. For this discussion of the rise in popularity and status of the poster in the 1960s, I have drawn upon Elizabeth E. Guffey's informative study, *Posters: A Global History* (London: Reaktion Books, 2015), and especially chapter 3, "New Art, New Space: 1960–1980."

43. Guffey, *Posters: A Global History*, 125 and 128.

44. John Borgzinner, "The Great Poster Wave," *Life* 63 (September 1, 1967), as quoted in Guffey, *Posters: A Global History*, 152–53.

45. For examples, see Guffey, *Posters: A Global History*, 126, 153, and 160. On the relationship between Pop art and the poster, see Guffey, 155.

46. The full title of the exhibition was *Amerikansk pop-konst: 106 former av kärlek och förtvivlan: Jim Dine, Roy Lichtenstein, Claes Oldenburg, James Rosenquist, George Segal, Andy Warhol, Tom Wesselman*, and it was on view from February 29 to April 12, 1964.

47. See the Moderna Museet's website collection entry for Andy Warhol, *Marilyn Monroe in Black and White (Twenty-Five Marilyns)*, NM 5885, at https://sis.modernamuseet.se.

48. See the Moderna Museet's website collection entry for Andy Warhol, "Fotoalbum volym 1," FM 1968 004 001, at https://sis.modernamuseet.se.

49. The particular 1962 *Marilyn* painting pictured in the photo album seems to be a version that was exhibited at the Moderna Museet 1964 exhibition on Pop art and sold at Christie's in 2014 (see https://www.christies.com/lotfinder/Lot/andy-warhol-1928-1987-white-marilyn-5792524-details.aspx). A vertical streak through Marilyn Monroe's hair on the viewer's right in the photo and in the Christie's sale work leads to this identification.

50. The SAS ticket was considered for possible use on the cover of the book, a plan that in the end was rejected along with a few other options. See Lucy Mulroney, *Andy Warhol, Publisher* (Chicago and London: University of Chicago Press, 2018), 170 n32.

51. "Shocking Pink Cows" ("Chockrosa kossor"), *Svenska Dagbladet*, February 2, 1968 (translation from McCoy, 2016 binder).

52. Bourdon, *Warhol*, 281.

53. Andreas Strobl, "Warhol über alles," *Messungen: Zeitschrift für*

Interpretationswissenschaften 1 (July 1991): 94–95, as quoted in Nina Schleif, "Carefully Unplanned: Books in Andy Warhol's Oeuvre," in *Reading Andy Warhol: Author Illustrator Publisher* (Ostfildern: Hatje Cantz, 2013), 59.

54. For the distinct versions of the catalogue/book, see Granath, "With Andy Warhol 1968," 00:13:00.

55. Schleif, "Carefully Unplanned," 59.

56. Mulroney, *Andy Warhol, Publisher*, 69. Mulroney considers the 1968 Moderna Museet publication to be one of Warhol's three "bad books" of the time, the other two being *Andy Warhol's Index (Book)* (1967) and *a: A novel* (1968).

57. Tony Scherman and David Dalton, *POP: The Genius of Andy Warhol* (New York: HarperCollins, 2009), 413.

58. Granath, "With Andy Warhol 1968," 00:13:00, and Willem de Rooij, "On Andy Warhol," in *Andy Warhol, A Guide to 706 Items*, 02:30:00–02:31:00.

59. Bourdon, *Warhol*, 281.

60. This experimental use of the *Marilyn* imagery perhaps has some connection to a mock-up for an accordion- or concertina-style book of around 1968 that used elements of the 1967 *Marilyn* print portfolio. On this maquette, which was discovered in Warhol's archives after his death, see Matt Wrbican, "Hold Close Our Fallen Star: Warhol's *Marilyn Monroe* Book Maquette," in *Reading Andy Warhol*, 186–201. By curious coincidence, a concertina-format book was used for an exhibition of Warhol's Ingrid Bergman prints at the Galerie Börjeson, located in Malmö, Sweden, in 1983; see Wrbican, 197 (where it is noted that three separate images were in this portfolio and that a series of thirty unique trial proofs were printed for each of the three images).

61. On this point, see Patrik Andersson, "The Inner and the Outer Space: Rethinking Movement in Art," in *Pontus Hultén and Moderna Museet: The Formative Years*, ed. Anna Tellgren, trans. Gabriella Berggren (Stockholm: Moderna Museet; London: Koenig Books, 2017), 47–48.

62. Pontus Hultén, "Förord," *Amerikansk pop-kunst: 106 former av kärlek och förtvivlan* (Stockholm: Moderna Museet, 1964), 15, as quoted in Andersson, "The Inner and the Outer Space," 47.

63. Hultén, "Förord," *Amerikansk pop-kunst*, 15, as quoted in Andersson, "The Inner and the Outer Space," 47.

64. Pontus Hultén, "Marcel Duchamp," in *Pontus Hultén Collection . . .* , 70.

65. "Biography Pontus Hultén," in *Pontus Hultén Collection . . .* , 432. On the *Movement in Art* exhibition, and its featuring of Duchamp, see Anna Lundström, "Movement in Art: The Layers of an Exhibition," in *Pontus Hultén and Moderna Museet*, 67–92.

66. Anna Tellgren, "Pontus Hultén and Moderna Museet: Research and Learning Based on an Art Collection, an Archive and a Library," in *Pontus Hultén and Moderna Museet*, 22.

67. Hultén, "Marcel Duchamp," in *Pontus Hultén Collection . . .* , 66.

68. Hultén, "Marcel Duchamp," 68. For other examples in the 1960s of seeing Duchamp's work as a statement against art as a commodity, see Jill Carrick, "The Assassination of Marcel Duchamp: Collectivism and Contestation in 1960s France," *Oxford Art Journal* 31, no. 1 (2008): 3–25.

69. Hultén, "Marcel Duchamp," 70. The relationship between art and philosophy was of fundamental interest to Hultén. As a student, he wrote his master's thesis in Art History on Jan Vermeer and Baruch Spinoza (1951); see Tellgren, "Pontus Hultén and Moderna Museet," 22.

70. *Blandaren* was founded by students at the Royal Institute of Technology in Stockholm and Hultén was on its editorial team; see Tellgren, "Pontus Hultén and Moderna Museet," 22; also https://blandaren.se/om-blandaren/.

71. This work, *Porte-bouteilles* (1986), is illustrated in *Pontus Hultén Collection . . .* , 67.

72. Several of these Ulf Linde replicas are listed in the online collection of Duchamp's work in the Moderna Museet: https://sis.modernamuseet.se/people/65/marcel-duchamp. An exhibition of them was held in 2011 (https://www.modernamuseet.se/stockholm/en/exhibitions/marcel-duchampulf-linde-place-the-academy-of-fine-arts/), memorialized in a catalogue edited by Jan Åman and Daniel Birnbaum, *De ou par: Marcel Duchamp par Ulf Linde* (Berlin: Sternberg Press, 2013).

73. Hultén, "Andy Warhol," in *Pontus Hultén Collection . . .* , 367.

74. Daniel Birnbaum, "Preface," *Pontus Hultén and Moderna Museet*, 11.

75. Andersson, "The Inner and the Outer Space," 51. A good overview of Sandberg's work is Ad Petersen, *Sandberg, Designer and Director of the Stedelijk* (Rotterdam: 010 Publishers, 2004).

76. Guffey, *Posters: A Global History*, 144 and 157.

77. Hultén, "Erró," in *Pontus Hultén Collection . . .* , 82.

78. Hultén, "Vladimir Tatlin," in *Pontus Hultén Collection . . .* , 340.

79. See Eileen Kinsella, "The Brillo-Box Scandal," *ARTnews*, posted online November 1, 2009; https://www.artnews.com/art-news/news/the-brillo-box-scandal-252/.

80. The now-dissolved Warhol Authentication Board issued an informed report on July 19, 2010, on the 1990 *Brillo Boxes*, which they called "Stockholm type boxes." The report noted Hultén's creative approach to curating, his previous use of replicas for exhibitions, and his admiration for Duchamp, but considered his written claims to the Authentication Board that the boxes were made in 1968 to be nothing more than falsehoods. I consulted a copy of this report in McCoy, 2016 binder.

81. This idea was proposed by the Swedish art critic Thomas Anderberg, who was quoted in a blog on the subject as having said, "I believe Hulten decided to show up the entire Warhol industry"; see Multiplesinc Projects, "Warhol Authentication Is a Messy Affair," August 1, 2016, https://www.multiplesinc.com/blog/44/.

Andy Warhol *Marilyn Monroe* Screenprints: A Pedagogical Evaluation

Kenneth Goldsmith

Editor's note: In 2016, Kenneth Goldsmith and Reva Wolf were hired to examine the McCoy Marilyn *screenprints. Wolf's report on the origins and materiality of the* Marilyns *evolved into the penetrating essay included in this volume. Goldsmith's 2017 report on the pedagogical value of the McCoy screenprints appears below. Affiliated with the University of Pennsylvania's English Department as a non-standing faculty member, Goldsmith had offered a full-year undergraduate seminar on Andy Warhol's 1965 ICA exhibition and had a long-standing scholarly interest in Warhol.*

The problematics surrounding the Warhol *Marilyn* screenprints are, pedagogically speaking, a goldmine. While I will leave the job to others to determine their authenticity, from my perspective as a faculty member at the University of Pennsylvania, the questions the works raise, simply as they are, are uniquely Warholian. The metaphysics surrounding these works are indeed the identical questions that Warhol himself raised over his decades of practice and the fact that such a vast body of work should fall into our possession should be cause for great celebration.

From the beginning of his career, Warhol questioned the long-cherished western values of genius, uniqueness, authenticity, and individuality: "I wish that I had stuck with the idea of just painting the same painting, like the soup can, and never painting another painting. When someone wanted one, you would just do another one." The idea of redundancy and repetition comes from consumer culture, a metric in which quantity means more than quality. In a sense, Warhol said, it didn't matter what you did, so long as there was a lot of it: "Don't pay any attention to what they write about you. Just measure it in inches." But of course, in a typical Warholian way, such statements were strategic smokescreens, ones which

enticed a gullible public to look in one direction while he did the complete opposite. In spite of his rhetoric, everything he did had a unique touch and auteurial air, expressed in ways that are almost inexplicable, notable by very specific identifiers of formal brilliance, camp, and perversity. Bad knockoffs are most often missing those qualities. I can't imagine, after having spent time with these prints, that anyone would have gone through the trouble to make so many variations of offbeat color combinations for commercial purposes. It simply wouldn't make sense. Nor would a commercial project have chosen such abrasive and unusual color combinations; were they to reach the market, few would've bought them. In this sense, these can only be art.

These works would be textbook examples to teach students about alternative authorial strategies. In fact, although played out on ink and paper, the modes of production, authorship, distribution and subsequent history resonate strongly with the digital age. In a moment where the worth of a cultural artifact is judged upon its replication rather than its uniqueness, these replicas, ironically, reek of authenticity for a twenty-first century audience. Each day we deal with digital bootlegs, rips, rags, and shreds, whose provenance is often untraceable. Instead of this being a problem, it's simply a condition. In fact, the cultural critics Hito Steyerl and Boris Groys have argued on behalf of the strengths of the "weak image," an artifact that although low resolution, is strong in terms of its availability and democracy. Warhol's oeuvre and his means of mechanical reproduction underscore this philosophy. "A Coke is a Coke and no amount of money can get you a better Coke than the one the bum on the corner is drinking. All the Cokes are the same and all the Cokes are good. Liz Taylor knows it, the President knows it, the bum knows it, and you know it." Extending his own argument, all Warhol screenprints are the same and all Warhol screenprints are good. Warhol's primary artifacts are weak images; a bootleg would be no different.

My final assessment is that having this trove of works on display at the University of Pennsylvania would be a touchstone for a frenzy of pedagogical activity. I can't imagine a sector of the university that wouldn't benefit from this: legal studies could tackle the copyright and production problems, historians could unravel the twists and turns of the period, art historians similarly could study the fabrication and provenance, poets and visual artists would find creative inspiration, and even business majors could view the works from a market angle; after all, Warhol himself is famous for saying, "making money is art and working is art and good business is the best art." In addition, the community outreach and educational effort surrounding the show could lead to numerous symposiums, readings, lectures, satellite exhibitions, and screenings.

Out of Sight

Installation Views

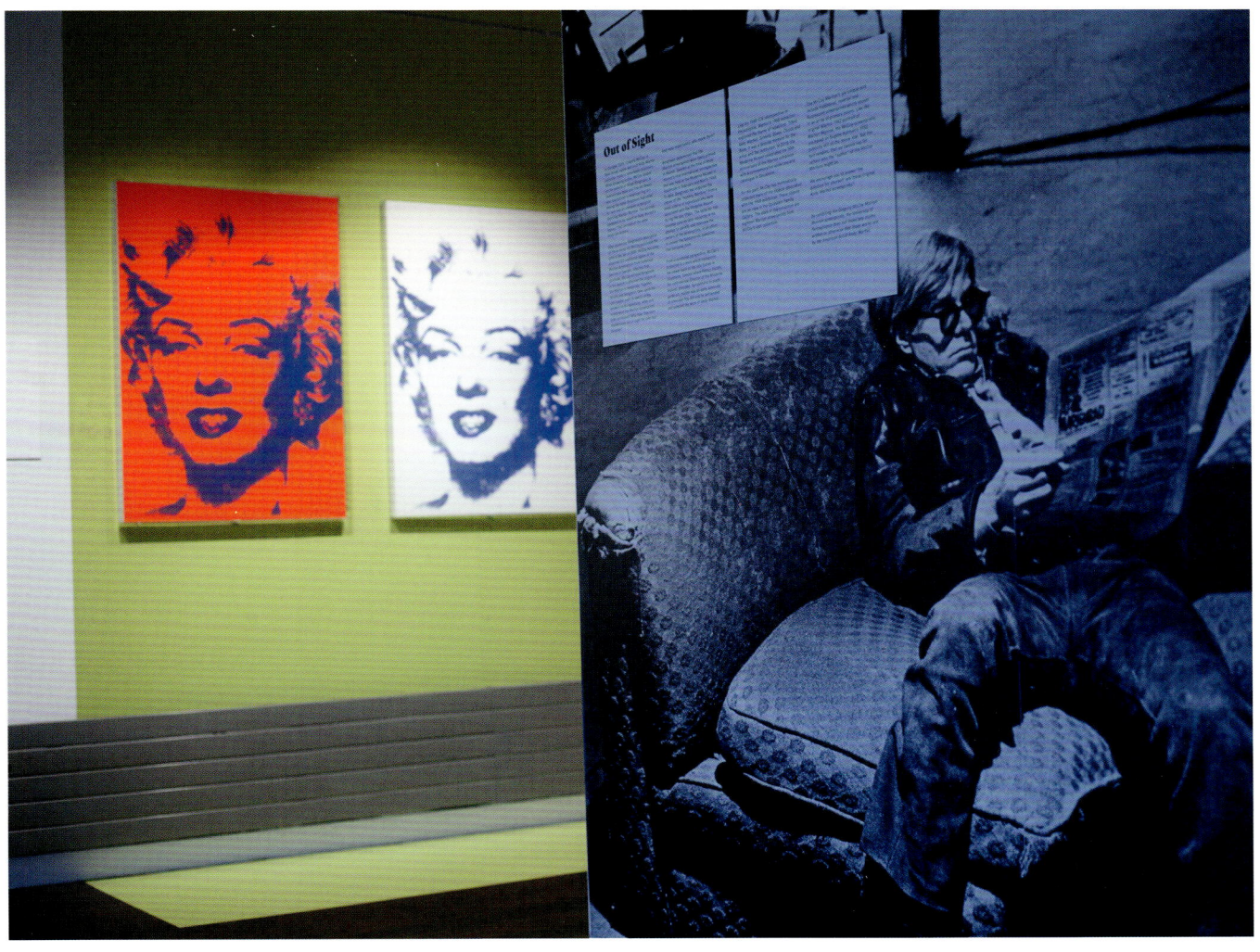

Interior shot of *Out of Sight: An Art Collector, A Discovery, and Andy Warhol* exhibition on view at the Goldstein Family Gallery, May 19–July 18, 2022. Photograph used courtesy of Christopher Lippa.

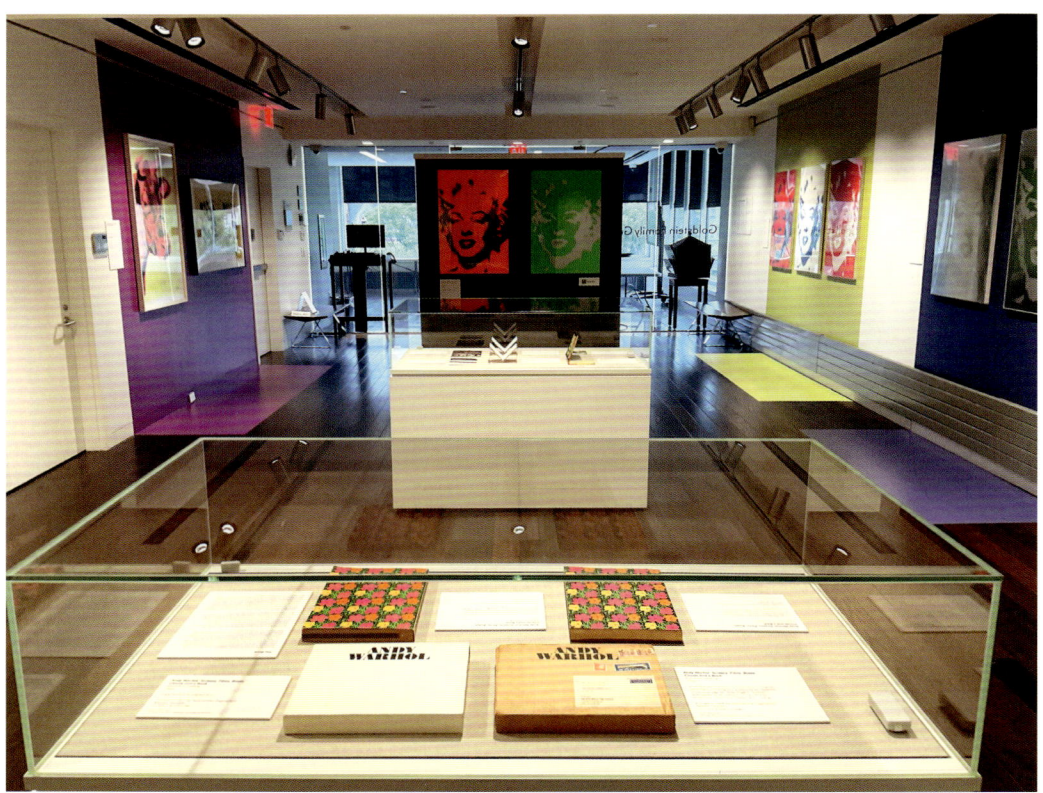

Interior shot of *Out of Sight: An Art Collector, A Discovery, and Andy Warhol* exhibition on view at the Goldstein Family Gallery, May 19–July 18, 2022. Photograph used courtesy of Christopher Lippa.

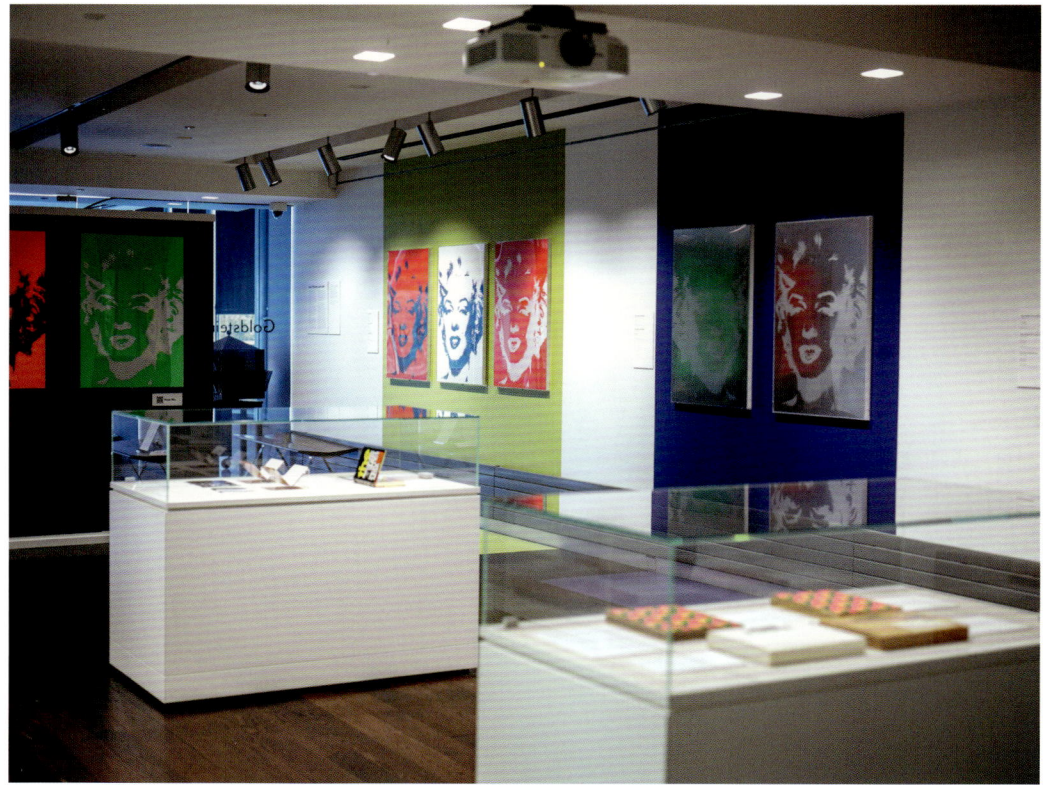

Interior shot of *Out of Sight: An Art Collector, A Discovery, and Andy Warhol* exhibition on view at the Goldstein Family Gallery, May 19–July 18, 2022. Photograph used courtesy of Christopher Lippa.

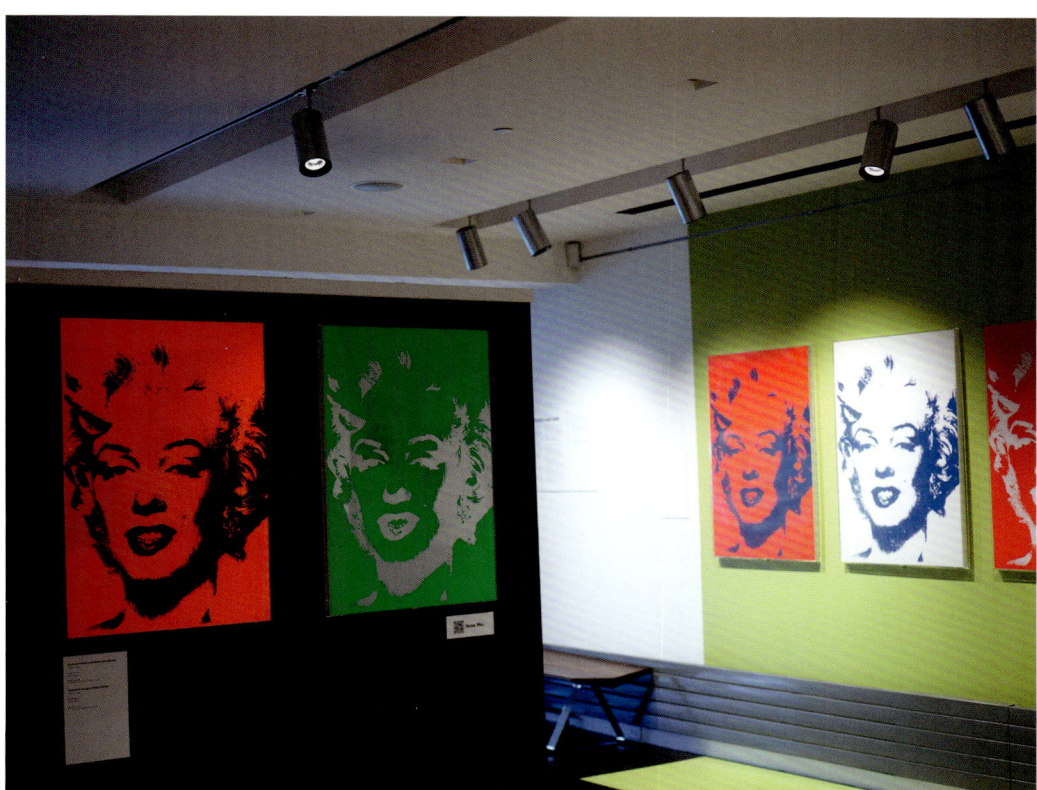

Interior shot of *Out of Sight: An Art Collector, A Discovery, and Andy Warhol*
exhibition on view at the Goldstein Family Gallery, May 19–July 18, 2022.
Photograph used courtesy of Christopher Lippa.

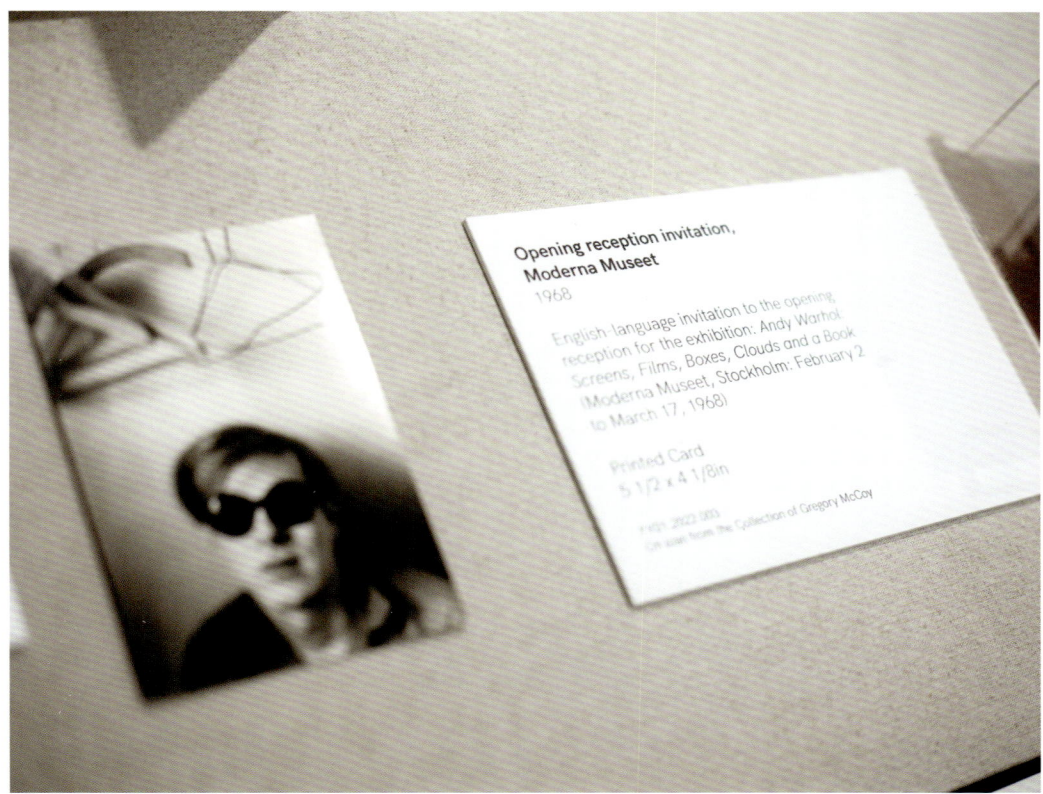

Interior shot of *Out of Sight: An Art Collector, A Discovery, and Andy Warhol*
exhibition on view at the Goldstein Family Gallery, May 19–July 18, 2022.
Photograph used courtesy of Christopher Lippa.

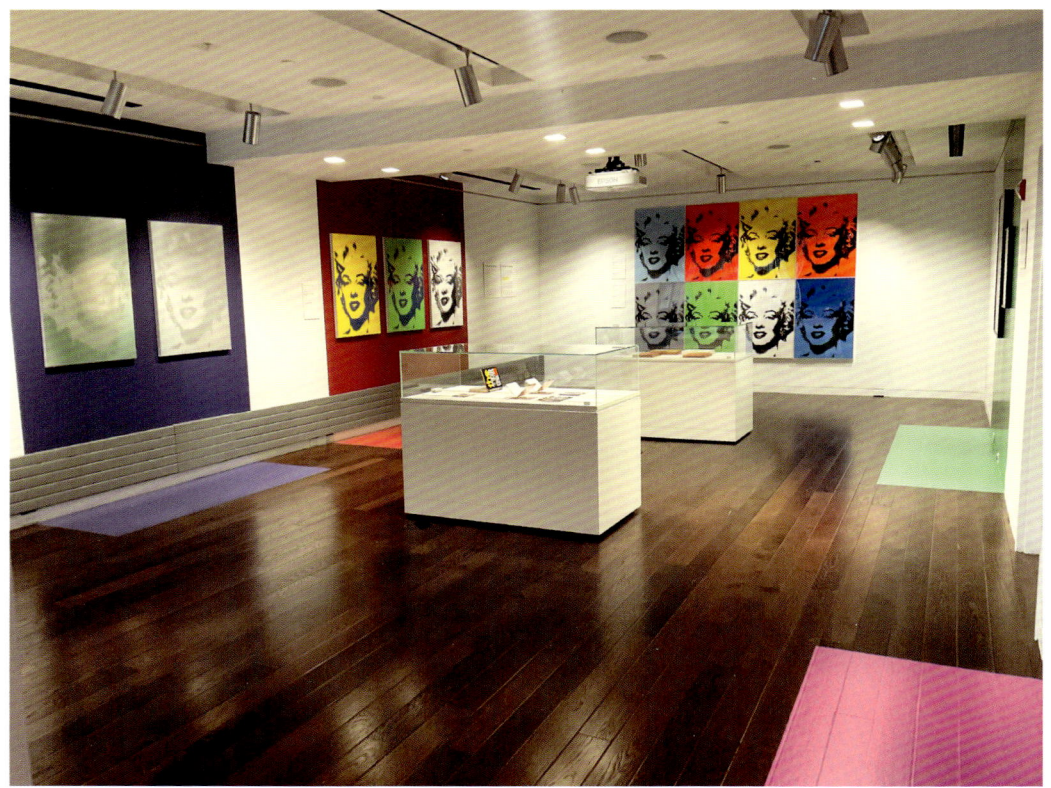

Interior shot of *Out of Sight: An Art Collector, A Discovery, and Andy Warhol*
exhibition on view at the Goldstein Family Gallery, May 19–July 18, 2022.
Photograph used courtesy of Christopher Lippa.

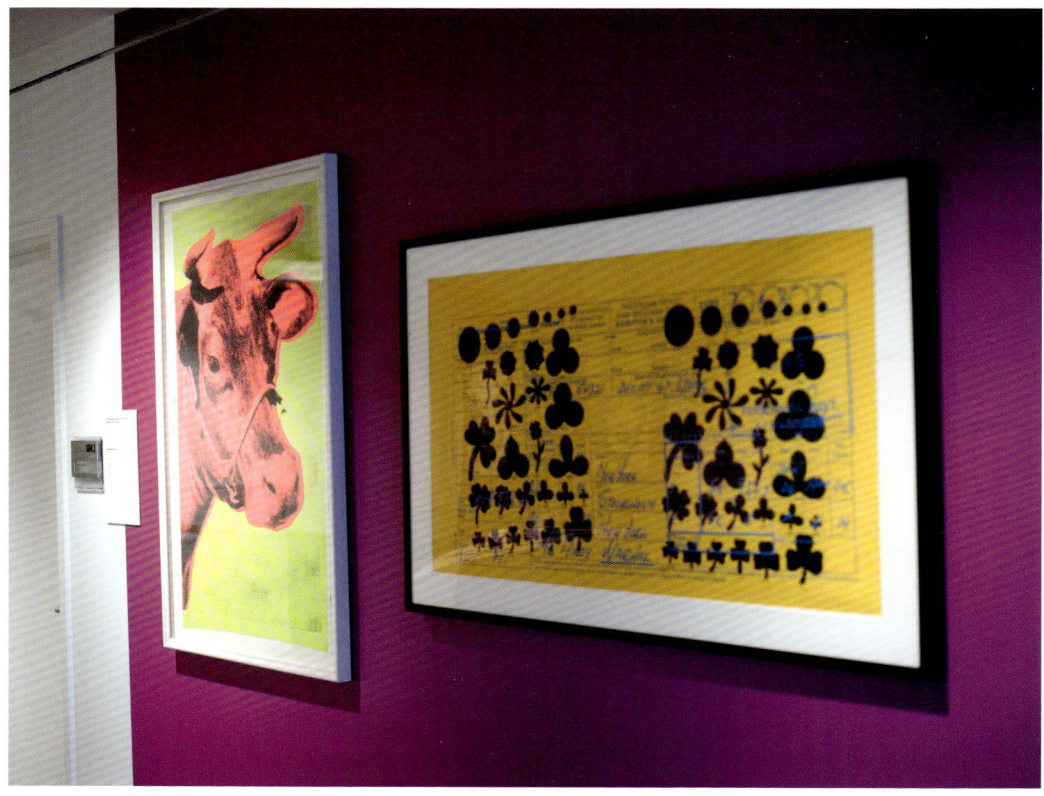

Interior shot of *Out of Sight: An Art Collector, A Discovery, and Andy Warhol*
exhibition on view at the Goldstein Family Gallery, May 19–July 18, 2022.
Photograph used courtesy of Christopher Lippa.

Part II

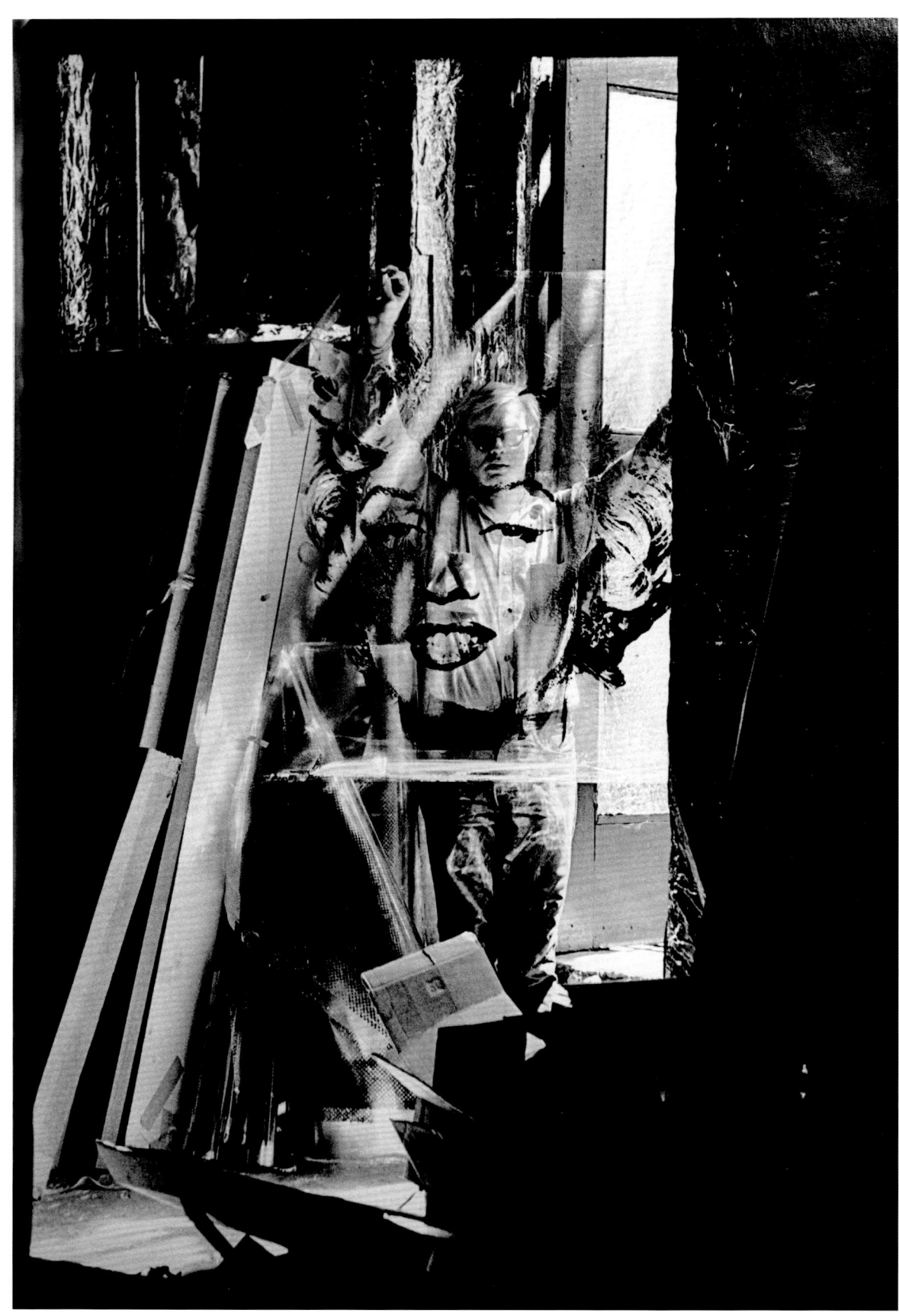

Figure 5.1   Photograph, *Marilyn Acetate 1*, 1964. Photograph of Andy
Warhol and Marilyn Monroe. Photograph by William John
Kennedy. Source: Alamy Stock Photos. Image used
with permission.

Notes on an Out of Sight Collection

Maureen McCormick

Cataloguing the heretofore unknown McCoy collection of screenprints has been an enormous, if dizzying, pleasure. Visitors to the exhibition will have experienced the superabundance of visual delight bordering on sensory overload that the collection provides. But cataloguing a newly discovered and unpublished collection is not without challenges. Chief among these was the lack of references or comparable works. The sheer number and size of the individual prints meant that the collection could never be viewed in its entirety; side-by-side comparisons were limited to two or three at a time. And, in order to preserve the acquisition history of the collection, the prints were catalogued as they were acquired rather than by paper/ink types. These constraints meant that certain patterns and variations revealed themselves only midcourse or in hindsight.

No doubt further examination, including a more technical examination such as a conservation scientist might undertake, will bring more observations to light. While analysis of several of the screenprints has been conducted—one in 2012 by Orion Analytical, LLC, and one in 2017 by the Williamstown Art Conservation Center, Inc.—in order to support the dating of the collection to the 1960s, new questions have arisen in the course of cataloguing the collection.[1] It is hoped that the information that follows may provide a sound basis for further research and study.

Screenprinting

Most readers will have a passing familiarity with the screenprinting process, whereby ink is pressed through a stencil made of a fine mesh fabric (originally silk, but now most commonly polyester), tautly stretched onto a wood frame and selectively masked off to allow the ink to pass through the mesh to the paper or other substrate below. The screen used for the McCoy *Marilyns* would have been produced by first coating the screen with a light-sensitive emulsion. Once the emulsion had dried, a photographic positive image on transparent acetate was laid on top of the screen and exposed to light, hardening the emulsion in the transparent/negative areas of the image. The emulsion beneath the areas blocked by the opaque/positive image would have remained water-soluble and easily washed away.

This is the same process that Warhol would have used in 1962 to produce the screen he used to create the painting in the collection of the Moderna Museet: *Marilyn Monroe in Black and White (Twenty-Five Marilyns)*, when he was beginning to employ screenprinting in his paintings *(Fig. 5.1)*. To produce the Stockholm painting, a single screen was repositioned to print each of the individual twenty-five frames, like a rubber stamp. That this painting was produced by hand is evident from the wide variation in image quality from frame to frame *(Fig. 4.11)*, which the artist makes no attempt to hide, either delighting in or at least unconcerned by the handmade quality.

Unlike the painting, however, the McCoy *Marilyns* were printed using what at that time was a state-of-the-art commercial screenprinting machine manufactured by Svecia,[2] a Swedish company, which had developed an innovative sliding table that greatly increased the reliability and consistency of commercial screenprinting. Though the process was mechanically assisted, the individual sheets of paper were hand-fed into the machine and ink levels carefully monitored and maintained by a master printer.[3]

Paper or Other Support

The majority of the *Marilyns* (315 of the 323) are printed on coated cover stock (.008 inch thick, or 80 lb.), the same type and weight as that used for the well-known Warhol quote posters that were produced by the Moderna Museet in connection with the 1968 exhibition, although the latter stock is uncoated.[4] Both the *Marilyn* screenprints and the Warhol quote posters measure 100 × 70 cm. (39½ × 27½ inches), a further connection with the Moderna Museet exhibition, though it should be noted that 100 × 70 cm. is a standard paper size in Europe that is designated as B1.

The remaining eight *Marilyns* are printed on heavier paperboard (.018 inch thick): two white, one tan, and the remaining five prints—known as Lac prints[5]—on paperboard that has been laminated, front and back, with silver foil.[6] As has already been noted by Reva Wolf,[7] the presence of these Lac prints in the collection suggests a tie with John Melin and Arne Wahlqvist, the graphic designer and master screenprinter who produced the *SAS Passenger Ticket* and the Warhol quote posters for the 1968 exhibition. Their fascination with this substrate is demonstrated by two posters designed by Melin and recently acquired by Gregory McCoy (*Figs. 5.2 and 5.3*). Both are included in the exhibition catalogue[8] produced by the Moderna Museet for its 1999–2000 exhibition dedicated to Melin, who is described as "one of the advertising gurus of the 60s and 70s . . . famous particularly for creating Moderna Museet's first graphic profile."[9]

Background and Image Colors

Of the screenprints on paper, forty-six are printed on plain white paper. The remaining prints have been printed with one of the following colors to create a solid background:

Tan (Pantone 7506-C), **Silver** (Pantone 536-C), **Light Blue** (Pantone 291-C), **Blue Ombre** (Pantone 2728-C at the top, fading to 2143-C at the bottom of the sheet), **Green** (Pantone 2269-C), **Fluorescent Green** (Pantone 802-C), **Yellow** (Pantone 107-C), **Orange** (Pantone 171-C), **Fluorescent Orange** (Pantone 805-C), **Red** (Pantone 1795-C).

The smoothness and consistency of most of the background colors suggests that the paper was commercially produced using offset lithography elsewhere. When examined under magnification, however, a few of the background colors appear to possibly have been hand-screenprinted, a considerably more difficult and time-consuming endeavor, a question that warrants further study.[10] The impression of a vast rainbow of color variations was achieved using only seven colors of ink:[11]

Black (Pantone 426-C), **Dark Gray** (Pantone 431-C), **Dark Blue** (Pantone 532-C), **Blue** (Pantone 2133-C), **Metallic Gold** (Pantone 871-C), **Metallic Silver** (Pantone 877-C), **White**.

The slight transparency of certain inks and the contrast between the color of the paper and the color of the ink made naked eye identification unreliable. For example, dark blue ink against a light color was easily identified as dark blue, but appeared black on a darker paper such as red or the blue ombre. The optical illusion known as complementary afterimage made identification of the ink colors on the fluorescent paper especially vexing.[12] Black ink would appear blue after just a few minutes of examination of a print on fluorescent orange paper, metallic silver ink would take on a lilac cast against fluorescent green paper, and so forth.

To counter these effects, a Pantone CAPSURE, a handheld color reading device, was used to identify ink colors. Even the CAPSURE was fooled by certain of the paper/ink color variations, depending on where the reading was taken. Several readings were thus taken on each print in areas where the dot pattern of the image was the most dense.

Inks

In addition to identifying pigments, the 2012 materials analysis identified the ink base (the liquid medium into which the pigments were mixed) for three of the background inks. The fluorescent orange ink and (non-fluorescent) green ink show features that indicate toluene-sulfonamide resin, possibly with melamine formaldehyde. The medium for the orange ink is a

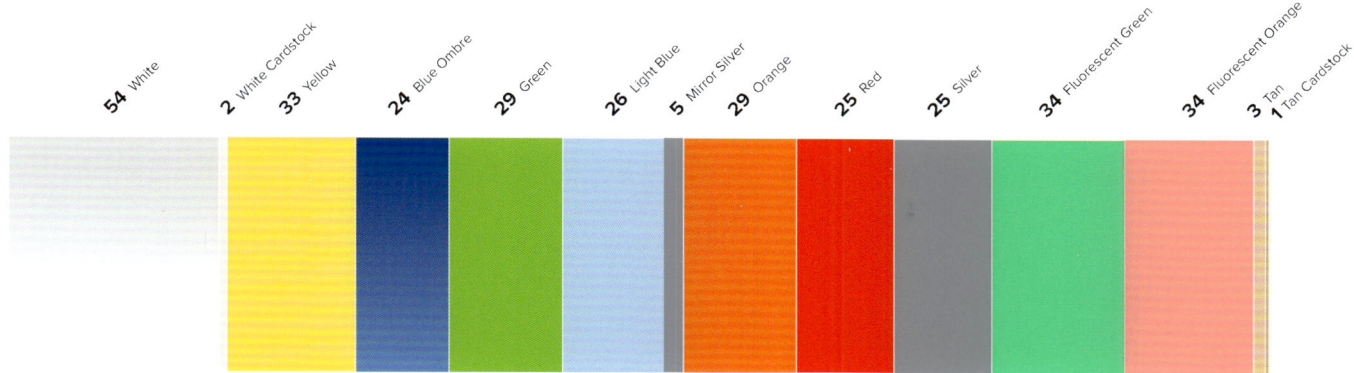

Table 1 / Paper or Support Type by Color

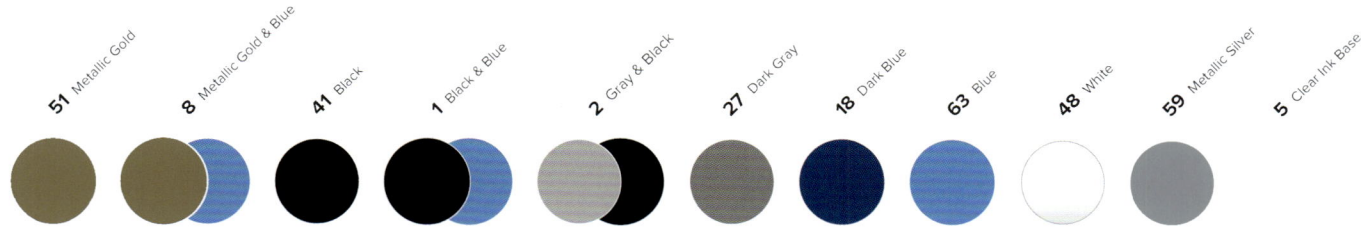

Table 2 / Ink Colors

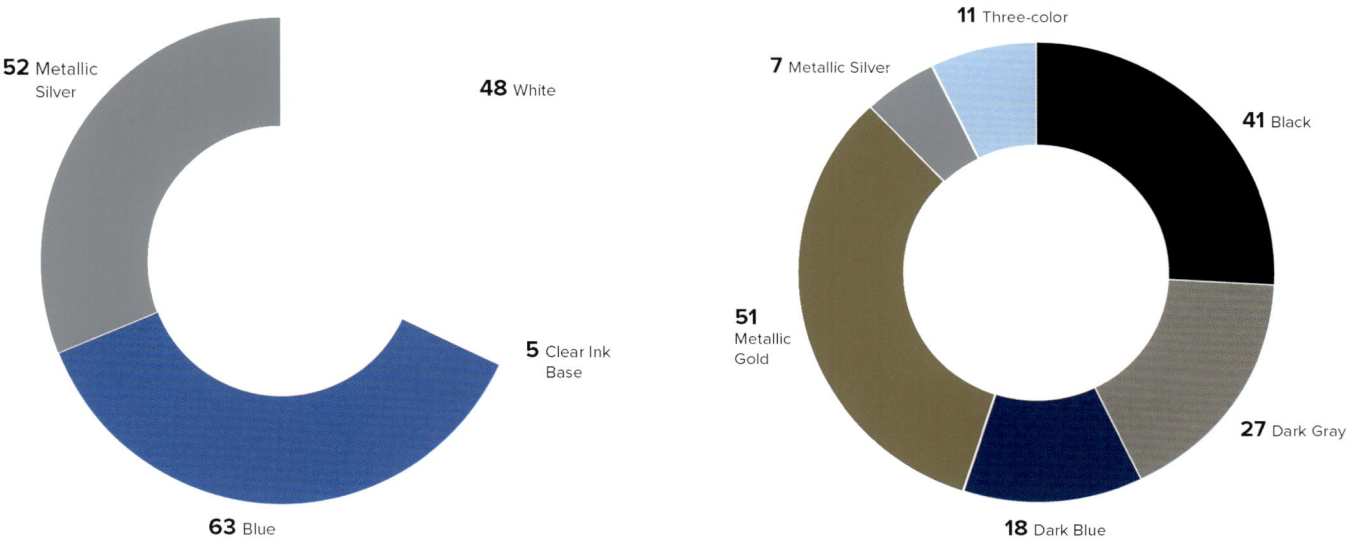

Table 3 / Ink Colors with No Inscriptions

Table 4 / Ink Colors with Inscriptions

cellulose ether. These findings are consistent with a dating to the 1960s, when oil-based screenprinting inks—which dry slowly through the process of oxidation—began to be replaced with inks that would dry more quickly by solvent evaporation.

Printed Caption

Nearly two thirds of the prints (204 of 323) include a printed caption that refers the viewer to the painting in the collection of the Moderna Museet. The inscription is found along the lower right edge of the print, and reads (in a single line from bottom to top):

ANDY WARHOL Marilyn Monroe in Black and White/Marilyn Monroe i svart och vitt 1962. Detalj. Akryl och screenprint pa duk. 208 × 140 cm. Moderna Museet, Stockholm

With one exception, the presence of the printed caption is dependent upon the color of the ink. Those printed with black, dark gray, dark blue, and metallic gold inks, irrespective of the paper color, include the caption. Those printed with blue, metallic silver, or white ink, do not. The exception is a group of seven prints that are printed with metallic silver ink on white paper, which do include the caption.

This raises the obvious question: why do some prints have the inscription while others do not? Were two screens produced, one with and one without the text, and if so, why? The most pragmatic explanation from a printmaking standpoint is that a single screen, one that included the inscription, was produced and the 204 prints were pulled. The inscription was then blocked out on the screen, and the remaining 119 prints pulled. But . . . why?

Three-Color Prints

The answer is likely found in eight of the ten three-color prints, so called as they have been printed with two different colors of ink, slightly off register, with the paper

color providing the third color. Seven of these are first printed with metallic gold ink, and one with black ink. All eight include the caption, which is printed in the first ink color and then overprinted with blue ink. Had the second pull included the inscription, the resulting line of type would have been visually disturbing. We can assume, then, that caption was masked off on the screen in order to overprint these eight prints with blue ink.

Two of the "three-color" prints remain to be considered. While *AWMM.1968.298 (Plate XXXII)* and *AWMM.1968.316 (Plate LXXIII)* have been catalogued as three-color prints, they stand apart from the eight discussed above. The first "color" laid down on the sheet is not a crisp, opaque layer of ink laid down on the surface of the paper, as is true of the rest of the collection, but is better described as a soft-edged, transparent gray stain *(Fig. 5.4)*. Rather than two slightly off register images, these images are off register by as much as an inch and a half *(Fig. 5.5)*. Might the first images have been made inadvertently, while cleaning traces of solvent from the screen (a common practice among screenprinters) and then overprinted with black ink in a spirit of experimentation, or thrift? To take this speculation to its admitted extreme: might this resulting print have been the impetus for the three-color prints? The *Marilyns* printed with white ink either lack the inscription altogether or only include a few fragmentary letters. Interestingly, those with fragmentary letters have the same fragmentary letters: the two capital *M's* in Moderna Museet. From this we can infer that these were printed at the end of the print run, when the masking was beginning to deteriorate.

A plausible order of events, then, could be: the screen, which included the caption, was produced; 204 two-color prints were made; *AWMM.1968.298 (Plate XLIX)* and *AWMM.1968.316 (Plate LXXIII)* were produced; the inscription was blocked off; the remaining three-color prints were overprinted with blue or black ink; the remaining two-color prints that lack the caption were printed, including those printed with white ink; and those bearing fragments of letters were likely among the last to be produced.

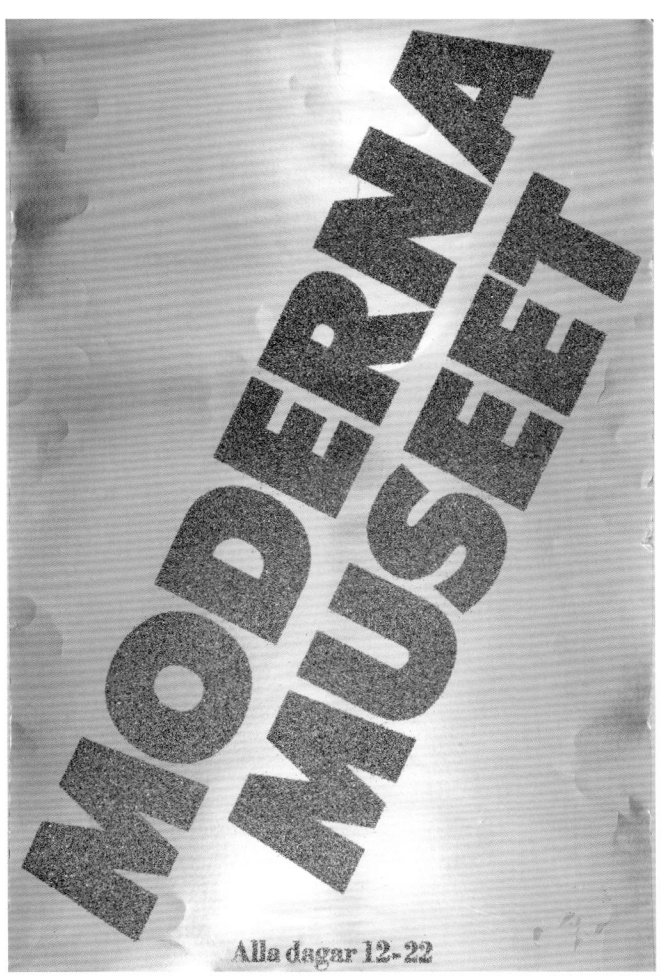

Figure 5.2   John Melin, Poster, 1970, screenprint, 39 ½ x 29 ½ in.
Included in the Moderna Museet exhibition *Graphic
Design: John Melin*, held October 30, 1999 to February 6,
2000. From the Gregory McCoy Collection. Image used
with permission.

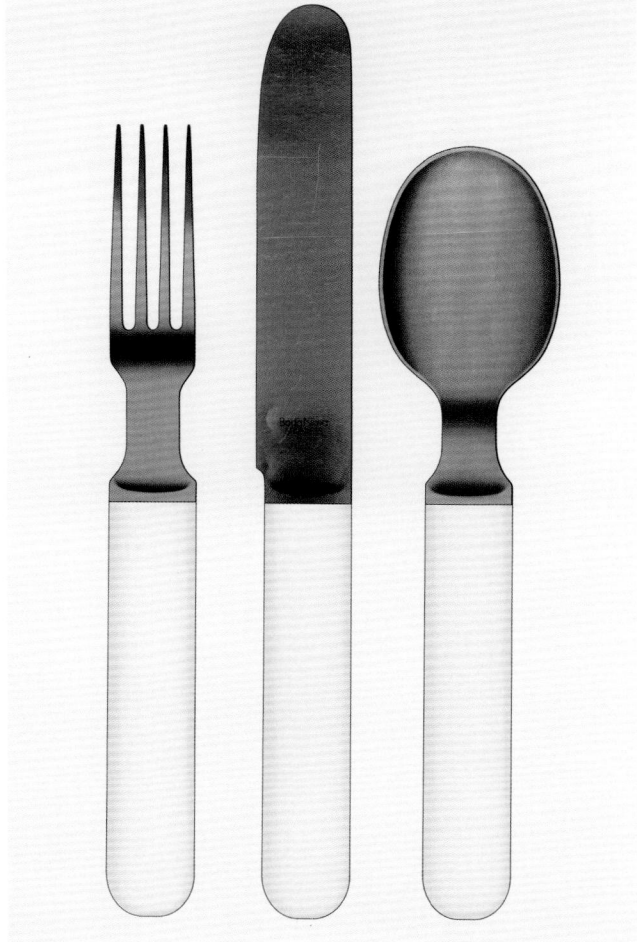

Figure 5.3   John Melin, Poster for the Boda Nova Kitchenware
Company, 1972, 39 ½ x 29 ½ in. From the
Gregory McCoy Collection. Image used with
permission.

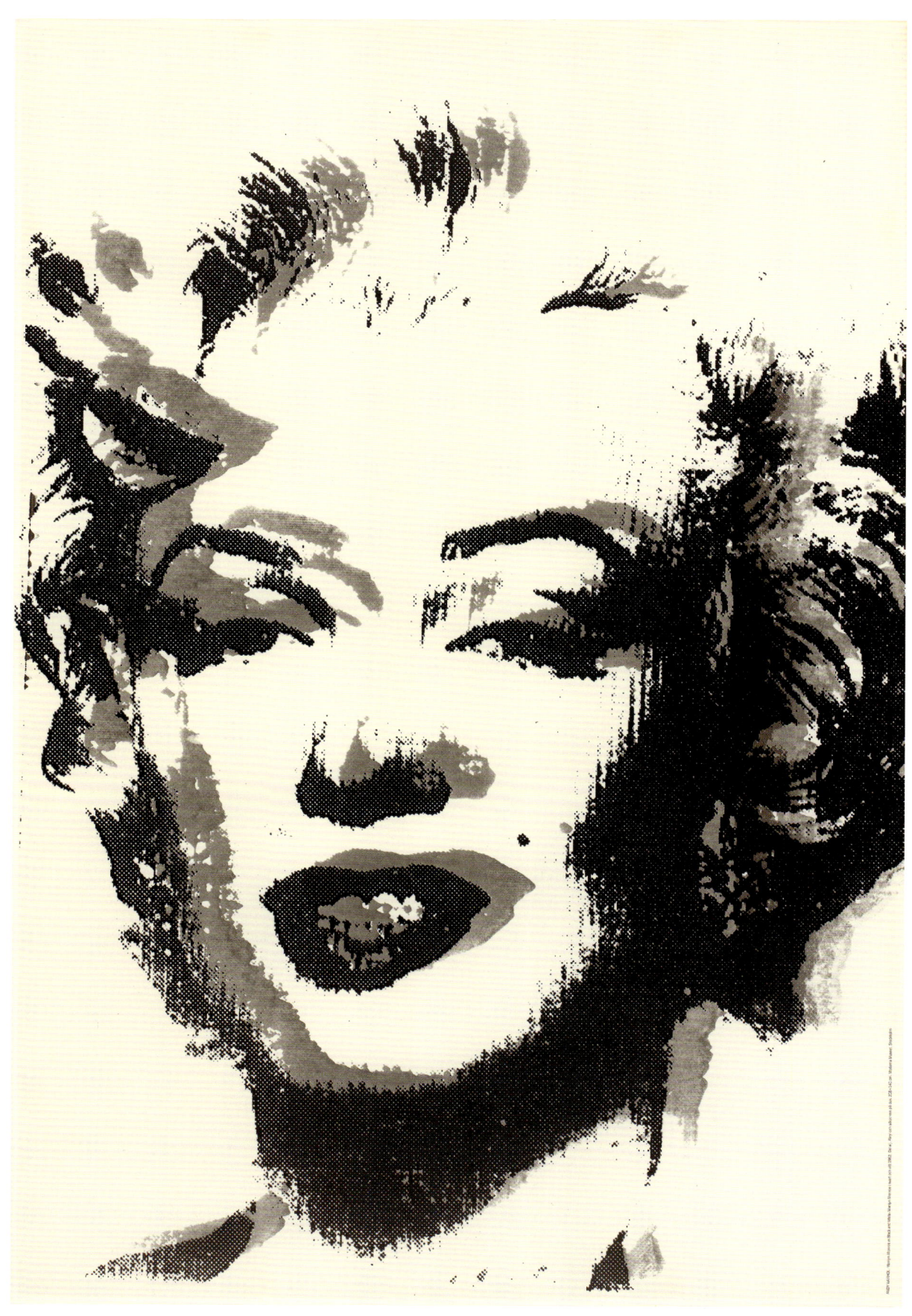

Figure 5.4   AWMM.1968.298 (Plate XLIX, p. 155), three-color screenprint: gray (or dilute black) and black inks on tan cardstock. From the Gregory McCoy Collection. Image used with permission.

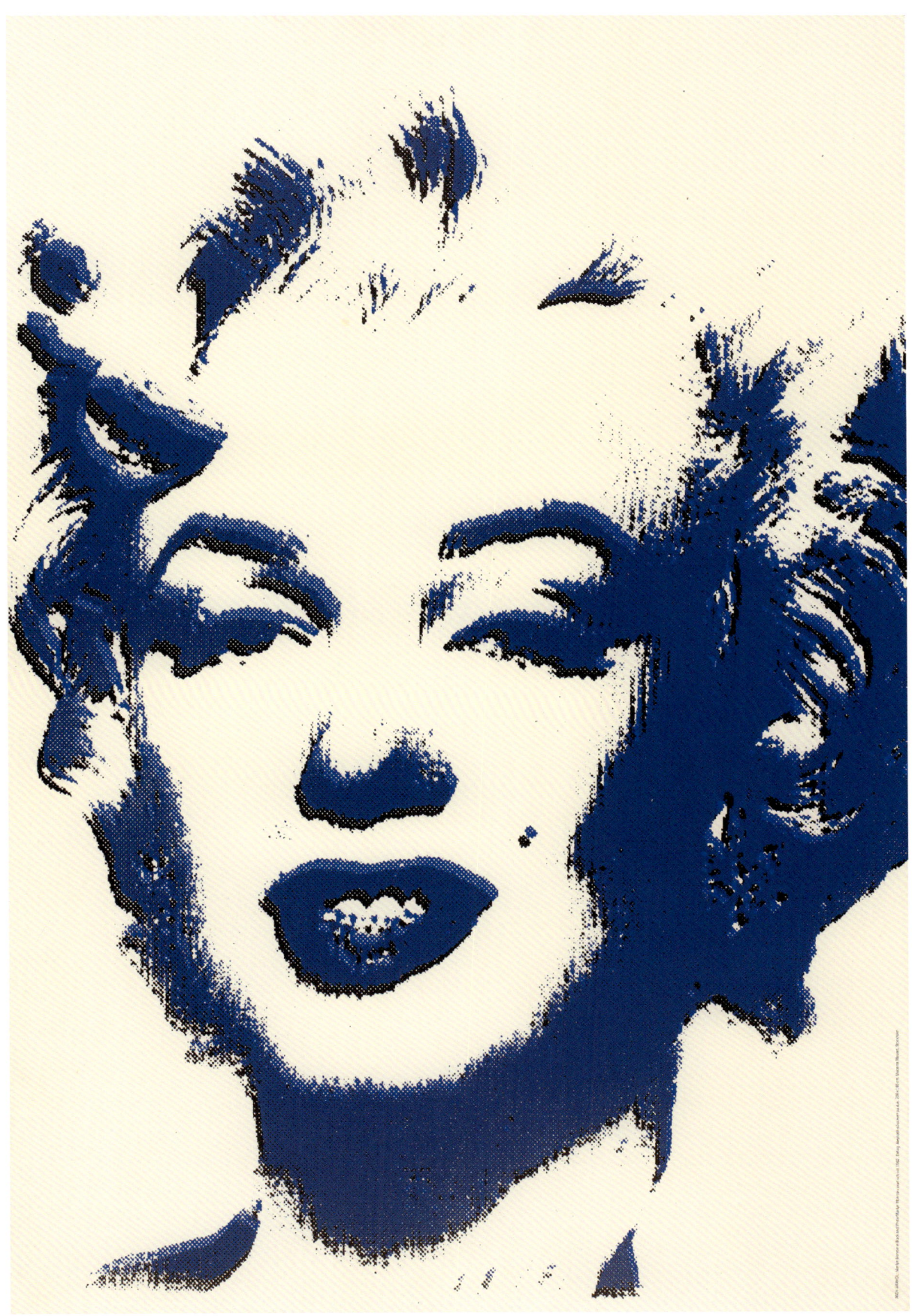

Figure 5.5   AWMM.1968.189 (Plate LXXII, p. 179), three-color
screenprint: black and blue inks on white cardstock. From the
Gregory McCoy Collection. Image used with permission.

Source Image

The inclusion of the caption on most of the prints is the best evidence that Moderna Museet directed the production of the prints, a literal *imprimatur*. Assuming this is the case, the first step in producing the screen would have been to take a photograph of one of the *Twenty-Five Marilyns*. Most of these frames can be easily eliminated, leaving three likely candidates *(Fig. 5.6)*. The iterative process of creating a high-contrast positive image for screenprinting invariably results in loss of detail, especially in the mid-tones, clearly seen when comparing the publicity photograph of Marilyn Monroe that Warhol used for Stockholm's painting *(Figs. 5.7 and 5.8)*. The McCoy *Marilyns* show minimal loss of detail of intensification of contrast *(Fig. 5.8)*, leaving this author to wonder whether the positive image used to make the screen for the McCoy *Marilyns* was the same one used to make the screen for the Stockholm *Marilyn*.[13] In other words, was it obtained from Warhol or the Factory? Regrettably, the global pandemic that has delayed the exhibition has likewise precluded a side-by-side comparison of a print with the painting to settle this tantalizing question.

Fluorescent Prints

Andy Warhol's use of fluorescent colors to flout the conventions of "fine art" had begun shortly before the Moderna Museet exhibition. The cover of the book that accompanied and was made part of the exhibition is printed with the well-known *Flowers* motif, as was the invitation to the opening reception *(Figs. 5.9 and 5.10)*. Both of these include green and orange inks that fluoresce under black light. That thirty-one of the McCoy *Marilyns* are printed on fluorescent green paper and thirty-three on fluorescent orange paper suggests another link between the McCoy *Marilyns* and the Moderna Museet exhibition.

Reversal Prints

The tonal values of the image and the background are reversed in 163 of the McCoy *Marilyns* such that the areas in shadow become the brightest area in the image, and vice versa, as in a photographic negative. Warhol would famously exploit this technique in the Reversal Series produced in the late 1970s to mid-1980s.

While most of the *Marilyns* can easily be categorized as either a true "reversal" or a "positive" image (e.g., white ink on red paper vs. black ink on yellow paper), others are not as clear-cut (e.g., metallic silver on white paper). In the cataloguing of the McCoy *Marilyns*, those printed with white, metallic silver, or metallic gold inks have been considered reversal prints; those printed with black, dark gray, dark blue, or blue inks have been considered positive images.

Two of the five Lac prints bear a ghostly mirror image of Marilyn Monroe on the verso, likely an unintended consequence of being stacked, without any interleaving, for decades *(AWMM.1968.021* and *AWMM.1968.058)*.

White on White

Visitors to the exhibition will have seen a video showing the prints on fluorescent paper luminesce when viewed under ultraviolet light and, in the case of reversal prints, the transformation of negative to positive images. The most dramatic transformation is seen with a group of seven white-on-white prints, which indeed can only be seen under ultraviolet light.[14] This group of prints points to Warhol's 1964 *White Painting*[15] and *Double Torso* from 1966 *(Fig. 3.12)*, both screenprinted paintings of a nude female torso using white silkscreen ink on a white ground that pose the question, "Is it pornography if you can't see it?" The white-on-white *Marilyns* seem to ask, "Is it art if you can't see it?" *(Figs. 5.12 and 5.13)*.

Conclusion

While the purpose of this essay is to detail the physical makeup of the collection, the question of whether or to what degree Warhol was involved is irresistible. That the Moderna Museet produced these prints seems indisputable. The presence of the Lac prints strongly suggests that John Melin and Arne Wahlqvist were involved. Given that *Marilyn Monroe in Black and White*

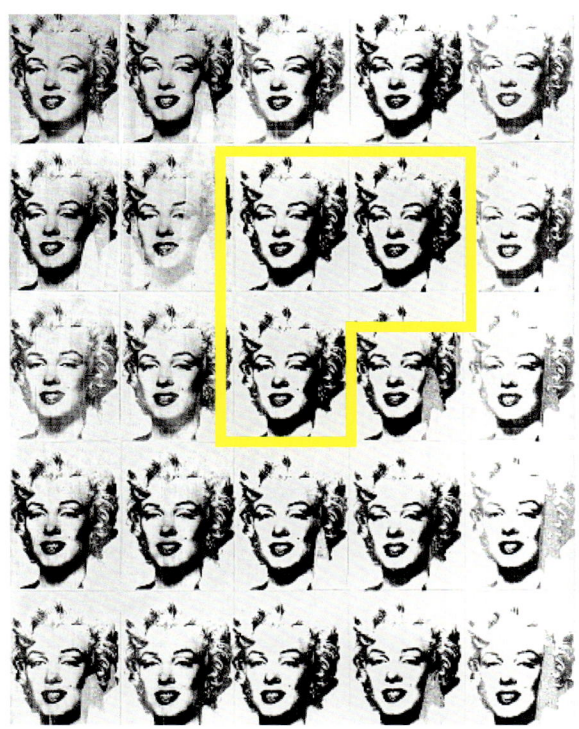

Figure 5.6   One of these three *Marilyns* was likely the source image for the McCoy *Marilyns*. Andy Warhol, *Twenty-Five Marilyns in Black and White*, 1962, in the permanent collection of the Moderna Museet, Stockholm, Sweden. Image used with permission.

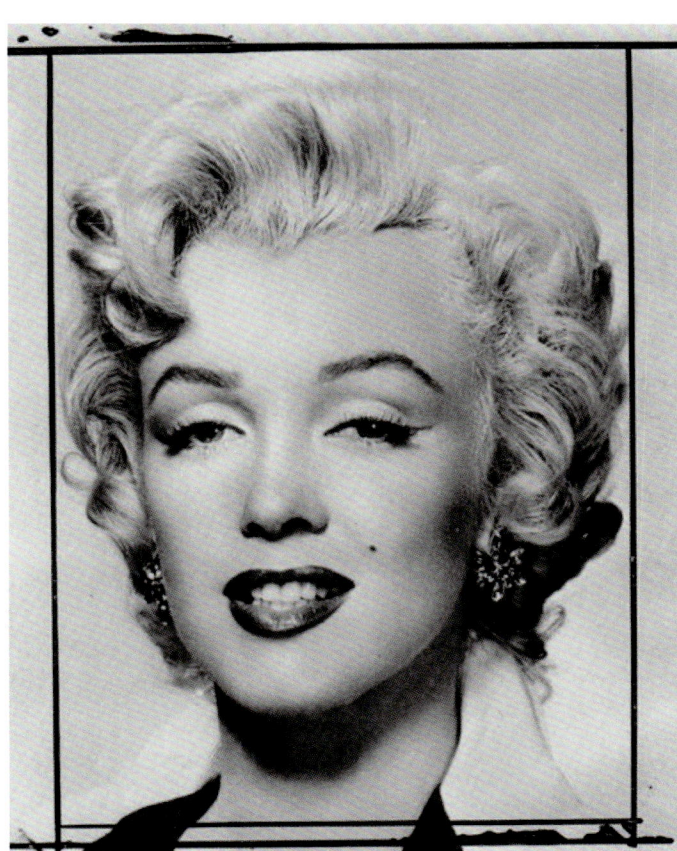

Figure 5.7   Eugene Korman, Marilyn Monroe, Twentieth Century Fox publicity still, 1952, showing Andy Warhol crop marks. Image in the public domain.

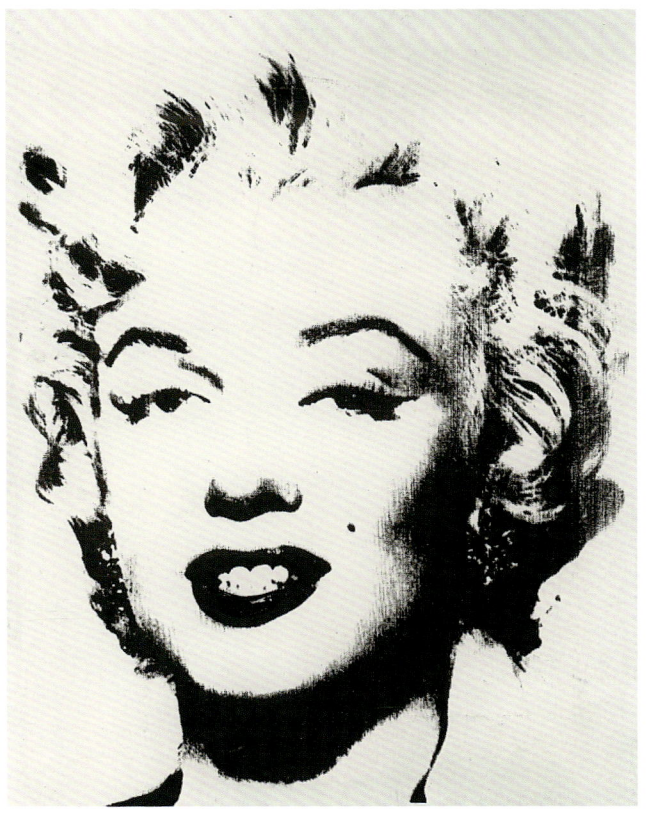

Figure 5.8   Detail of Andy Warhol, *Twenty-Five Marilyns in Black and White*, 1962, in the permanent collection of the Moderna Museet, Stockholm, Sweden. Image used with permission.

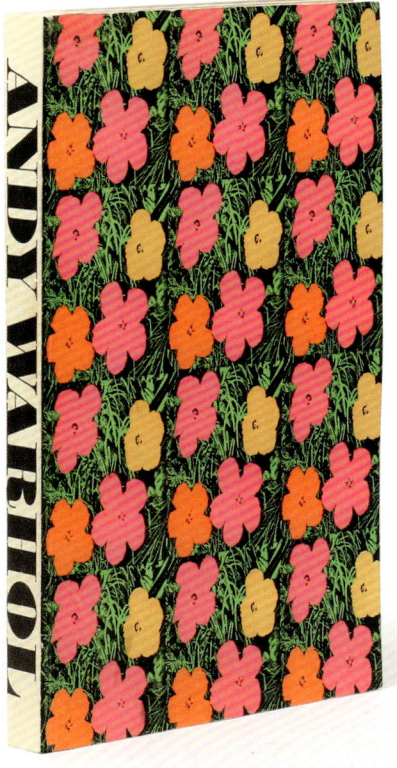

Figure 5.9   *Andy Warhol* (Stockholm: Moderna Museet, 1968), front cover and spine, 11 ¼ x 8 ¾ x 1 ⅜ in.

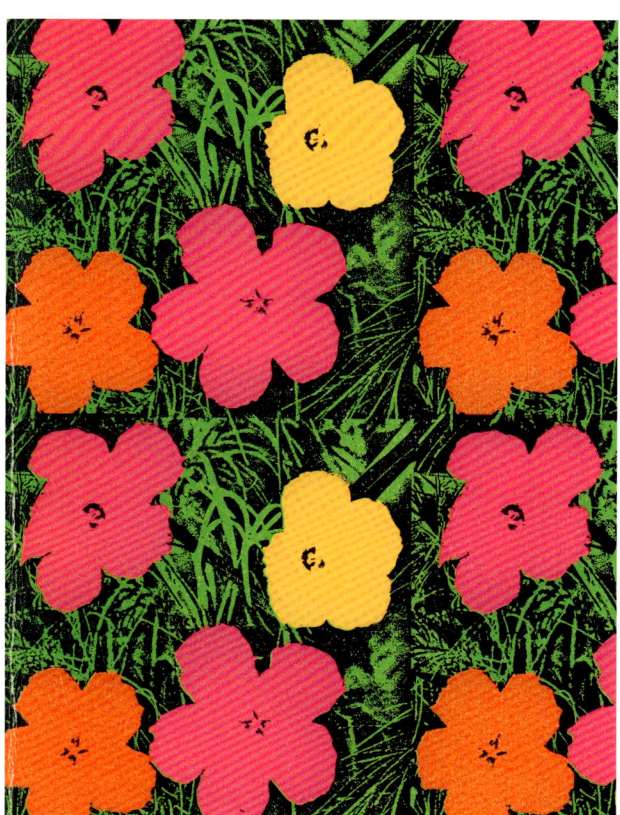

Figure 5.10   Invitation to opening of Andy Warhol exhibition, Moderna Museet, 1968, recto, 5 ½ x 4 ⅛ in. (folded). From the Gregory McCoy Collection. Image used with permission.

Andy Warhol

Screens, Films, Boxes, Clouds and a Book, 1968

Utställningen öppnas lördagen den 10 februari klockan 12

Kortet gäller öppningsdagen för två personer

Moderna Museet Nationalmuseum Stockholm

Förhandsvisning fredagen den 9 febr. klockan 19.30 för Moderna Museets Vänner.
Pop (Pärsson Sound), dans, öl och smörgåsar.
Entré 10 kronor.

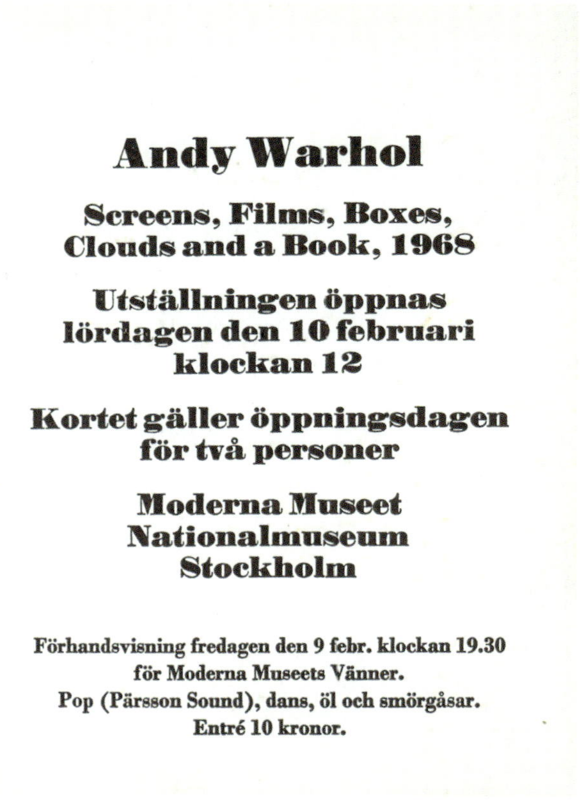

Figure 5.11   Invitation to opening of Andy Warhol exhibition, Moderna Museet, 1968, verso. From the Gregory McCoy Collection. Image used with permission.

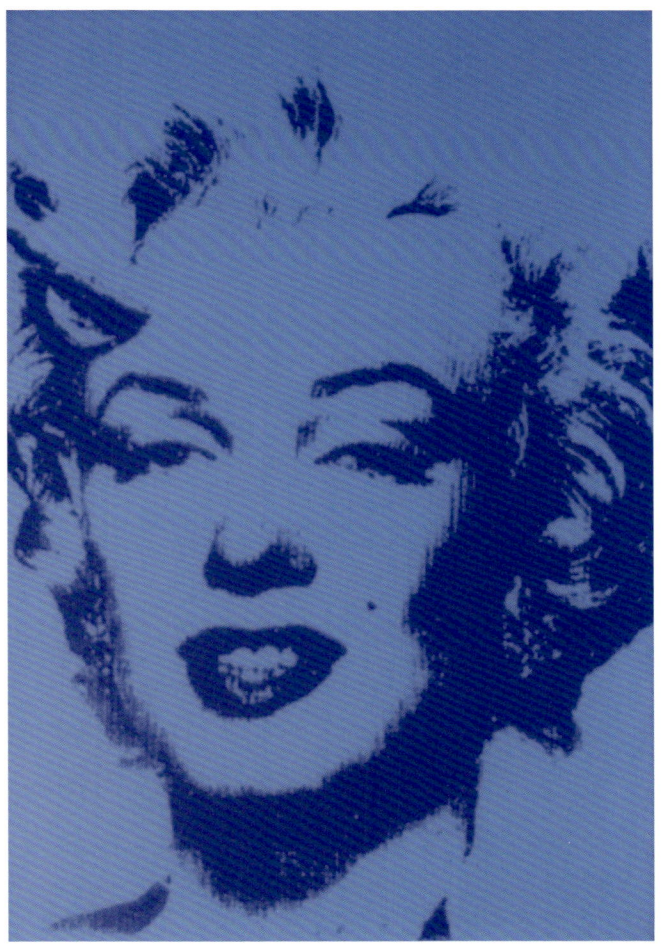

Figure 5.12	AWMM.1968.242 (Plate LXX, p. 177). From the Gregory McCoy Collection. Image used with permission.

Figure 5.13	AWMM.1968.242, seen under ultraviolet light. From the Gregory McCoy Collection. Image used with permission.

was not included in the 1968 exhibition, it seems unlikely that the museum's intention was to produce a poster to promote the exhibition. And clearly the motivation was not to produce a faithful reproduction of the 1962 painting; otherwise, the screenprints, like the text posters and the painting itself, would have been printed only in black and white.

Instead, a great deal of time, resources, and creativity went into producing who knows how many prints in a riot of color combinations and visual effects. In the field of medical diagnostics, interns are warned, "When you hear hoofbeats, don't look for zebras," which is to say that the most obvious diagnosis is generally the correct one. To imagine that Pontus Hultén and/or John Melin and/or Arne Wahlqvist produced the McCoy *Marilyns* without any input whatsoever by Warhol himself, and did so by so masterfully employing the artist's tropes before they had become tropes (to wit, the white-on-white prints), seems, to me, to perhaps be looking for zebras.

Bengt Andersson's *beslutsänger* ("decision anxiety") over whether or not to sell the prints could, as Reva Wolf suggests, have been worry about becoming embroiled in another Warhol attribution controversy, but his parting words (in his email of June 2021 to Börje Bengtsson[16]) seem to belie this. After protesting a bit too much, in my view, about the fact that it was impossible to know for sure when or why the prints were made, he reluctantly offers to sell them, but adds: "In conclusion, I'd be much happier if you instead came back to me with a proposal for an exhibition in your gallery!" Implied but not stated is the fear that he will someday come to regret *the one that got away*.

Whether or not the authorship of the McCoy *Marilyns* can ever be conclusively ascertained, what can be said about the collection can be said with confidence. Whomever conceived of or directed the production of the collection, an artist with a keen graphic sensibility and a master printmaker were at the helm. The technical quality of the printing is impeccable. The handful of prints that are inconsistent (ink not as densely applied, or slight "ghosting" of the image) are the exceptions that prove the rule.[17] That a visually sophisticated, irreverent, and playful artist/designer/printer chose the paper and ink color combinations is on ample display in the exhibition and within these pages.

1. Both analyses were performed using FTIR (Fourier transform infrared miscrospectroscopy) and Raman spectra (dispersive confocal Raman microspectroscopy). The pigments and other materials that were identified neither definitively confirm nor counterindicate a dating to the 1960s; the pigments analyzed were in use in the 1960s and are still in use today. However, a class of red and yellow pigments that are currently used in printing inks (diketopyrollo pyrrole pigments), but were not manufactured until the mid-1980s, were *not* detected.

2. Wikipedia, s.v. "Svecia (company)," last modified February 19, 2022, 02:57, https://en.wikipedia.org/wiki/Svecia_screen_printing_machines.

3. According to Bengt Andersson, who purchased the printing company Reklamteknik where a number of the *Marilyns* were found.

4. Discussed by Reva Wolf, "Marilyn Mystery" in the present publication.

5. As mentioned by Reva Wolf in "Marilyn Mystery," the term Lac print was used and perhaps coined by John Melin and Arne Wahlqvist, presumably as shorthand for "lacquer."

6. This substrate became less popular after the advent of metallicized polyester film (the best known of which is Mylar). According to a timeline on its website (usa.dupontteijinfilms.com), Mylar was invented by Dupont in 1954 in Circleville, Ohio. Production of Mylar in Europe did not begin until 1965 in Luxembourg. Further research is needed to determine when Mylar-coated papers became available for printing purposes in Europe, which might shed further light on the question of dating of the collection.

7. See "Marilyn Mystery."

8. *John Melin: till Exempel* (Stockholm: Moderna Museet, 2000), 41, 119.

9. "Graphic Design: John Melin," https://www.modernamuseet.se/stockholm/en/exhibitions/graphic-design-john-melin1/.

10. Examination took place at the Conservation Center for Art & Historic Artifacts (ccaha.org) by Heather Hendry, Senior Paper Conservator, on 27 February 2020. The backgrounds that may have been screenprinted are: fluorescent orange, fluorescent green, and silver, and possibly the green and orange as well.

11. An eighth "color" of ink may be that used on the Lac-prints, which appears (under magnification at CCAHA, see endnote 5) to have been printed with a ink base, without any pigments mixed into it. Materials analysis is required to confirm this observation.

12. A complementary afterimage is the result of the overstimulation of the eye's photoreceptors that are responsible for discerning color (the cones). When the cones are overexposed to one color, the afterimage seen will approximate its complementary color. The reader can experience this phenomenon by staring at one of the *Marilyns* printed on fluorescent paper for a minute or so, and then looking away to a white surface and blinking a few times.

13. This observation is based on a comparison of digital images of both, using Adobe Photoshop on an iMac 24-inch, M1, 2021.

14. Although all prints on white paper will luminesce under black light, only those printed with white ink have been catalogued as fluorescent, since these can only be seen under black light. The short video illustrating the transition from day light to ultraviolet light can be viewed here: https://youtu.be/svX04e8jBkw.

15. See the website of the Norton Simon Museum: https://www.nortonsimon.org/art/detail/P.1969.073.

16. Email from Bengt Andersson to Börje Bengtsson, April 26, 2015, as translated by Nicola Knipe, June 7, 2021, and provided to the author.

17. "Ghosting" is caused by the movement of the screen following a squeegee stroke, and results in a faint, accidental, offset image.

Catalogue Raisonné of the McCoy *Marilyns*

Including Text Posters and Other Works

The McCoy *Marilyns* each measure 100 cm. (39½ in.) in height by 70 cm. (27½ in.) in width. Unless otherwise indicated, paper is coated cover stock (.008 in. thick or 80 lb.).

Prints are designated as two-color or three-color. Although the background color was most likely printed by offset lithography by the company that supplied the paper stock, for the purposes of this catalogue the paper color is considered one of the colors.

Nearly two-thirds of the prints include the following caption, located along the lower right edge of the sheet, printed in a single line from bottom to top:

> **ANDY WARHOL Marilyn Monroe in Black and White/Marilyn Monroe i svart och vitt1962. Detalj. Akryl och screenprint pa duk. 208 × 140 cm. Moderna Museet, Stockholm**

In the case of three-color prints that bear the caption, the caption is printed with the first color of ink used.

The McCoy Collection also includes examples of each of the seven posters produced by the Moderna Museet to advertise the 1968 Warhol exhibition, each with a quote by Andy Warhol. Each measure 100 cm (39 ½ in.) in height by 70 cm (27 ½ in.) in width. The paper is uncoated cover stock (.008 in. thick or 80 lb.).

Prints included in the exhibition *Out of Sight: An Art Collector, A Discovery and Andy Warhol* are indicated with an asterisk (*) after its collection number.

Prints illustrated in this section of the catalogue are indicated by **(illustrated)** in bold after their collection number.

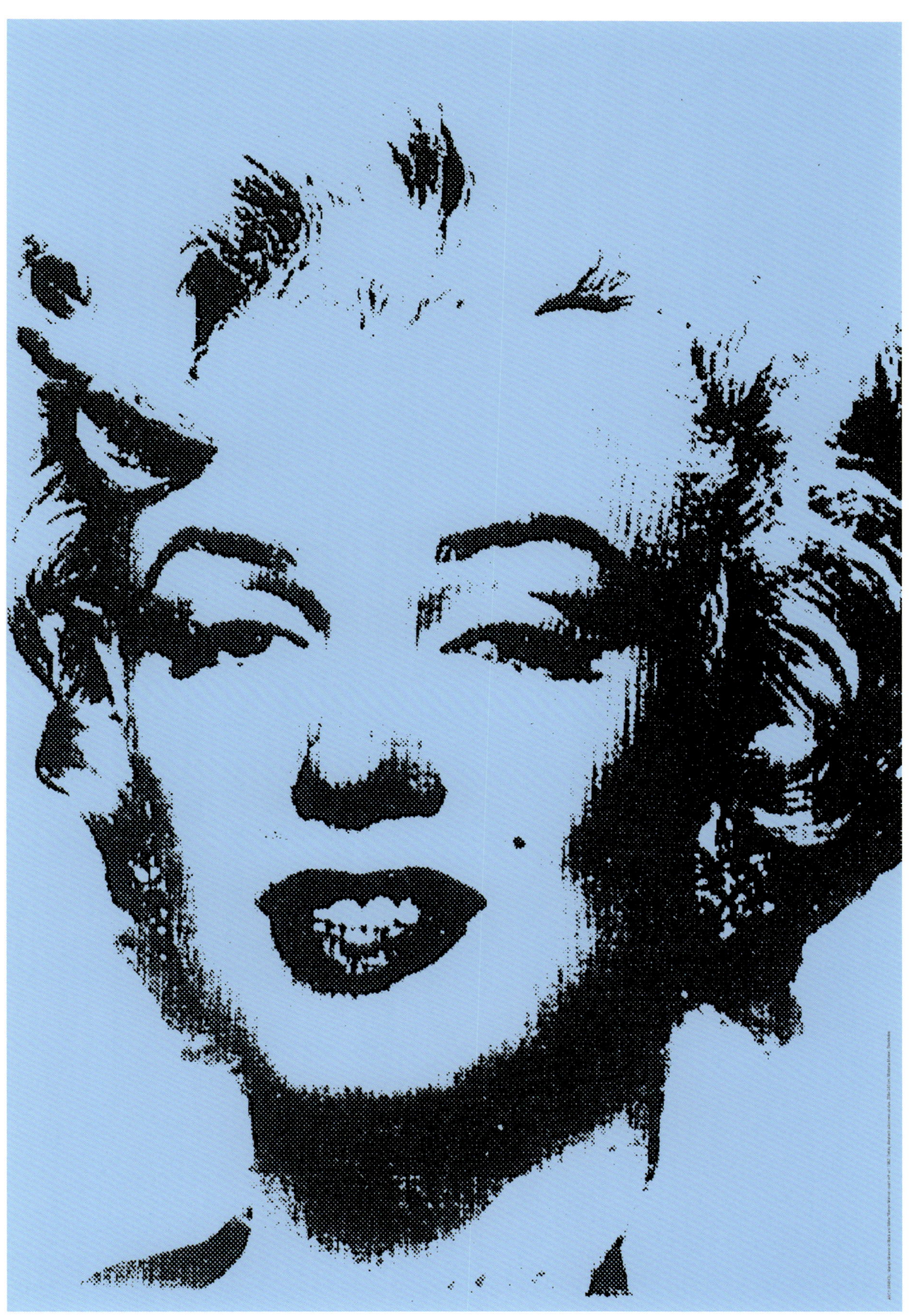

Plate I   Two-color screenprints: black ink on light blue paper; Number of prints: four; Caption: yes; Collection numbers: AWMM.1968.142 **(illustrated)***, AWMM.1968.164, AWMM.1968.182, AWMM.1968.293.

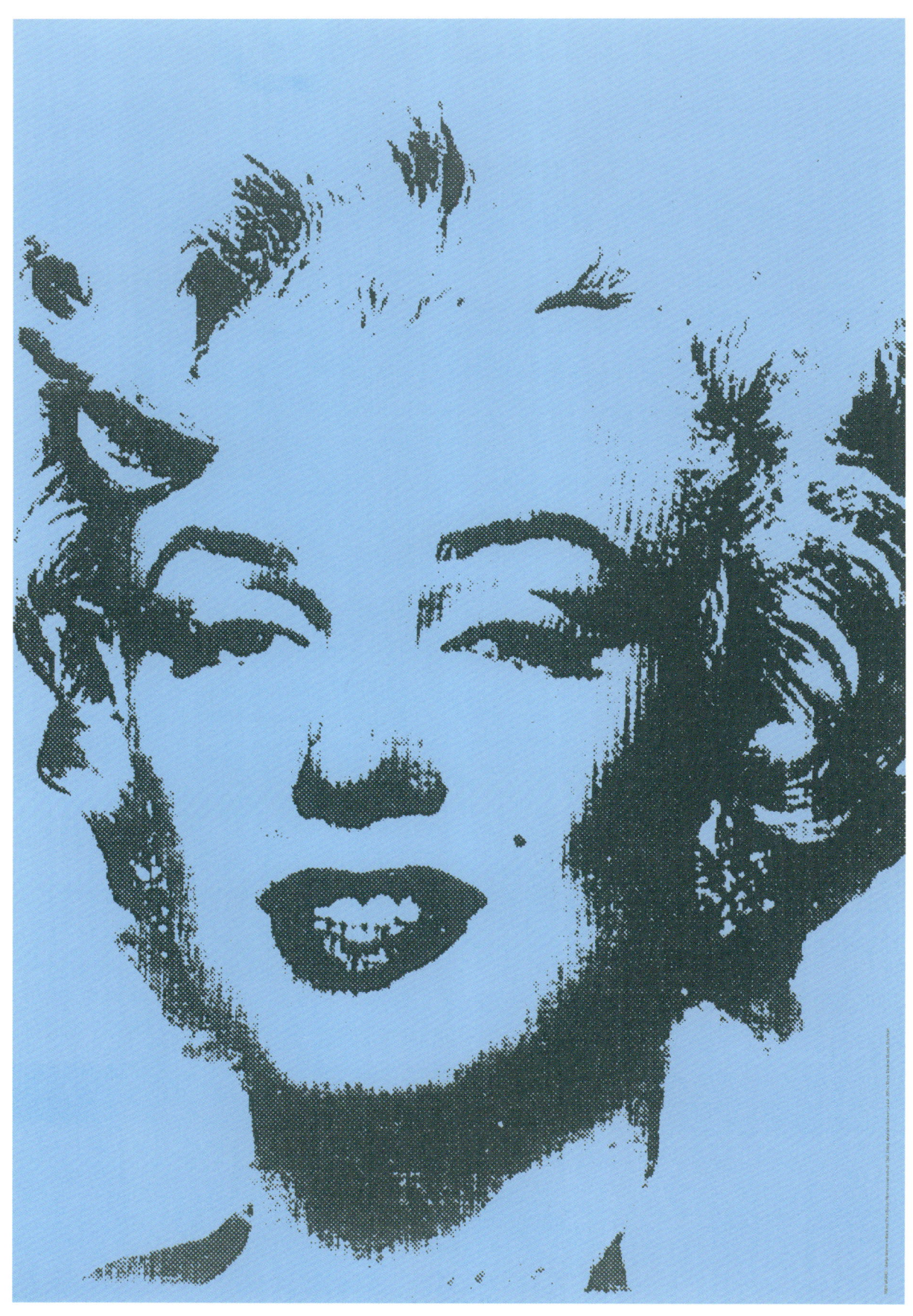

Plate II   Two-color screenprints: dark gray ink on light blue paper; Number of prints:
three; Caption: yes; Collection numbers: AWMM.1968.001,
AWMM.1968.287 **(illustrated)**, AWMM.1968.310.

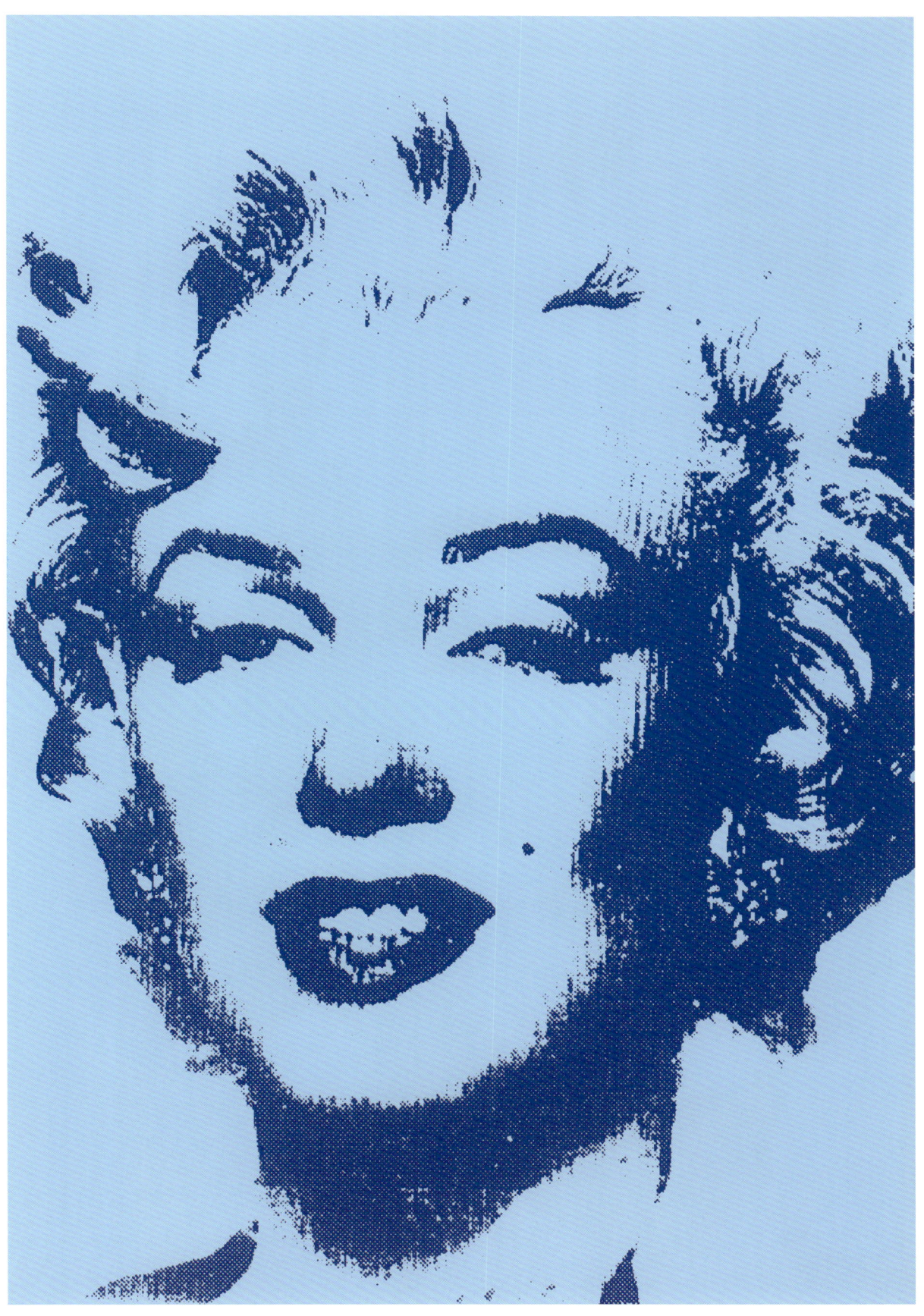

Plate III   Two-color screenprints: blue ink on light blue paper; Number of prints: six;
Caption: no; Collection numbers: AWMM.1968.102 **(illustrated)**, AWMM.1968.178,
AWMM.1968.183, AWMM.1968.195, AWMM.1968.216, AWMM.1968.290.

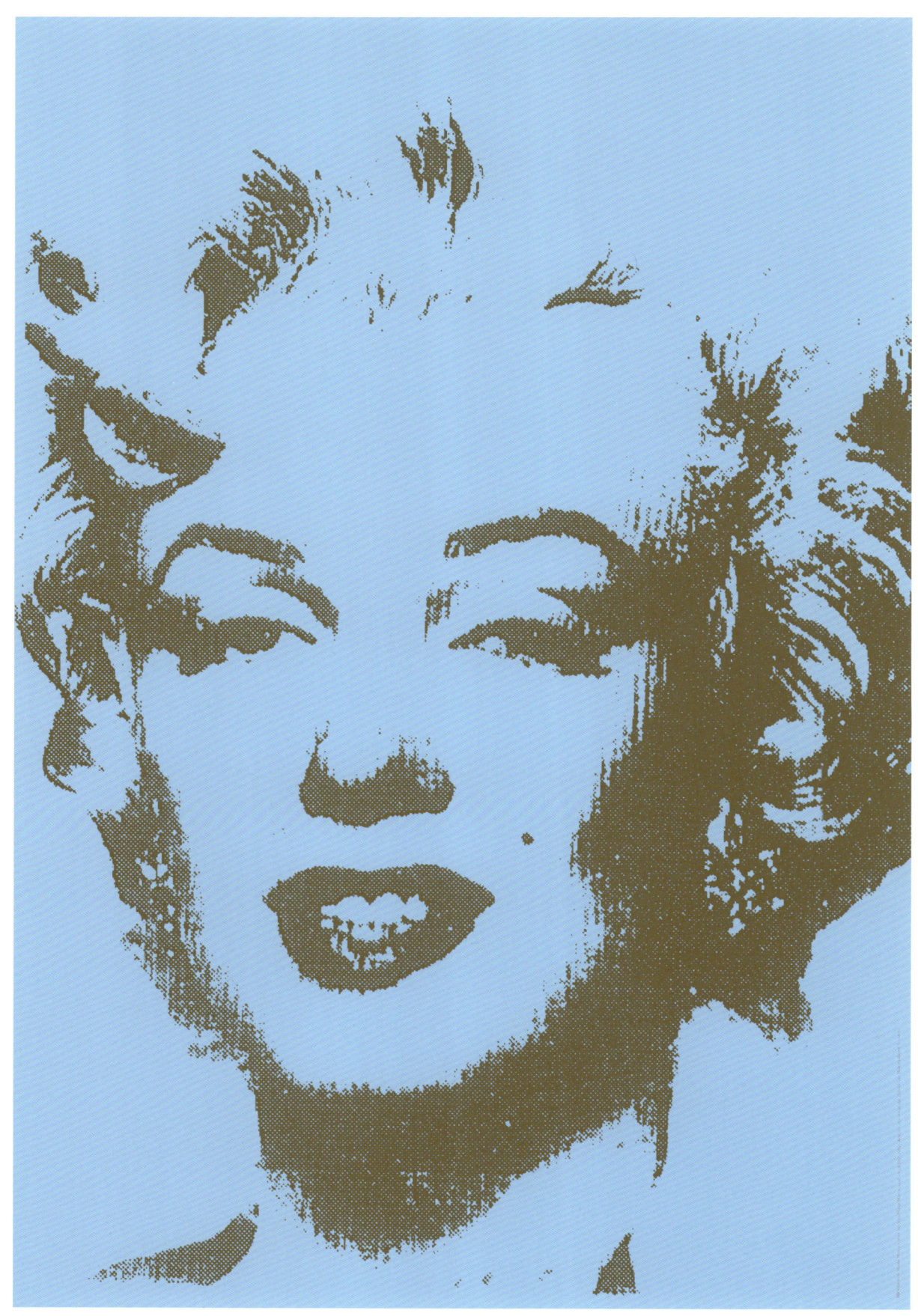

Plate IV   Two-color reversal screenprints: metallic gold ink on light blue paper; Number
of prints: five; Caption: yes; Collection numbers: AWMM.1968.017 **(illustrated)**,
AWMM.1968.023, AWMM.1968.063, AWMM.1968.141, AWMM.1968.321.

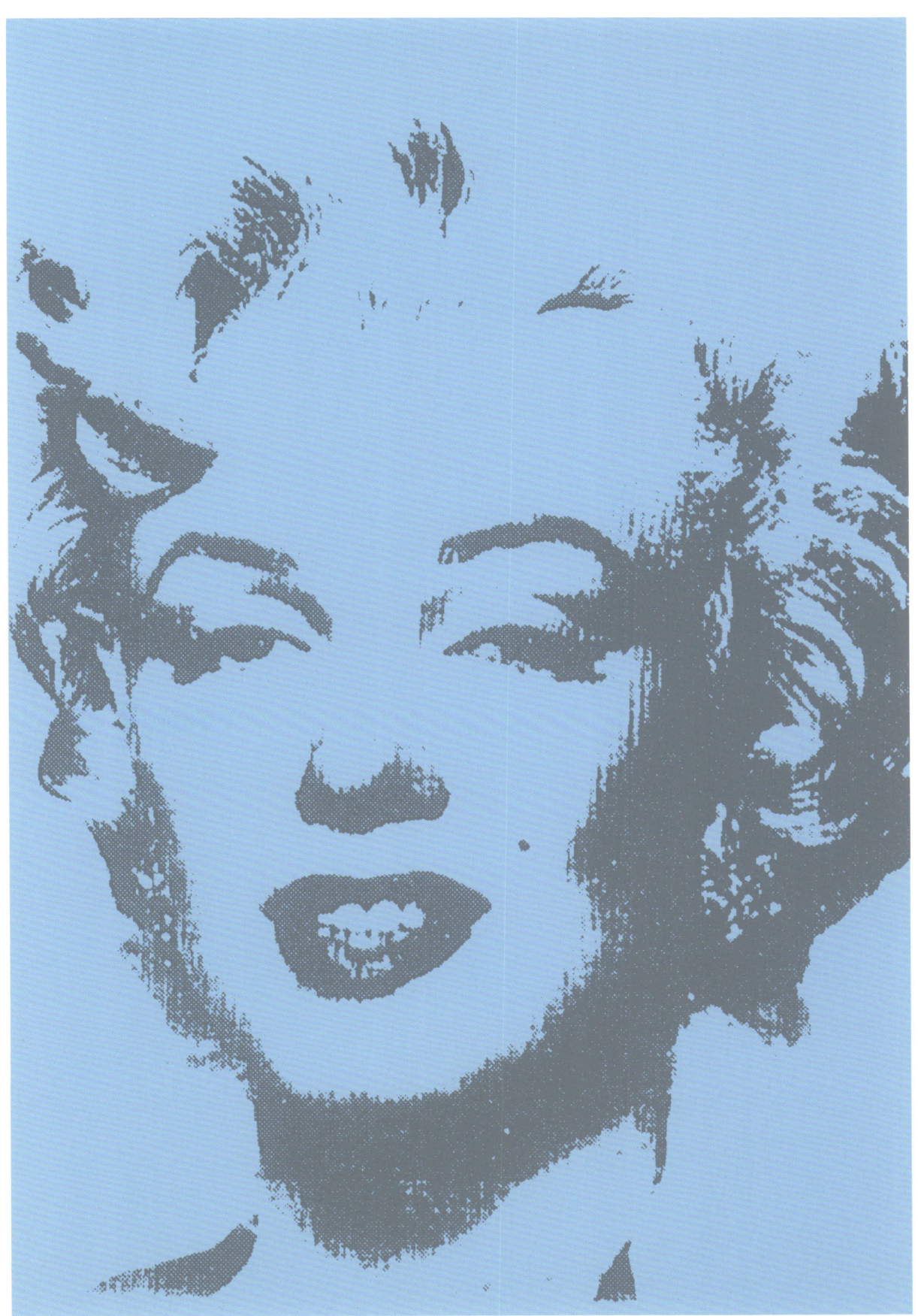

Plate V   Two-color reversal screenprints: metallic silver ink on light blue paper; Number
of prints: four; Caption: no; Collection numbers: AWMM.1968.143 **(illustrated)**,
AWMM.1968.161, AWMM.1968.165, AWMM.1968.269.

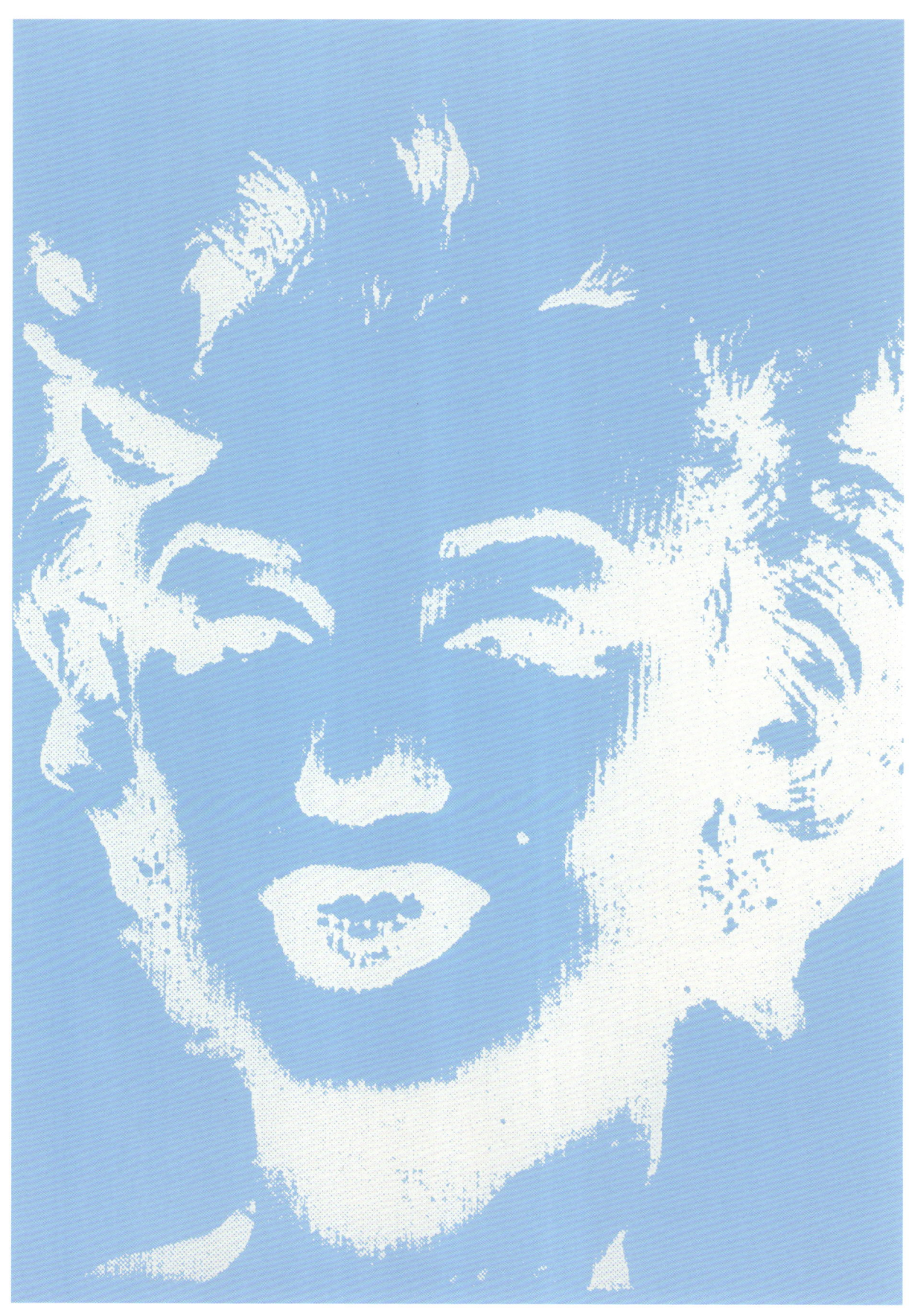

Plate VI   Two-color reversal screenprints: white ink on light blue paper; Number of prints: four;
Caption: no; Collection numbers: AWMM.1968.100 **(illustrated)**, AWMM.1968.176,
AWMM.1968.194, AWMM.1968.231.

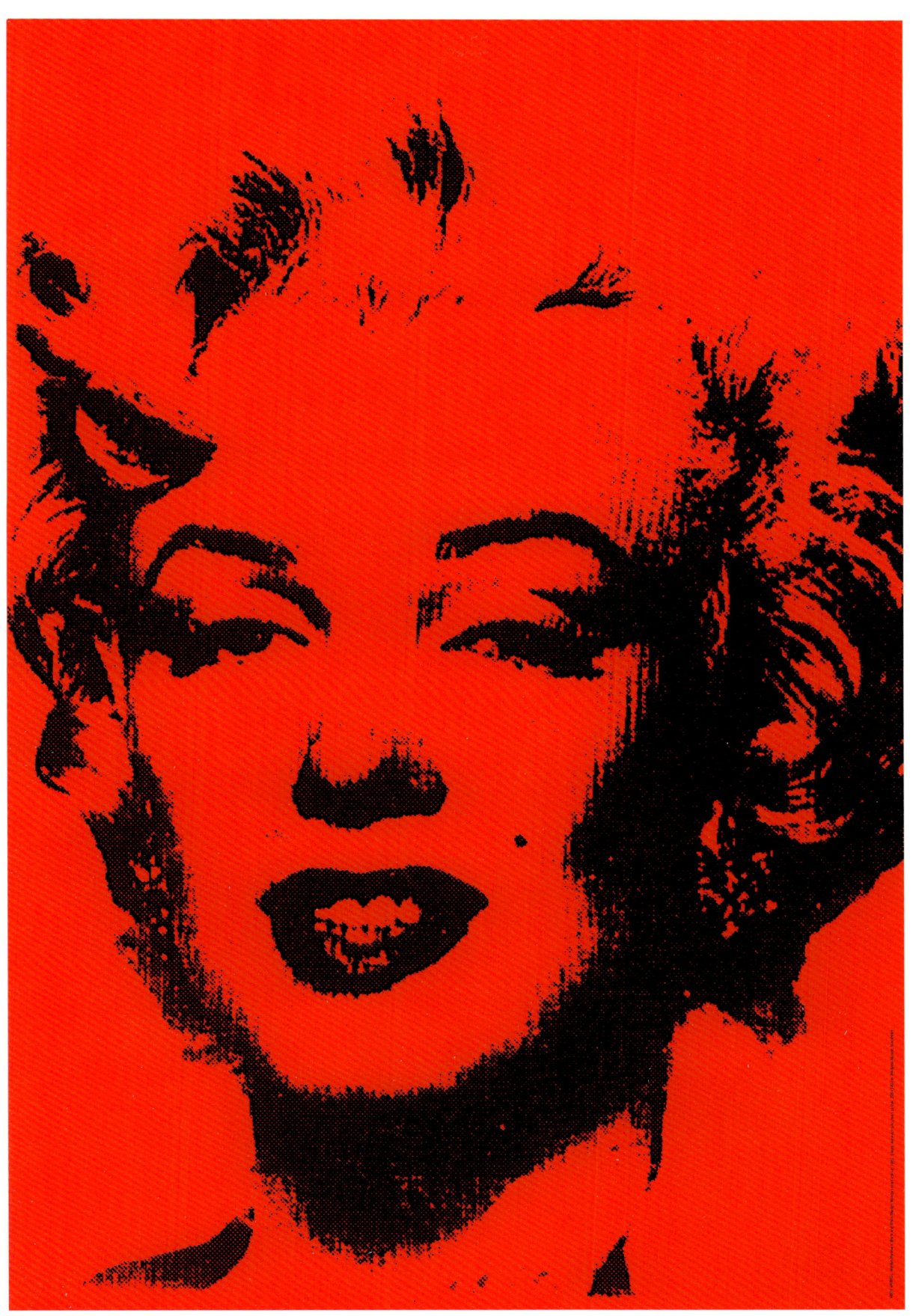

Plate VII   Two-color screenprint: black ink on red paper;
Number of prints: one; Caption: yes; Collection
number: AWMM.1968.085*.

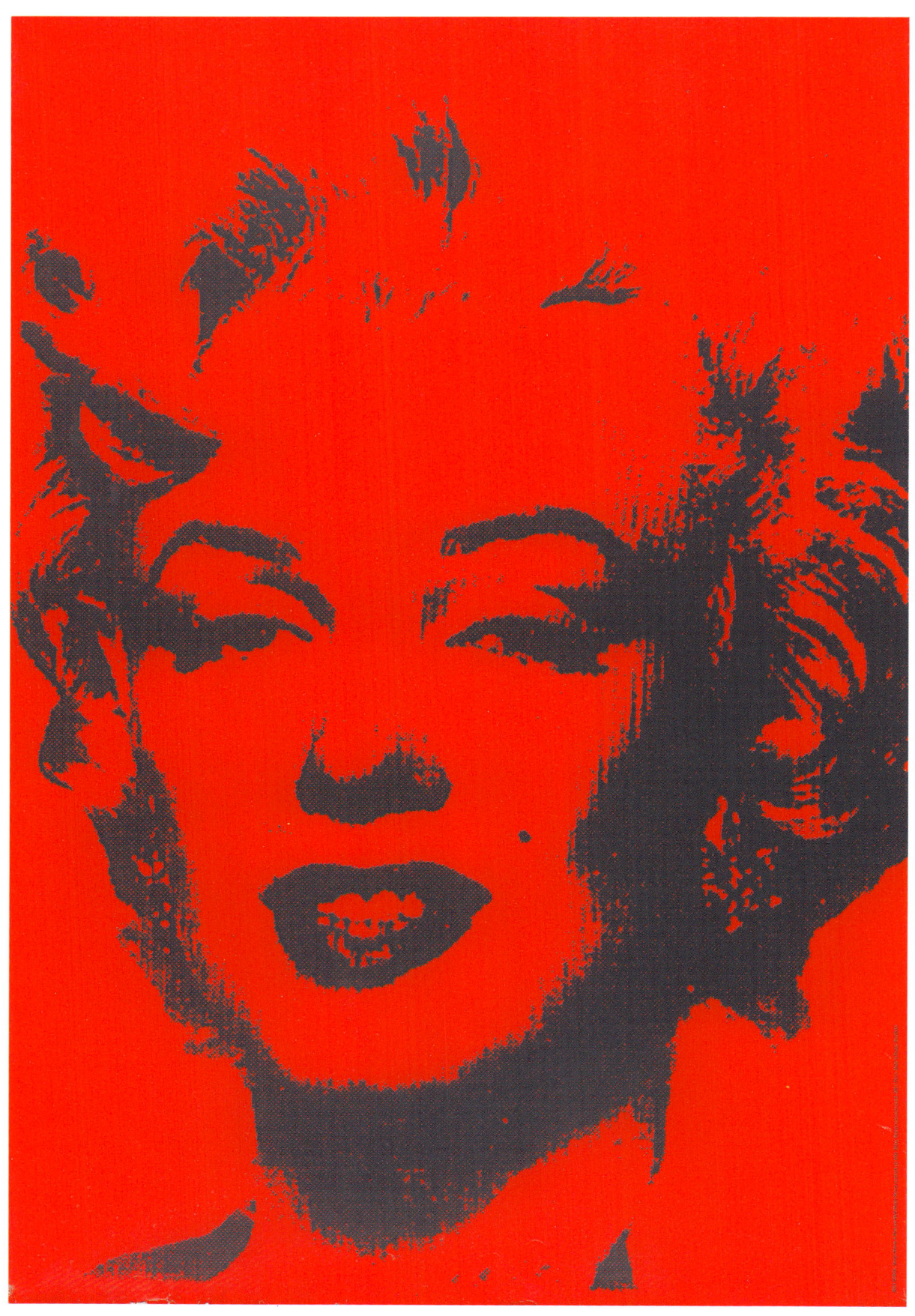

Plate VIII   Two-color screenprints: dark gray ink on red paper; Number of
prints: two; Caption: yes; Collection numbers: AWMM.1968.009
(illustrated), AWMM.1968.188.

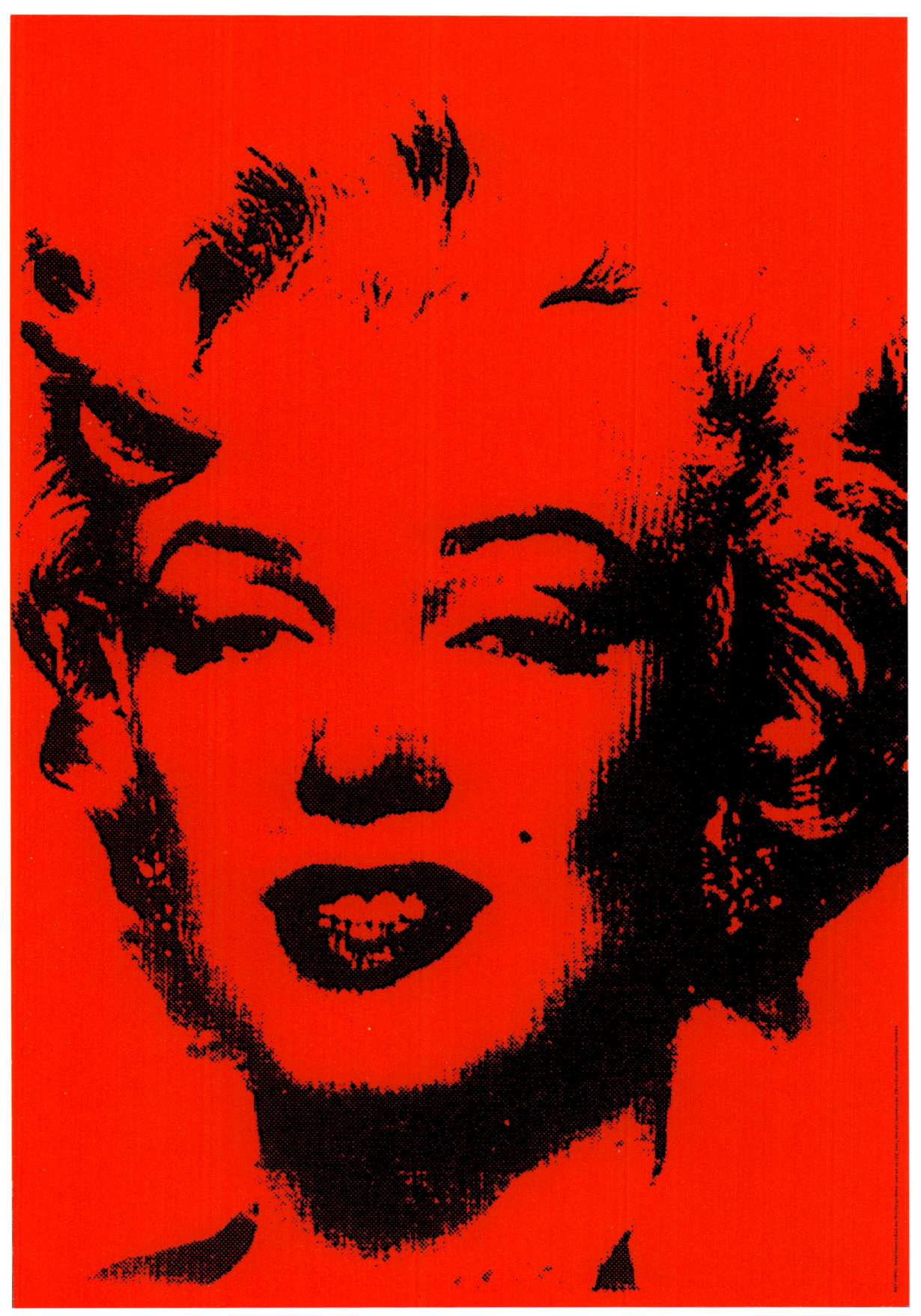

Plate IX   Two-color screenprints: dark blue ink on red paper; Number of
prints: three; Caption: yes; Collection numbers: AWMM.1968.002
(illustrated), AWMM.1968.125, AWMM.1968.187.

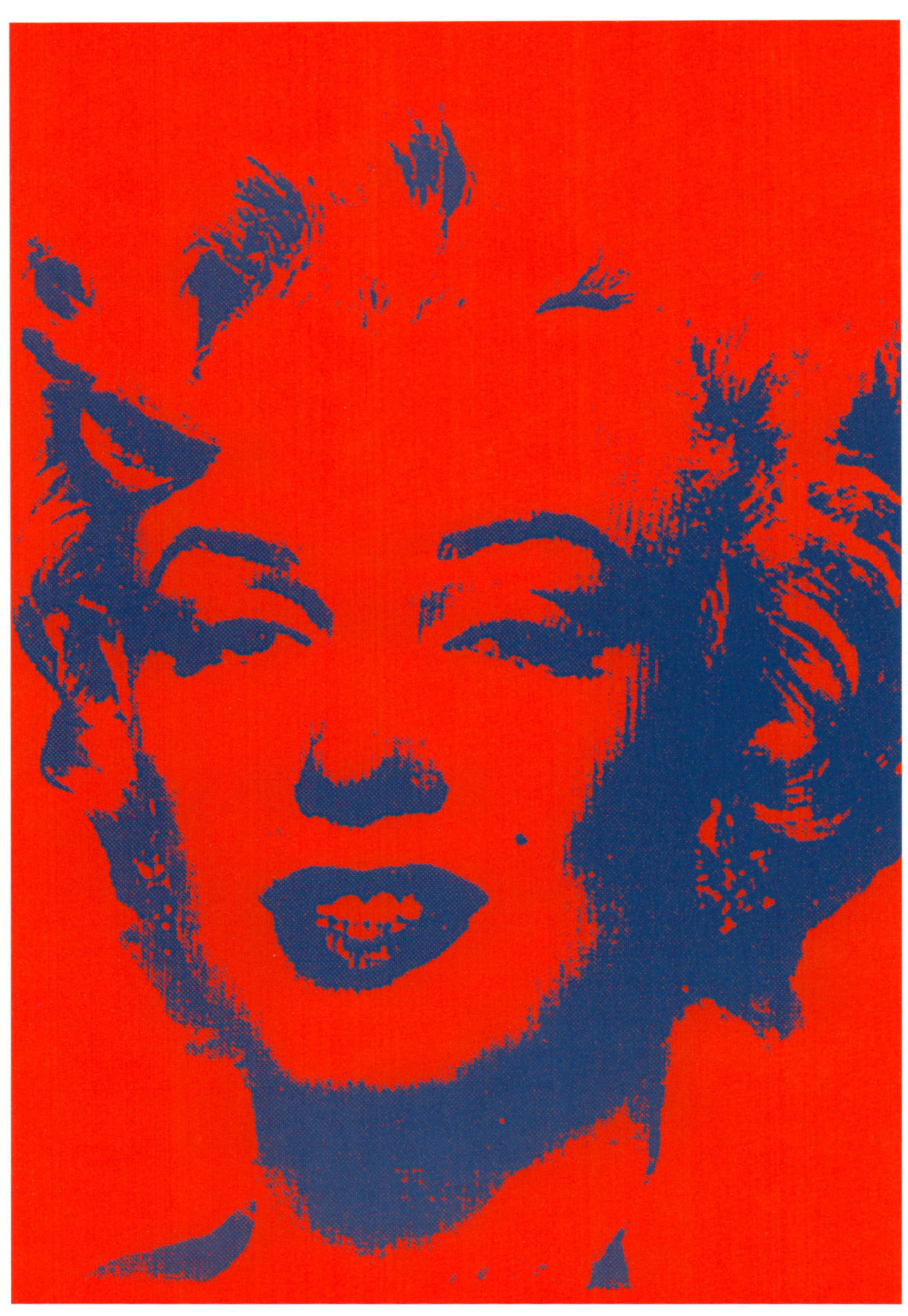

Plate X   Two-color screenprints: blue ink on red paper; Number of prints: five;
Caption: no; Collection numbers: AWMM.1968.064*, AWMM.1968.065
(illustrated), AWMM.1968.122, AWMM.1968.154, AWMM.1968.254.

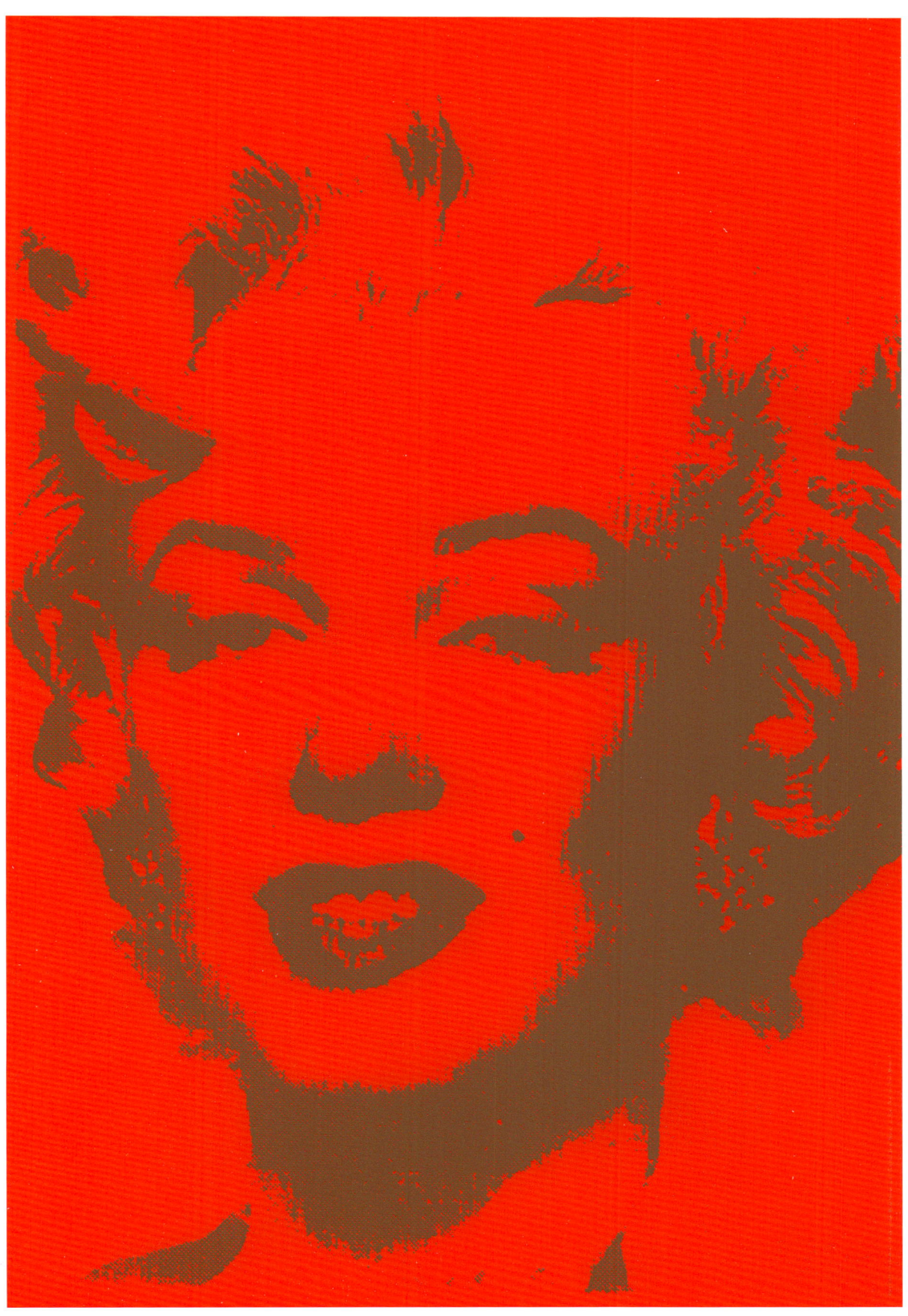

Plate XI   Two-color reversal screenprints: metallic gold ink on red paper; Number
of prints: four; Caption: yes; Collection numbers: AWMM.1968.008,
AWMM.1968.019 **(illustrated)**, AWMM.1968.282, AWMM.1968.300.

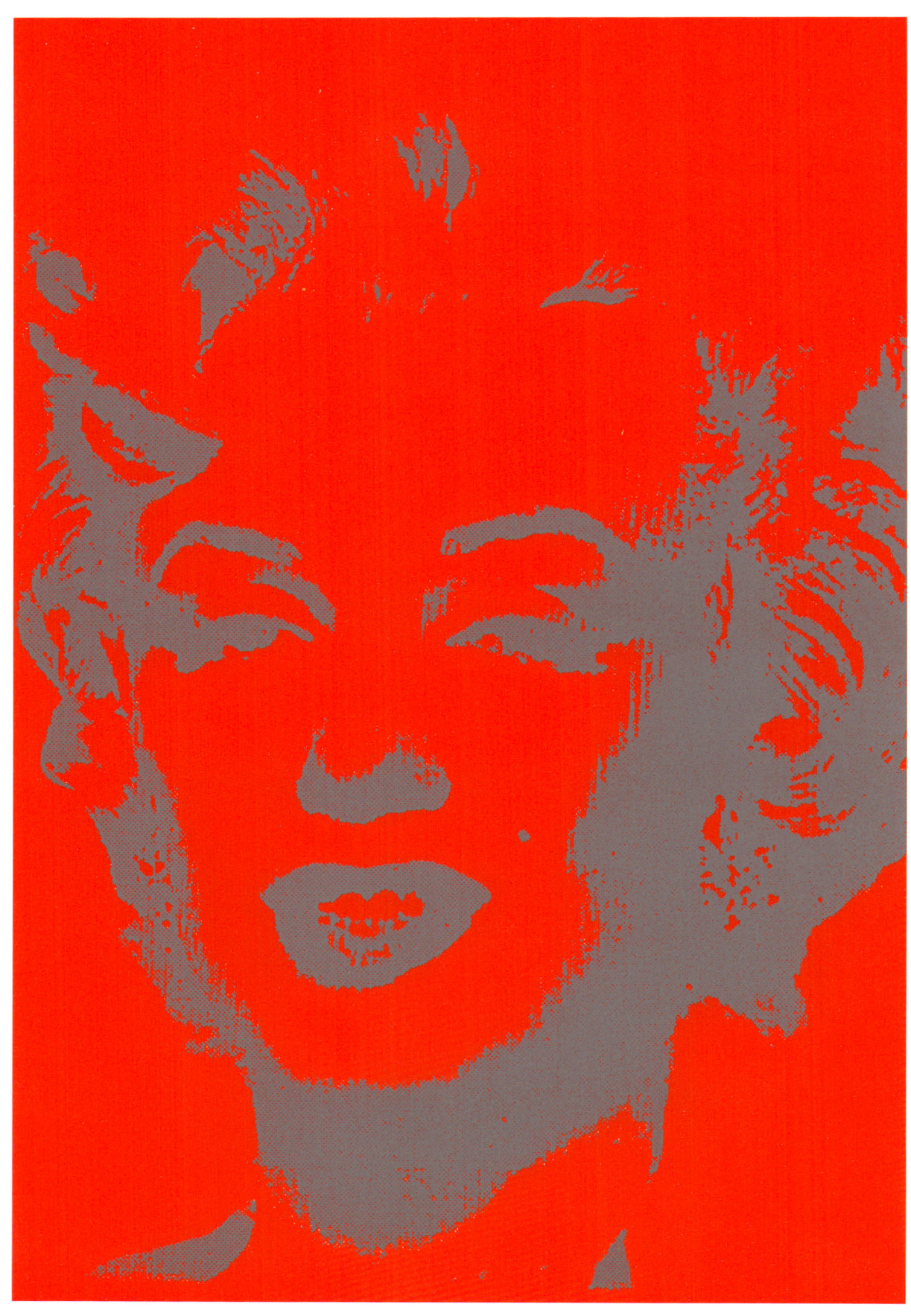

Plate XII   Two-color reversal screenprints: metallic silver ink on red paper; Number of prints: six;
Caption: no; Collection numbers: AWMM.1968.090, AWMM.1968.160, AWMM.1968.167,
AWMM.1968.172, AWMM.1968.235, AWMM.1968.245 **(illustrated)**.

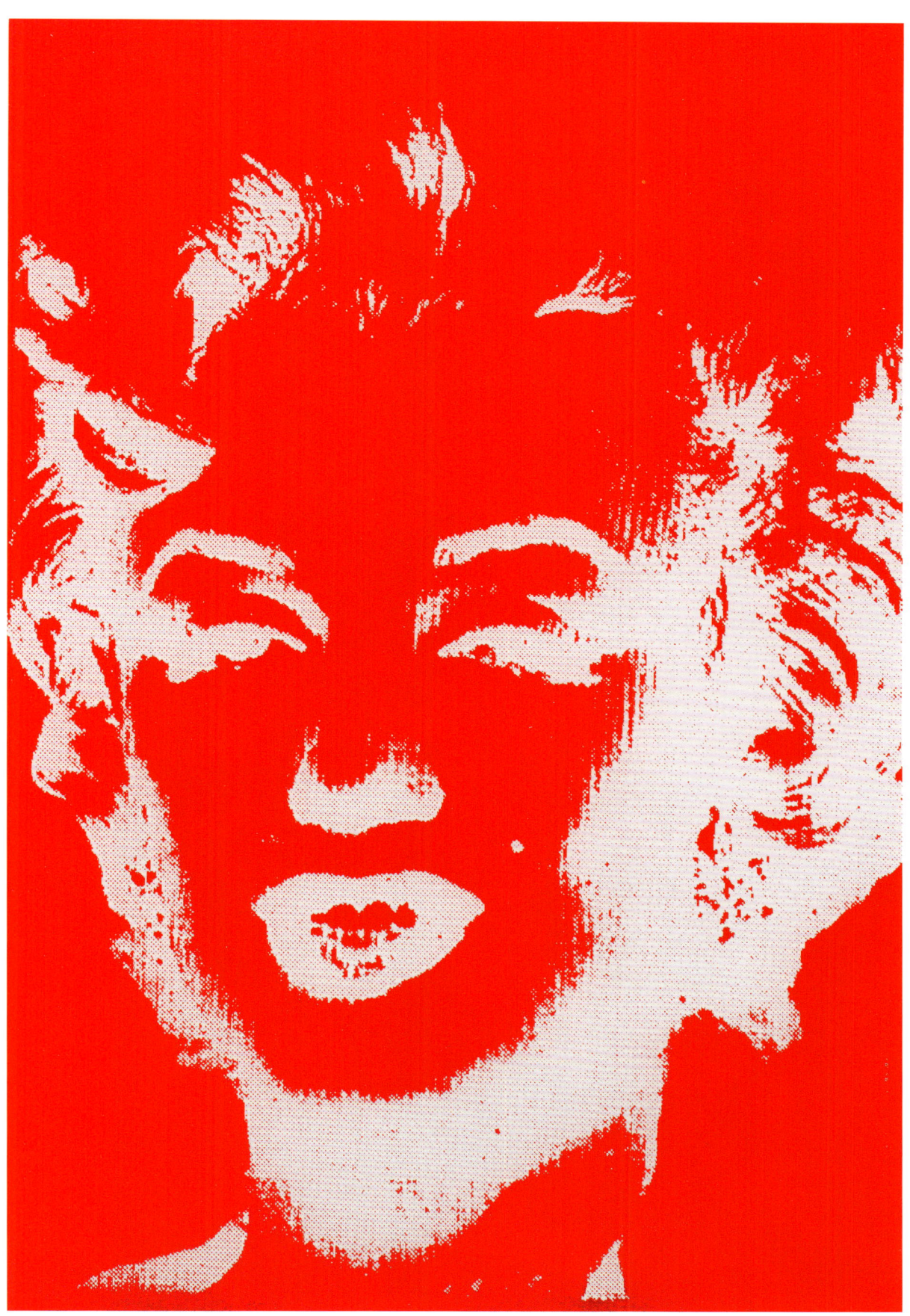

Plate XIII Two-color reversal screenprints: white ink on red paper; Number of prints: four; Caption: no; Collection numbers: AWMM.1968.115, AWMM.1968.152, AWMM.1968.171, AWMM.1968.236 **(illustrated)***.

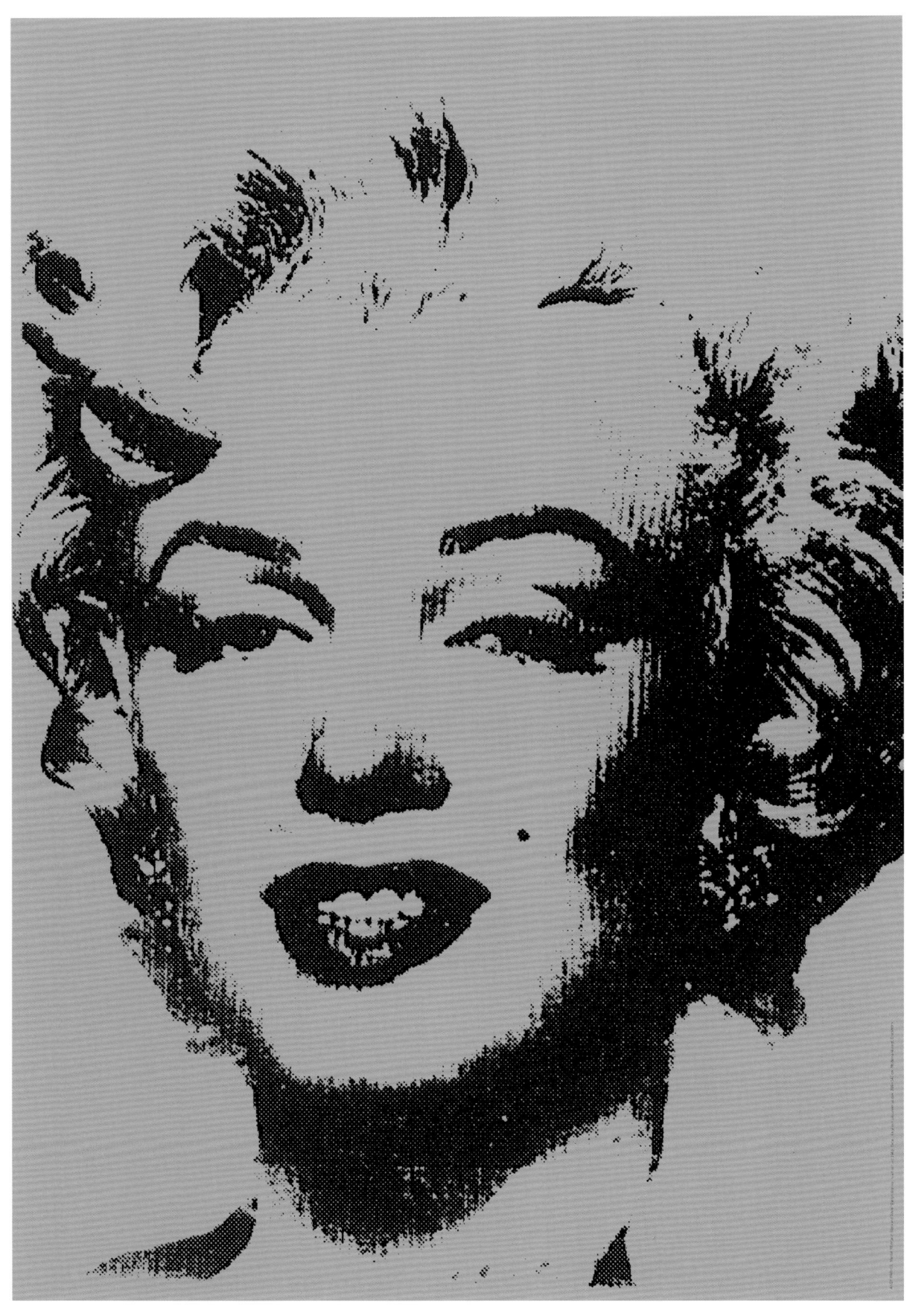

Plate XIV   Two-color screenprints: black ink on silver paper; Number of prints: three;
Caption: yes; Collection numbers: AWMM.1968.003, AWMM.1968.191
(illustrated)*, AWMM.1968.257.

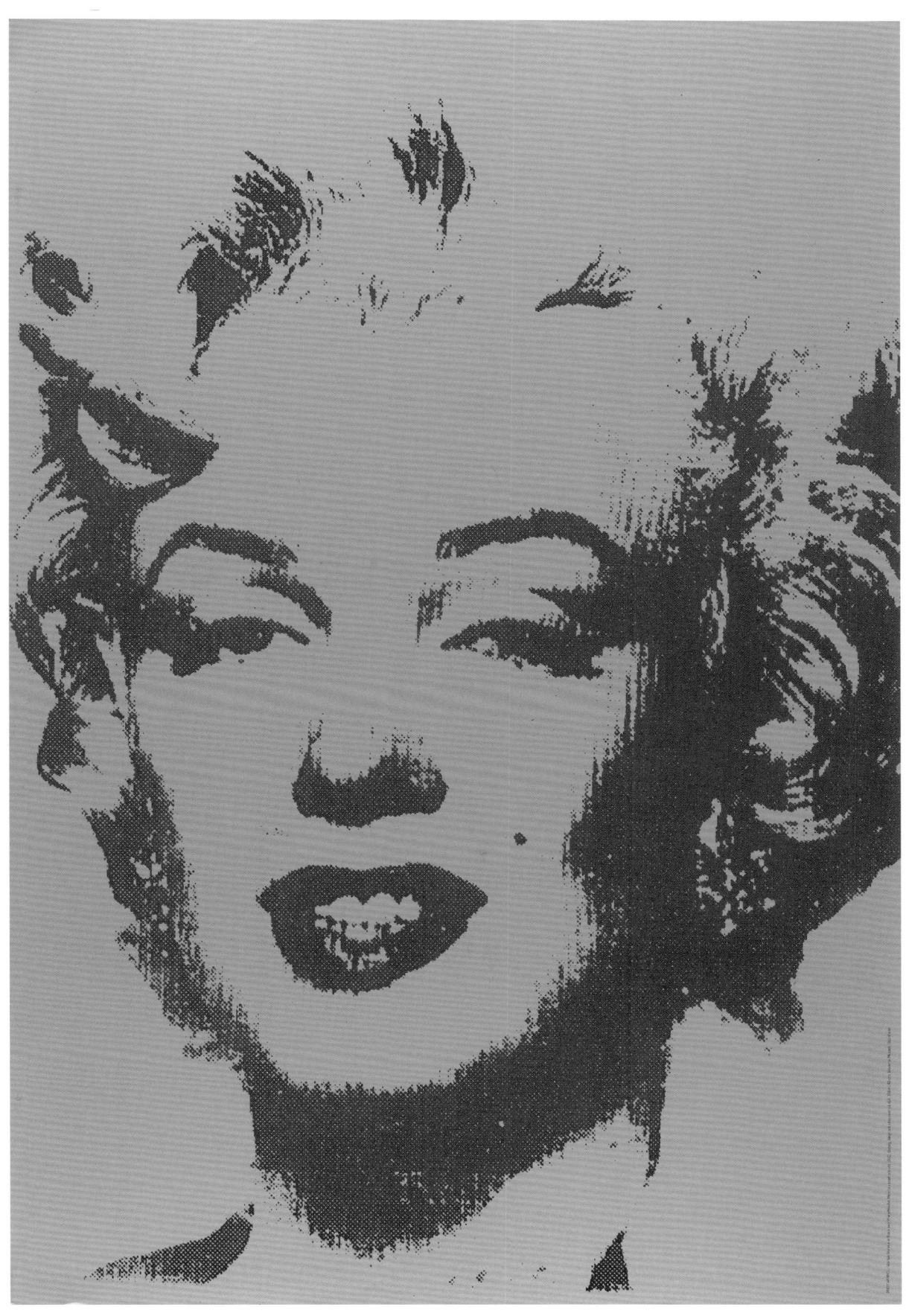

Plate XV   Two-color screenprints: dark gray ink on silver paper; Number of
prints: two; Caption: yes; Collection numbers: AWMM.1968.206,
AWMM.1968.301 **(illustrated)**.

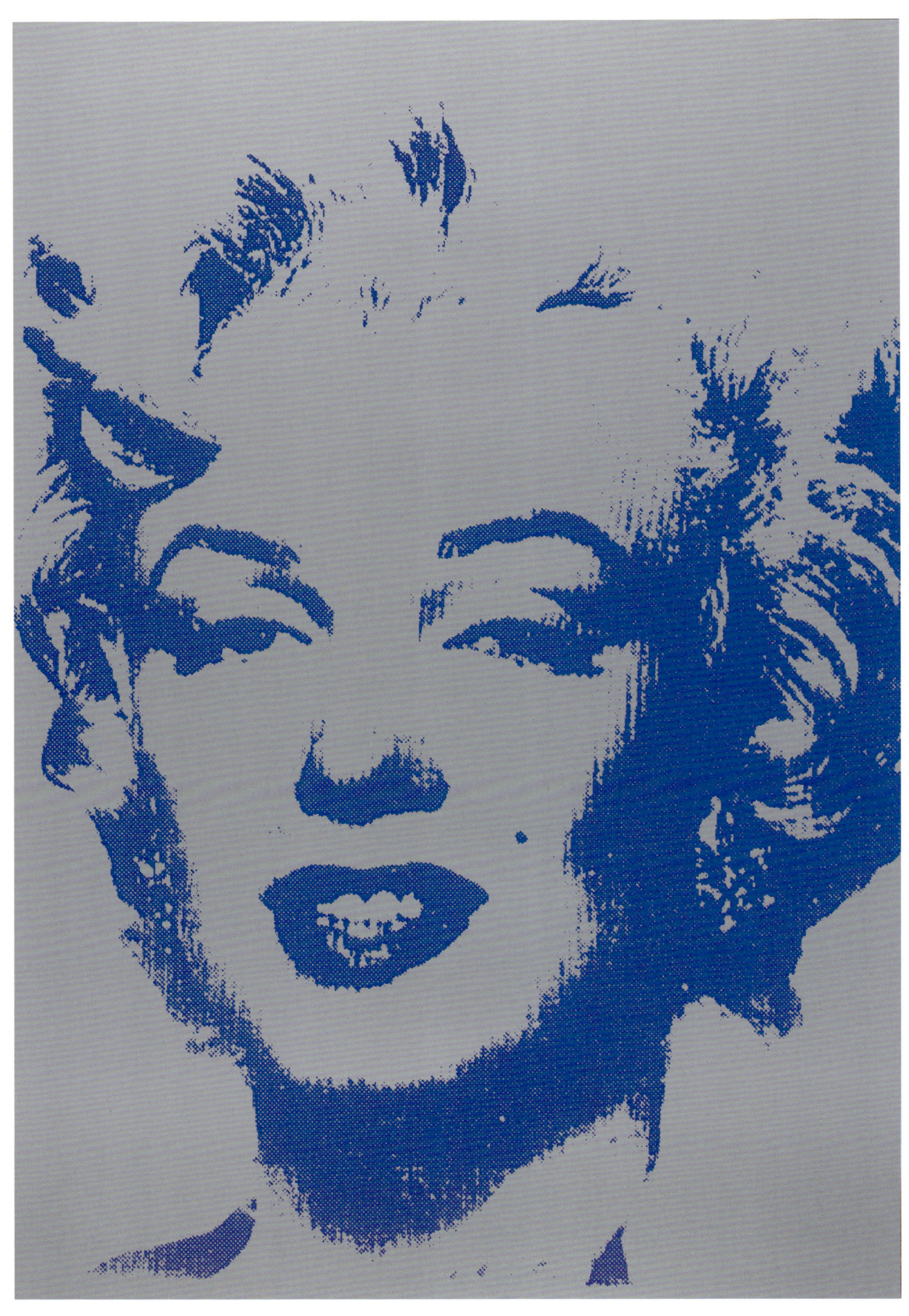

Plate XVI   Two-color screenprints: blue ink on silver paper; Number of prints: nine; Caption: no; Collection numbers: AWMM.1968.050, AWMM.1968.051, AWMM.1968.052, AWMM.1968.068, AWMM.1968.069, AWMM.1968.103, AWMM.1968.204, AWMM.1968.243 **(illustrated)**, AWMM.1968.284.

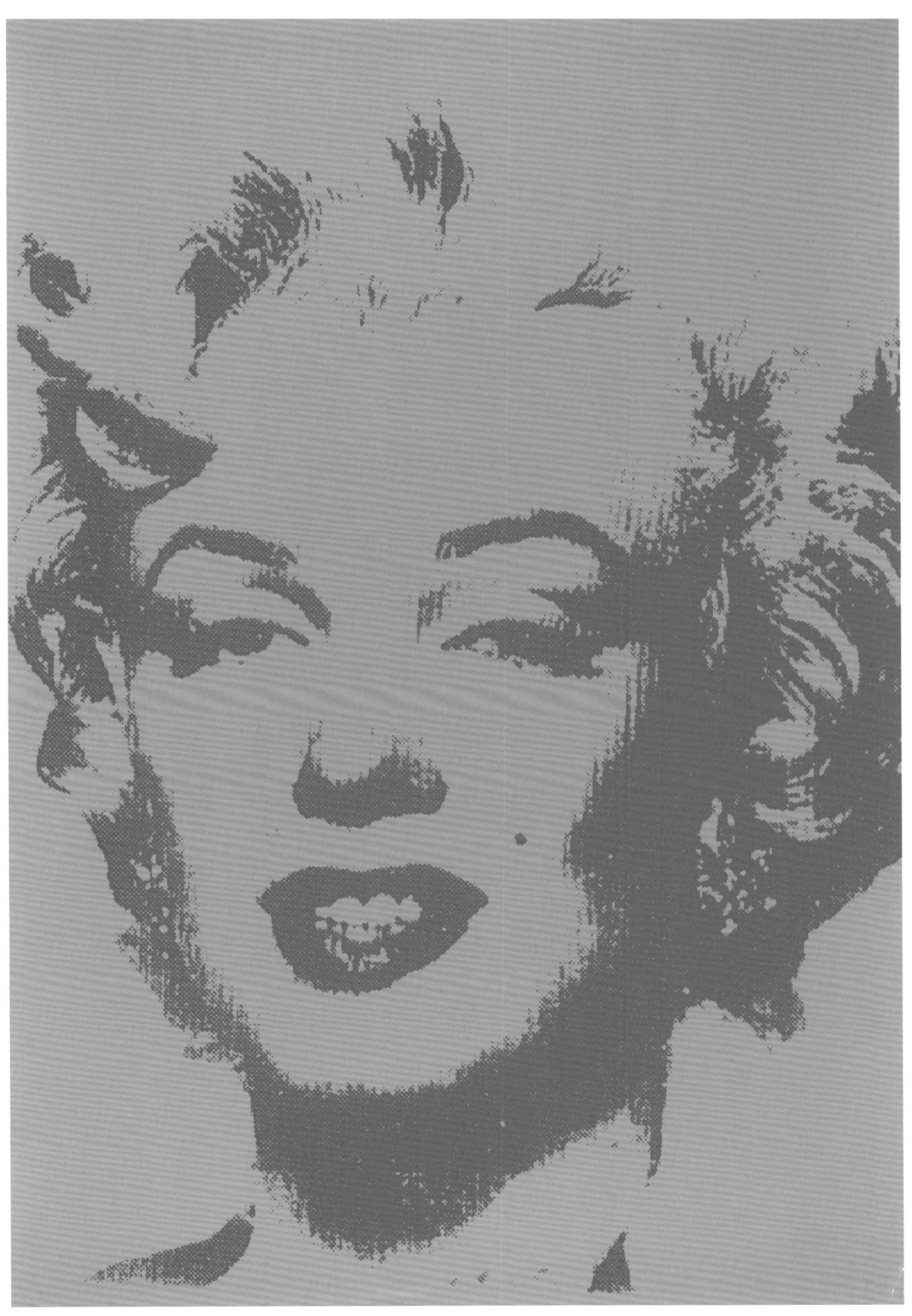

Plate XVII   Two-color reversal screenprints: metallic gold ink on silver
paper; Number of prints: two; Caption: yes; Collection numbers:
AWMM.1968.250, AWMM.1968.299 **(illustrated)**.

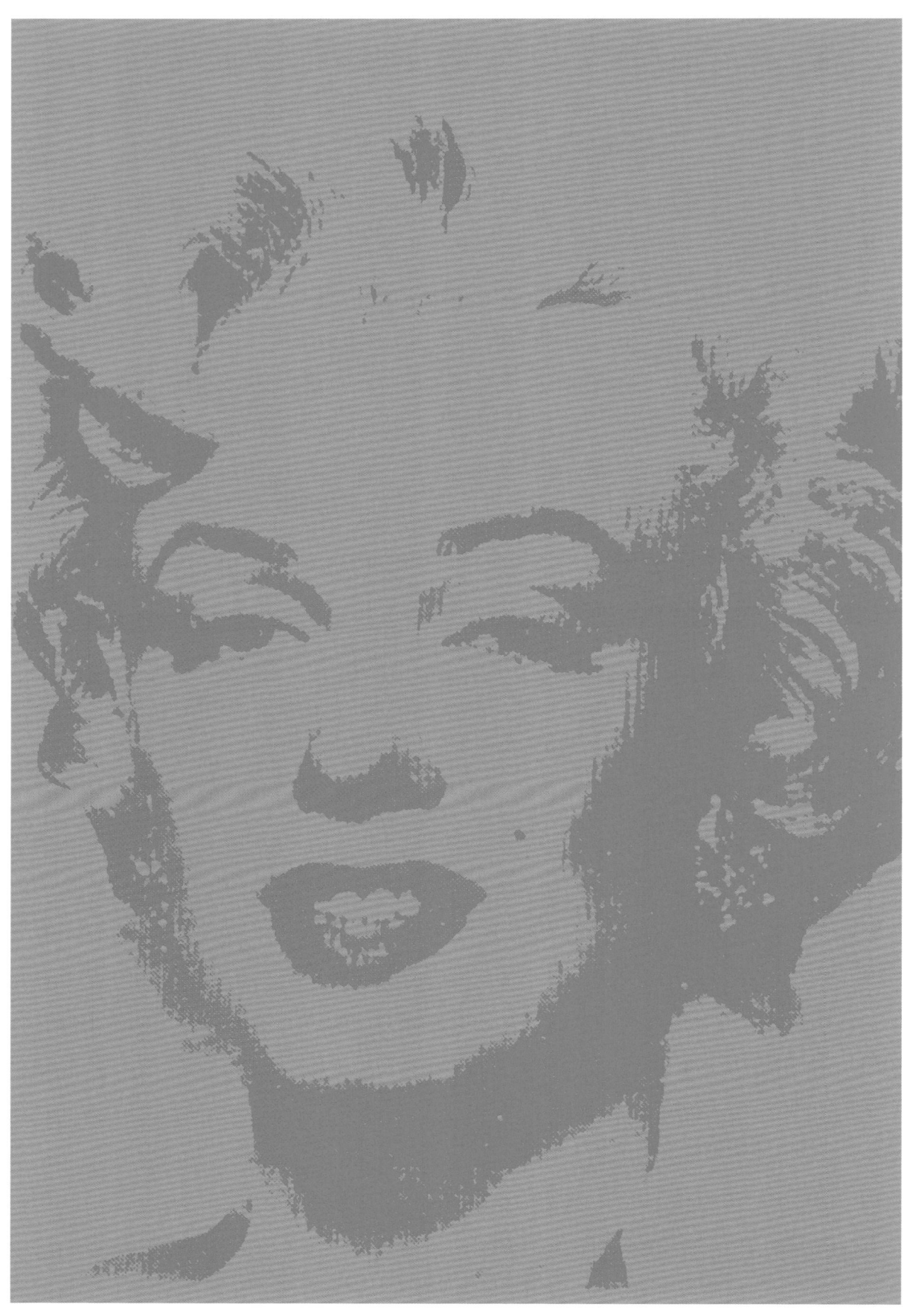

Plate XVIII   Two-color reversal screenprints: metallic silver ink on silver paper; Number of
prints: five; Caption: no; Collection numbers: AWMM.1968.098, AWMM.1968.166,
AWMM.1968.175, AWMM.1968.207, AWMM.1968.241 **(illustrated)**.

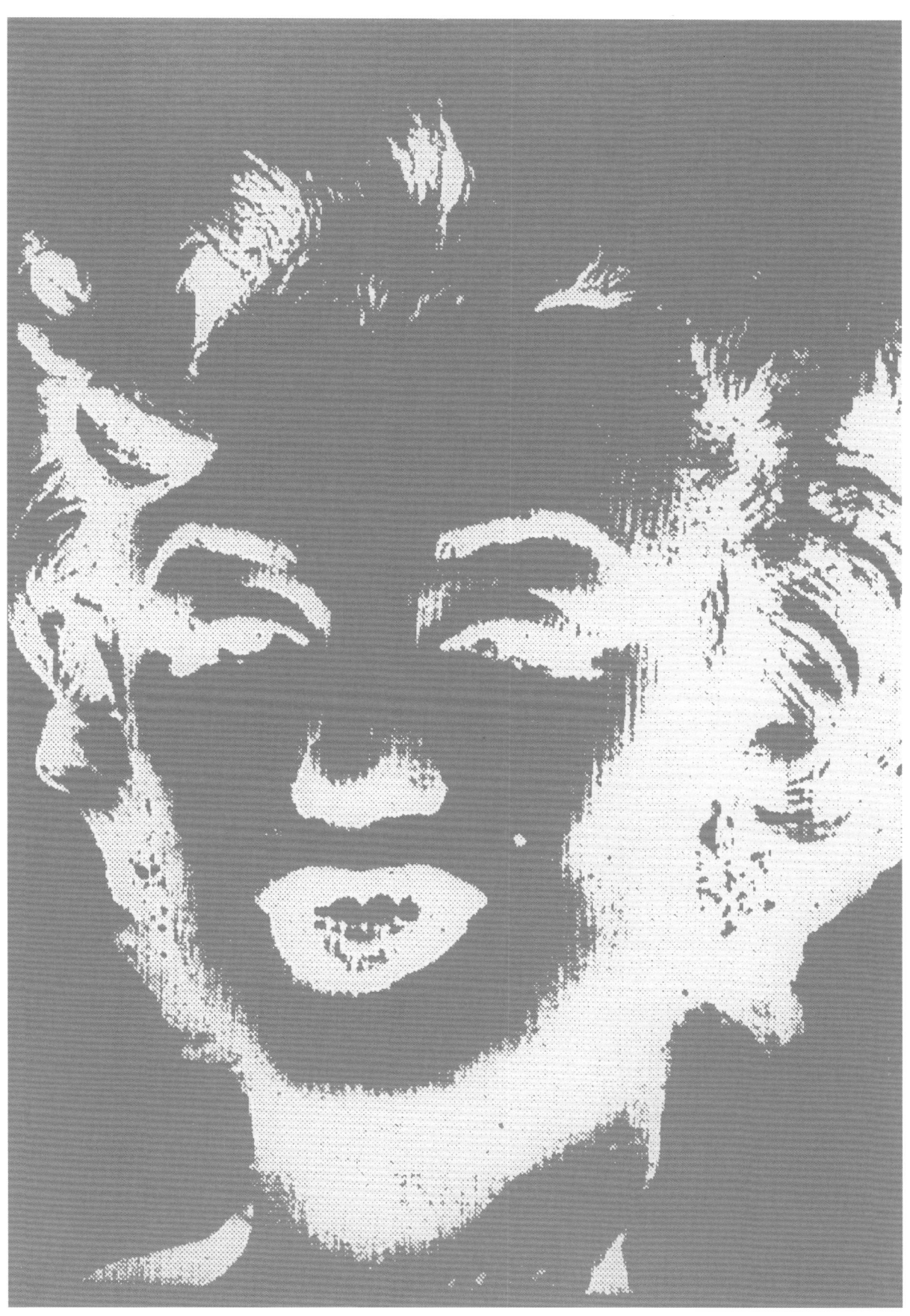

Plate XIX   Two-color reversal screenprints: white ink on silver paper; Number
of prints: four; Caption: no; Collection numbers: AWMM.1968.099
(illustrated), AWMM.1968.153, AWMM.1968.205, AWMM.1968.258.

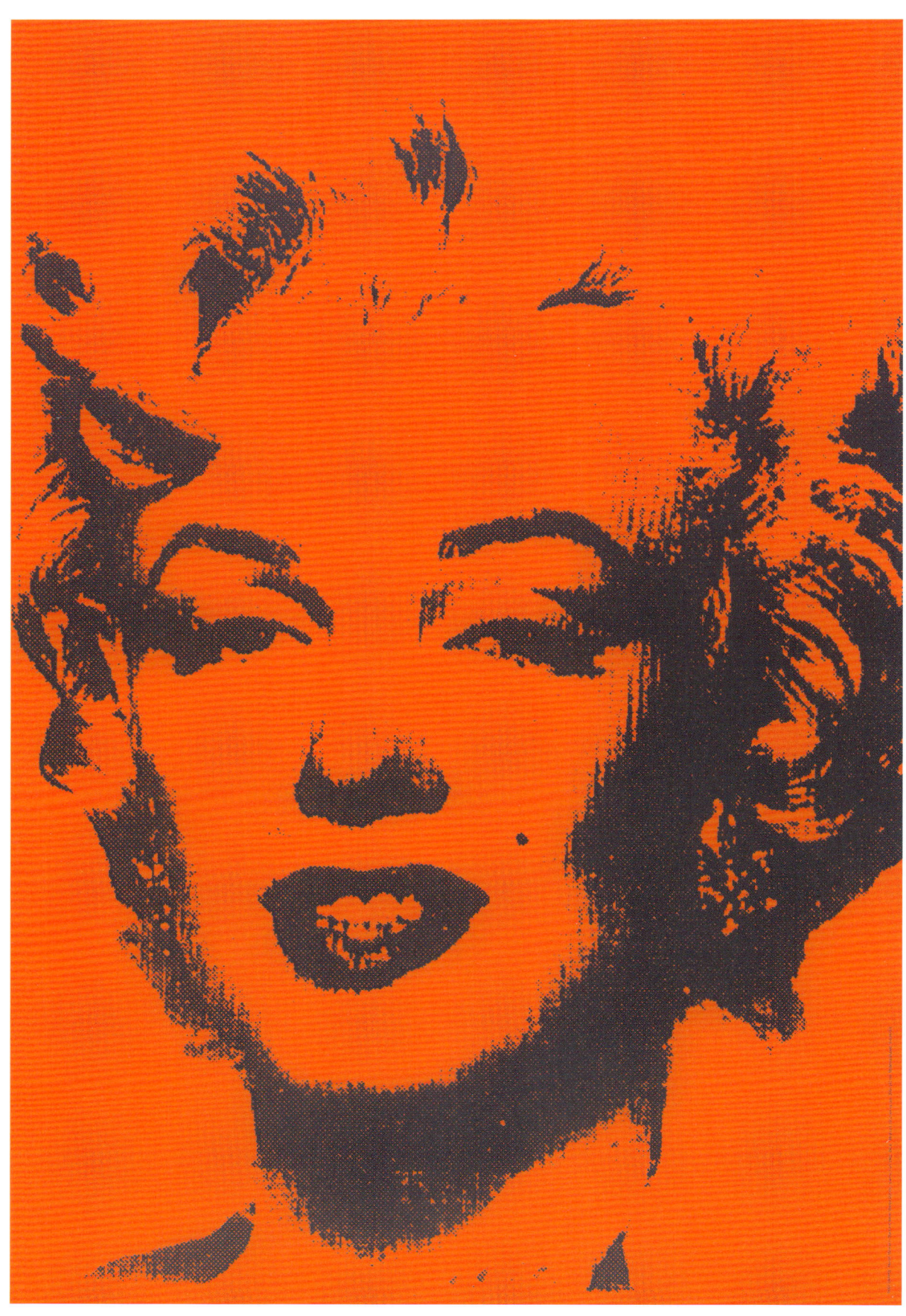

Plate XX   Two-color screenprints: dark gray ink on orange paper; Number of prints: four; Caption: yes; Collection numbers: AWMM.1968.013, AWMM.1968.263, AWMM.1968.132 **(illustrated)**, AWMM.1968.265.

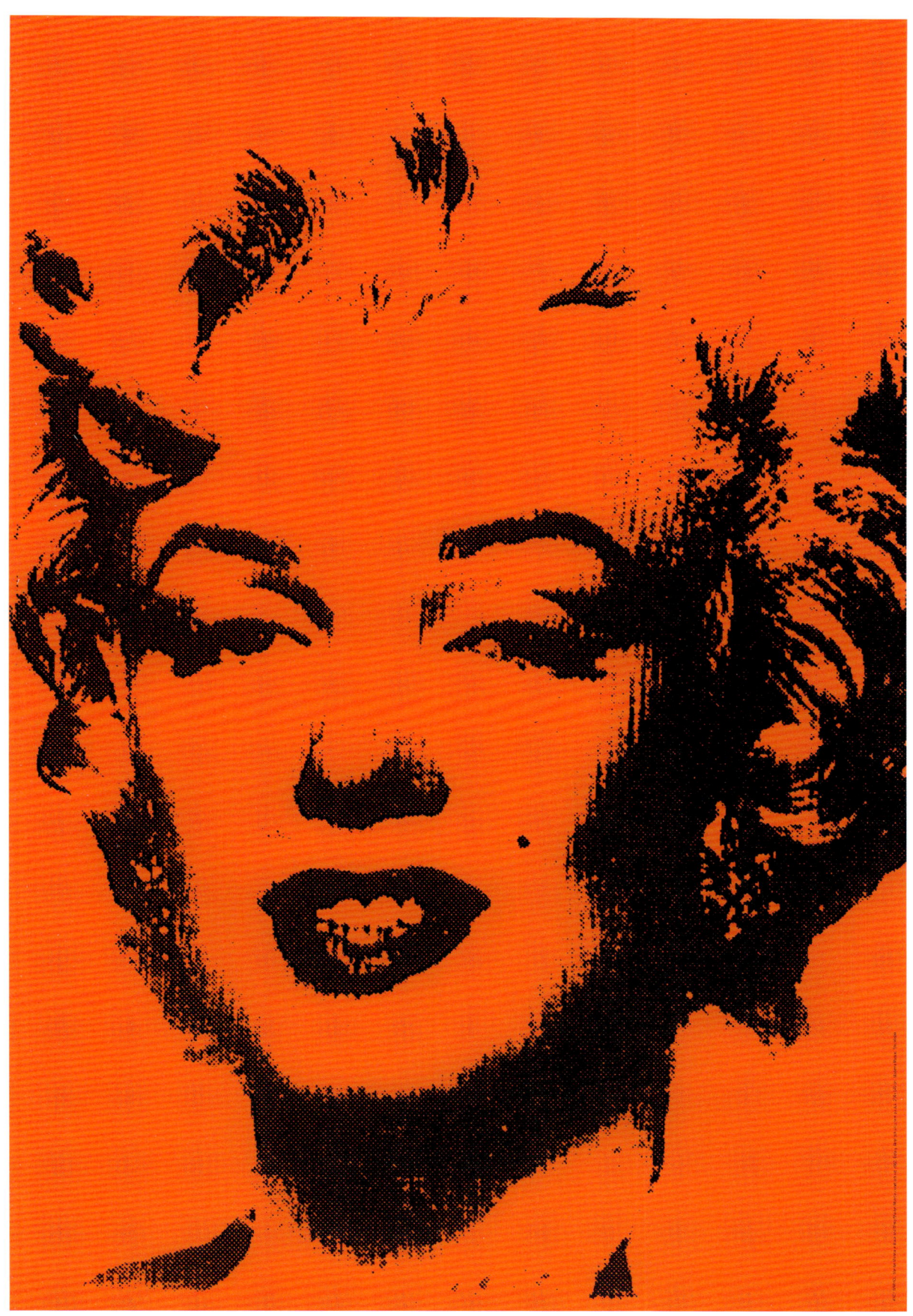

Plate XXI   Two-color screenprints: dark blue ink on orange paper; Number of
prints: three; Caption: yes; Collection numbers: AWMM.1968.010,
AWMM.1968.106, AWMM.1968.114 **(illustrated)***.

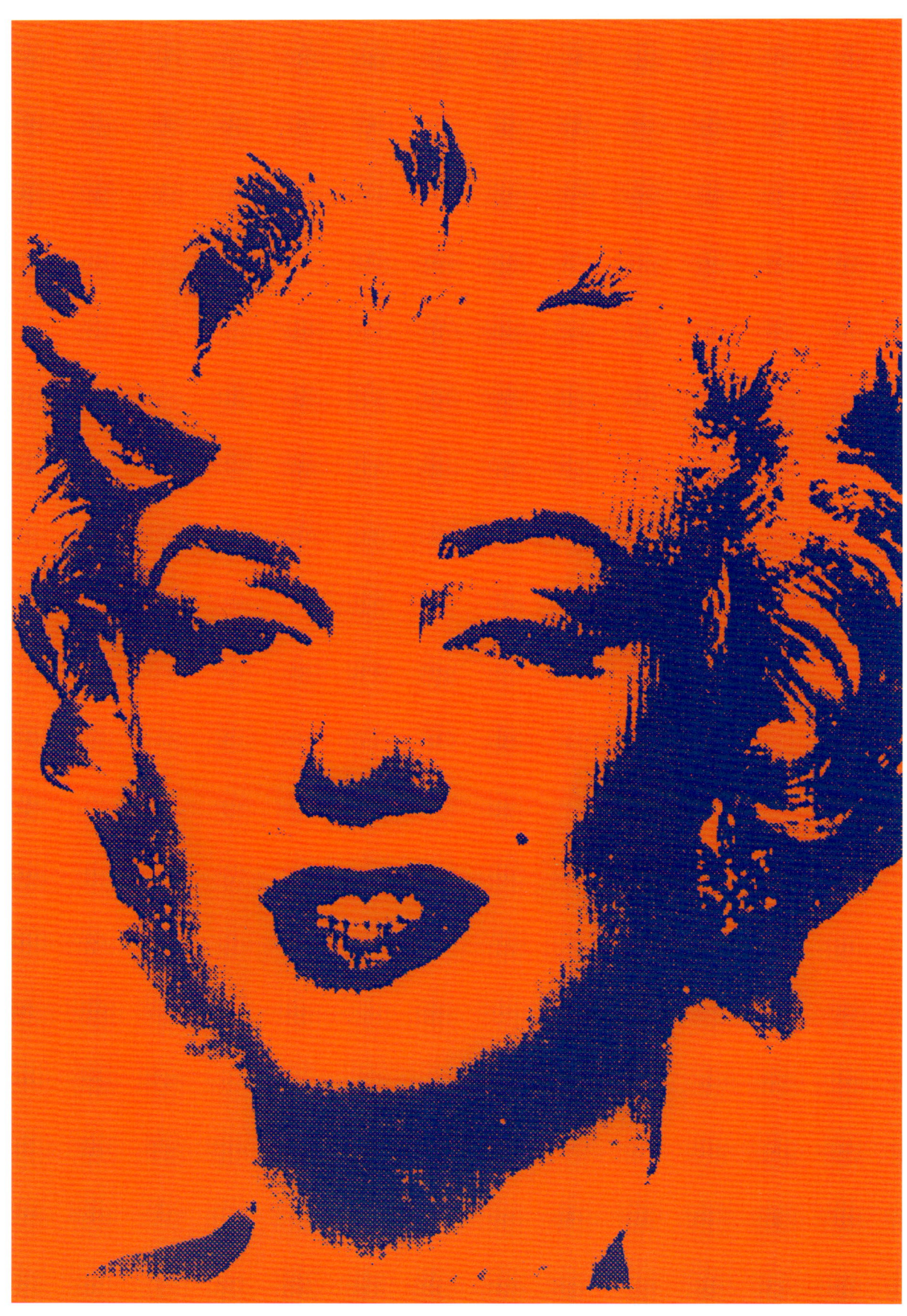

Plate XXII Two-color screenprints: blue ink on orange paper; Number of prints: seven; Caption: no; Collection numbers: AWMM.1968.049, AWMM.1968.070, AWMM.1968.071, AWMM.1968.084 **(illustrated)**, AWMM.1968.126, AWMM.1968.217, AWMM.1968.239.

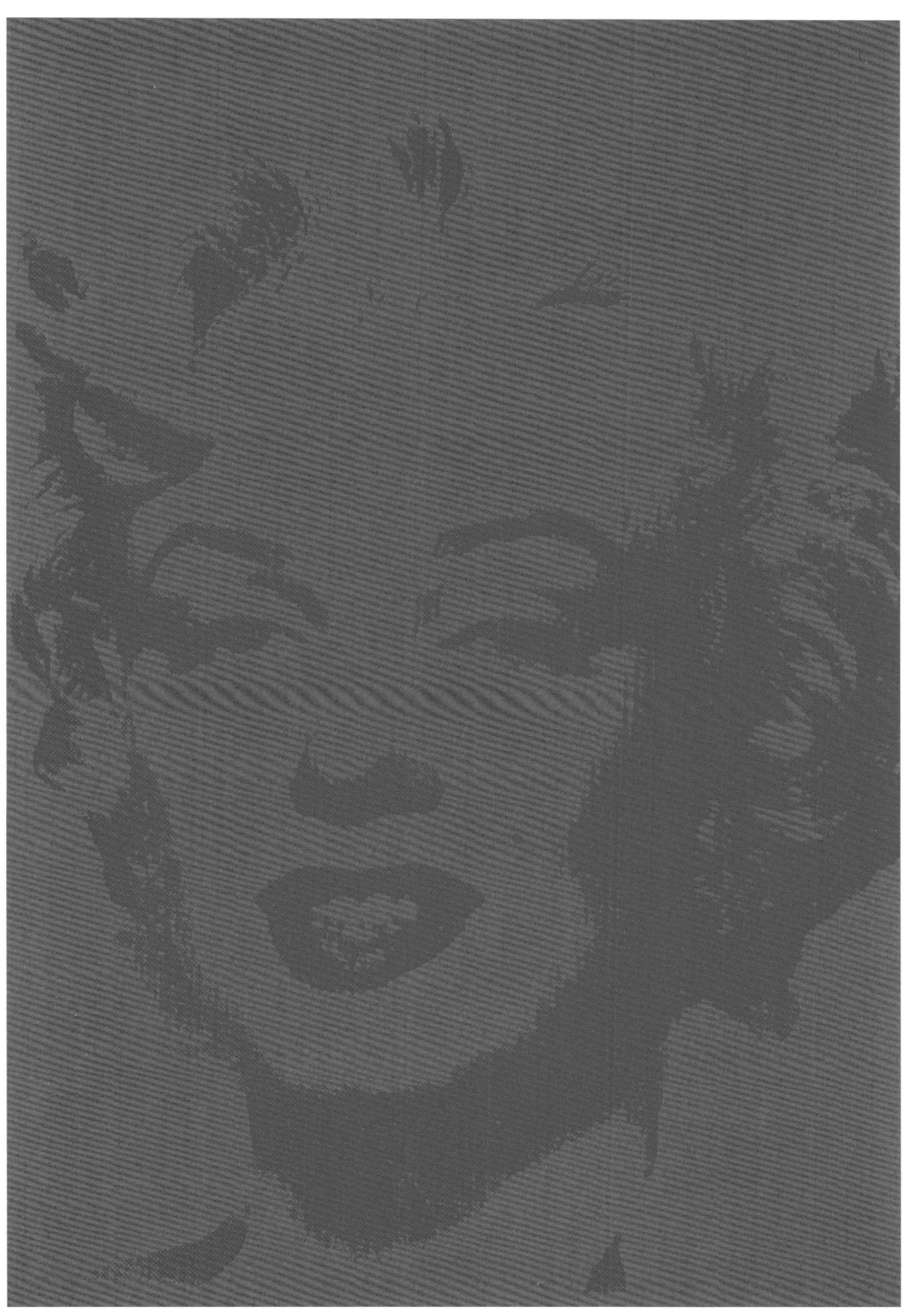

Plate XXIII   Two-color reversal screenprints: metallic gold ink on orange paper; Number of prints: five; Caption: yes; Collection numbers: AWMM.1968.035 **(illustrated)**, AWMM.1968.192, AWMM.1968.202, AWMM.1968.212, AWMM.1968.309.

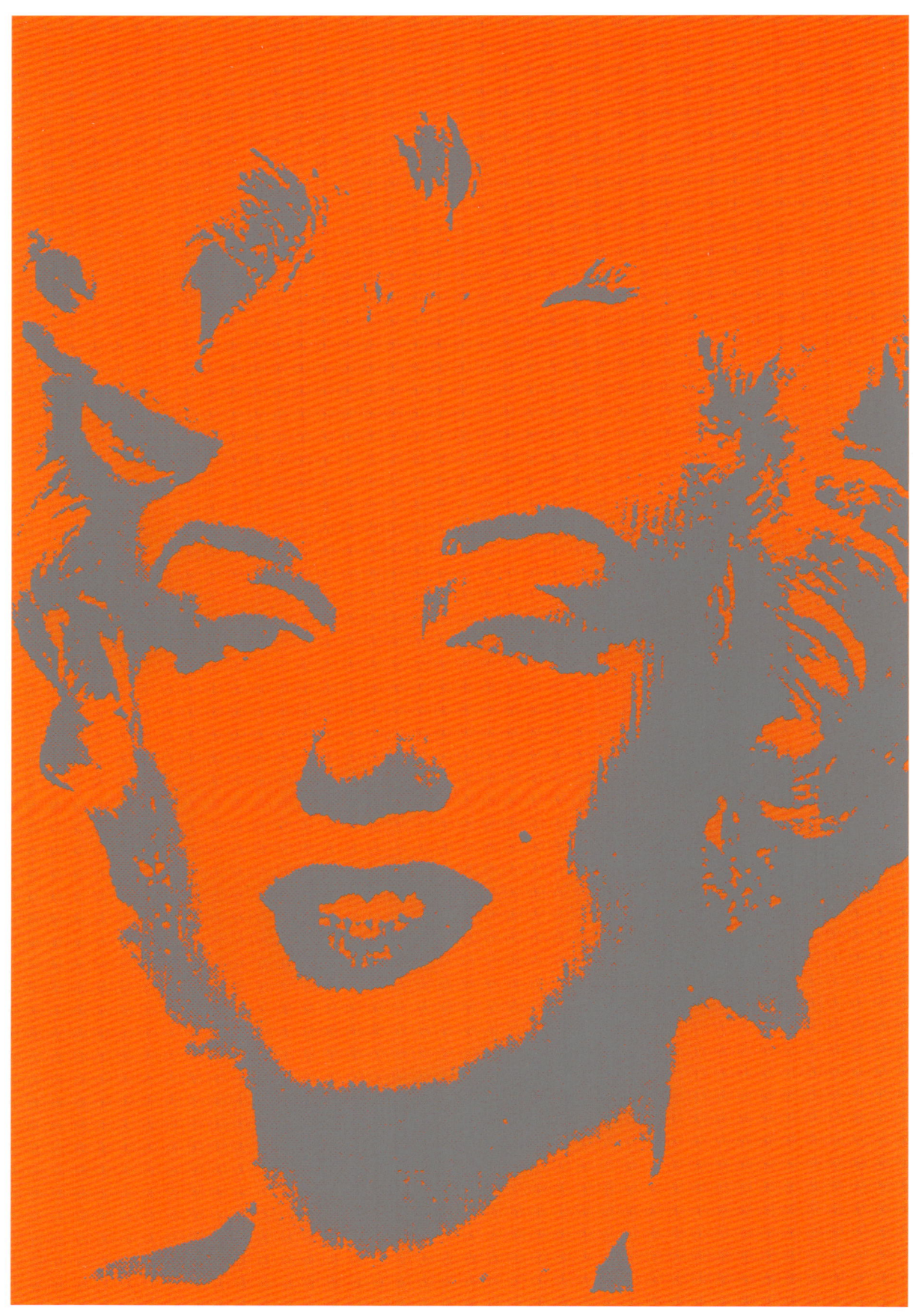

Plate XXIV   Two-color reversal screenprints: metallic silver ink on orange paper; Number of prints:
seven; Caption: no; Collection numbers: AWMM.1968.060 **(illustrated)**, AWMM.1968.072,
AWMM.1968.086, AWMM.1968.116, AWMM.1968.228, AWMM.1968.238, AWMM.1968.240.

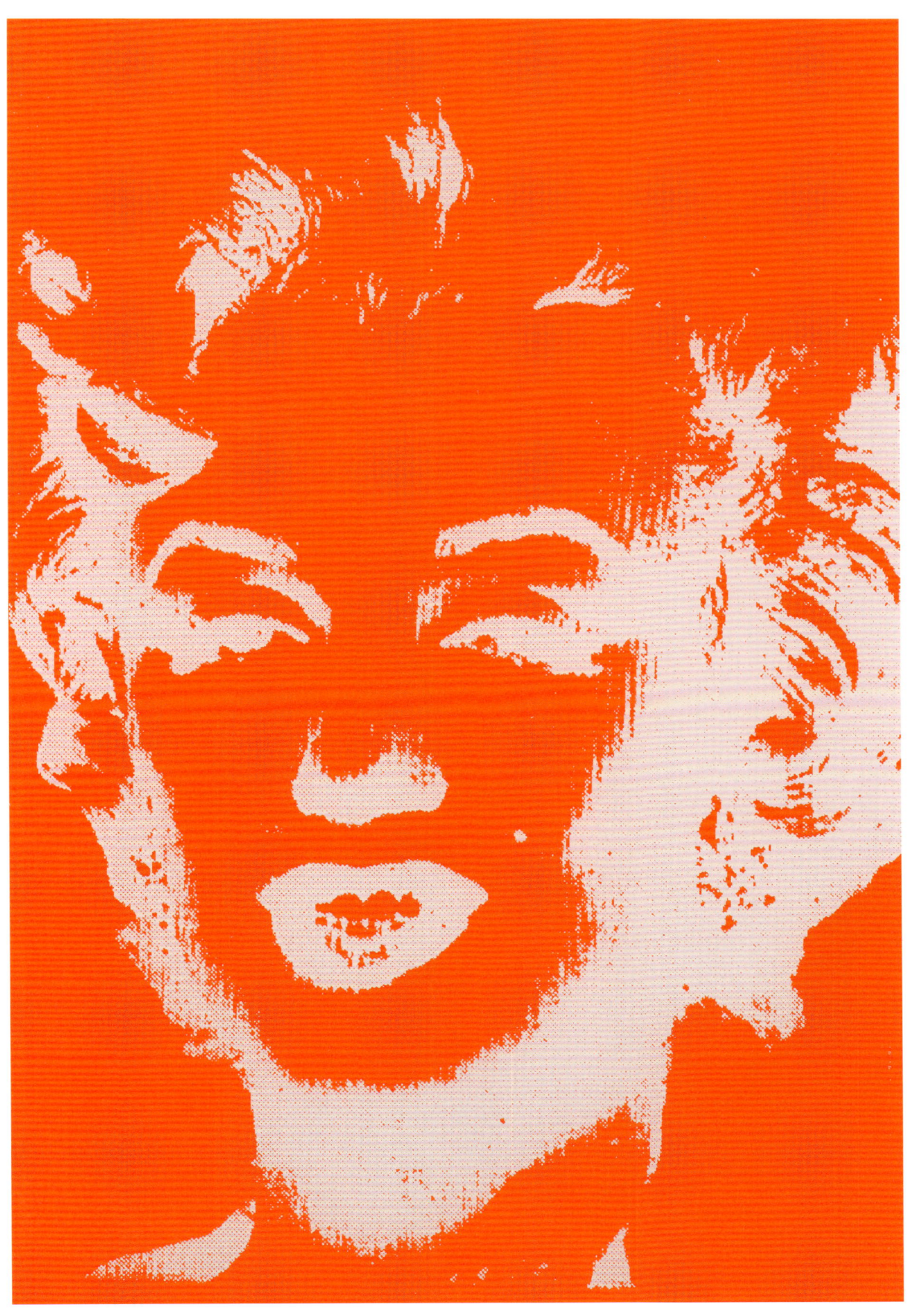

Plate XXV Two-color reversal screenprints: white ink on orange paper; Number of prints: three; Caption: no; Collection numbers: AWMM.1968.127 **(illustrated)**, AWMM.1968.224, AWMM.1968.237.

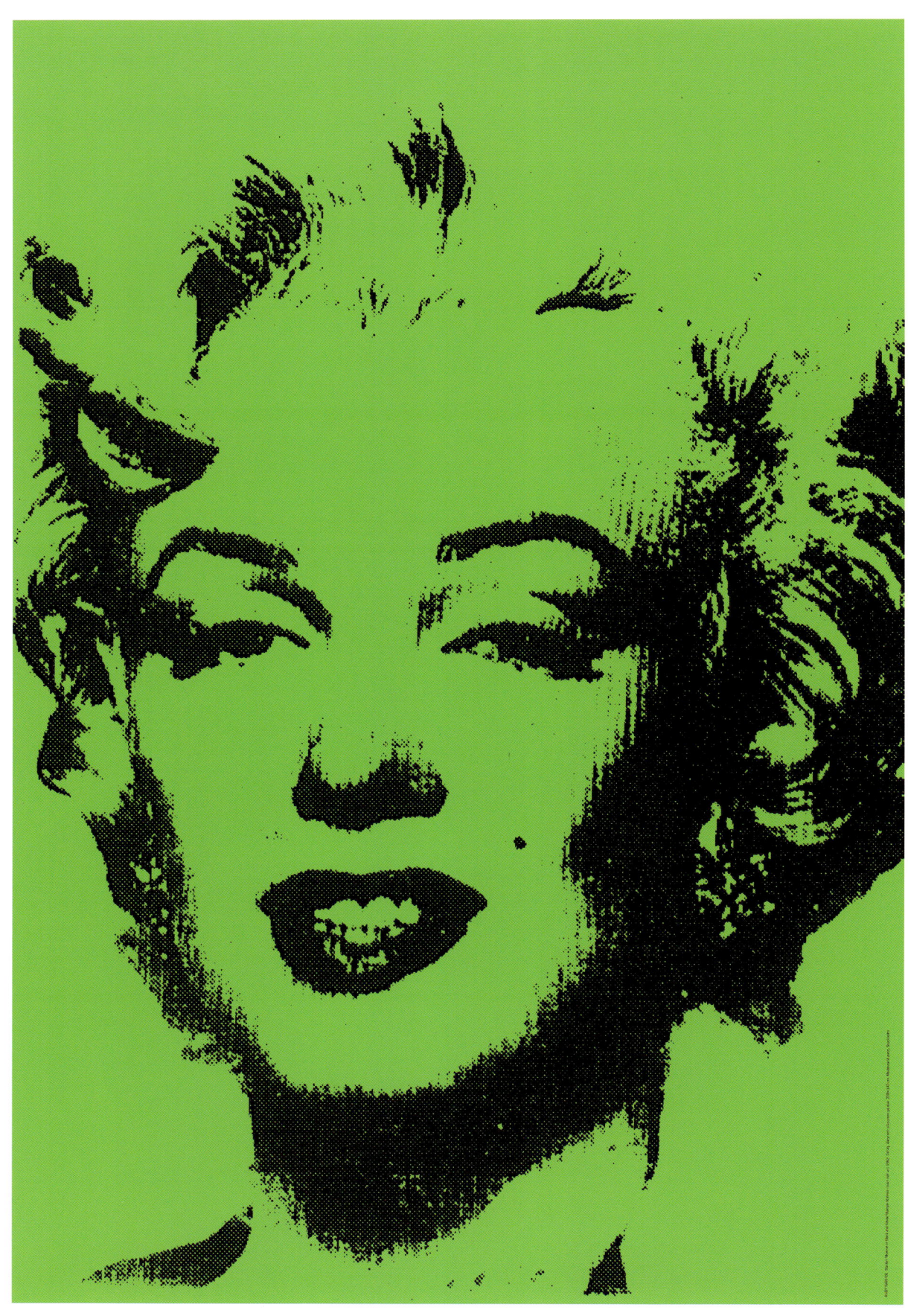

Plate XXVI   Two-color screenprints: black ink on green paper; Number of prints: five;
Caption: yes; Collection numbers: AWMM.1968.007, AWMM.1968.083,
AWMM.1968.120, AWMM.1968.139, AWMM.1968.234 **(illustrated)***.

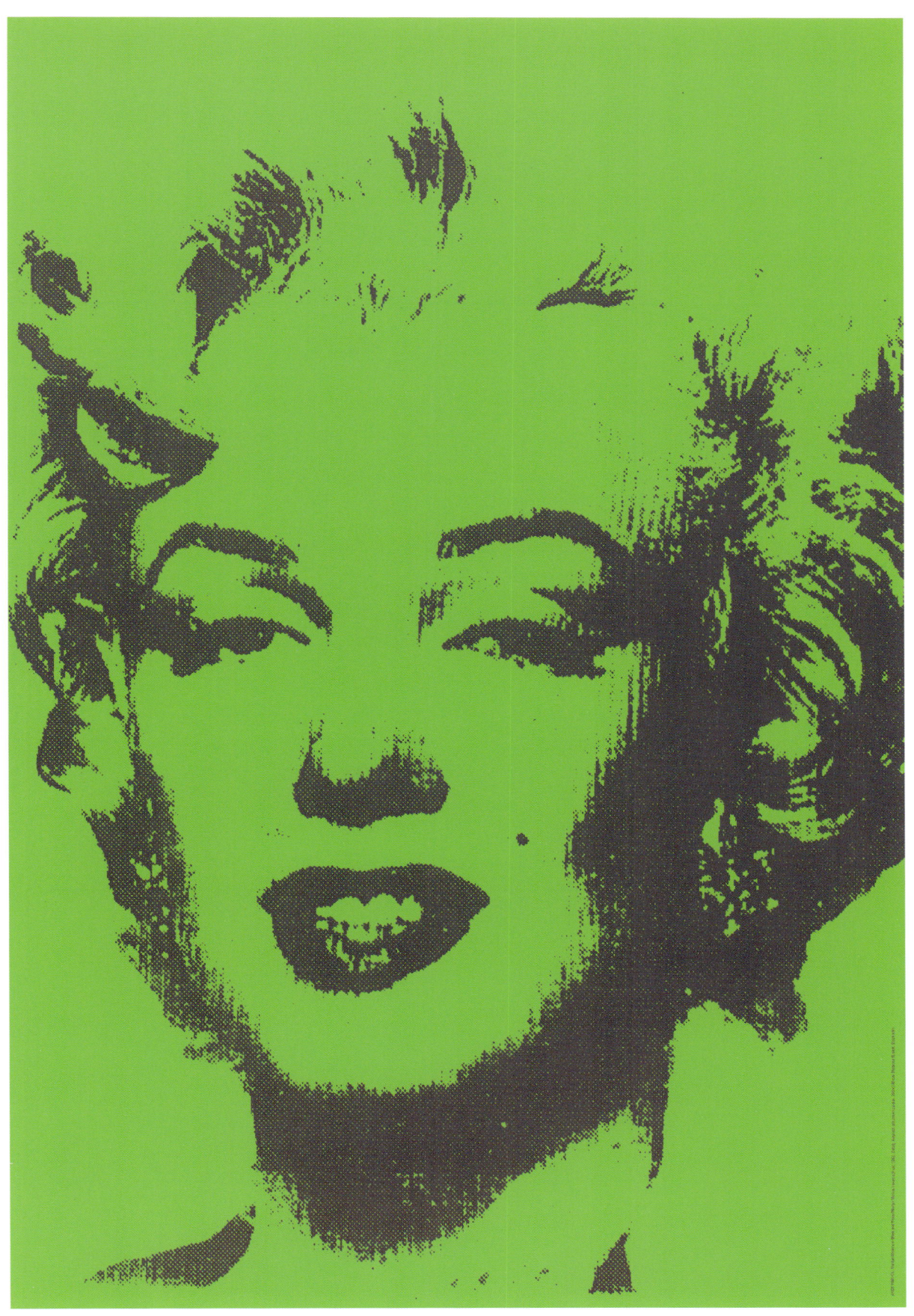

Plate XXVII   Two-color screenprints: dark gray ink on green paper; Number of
prints: two; Caption: yes; Collection numbers: AWMM.1968.128
(illustrated), AWMM.1968.312.

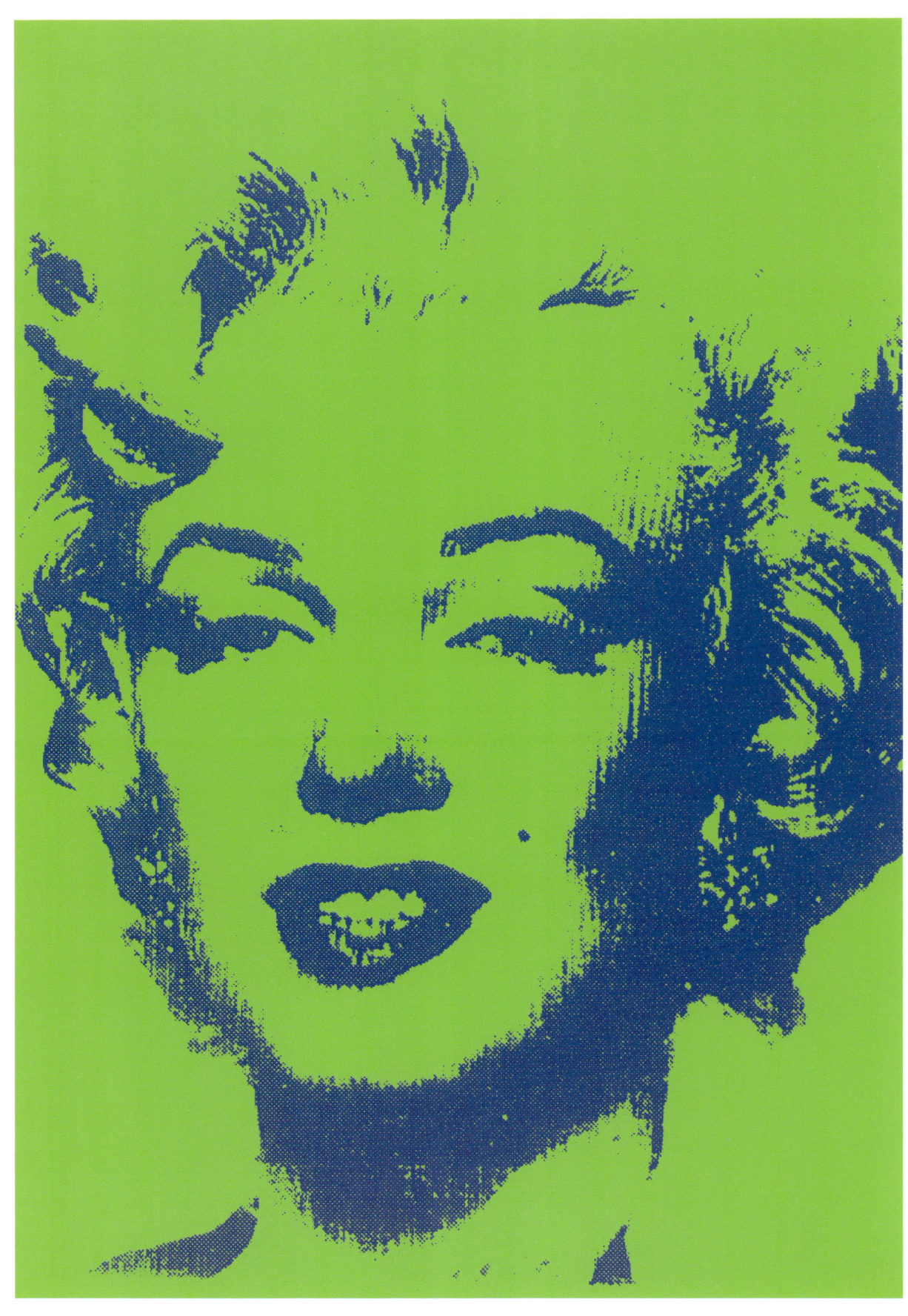

Plate XXVIII   Two-color screenprints: blue ink on green paper; Number of prints: five;
Caption: no; Collection numbers: AWMM.1968.055, AWMM.1968.108
(illustrated), AWMM.1968.185, AWMM.1968.198, AWMM.1968.218.

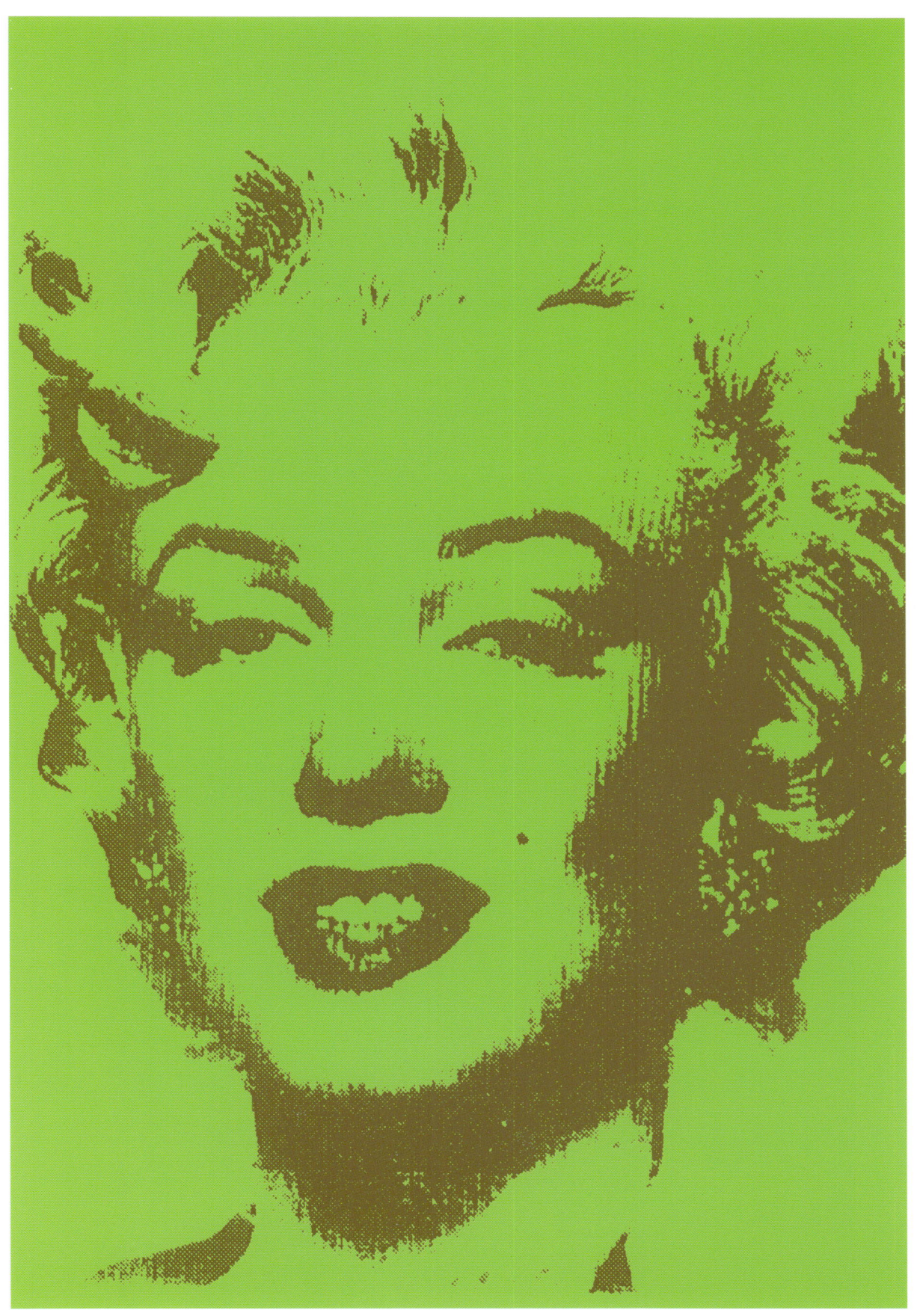

Plate XXIX   Two-color reversal screenprints: metallic gold ink on green paper; Number of prints: seven;
Caption: yes; Collection numbers: AWMM.1968.048, AWMM.1968.057 **(illustrated)**,
AWMM.1968.073, AWMM.1968.089, AWMM.1968.110, AWMM.1968.138, AWMM.1968.233.

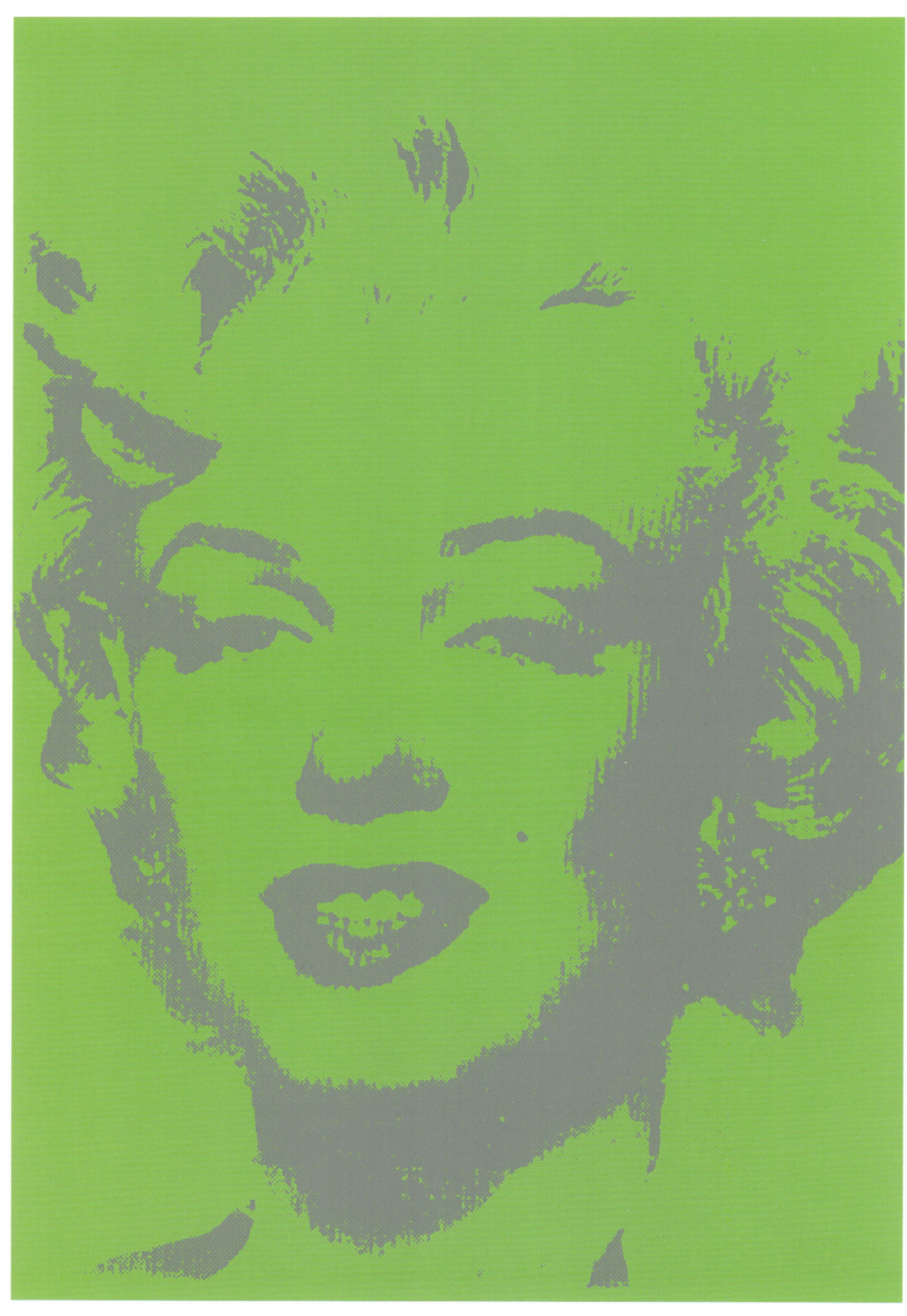

Plate XXX   Two-color reversal screenprints: metallic silver ink on green paper; Number of prints: five; Caption: no; Collection numbers: AWMM.1968.040, AWMM.1968.101 **(illustrated)**, AWMM.1968.177, AWMM.1968.199, AWMM.1968.225.

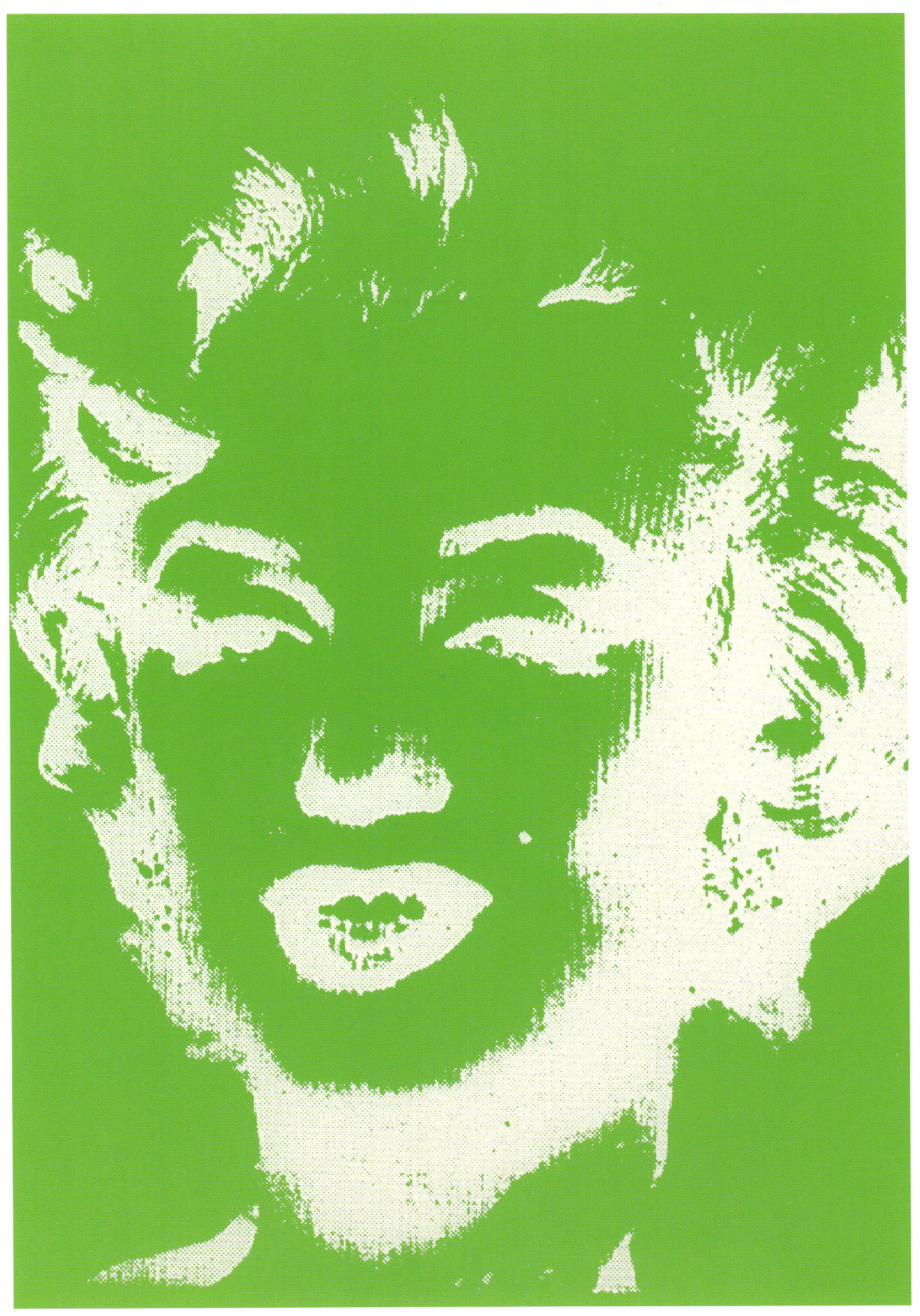

Plate XXXI   Two-color reversal screenprints: white ink on green paper; Number of prints: four; Caption: no; Collection numbers: AWMM.1968.018 **(illustrated)**, AWMM.1968.031, AWMM.1968.121, AWMM.1968.227.

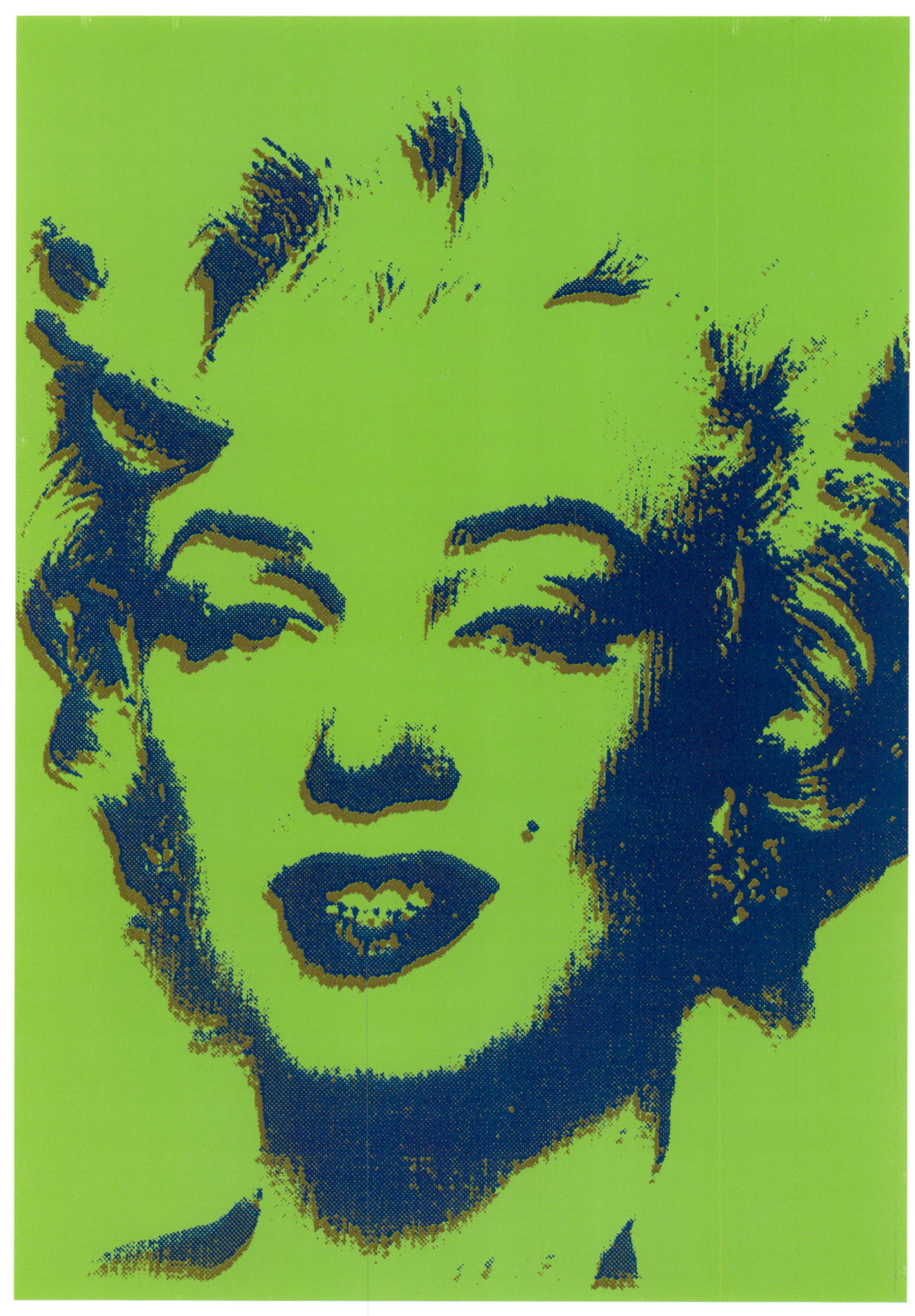

Plate XXXII   Three-color screenprint: metallic gold ink and blue ink on green paper; Number of prints: one; Caption: yes; Collection number: AWMM.1968.288*.

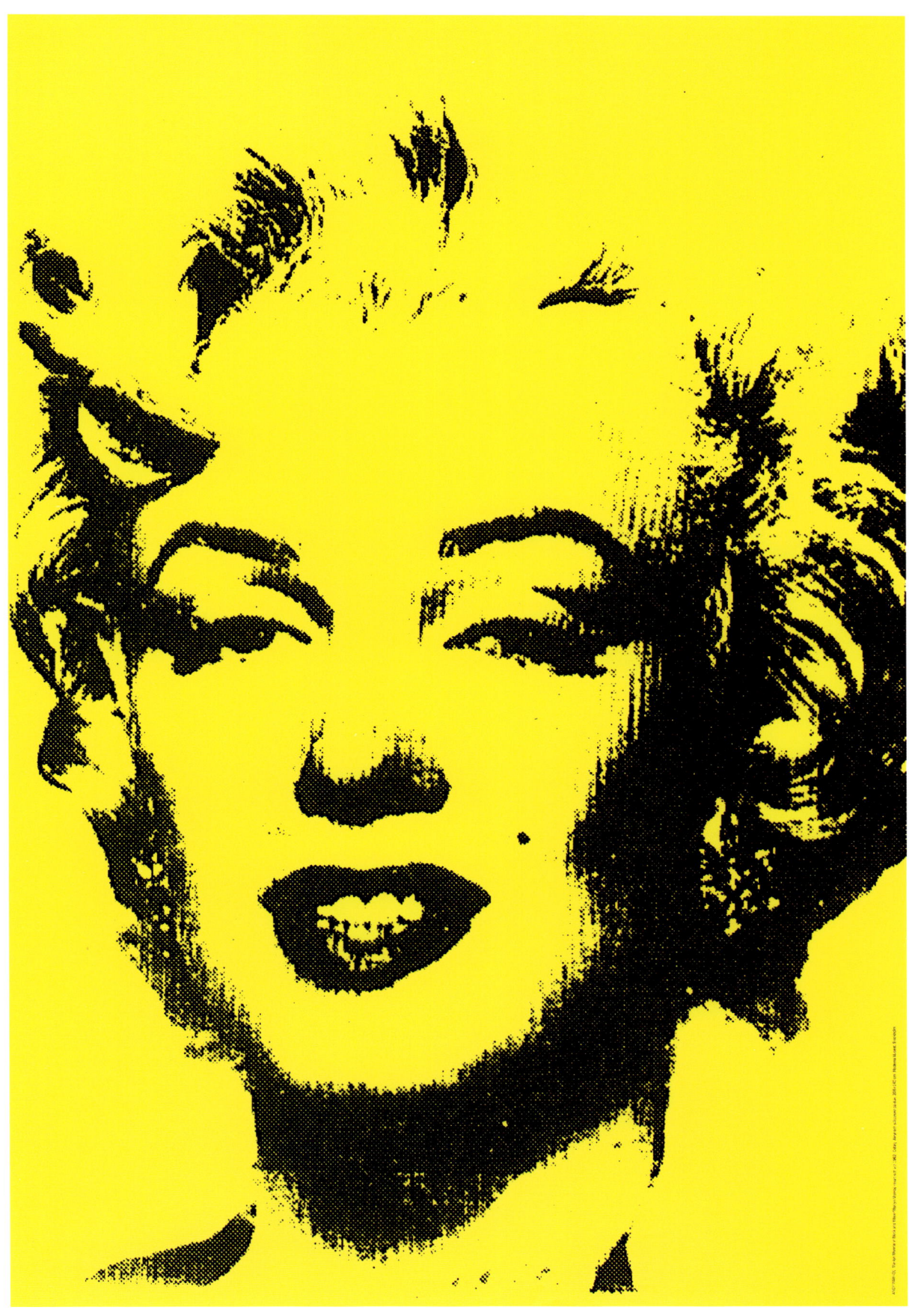

Plate XXXIII   Two-color screenprints: black ink on yellow paper; Number of prints: seven; Caption: yes;
Collection numbers: AWMM.1968.004 **(illustrated)***, AWMM.1968.037, AWMM.1968.088,
AWMM.1968.111, AWMM.1968.119, AWMM.1968.190, AWMM.1968.213.

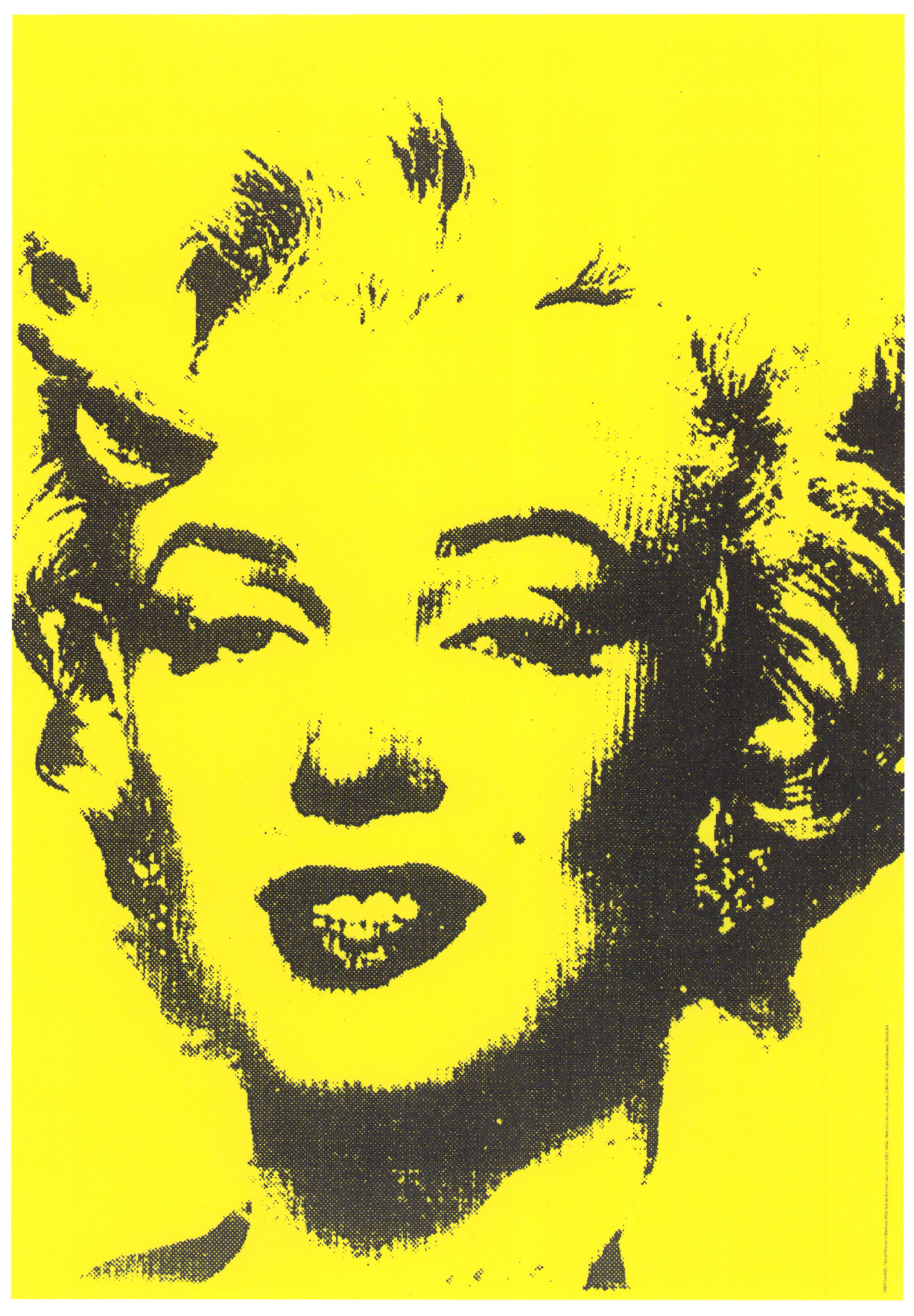

Plate XXXIV   Two-color screenprints: dark gray ink on yellow paper; Number of
prints: two; Caption: yes; Collection numbers: AWMM.1968.028,
AWMM.1968.264 **(illustrated)**.

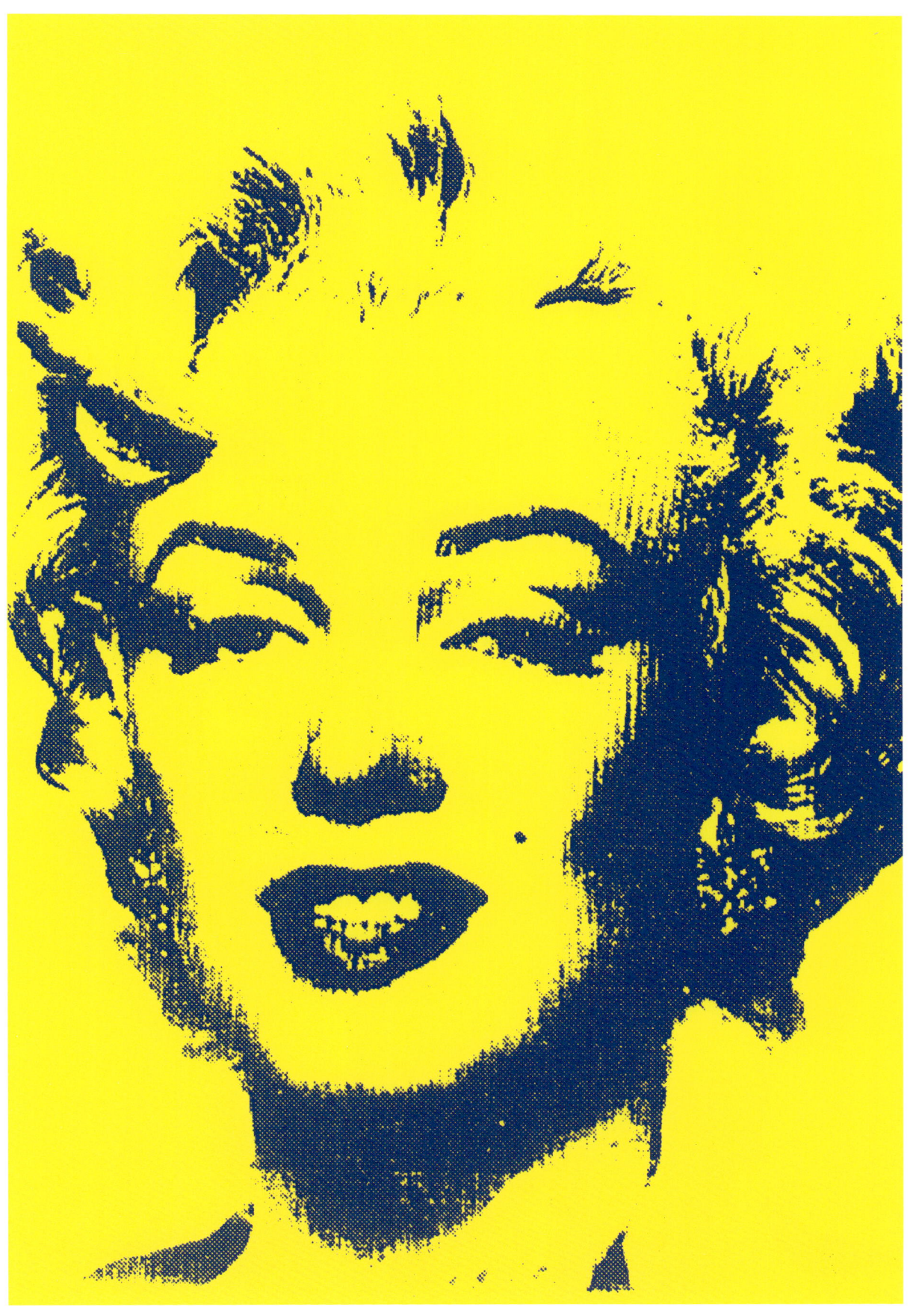

Plate XXXV   Two-color screenprints: blue ink on yellow paper; Number of prints: five; Caption: no; Collection number: AWMM.1968.137 **(illustrated)**, AWMM.1968.151, AWMM.1968.163, AWMM.1968.220, AWMM.1968.275.

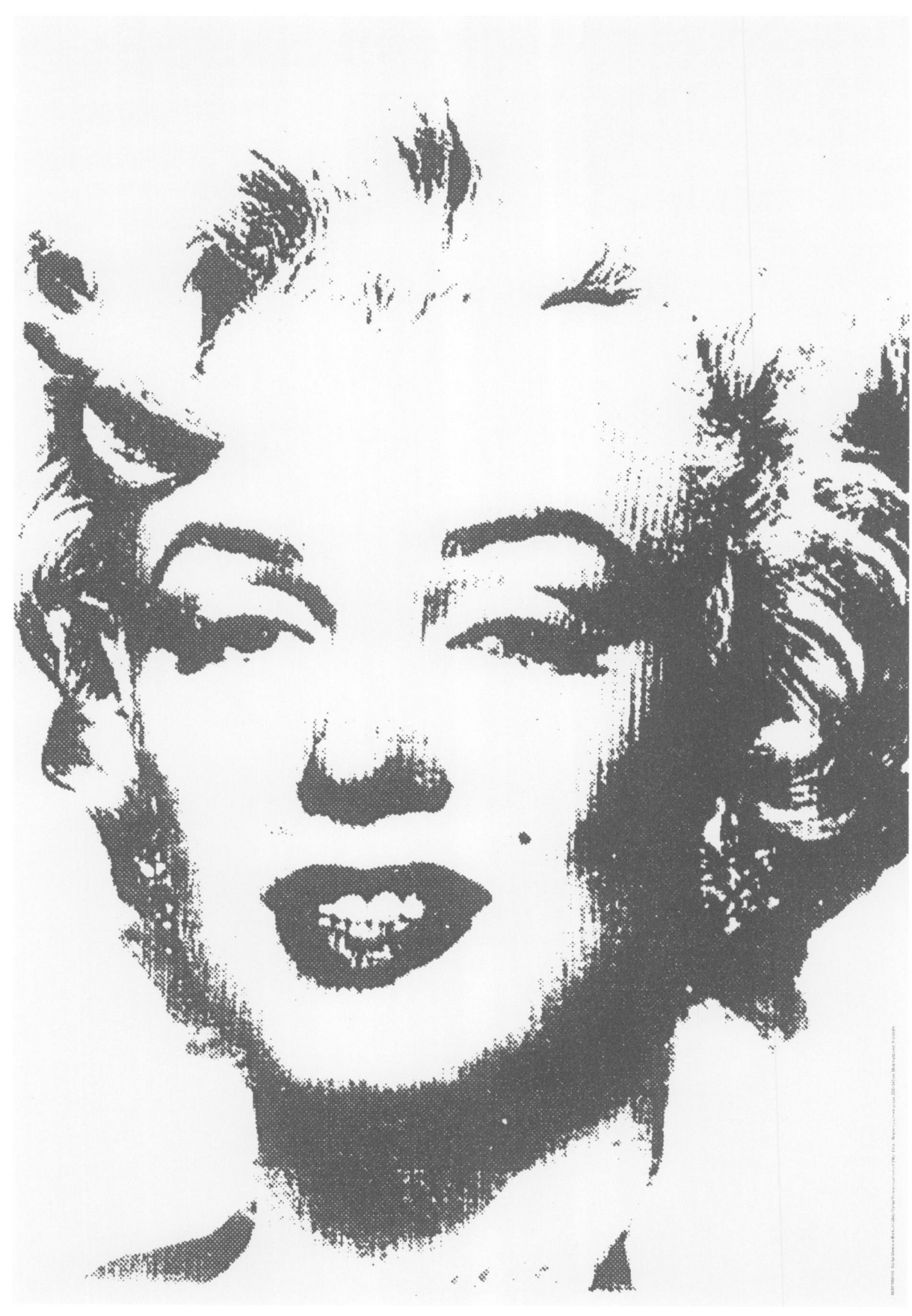

Plate XXXVI   Two-color reversal screenprints: metallic gold ink on yellow paper; Number of prints: seven;
Caption: yes; Collection numbers: AWMM.1968.026, AWMM.1968.066, AWMM.1968.067
(illustrated), AWMM.1968.087, AWMM.1968.155, AWMM.1968.210, AWMM.1968.285.

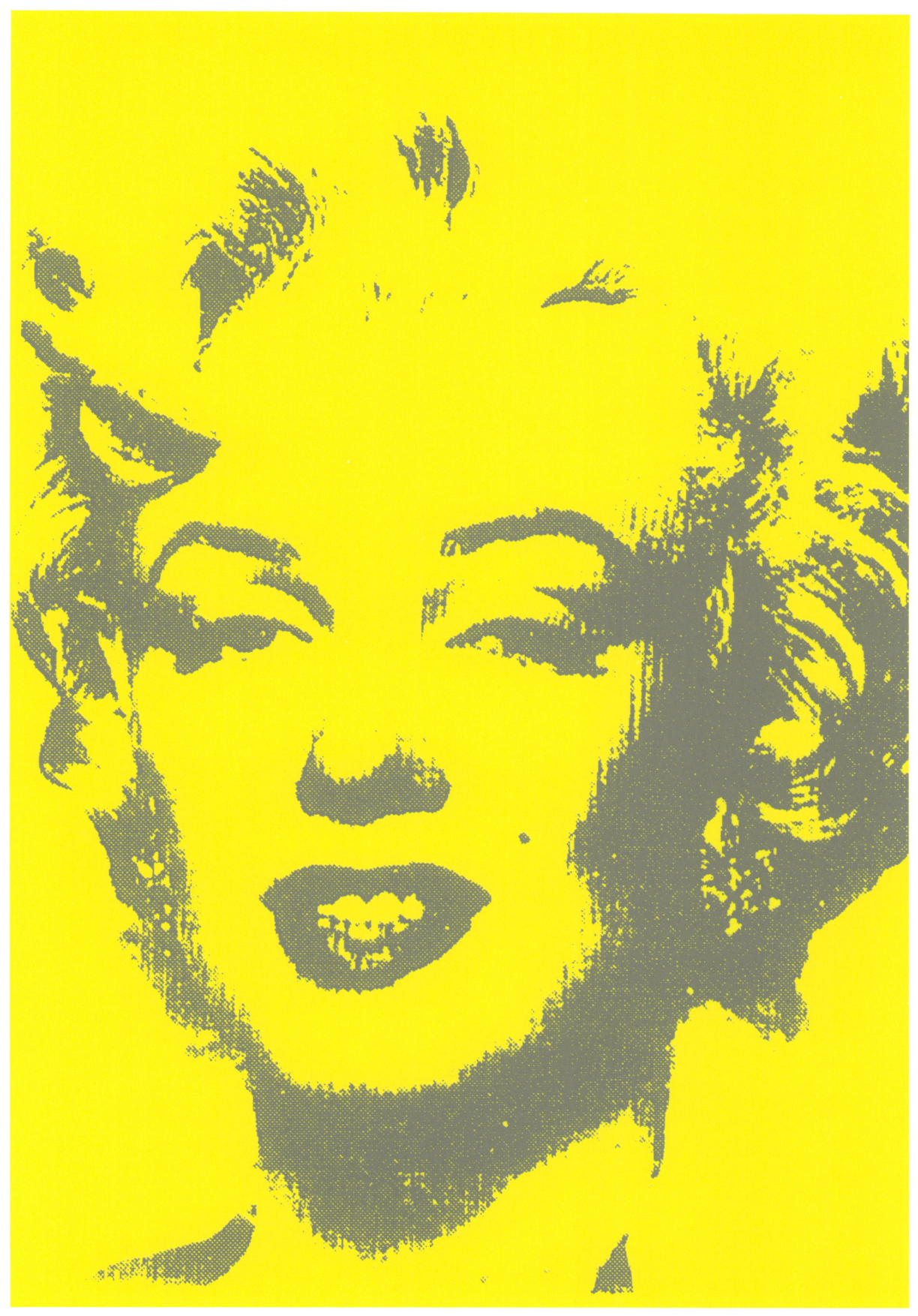

Plate XXXVII   Two-color reversal screenprints: metallic silver ink on yellow paper; Number of prints: eight; Caption: no; Collection numbers: AWMM.1968.056, AWMM.1968.109 **(illustrated)**, AWMM.1968.113, AWMM.1968.148, AWMM.1968.173, AWMM.1968.226, AWMM.1968.247, AWMM.1968.274.

Plate XXXVIII   Two-color reversal screenprints: white ink on yellow paper; Number
of prints: three; Caption: no; Collection numbers: AWMM.1968.027,
AWMM.1968.184, AWMM.1968.229 **(illustrated)**.

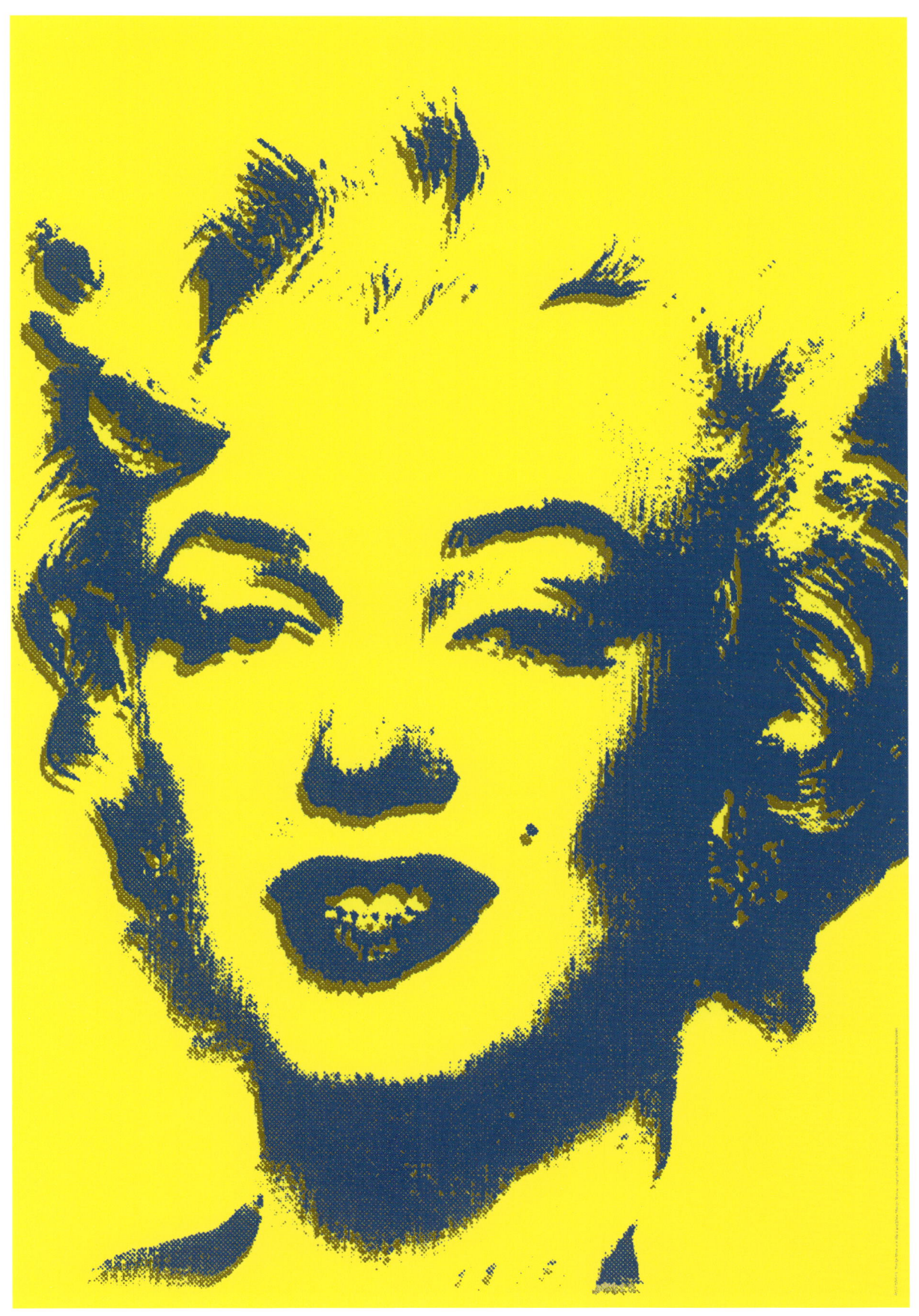

Plate XXXIX   Three-color screenprint: metallic gold ink and blue ink on
yellow paper; Number of prints: one; Caption: yes; Collection
number: AWMM.1968.022*.

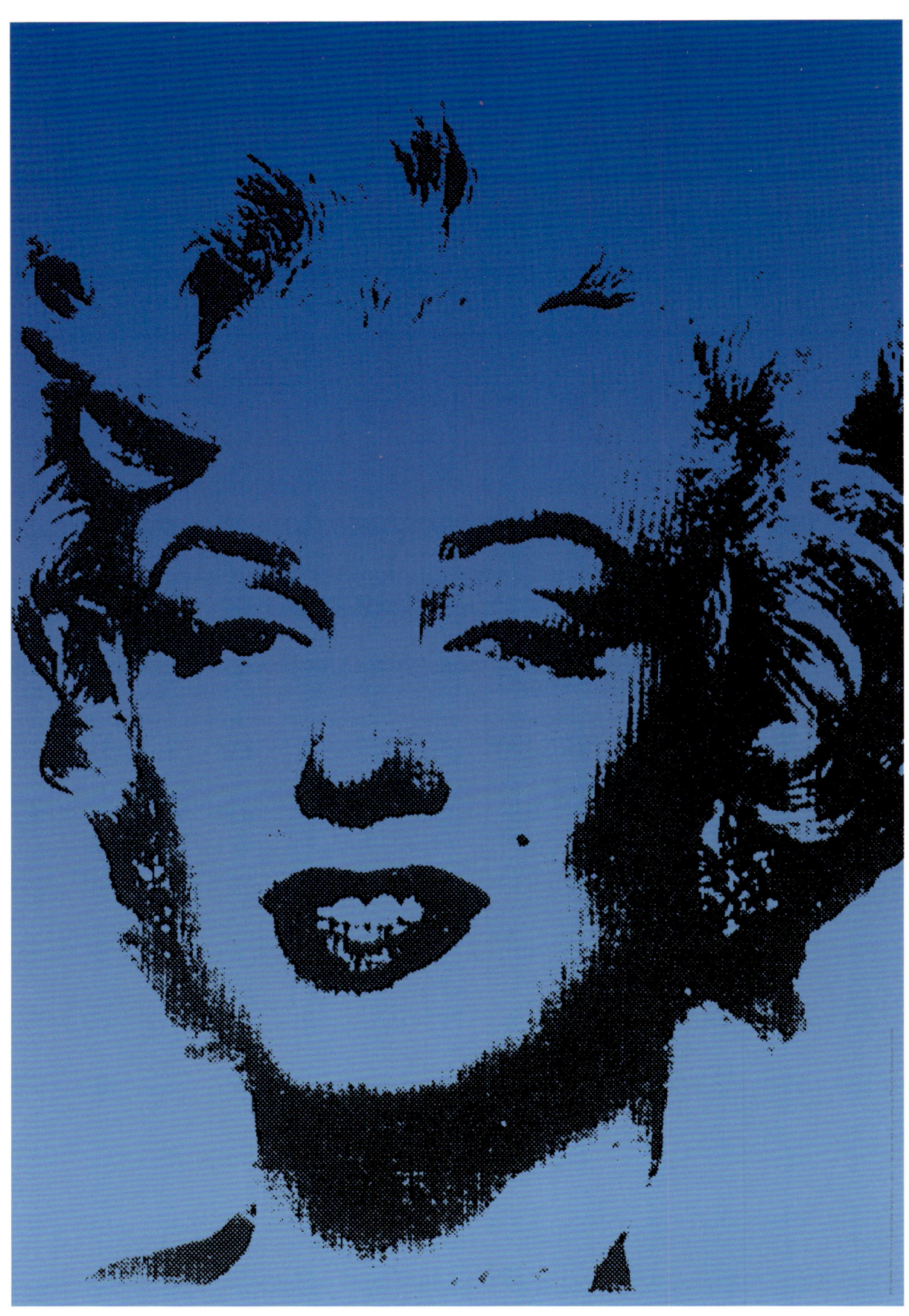

Plate XL   Two-color screenprints: black ink on blue ombre paper; Number
of prints: four; Caption: yes; Collection number: AWMM.1968.118
(illustrated)*, AWMM.1968.283, AWMM.1968.303, AWMM.1968.305.

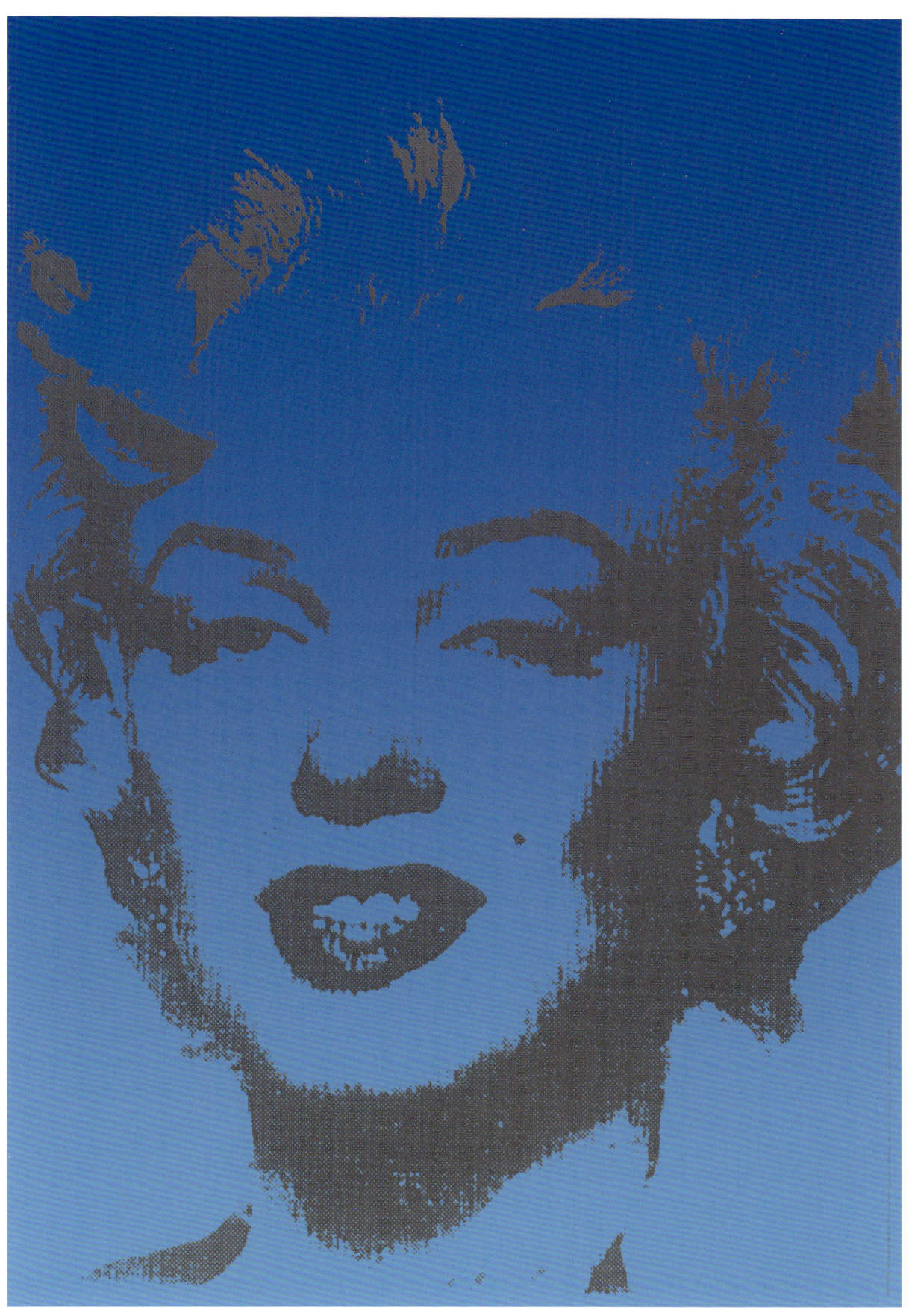

Plate XLI   Two-color screenprints: dark gray ink on blue ombre paper; Number
of prints: three; Caption: yes; Collection number: AWMM.1968.105
(illustrated), AWMM.1968.196, AWMM.1968.251.

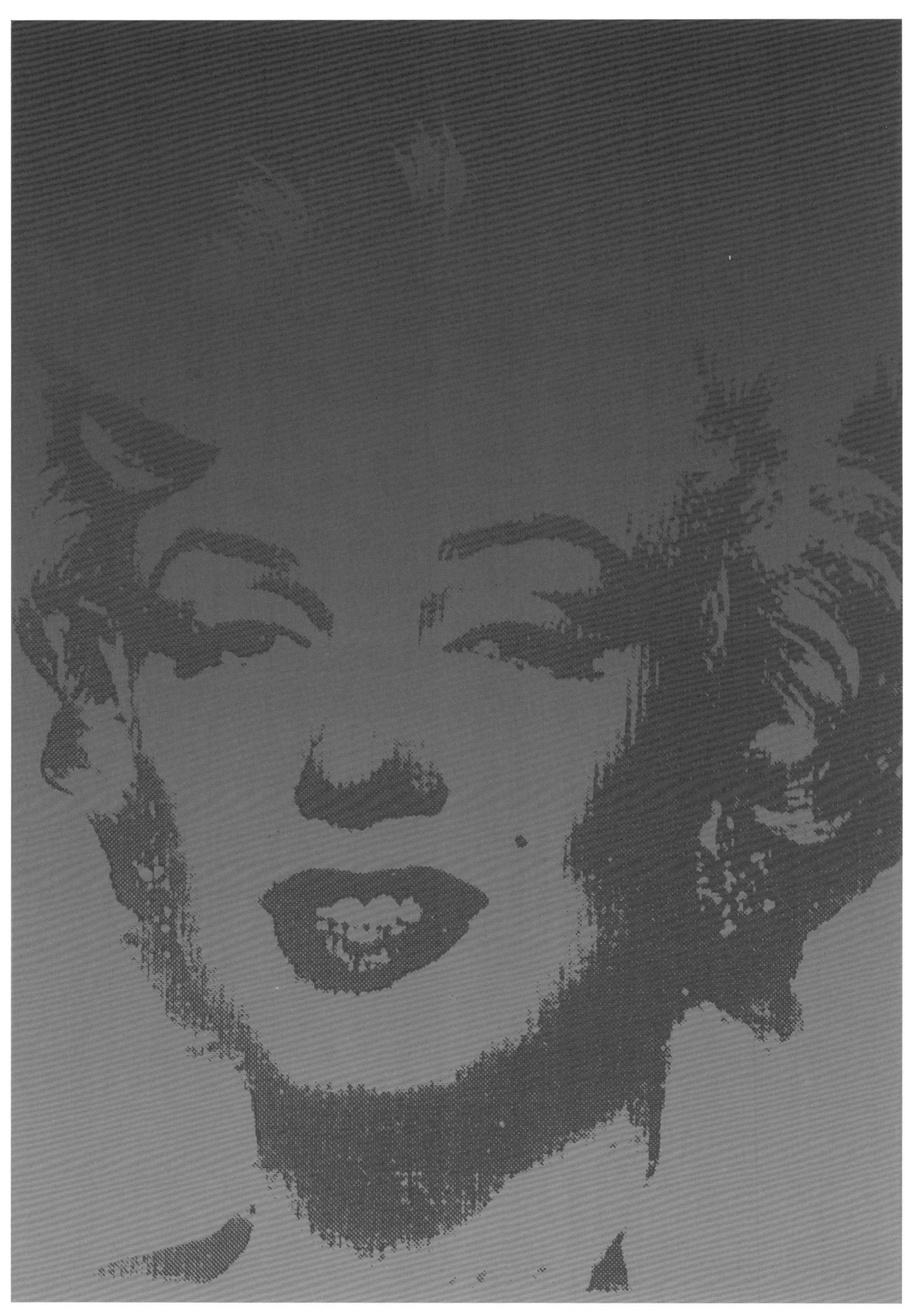

Plate XLII   Two-color screenprints: blue ink on blue ombre paper; Number of
prints: three; Caption: no; Collection number: AWMM.1968.159,
AWMM.1968.174 **(illustrated)**, AWMM.1968.281.

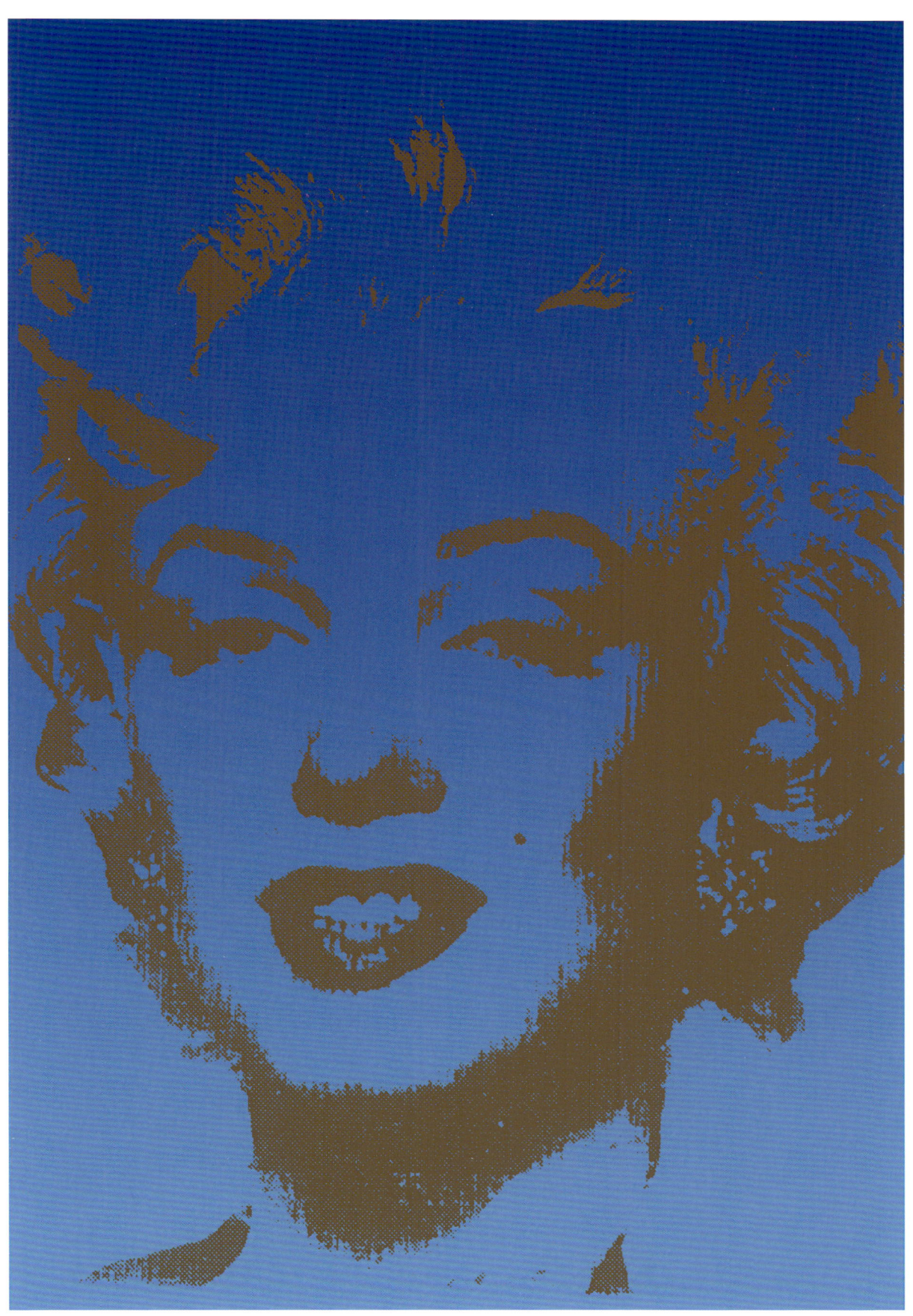

Plate XLIII Two-color reversal screenprints: metallic gold ink on blue ombre paper;
Number of prints: four; Caption: yes; Collection numbers: AWMM.1968.016,
AWMM.1968.107, AWMM.1968.145 **(illustrated)**, AWMM.1968.147.

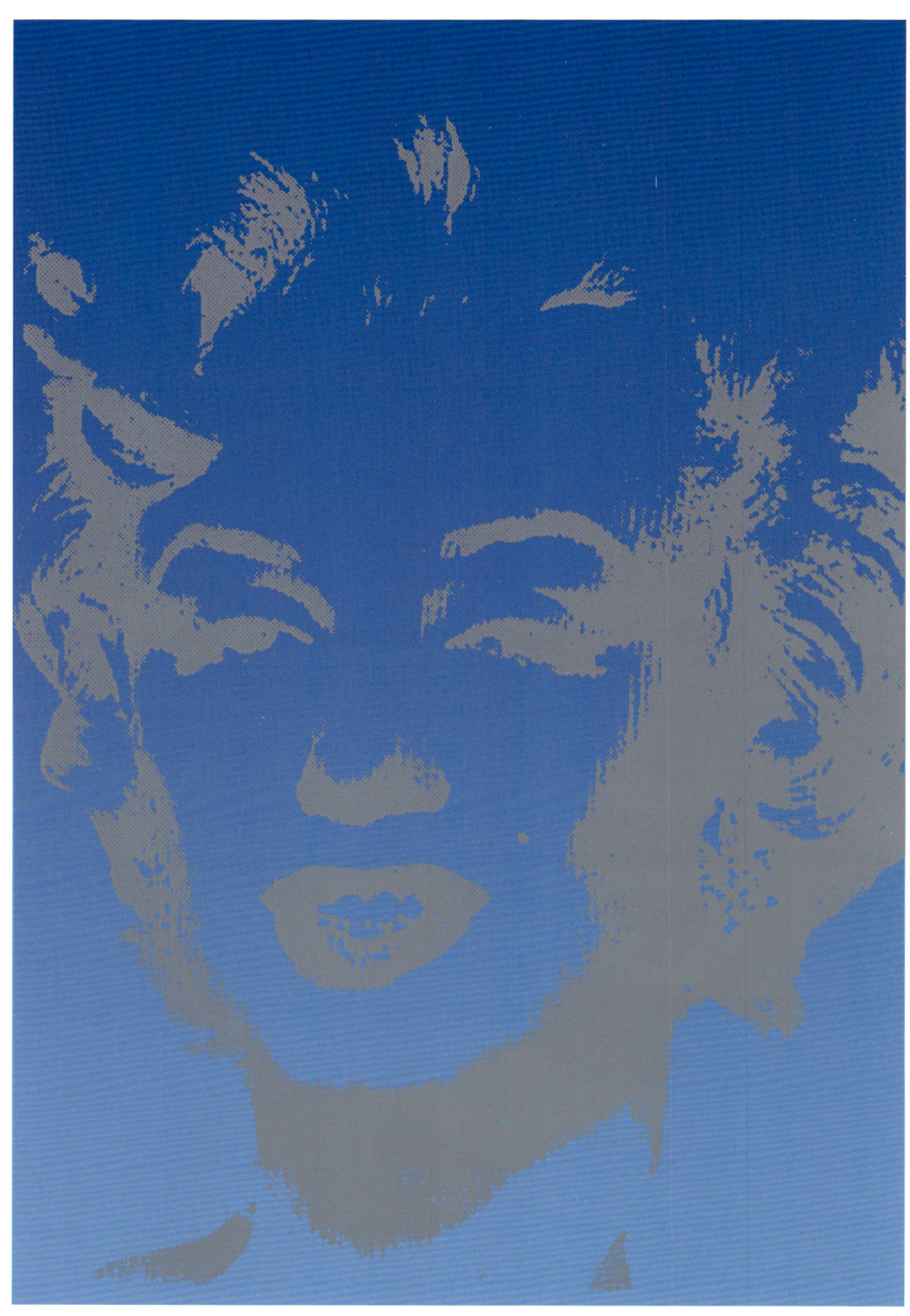

Plate XLIV   Two-color reversal screenprints: metallic silver ink on blue ombre
paper; Number of prints: three; Caption: no; Collection numbers:
AWMM.1968.038 **(illustrated)**, AWMM.1968.144, AWMM.1968.317.

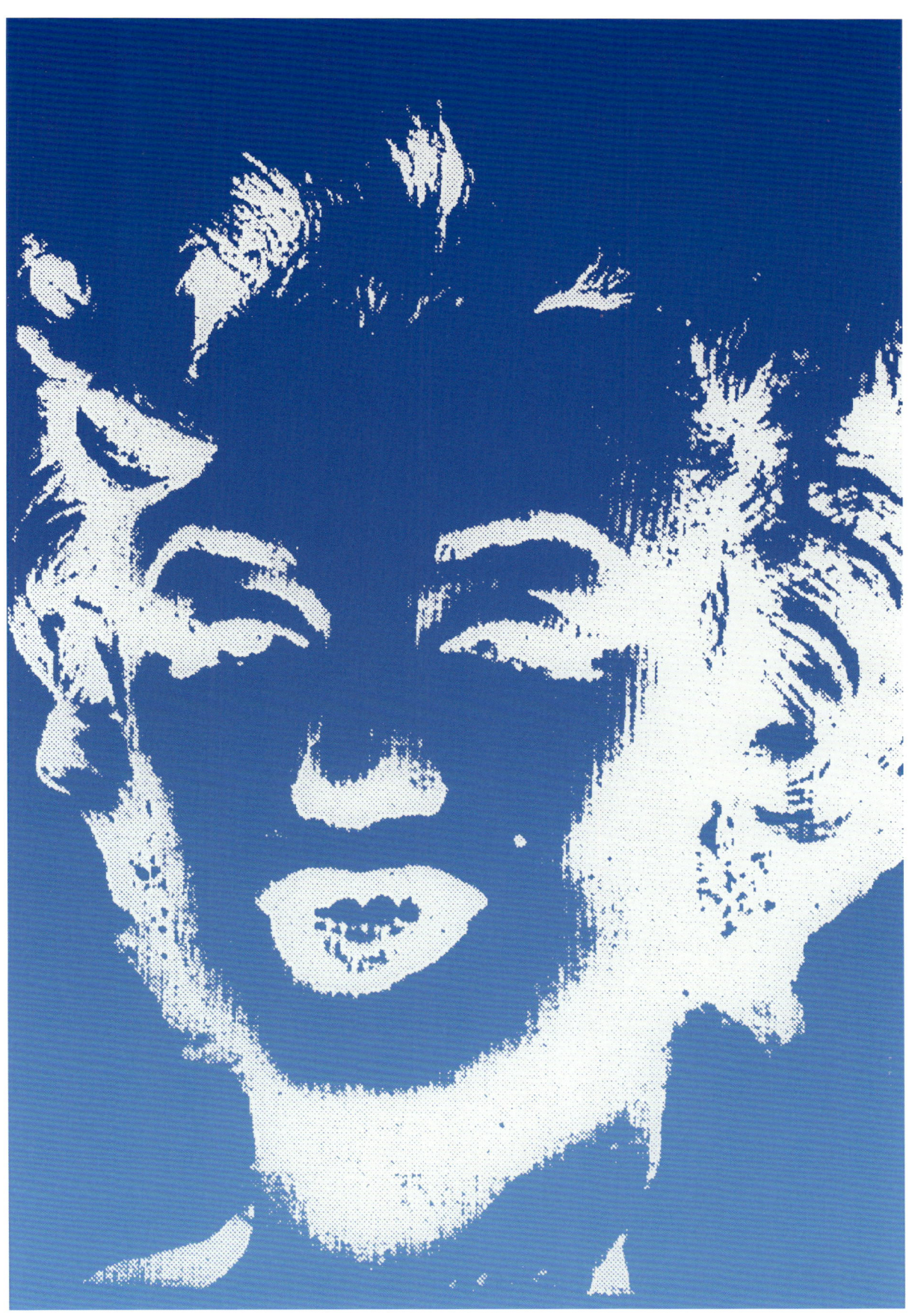

Plate XLV   Two-color reversal screenprints: white ink on blue ombre paper; Number of prints: six;
Caption: no; Collection number: AWMM.1968.097, AWMM.1968.193, AWMM.1968.197,
AWMM.1968.253, AWMM.1968.259 **(illustrated)**, AWMM.1968.308.

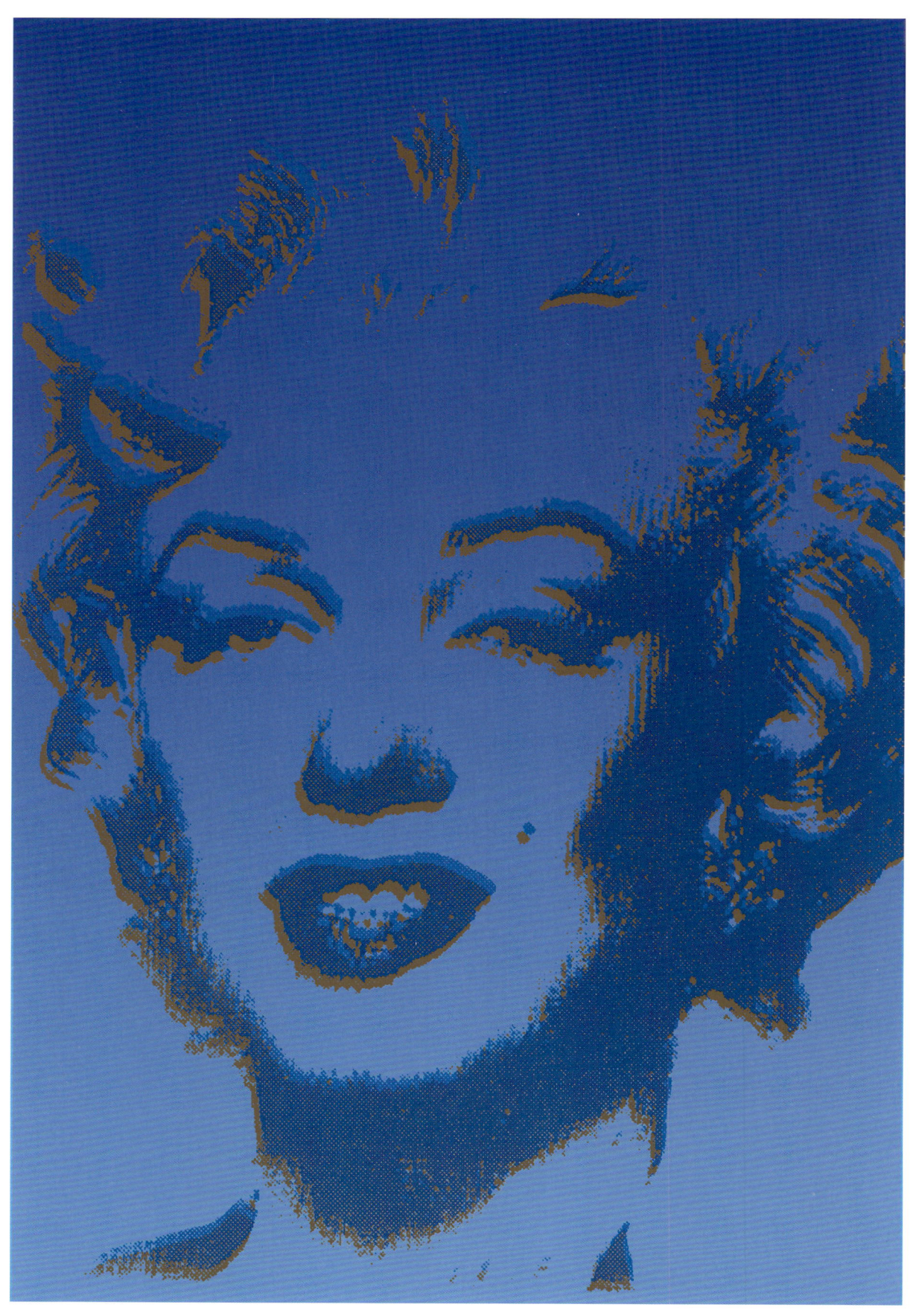

Plate XLVI   Three-color screenprint: metallic gold ink and blue ink on blue
ombre paper; Number of prints: one; Caption: yes (illegible);
Collection number: AWMM.1968.158.

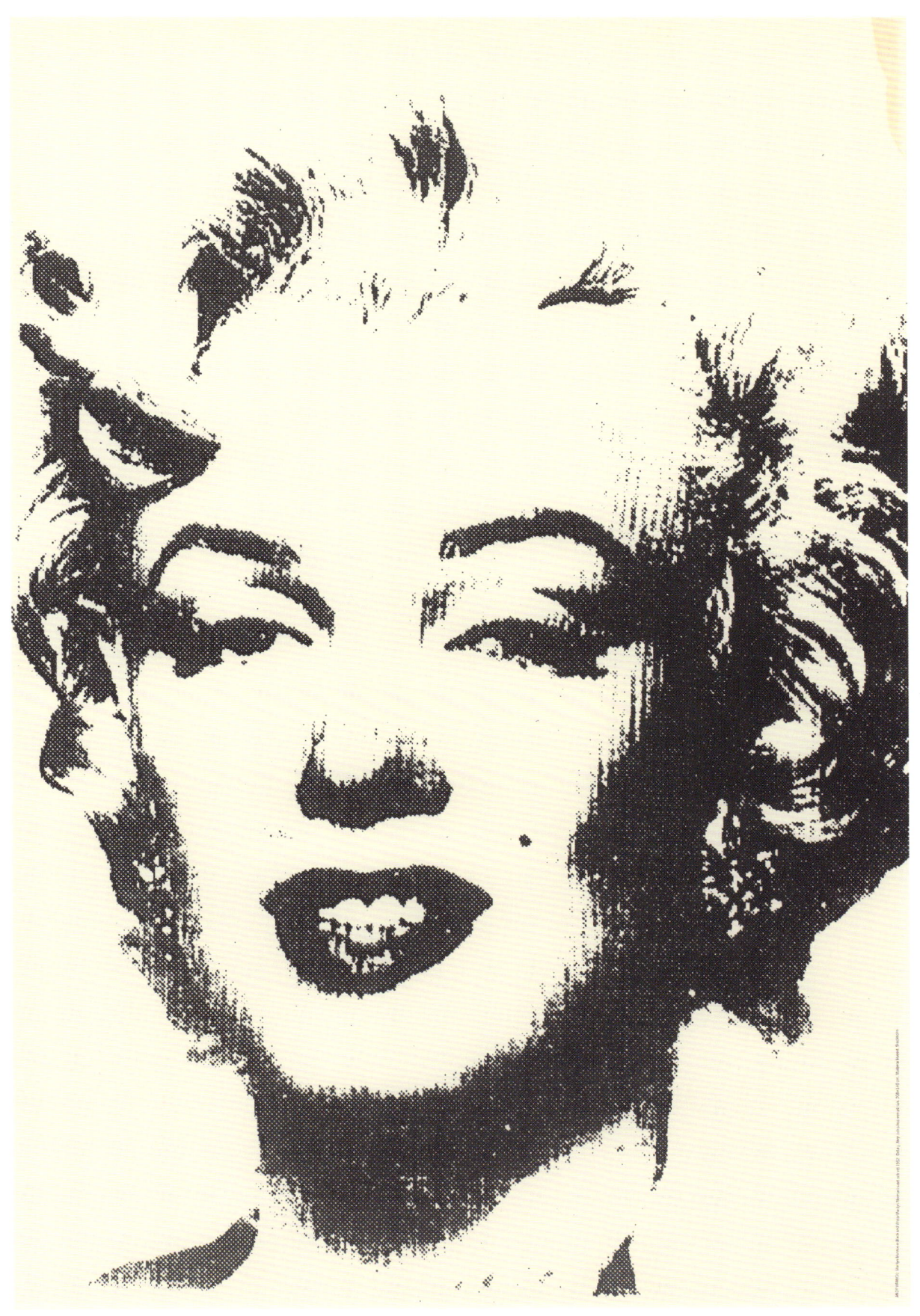

Plate XLVII   Two-color screenprint: dark gray ink on tan
paper; Number of prints: one; Caption: yes;
Collection number: AWMM.1968.296.

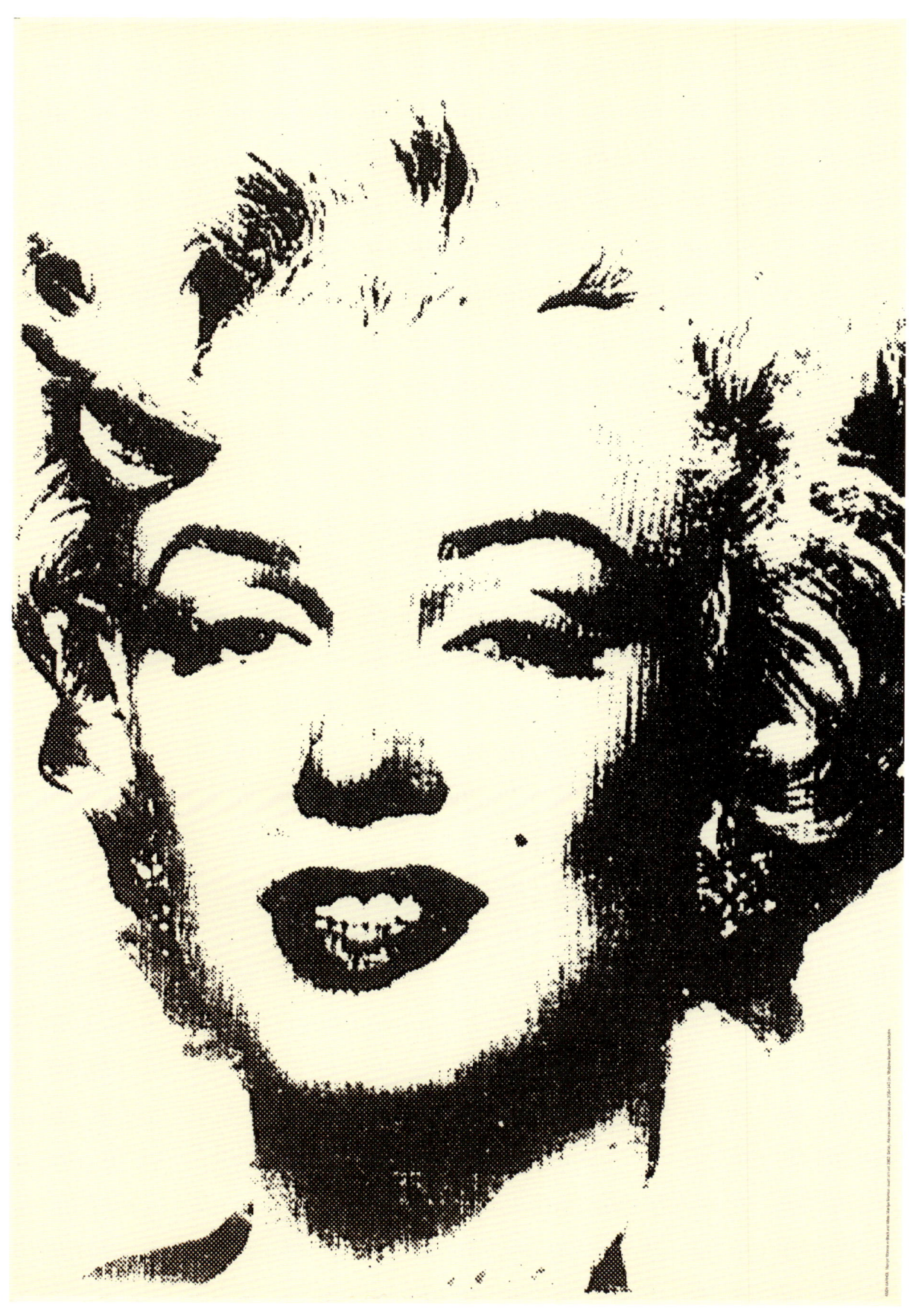

Plate XLVIII   Two-color screenprints: black ink on tan cardstock; Number of
prints: two; Caption: yes; Collection numbers: AWMM.1968.297
(illustrated), AWMM.1968.304.

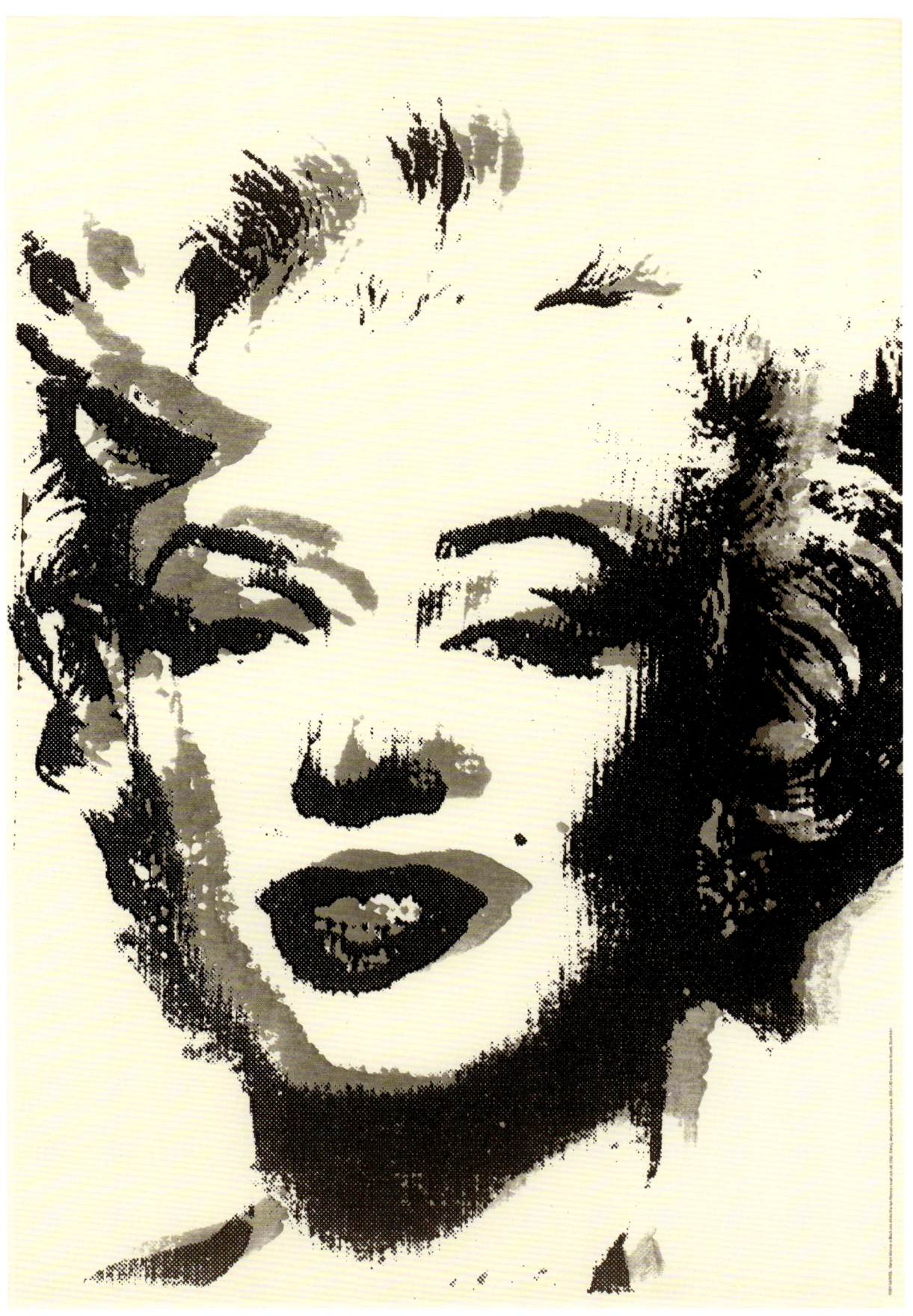

Plate XLIX   Three-color screenprint: gray (or dilute black) and black inks on tan cardstock; Number of prints: one; Caption: yes; Collection number: AWMM.1968.298.

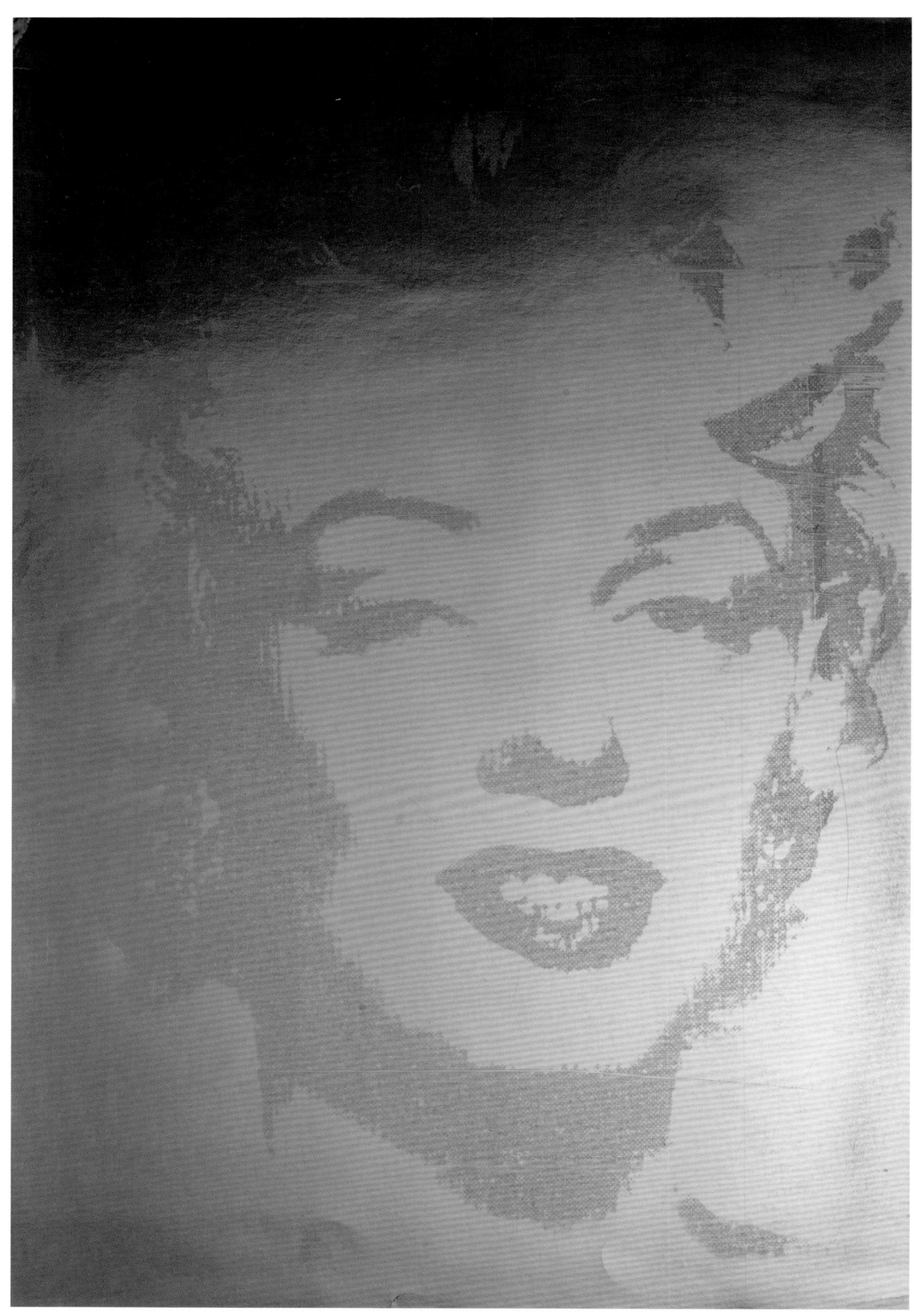

Plate L.A   Two-color reversal screenprint: clear ink base on paperboard that has been laminated on both sides with silver foil (Lac-prints); Number of prints: five; Caption: none; Note: the verso of prints marked (†) bear an offset mirror image; Collection numbers: AWMM.1968.020, AWMM.1968.021 **(illustrated)**†, AWMM.1968.058*, AWMM.1968.294, AWMM.1968.295†*.

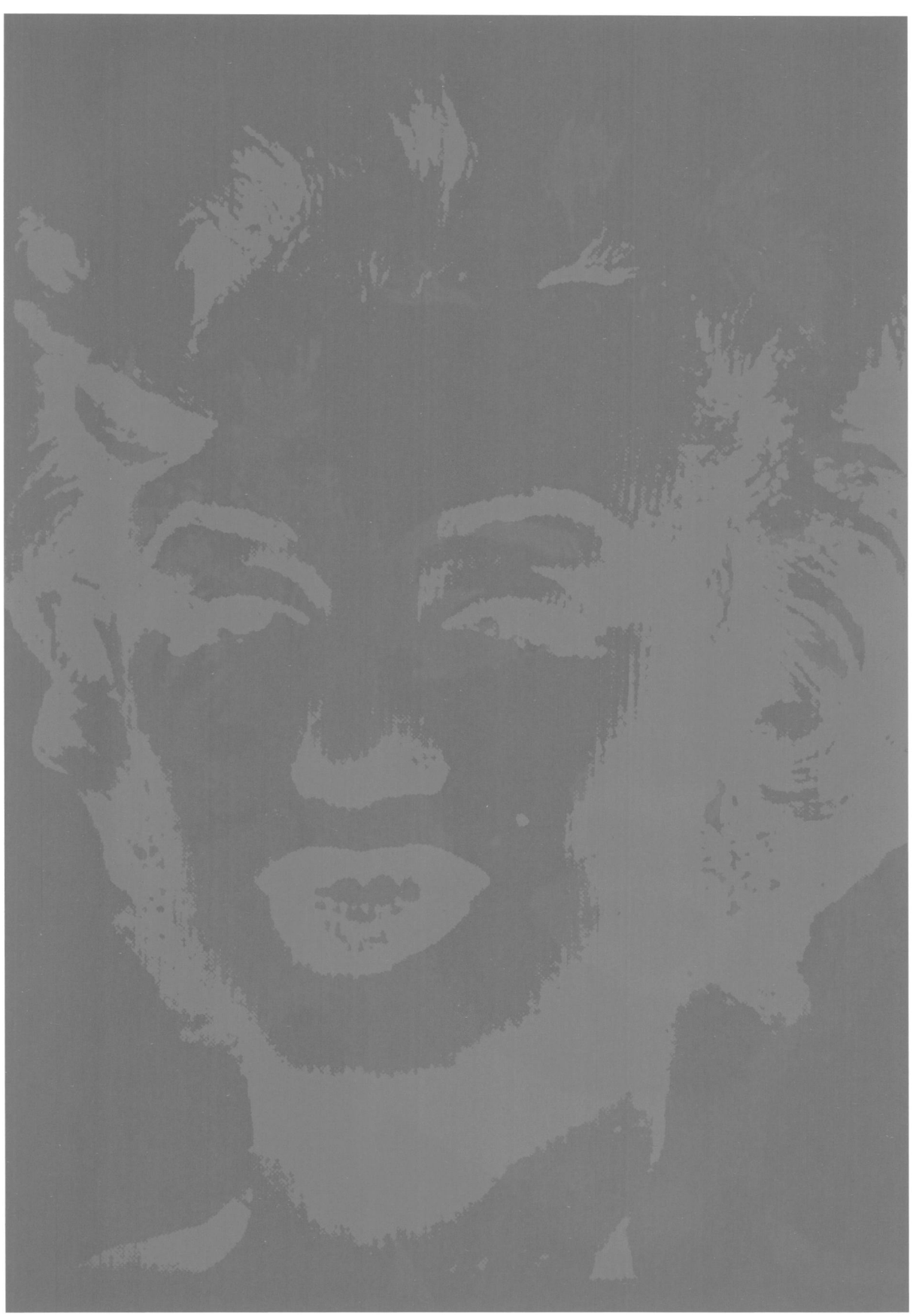

Plate L.B Two-color reversal screenprint: clear ink base on paperboard that has been laminated on both sides with silver foil (Lac-prints); Number of prints: five; Caption: none; Note: the verso of prints marked (†) bear an offset mirror image; Collection numbers: AWMM.1968.020, AWMM.1968.021†, AWMM.1968.058 **(illustrated)***, AWMM.1968.294, AWMM.1968.295†*.

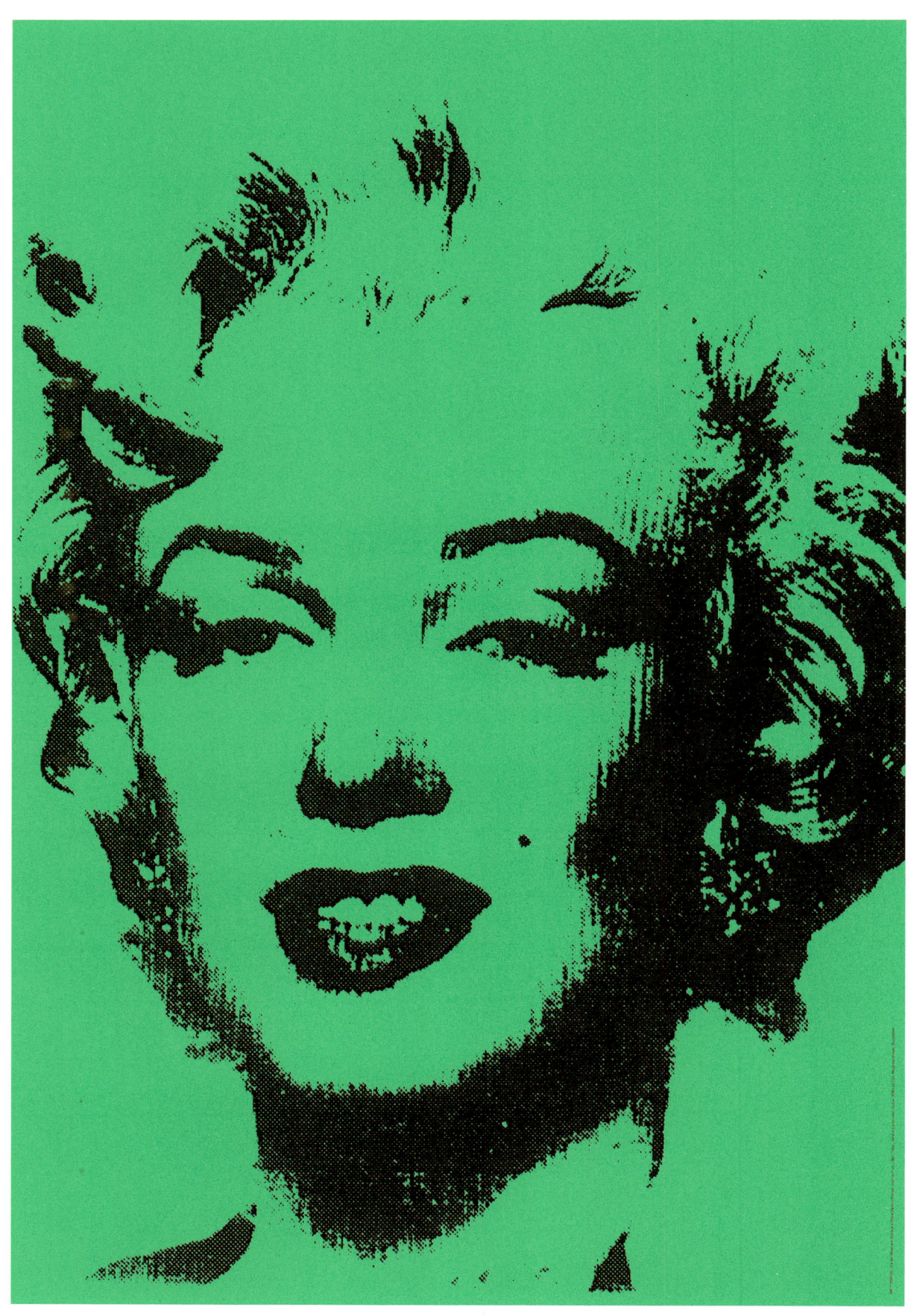

Plate LI Two-color screenprints: black ink on fluorescent green paper; Number of prints: five; Caption: yes; Collection numbers: AWMM.1968.012, AWMM.1968.146 **(illustrated)**, AWMM.1968.232, AWMM.1968.248, AWMM.1968.311.

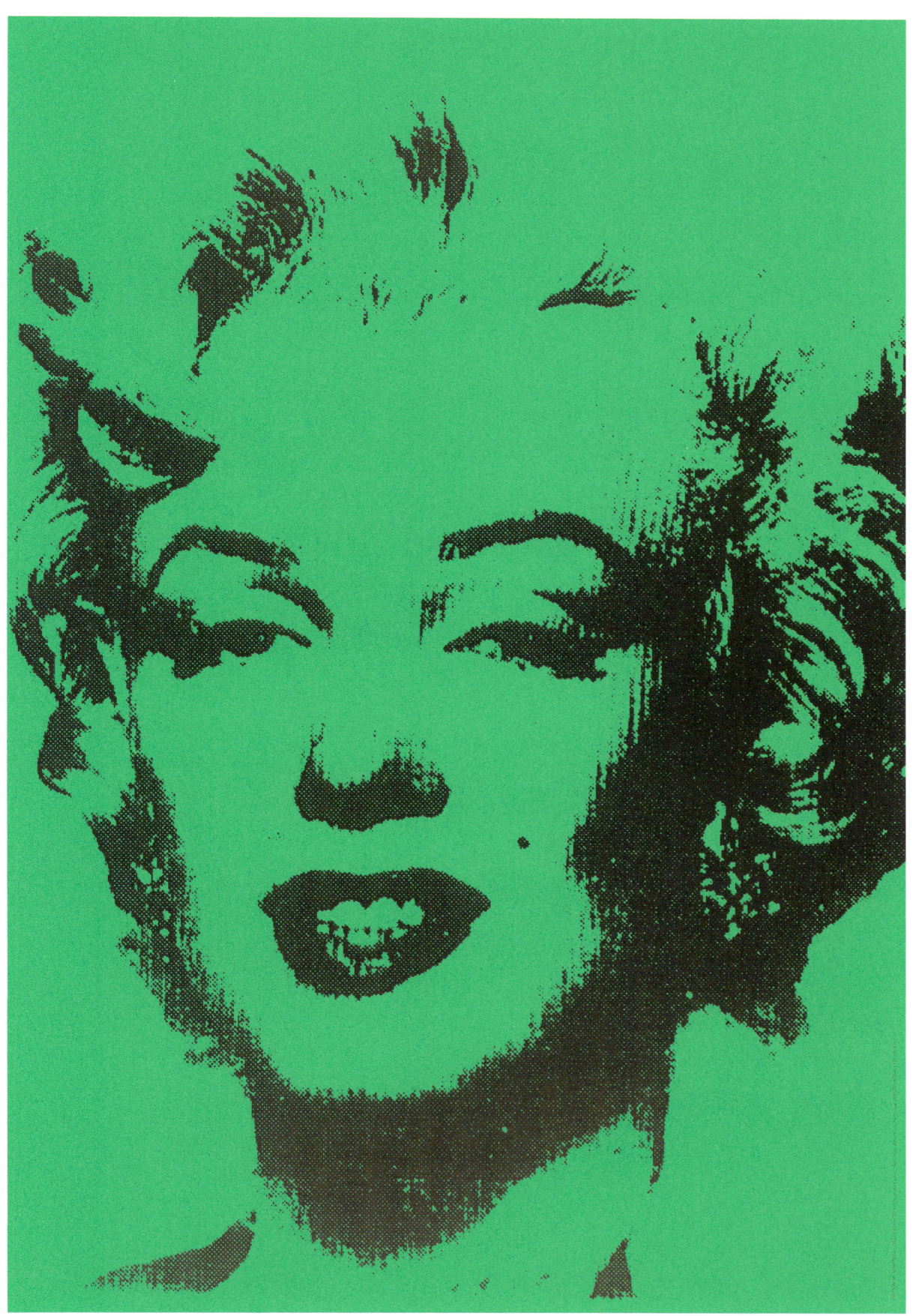

Plate LII   Two-color screenprints: dark gray ink on fluorescent green paper; Number of prints: four; Caption: yes; Collection numbers: AWMM.1968.061 **(illustrated)**, AWMM.1968.123, AWMM.1968.208, AWMM.1968.266.

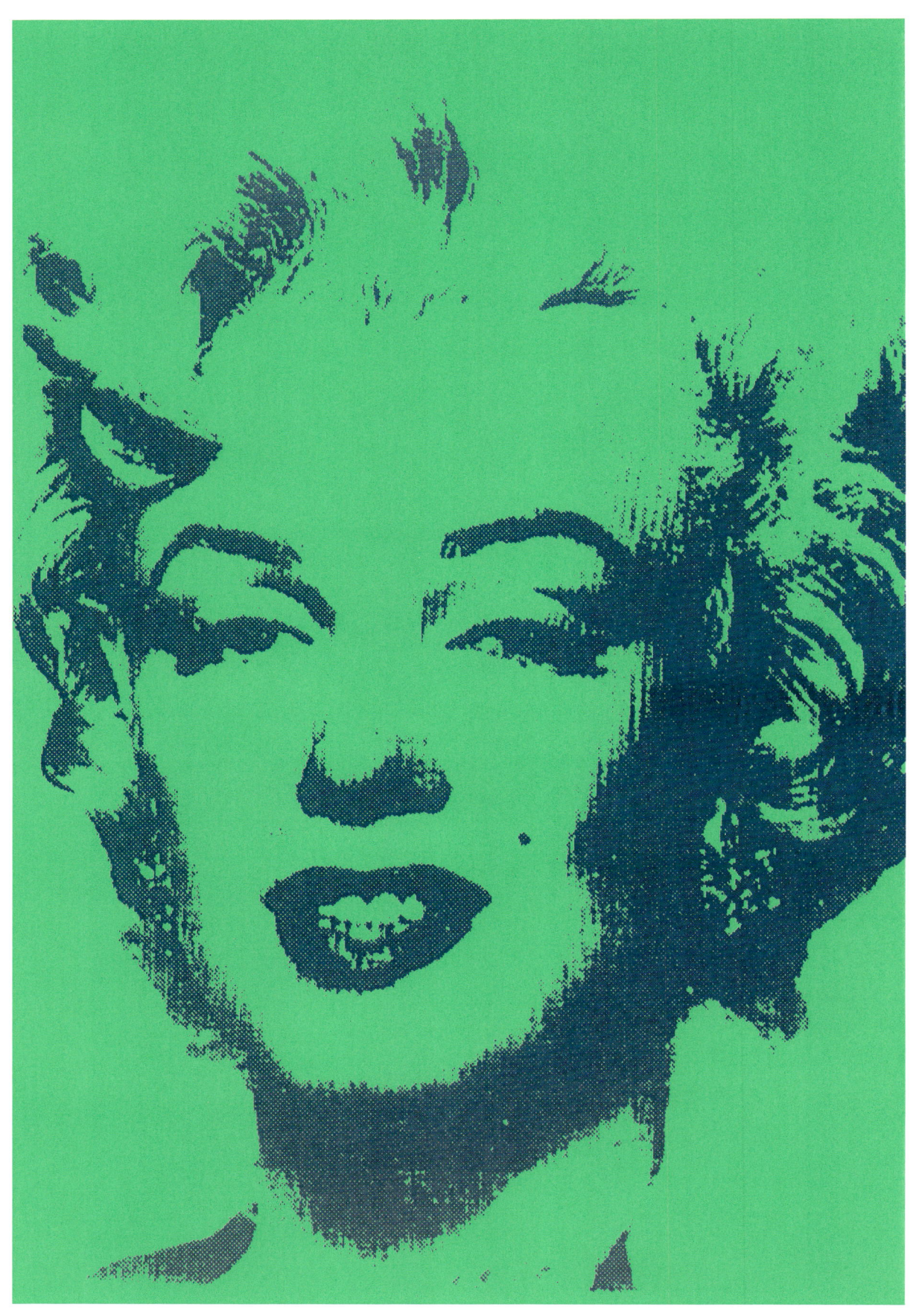

Plate LIII   Two-color screenprints: blue ink on fluorescent green paper; Number of prints: six;
Caption: no; Collection numbers: AWMM.1968.062, AWMM.1968.104 **(illustrated)**,
AWMM.1968.131, AWMM.1968.272, AWMM.1968.286, AWMM.1968.307.

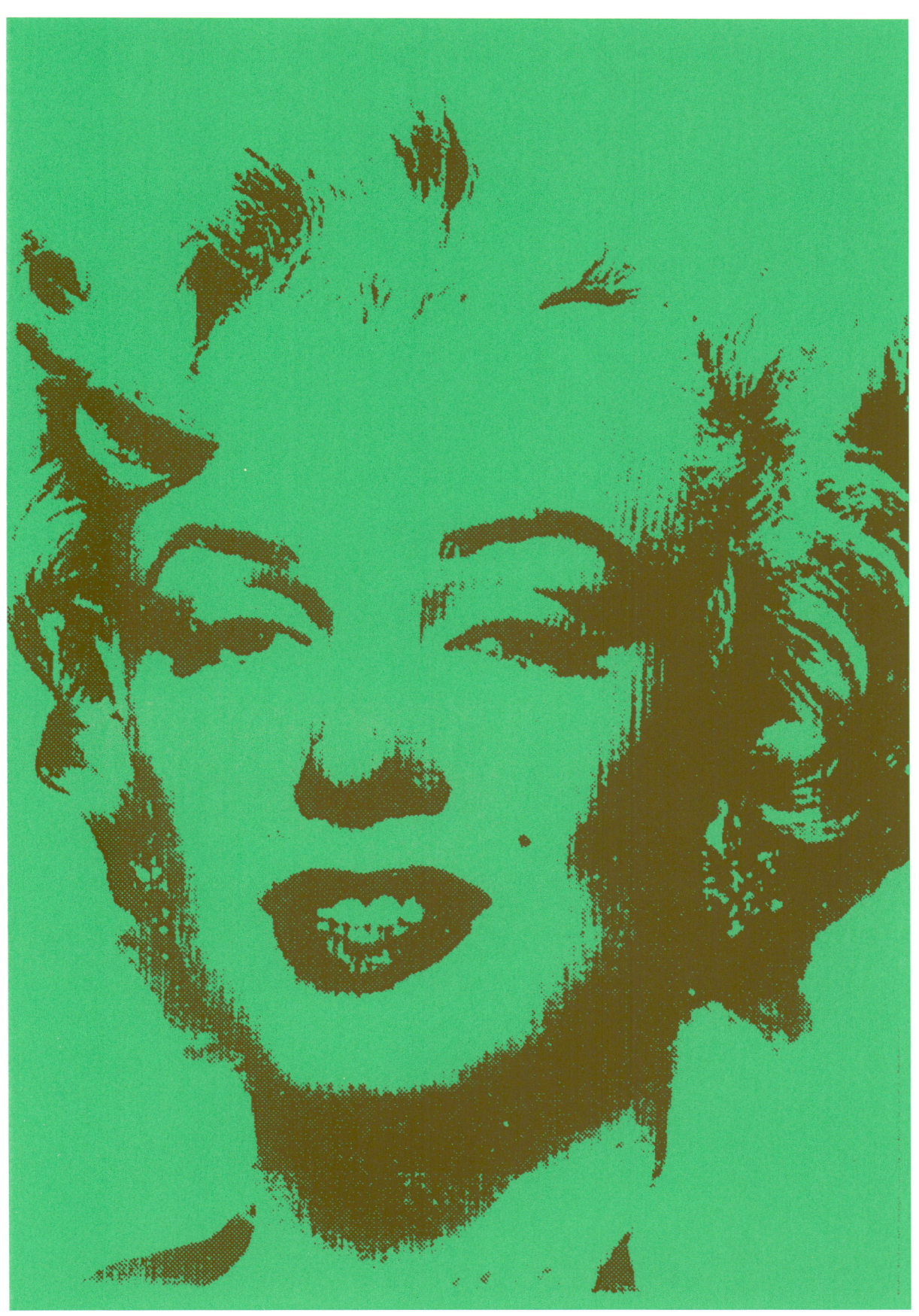

Plate LIV   Two-color reversal screenprints: metallic gold ink on fluorescent green paper;
Number of prints: three; Caption: yes; Collection numbers: AWMM.1968.005,
AWMM.1968.180 **(illustrated)**, AWMM.1968.211.

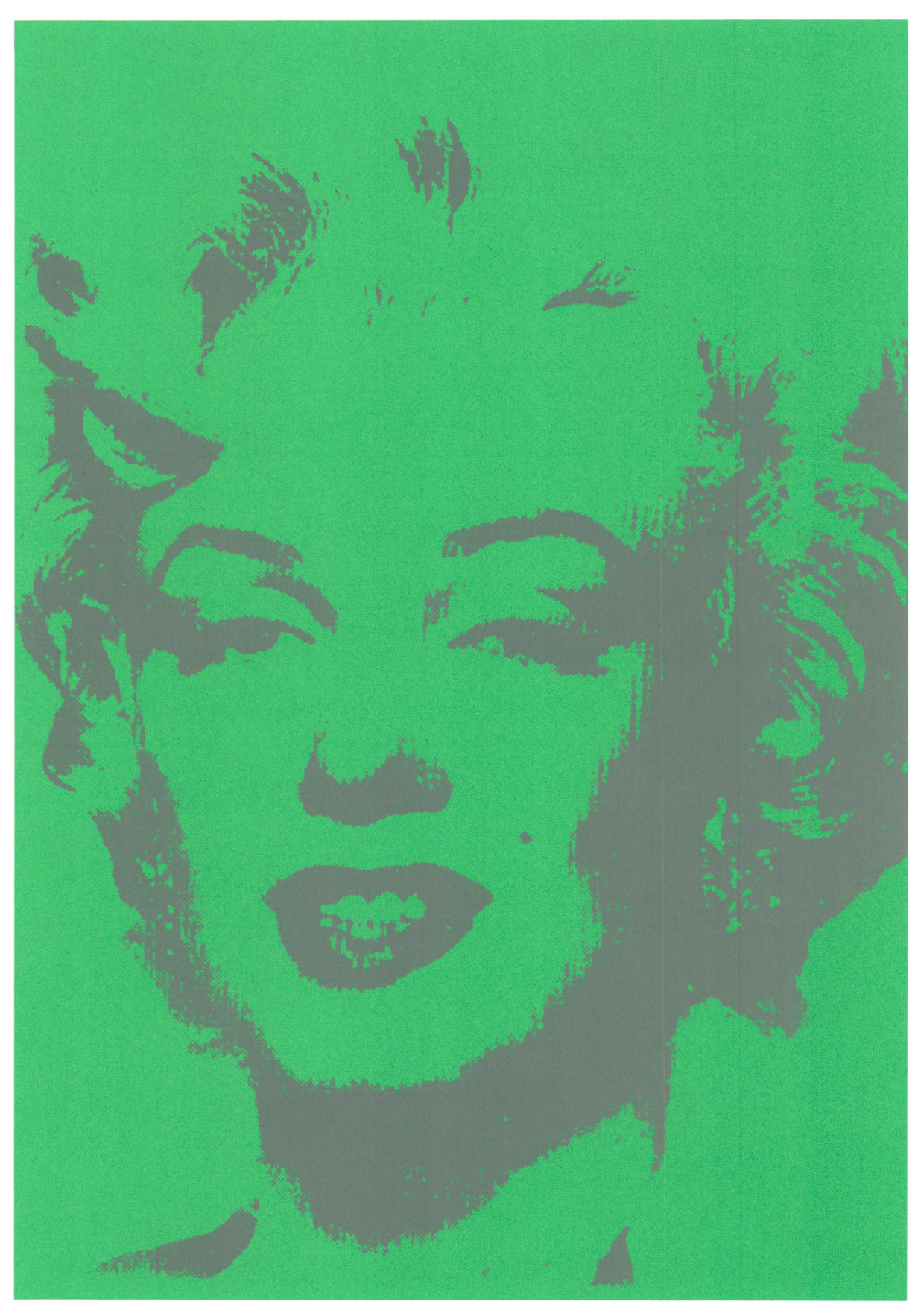

Plate LV   Two-color reversal screenprints: metallic silver ink on fluorescent green paper; Number
of prints: five; Caption: no; Collection numbers: AWMM.1968.034 **(illustrated)**,
AWMM.1968.082*, AWMM.1968.203, AWMM.1968.271, AWMM.1968.292.

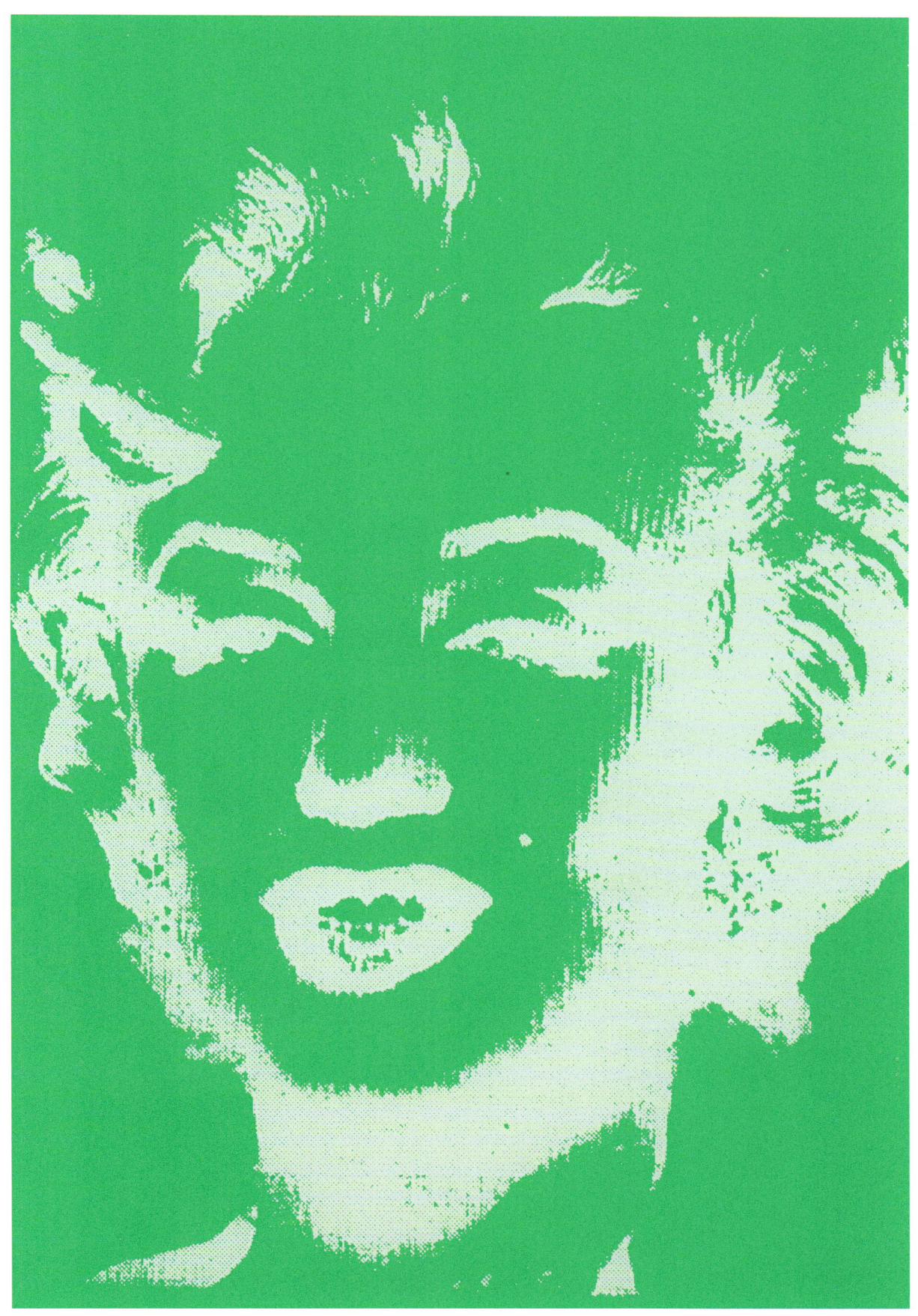

Plate LVI   Two-color reversal screenprints: white ink on fluorescent green paper; Number of prints:
six; Caption: no; Collection numbers: AWMM.1968.094, AWMM.1968.129 **(illustrated)**,
AWMM.1968.179, AWMM.1968.186, AWMM.1968.222, AWMM.1968.270.

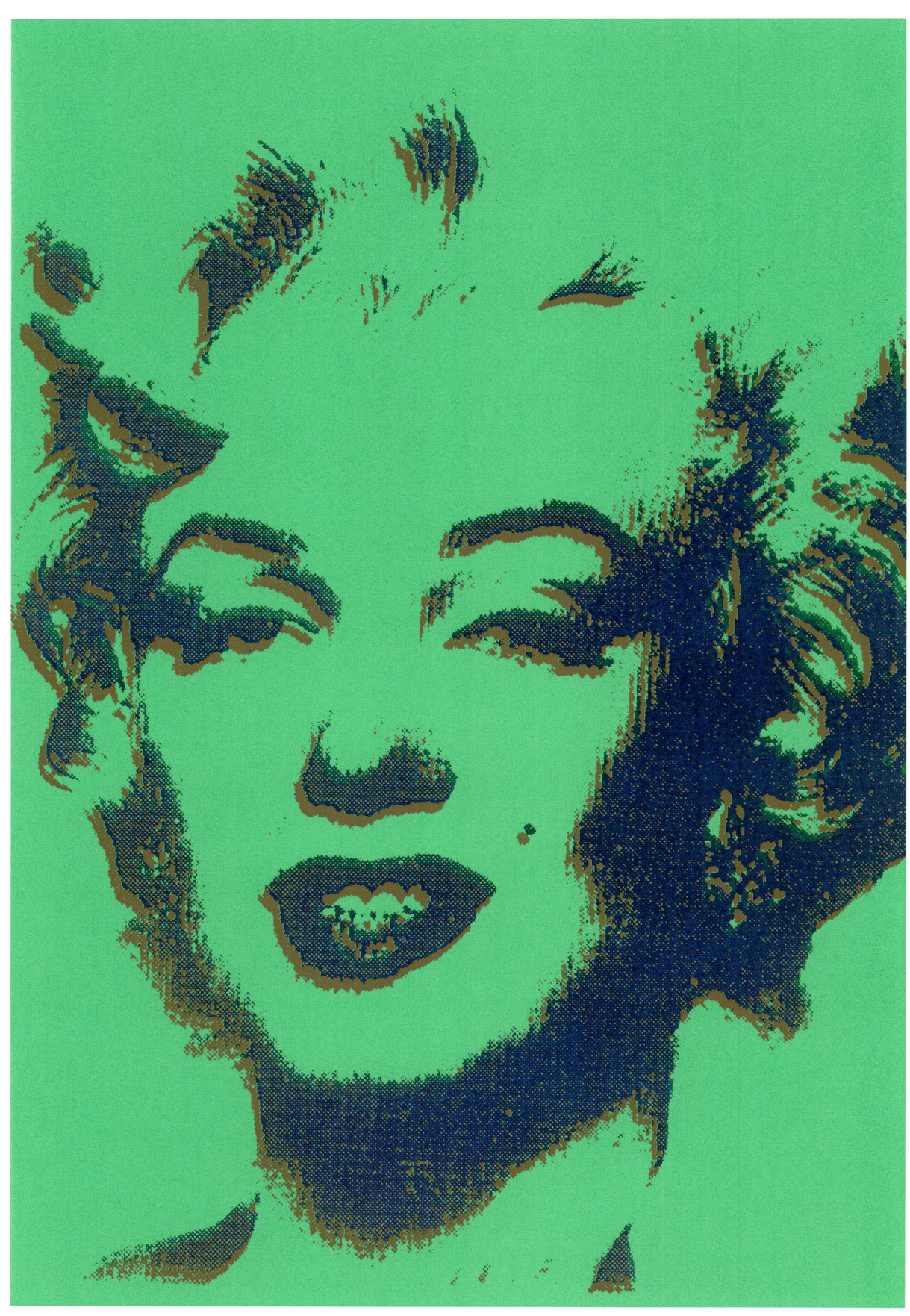

Plate LVII   Three-color screenprints: metallic gold ink and blue ink on fluorescent green paper; Number
of prints: five; Caption: yes; Collection numbers: AWMM.1968.014, AWMM.1968.015,
AWMM.1968.130, AWMM.1968.252 **(illustrated)**, AWMM.1968.322.

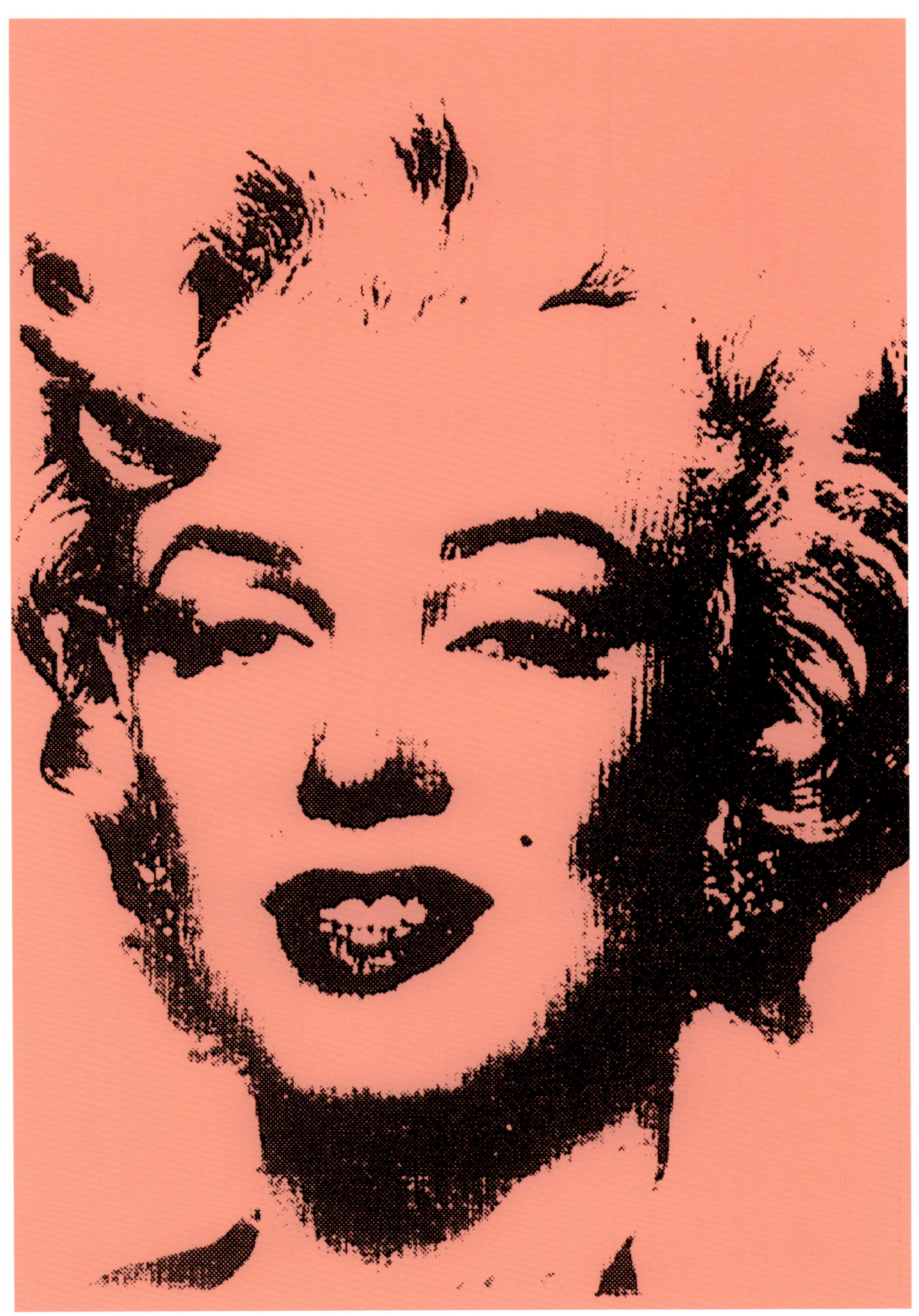

Plate LVIII Two-color screenprints: black ink on fluorescent orange paper;
Number of prints: two; Caption: yes; Collection numbers:
AWMM.1968.209*, AWMM.1968.289 **(illustrated)**.

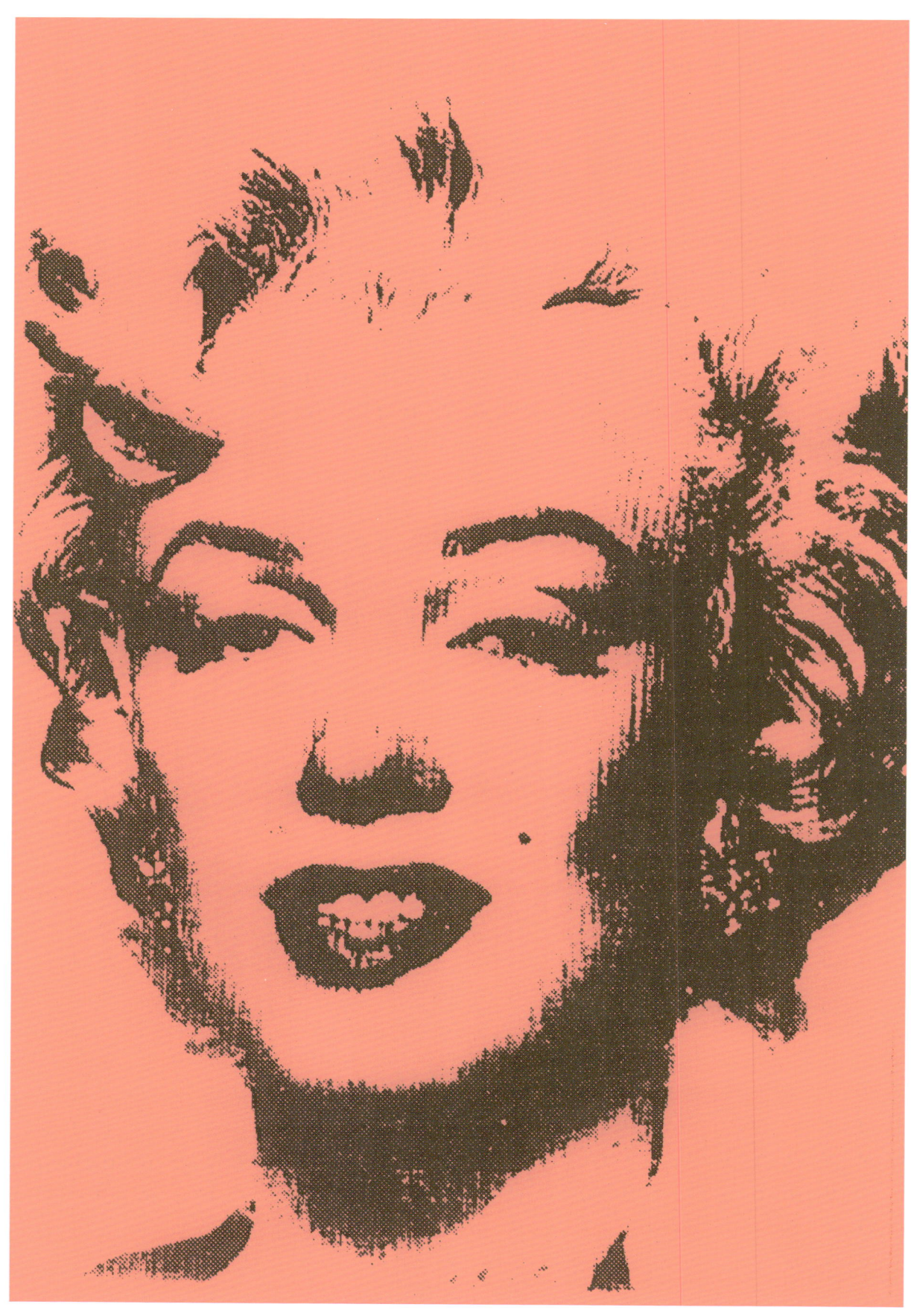

Plate LIX   Two-color screenprints: dark gray ink on fluorescent orange paper; Number of prints: three; Caption: yes; Collection numbers: AWMM.1968.091 **(illustrated)**, AWMM.1968.124, AWMM.1968.181.

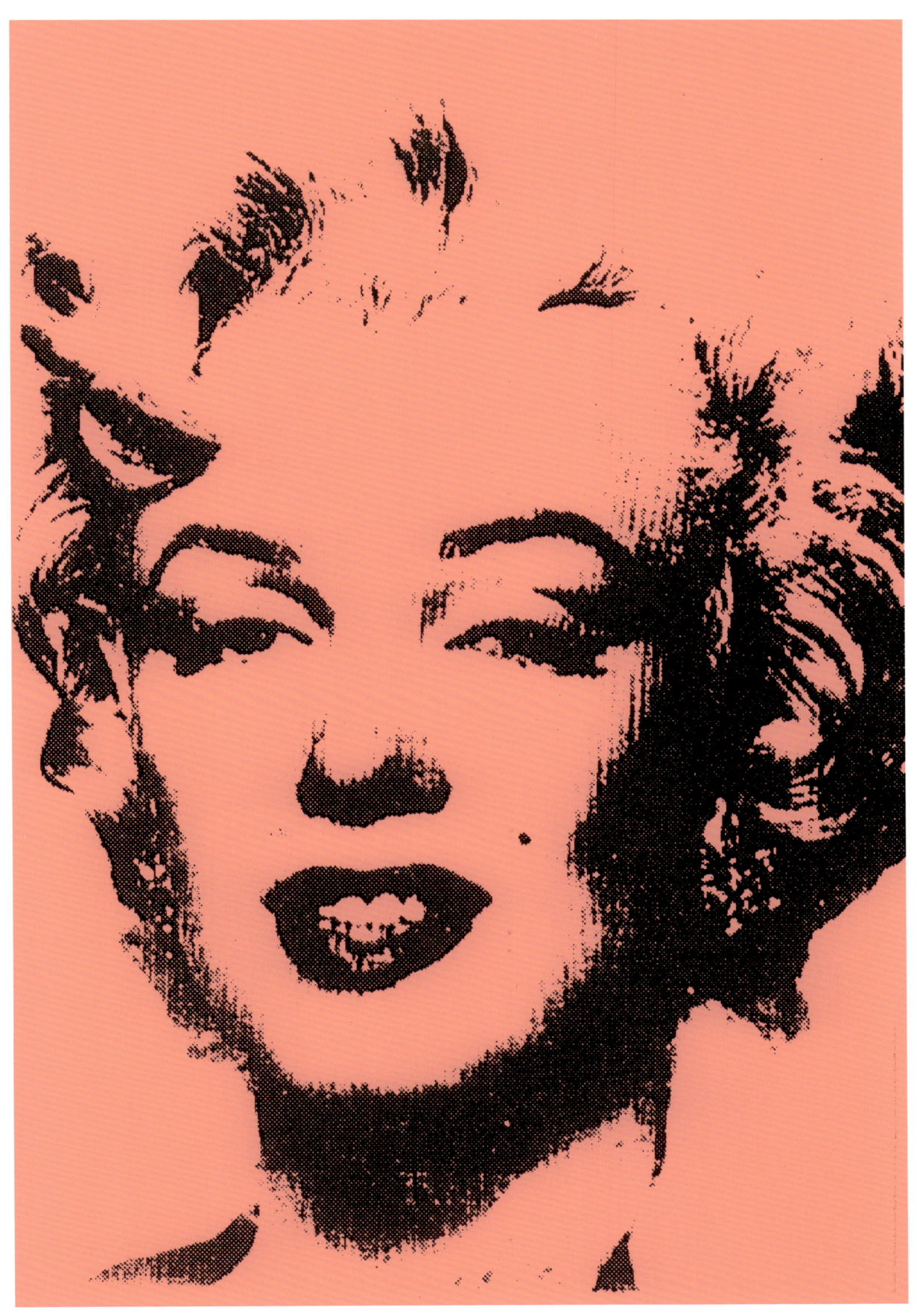

Plate LX   Two-color screenprints: dark blue ink on fluorescent orange
paper; Number of prints: three; Caption: yes; Collection numbers:
AWMM.1968.011, AWMM.1968.095 **(illustrated)**, AWMM.1968.135.

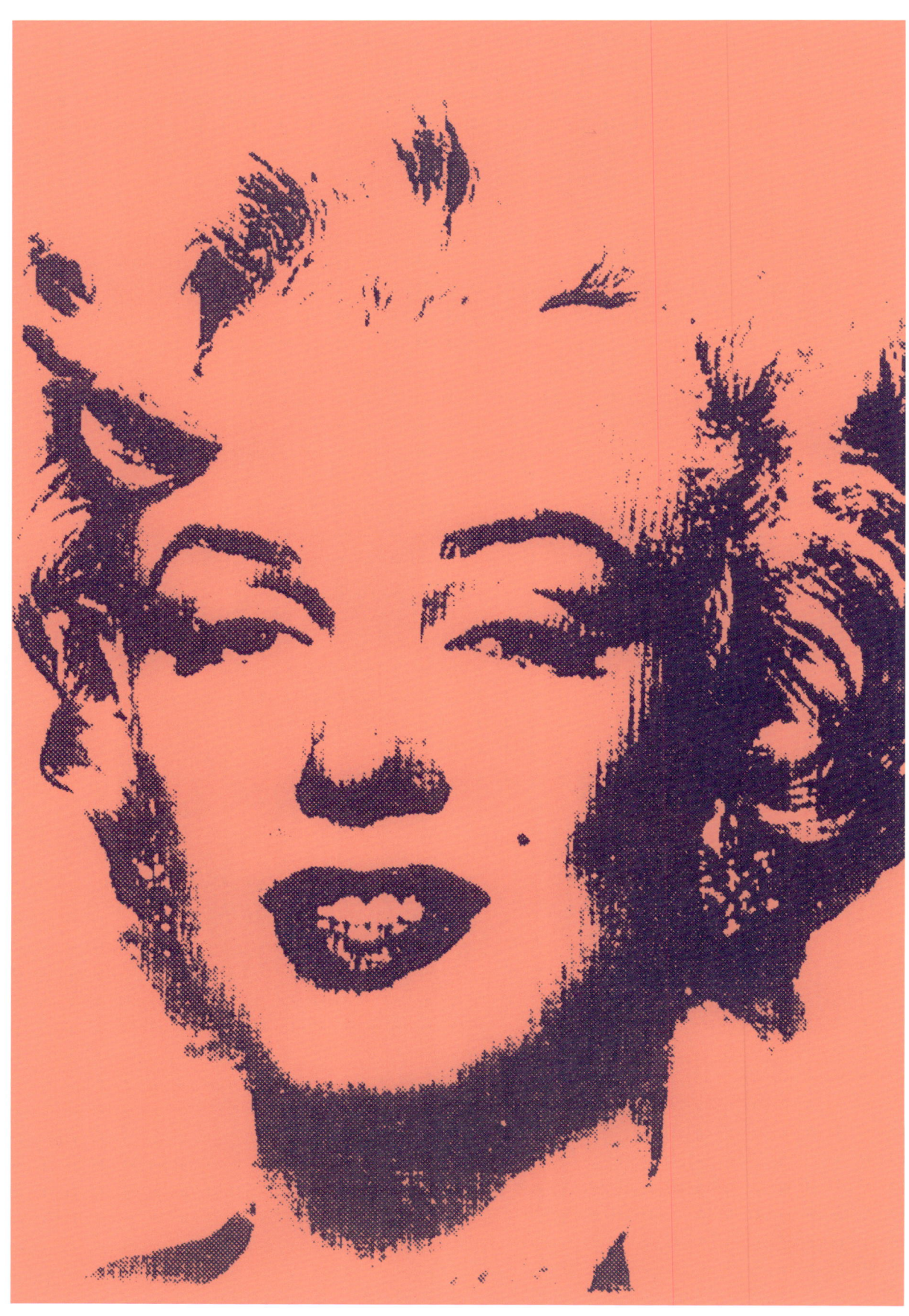

Plate LXI   Two-color screenprints: blue ink on fluorescent orange paper; Number of prints: seven;
Caption: no; Collection numbers: AWMM.1968.039, AWMM.1968.044, AWMM.1968.045,
AWMM.1968.059, AWMM.1968.136, AWMM.1968.157, AWMM.1968.215 **(illustrated)**.

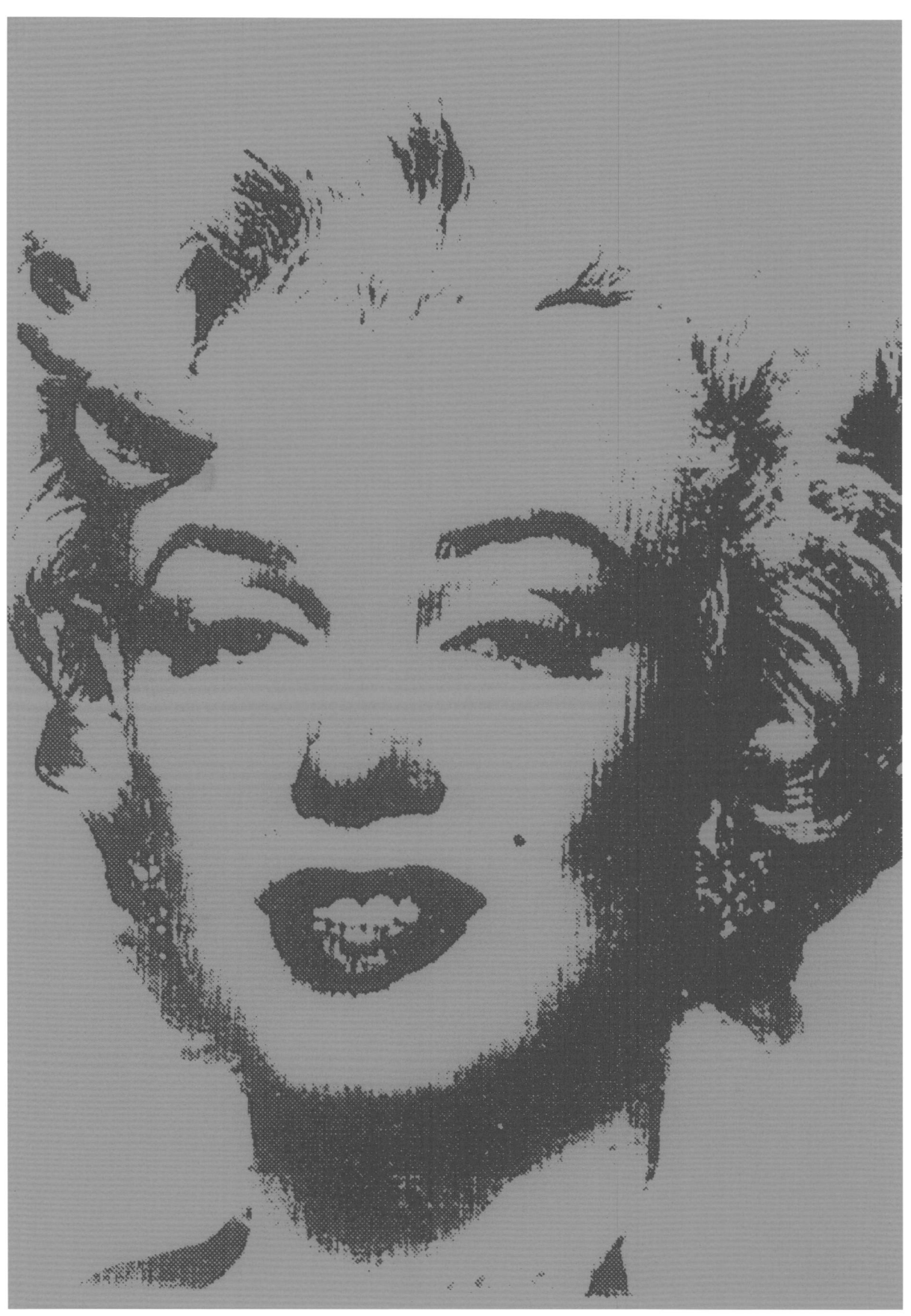

Plate LXII   Two-color reversal screenprints: metallic gold ink on fluorescent orange paper;
Number of prints: three; Caption: yes; Collection numbers: AWMM.1968.133,
AWMM.1968.214, AWMM.1968.249 **(illustrated)**.

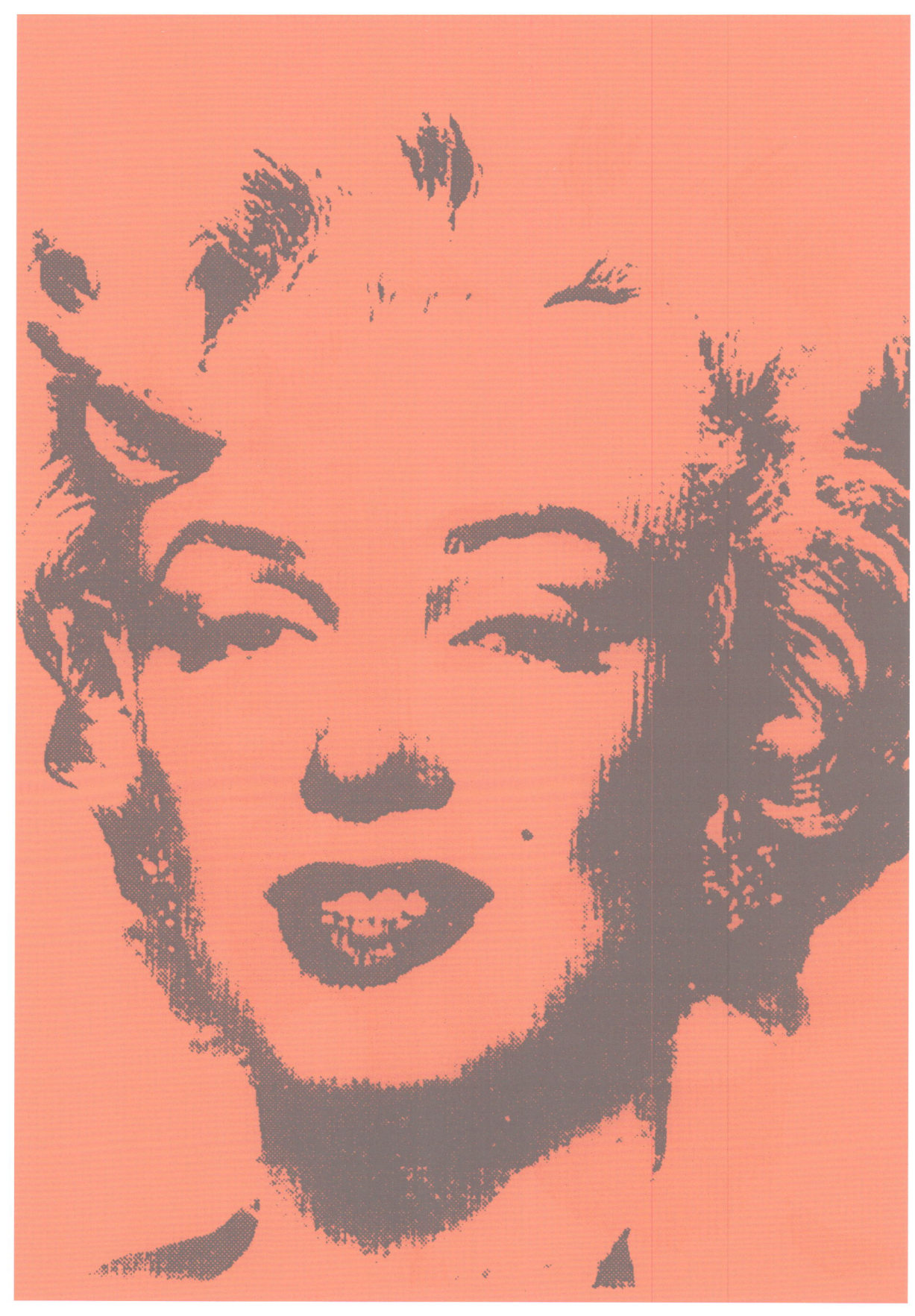

Plate LXIII　　Two-color reversal screenprints: metallic silver ink on fluorescent orange paper; Number of prints: eight; Caption: no; Collection numbers: AWMM.1968.036, AWMM.1968.041, AWMM.1968.046, AWMM.1968.047, AWMM.1968.081 **(illustrated)**, AWMM.1968.168, AWMM.1968.230, AWMM.1968.291.

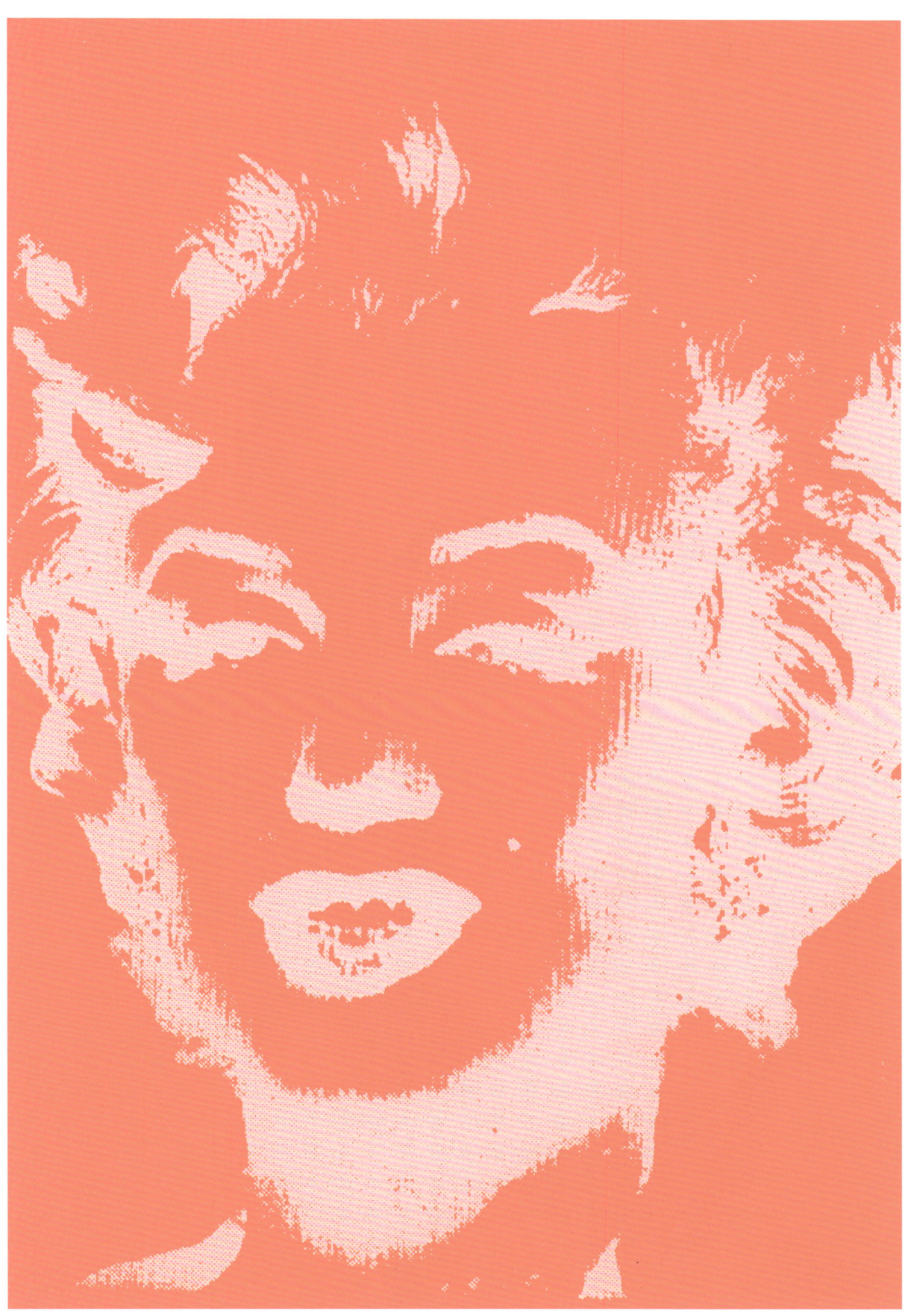

Plate LXIV Two-color reversal screenprints: white ink on fluorescent orange paper; Number of prints: seven; Caption: no; Collection numbers: AWMM.1968.006, AWMM.1968.029, AWMM.1968.096, AWMM.1968.134, AWMM.1968.169, AWMM.1968.170, AWMM.1968.223 **(illustrated)**.

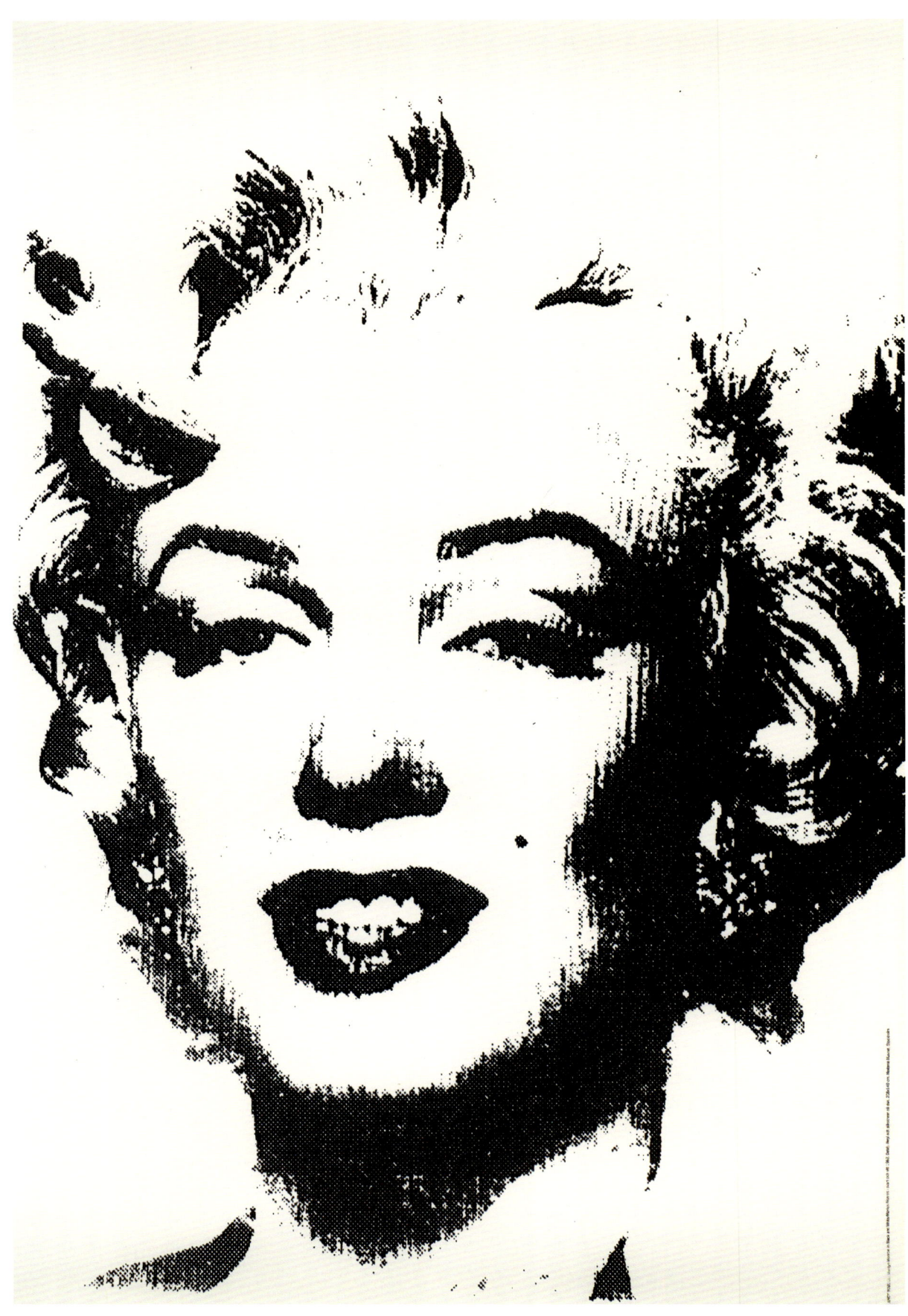

Plate LXV Two-color screenprints: black ink on white paper; Number of prints: seven; Caption: yes; Collection numbers: AWMM.1968.313, AWMM.1968.314*, AWMM.1968.315, AWMM.1968.318, AWMM.1968.319 **(illustrated)**, AWMM.1968.320, AWMM.1968.323.

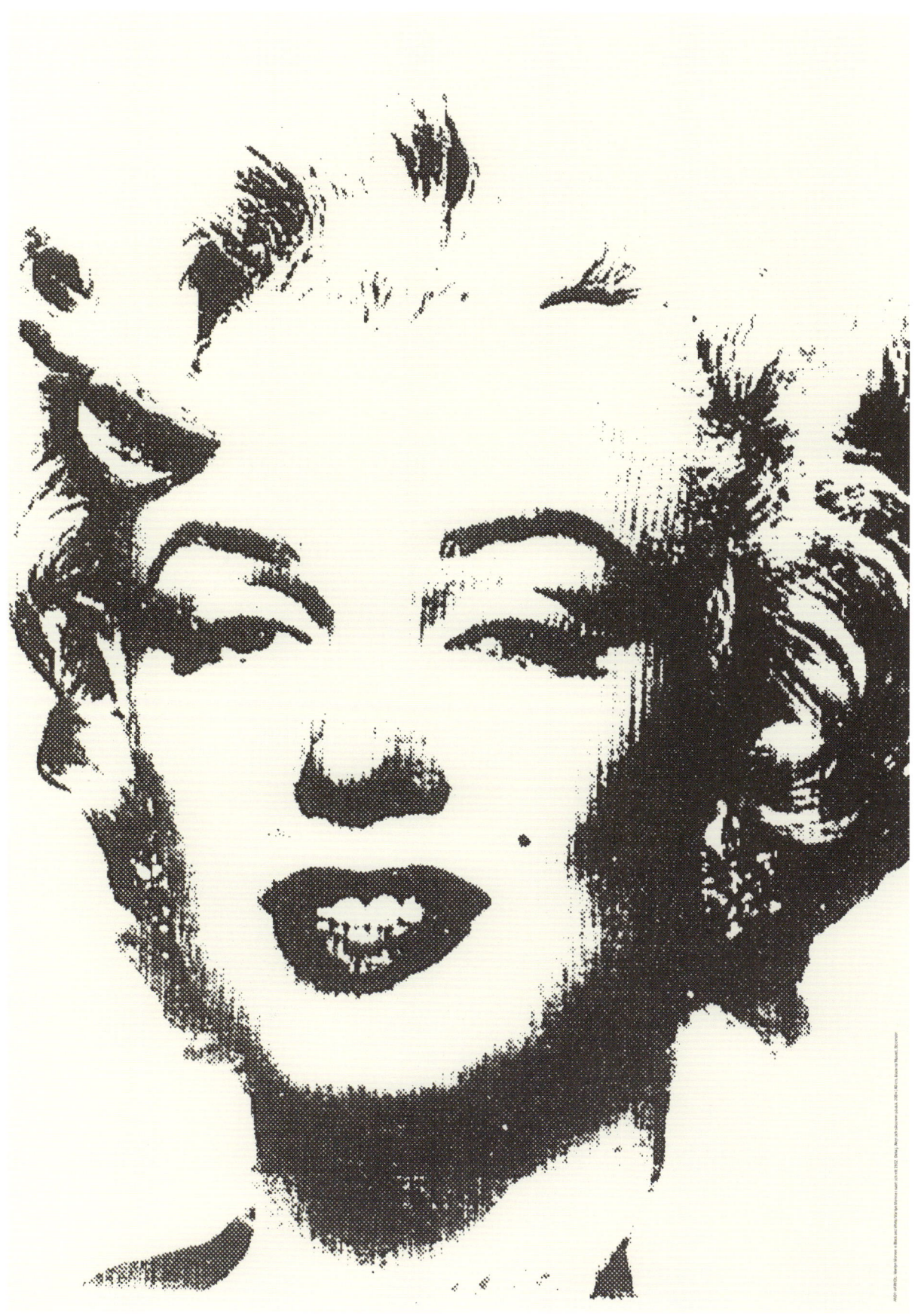

Plate LXVI   Two-color screenprints: dark gray ink on white paper; Number of prints: ten; Caption: yes; Collection numbers: AWMM.1968.024, AWMM.1968.033, AWMM.1968.140, AWMM.1968.246, AWMM.1968.256, AWMM.1968.262, AWMM.1968.268, AWMM.1968.278 **(illustrated)**, AWMM.1968.279, AWMM.1968.280.

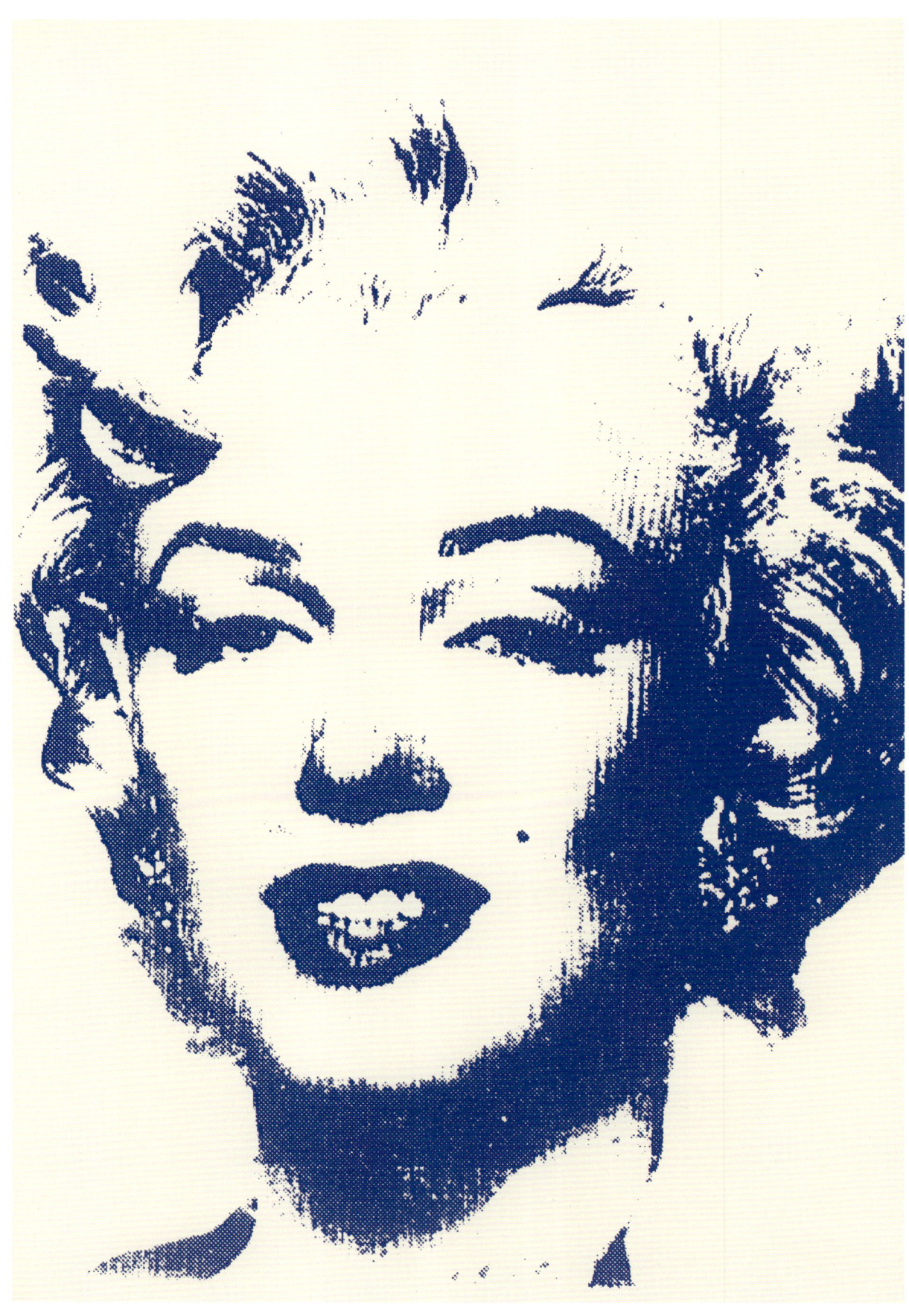

Plate LXVII   Two-color screenprints: blue ink on white paper; Number of prints: ten; Caption: no; Collection numbers:
AWMM.1968.030, AWMM.1968.042 **(illustrated)***, AWMM.1968.053, AWMM.1968.080, AWMM.1968.112,
AWMM.1968.150, AWMM.1968.156, AWMM.1968.219, AWMM.1968.221, AWMM.1968.244.

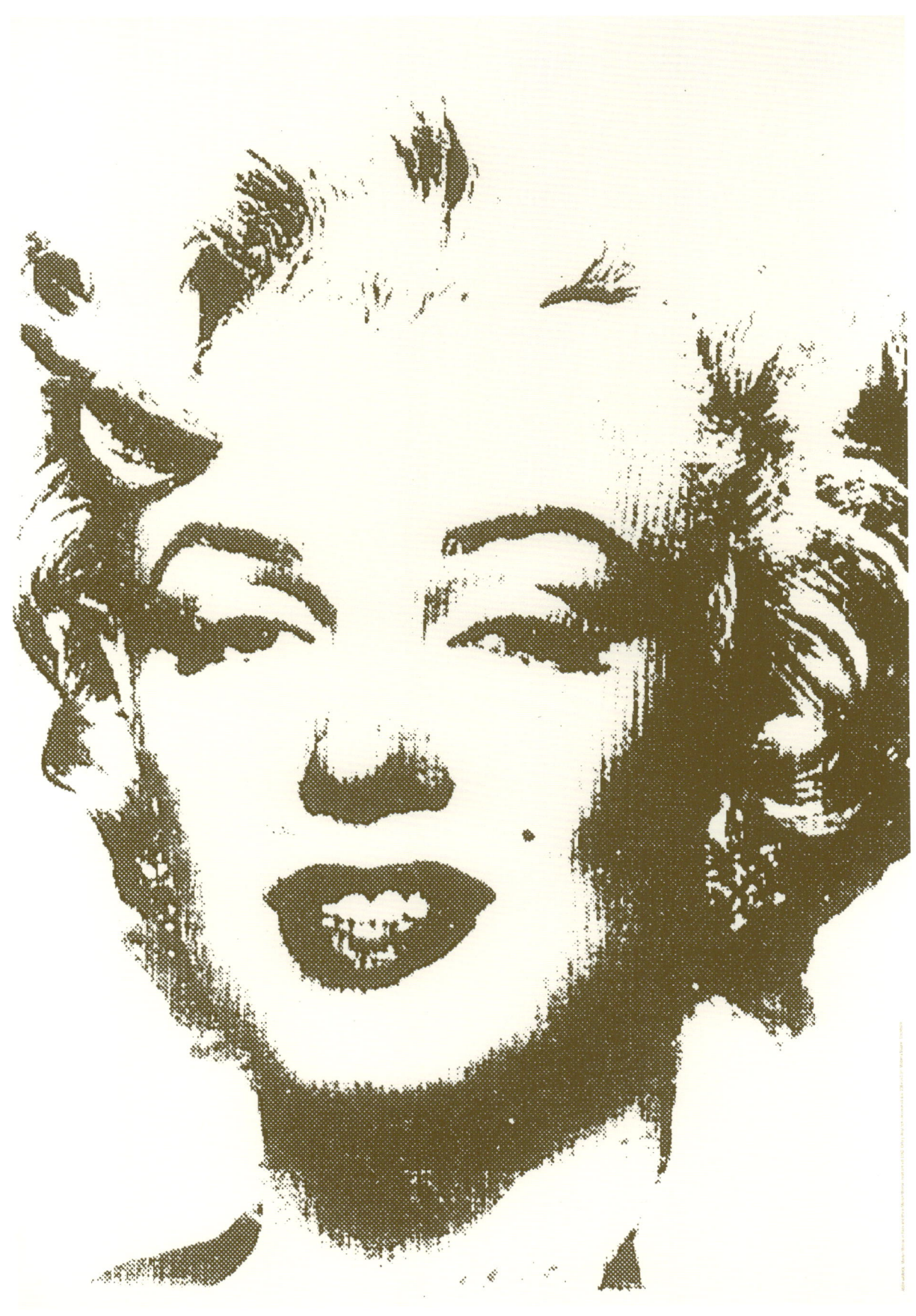

Plate LXVIII Two-color reversal screenprints: metallic gold ink on white paper; Number of prints: eleven; Caption: yes; Collection numbers: AWMM.1968.078, AWMM.1968.079, AWMM.1968.092 **(illustrated)**, AWMM.1968.149, AWMM.1968.200, AWMM.1968.255, AWMM.1968.261, AWMM.1968.267, AWMM.1968.276, AWMM.1968.277, AWMM.1968.302.

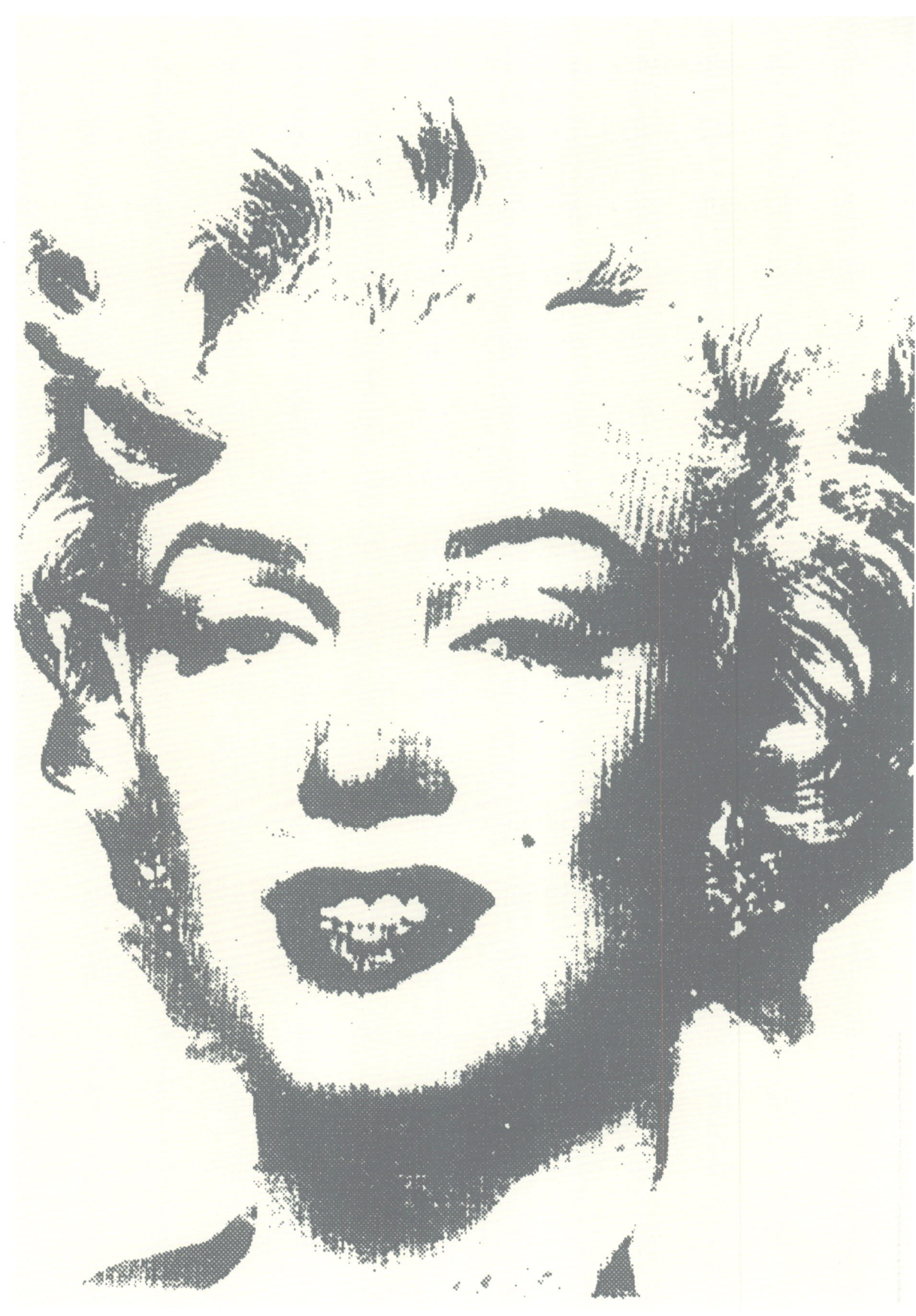

Plate LXIX   Two-color reversal screenprints: metallic silver ink on white paper; Number of prints: eight; Caption:
yes; Collection numbers: AWMM.1968.054, AWMM.1968.077, AWMM.1968.093, AWMM.1968.117
(illustrated), AWMM.1968.162, AWMM.1968.201, AWMM.1968.273, AWMM.1968.306.

Plate LXX Two-color reversal screenprints: white ink on white paper; Number of prints: seven;
Caption: no; Collection numbers: AWMM.1968.025, AWMM.1968.032, AWMM.1968.043,
AWMM.1968.074, AWMM.1968.075, AWMM.1968.076, AWMM.1968.242 **(illustrated)**.

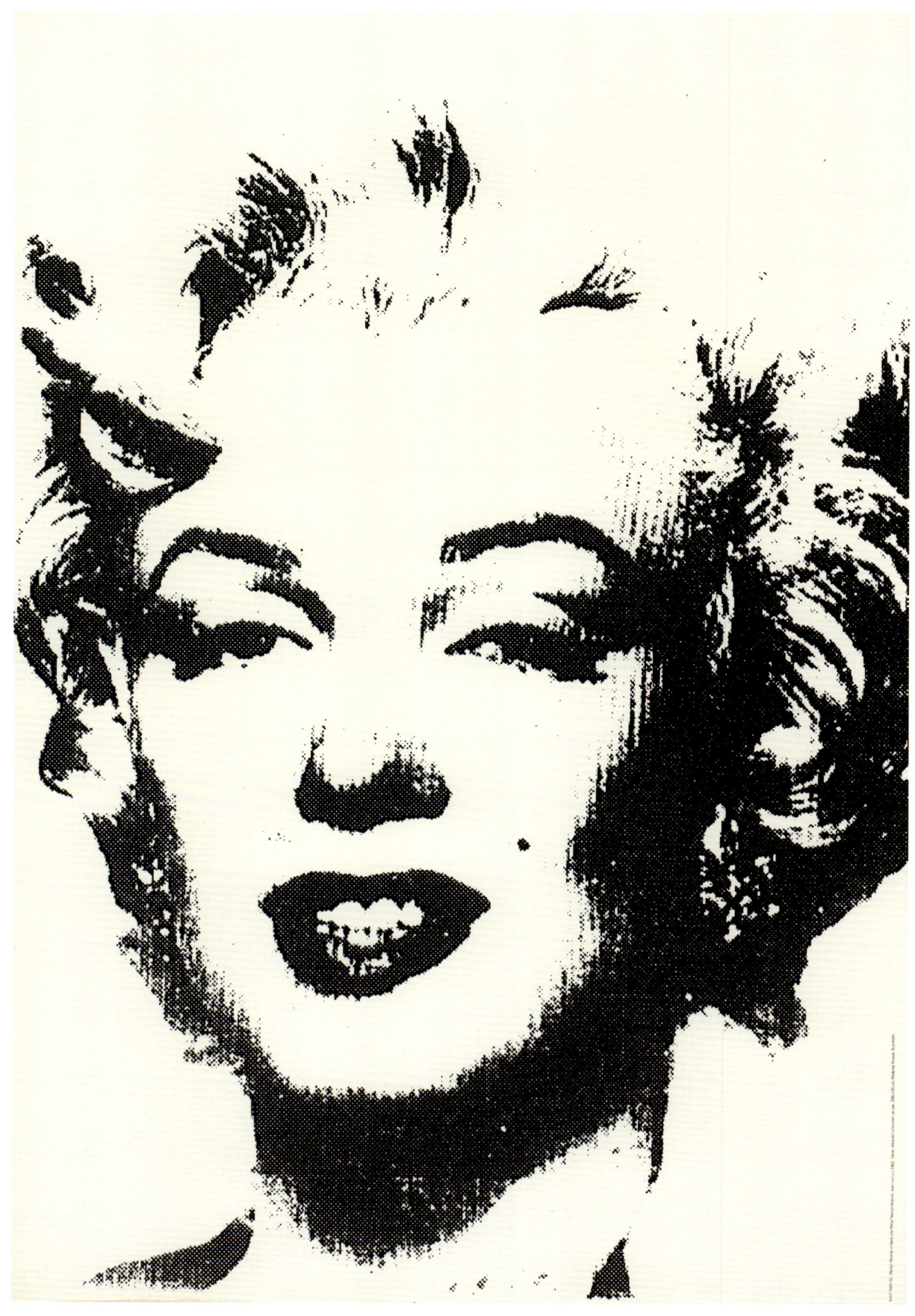

Plate LXXI   Two-color screenprint: black ink on white cardstock;
Number of prints: one; Caption: yes; Collection
number: AWMM.1968.260.

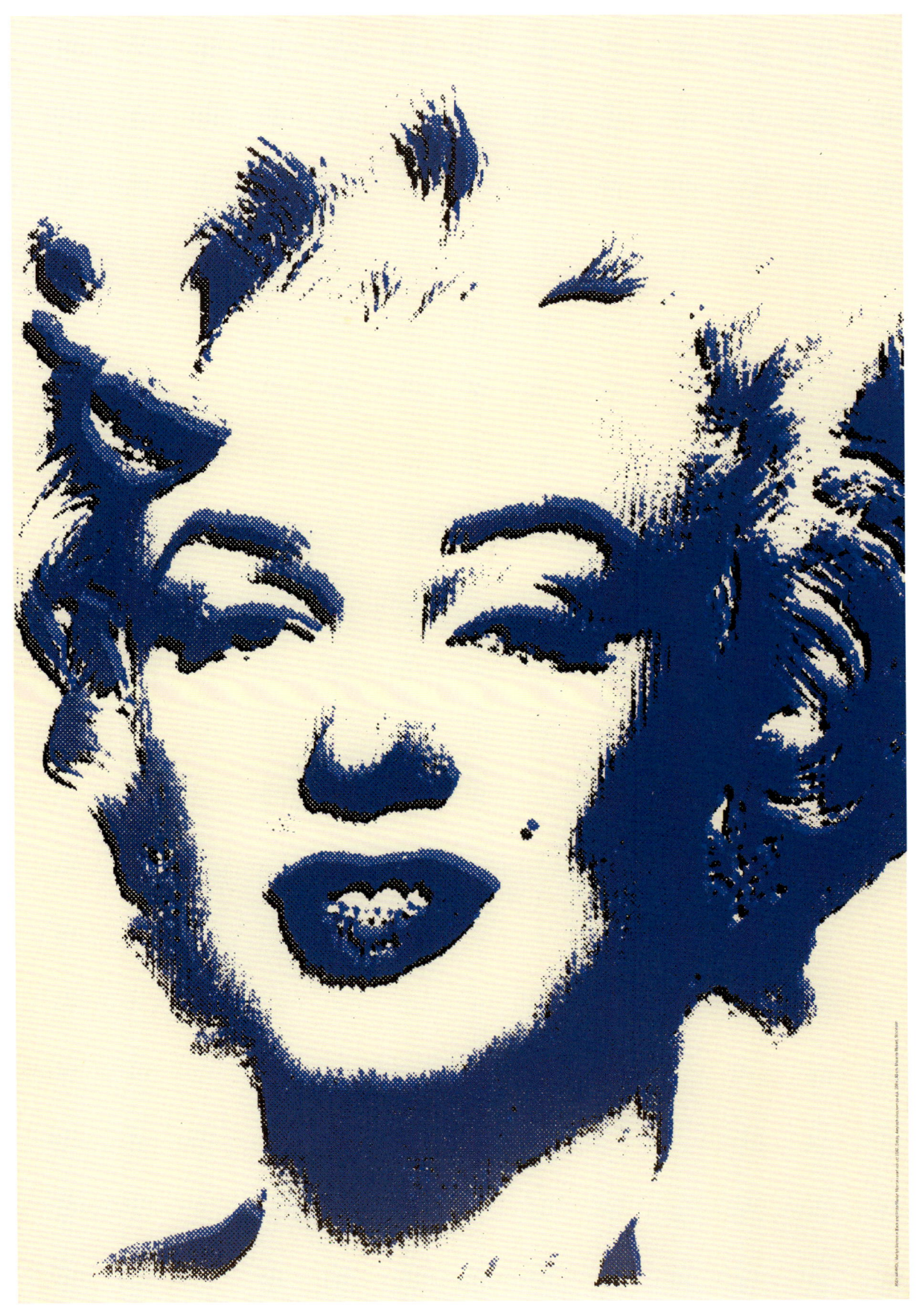

Plate LXXII   Three-color screenprint: black and blue inks on white
cardstock; Number of prints: one; Caption: yes; Collection
number: AWMM.1968.189.

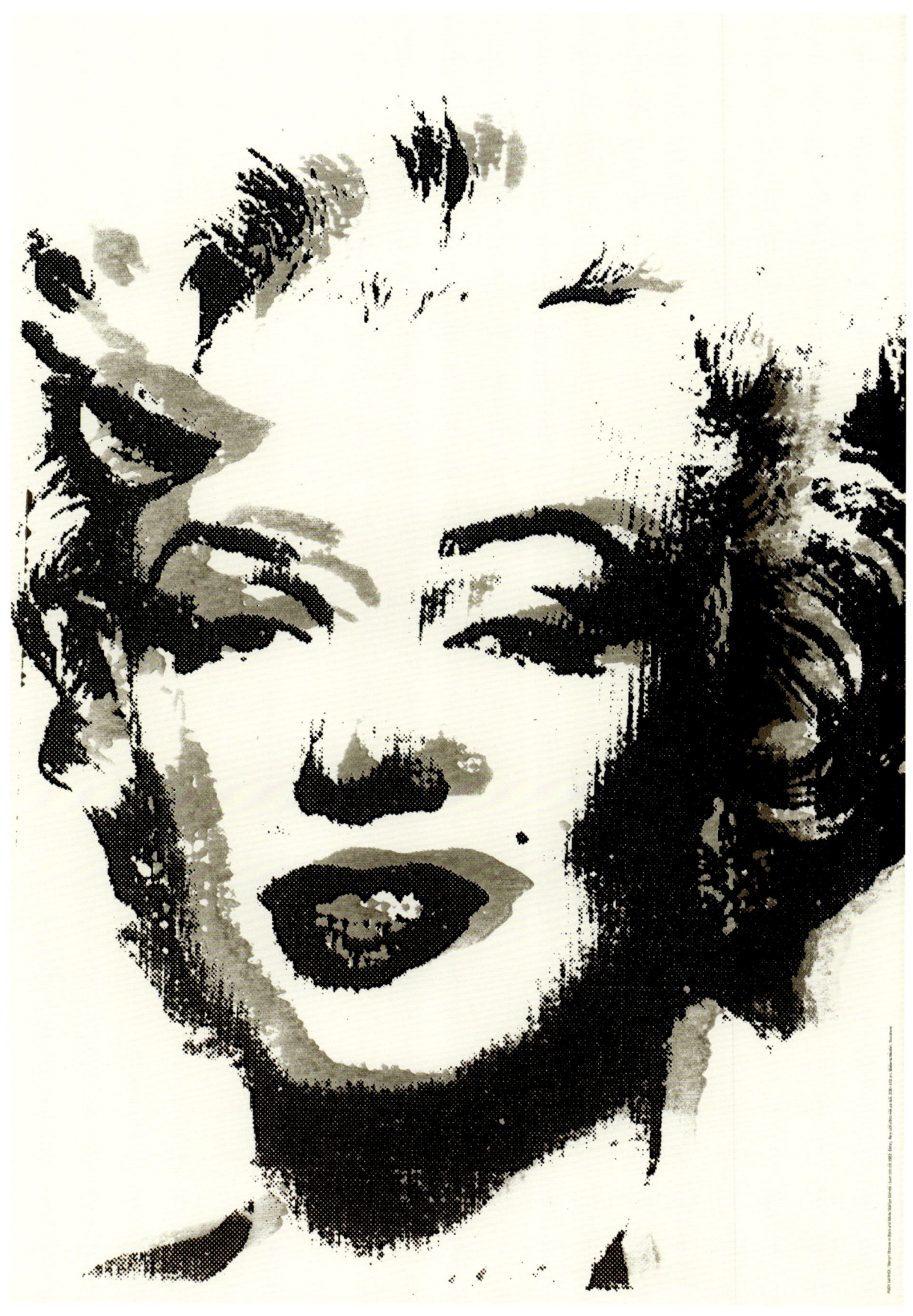

Plate LXXIII   Three-color screenprint: gray (or dilute black) and
black inks on white paper; Number of prints: one;
Caption: yes; Collection number: AWMM.1968.316.

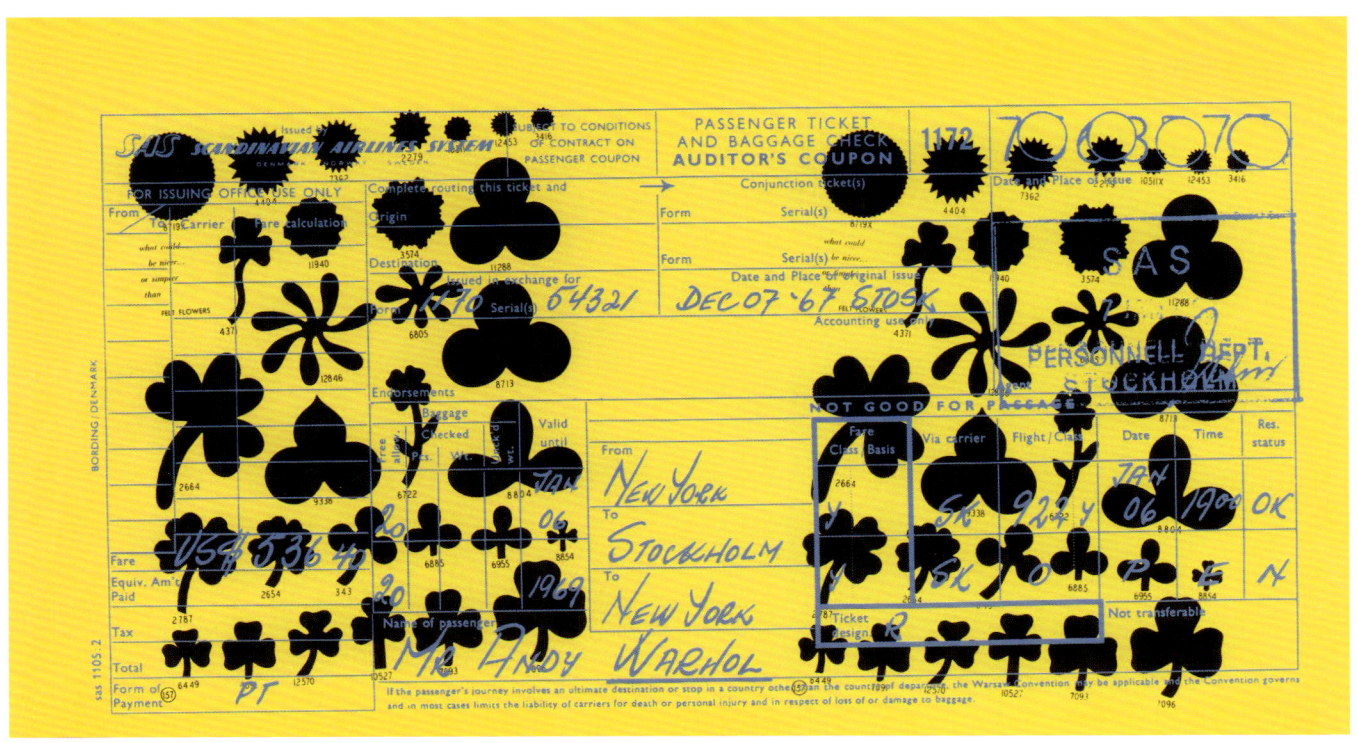

Plate LXXIV   Andy Warhol, *SAS Passenger Ticket*, 1968; Signed on the back;
26 ¾ × 48 ¾ in.; 31 ¼ × 52 × 1 ½ in. (framed); Collection
number: YY01.2019.2003.

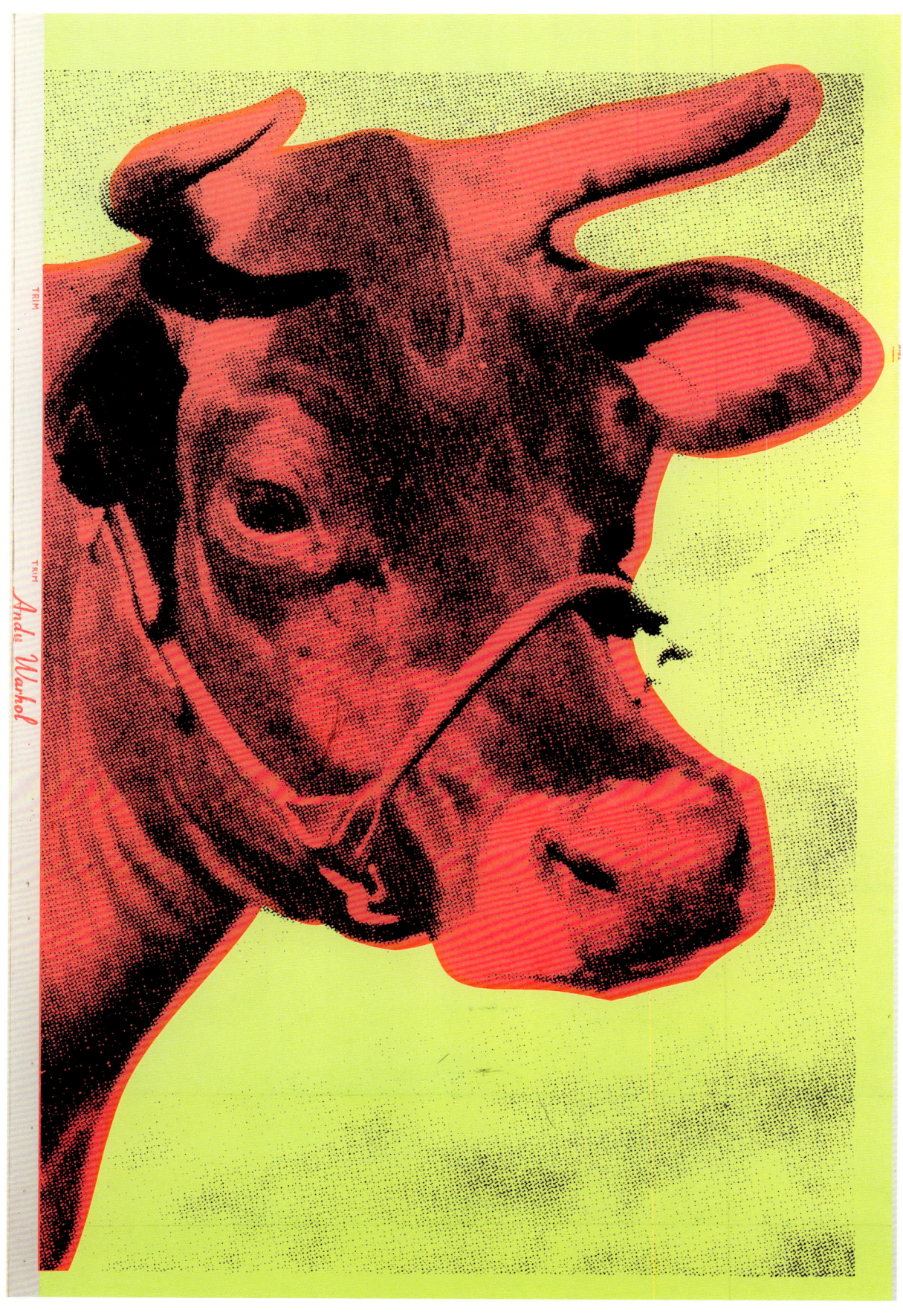

Plate LXXV   Wallpaper produced for Andy Warhol; Exhibition Moderna Museet ca. 1966 for
display on the façade; 46 × 30 in. (sight); 50 ½ × 34 × 1 ½ in. (framed); Ex collection
(and framed by) Olle Granath; Collection number: YY01.2021.002.

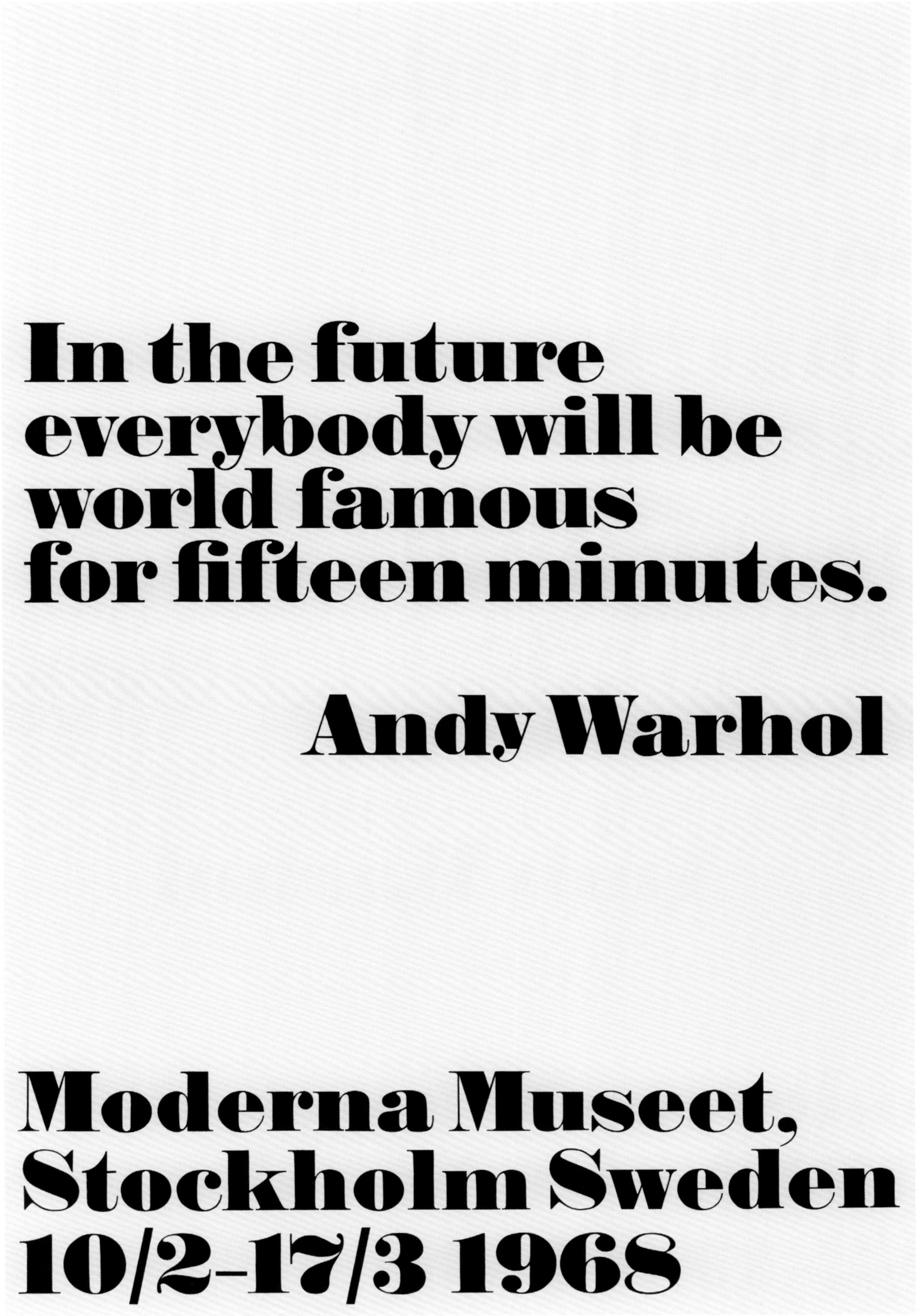

In the future everybody will be world famous for fifteen minutes.

Andy Warhol

Moderna Museet, Stockholm Sweden 10/2-17/3 1968

Plate LXXVI   White Paper Black Type; Number of prints: 3; Collection
numbers: AWTP.1968.001, AWTP.1968.002, AWTP.1968.015
(illustrated)*; NB 002 has pencil illegible signature.

"Do you think pop art is..."
"No."
"What?"
"No."
"Do you think pop art is..."
"No... No I don't."

Andy Warhol

Moderna Museet, Stockholm Sweden 10/2-17/3 1968

I like boring things...

Andy Warhol

Moderna Museet, Stockholm Sweden 10/2-17/3 1968

Plate LXXVIII   White Paper Black Type; Number of prints: 3; Collection
numbers: AWTP.1968.005, AWTP.1968.009, AWTP.1968.011
(illustrated).

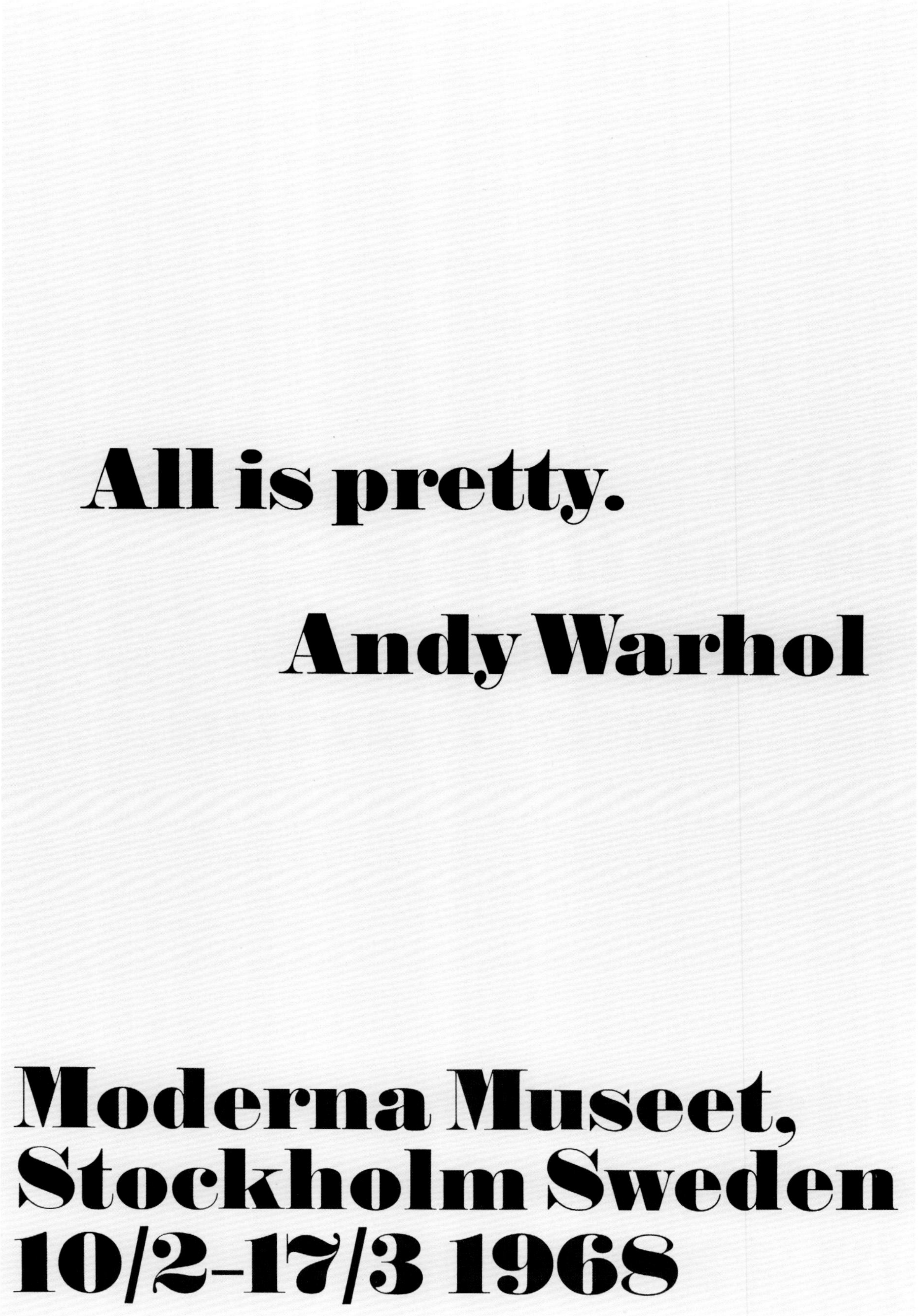

All is pretty.

Andy Warhol

Moderna Museet, Stockholm Sweden 10/2-17/3 1968

Plate LXXIX White Paper Black Type; Number of prints: 1; Collection number: AWTP.1968.003.

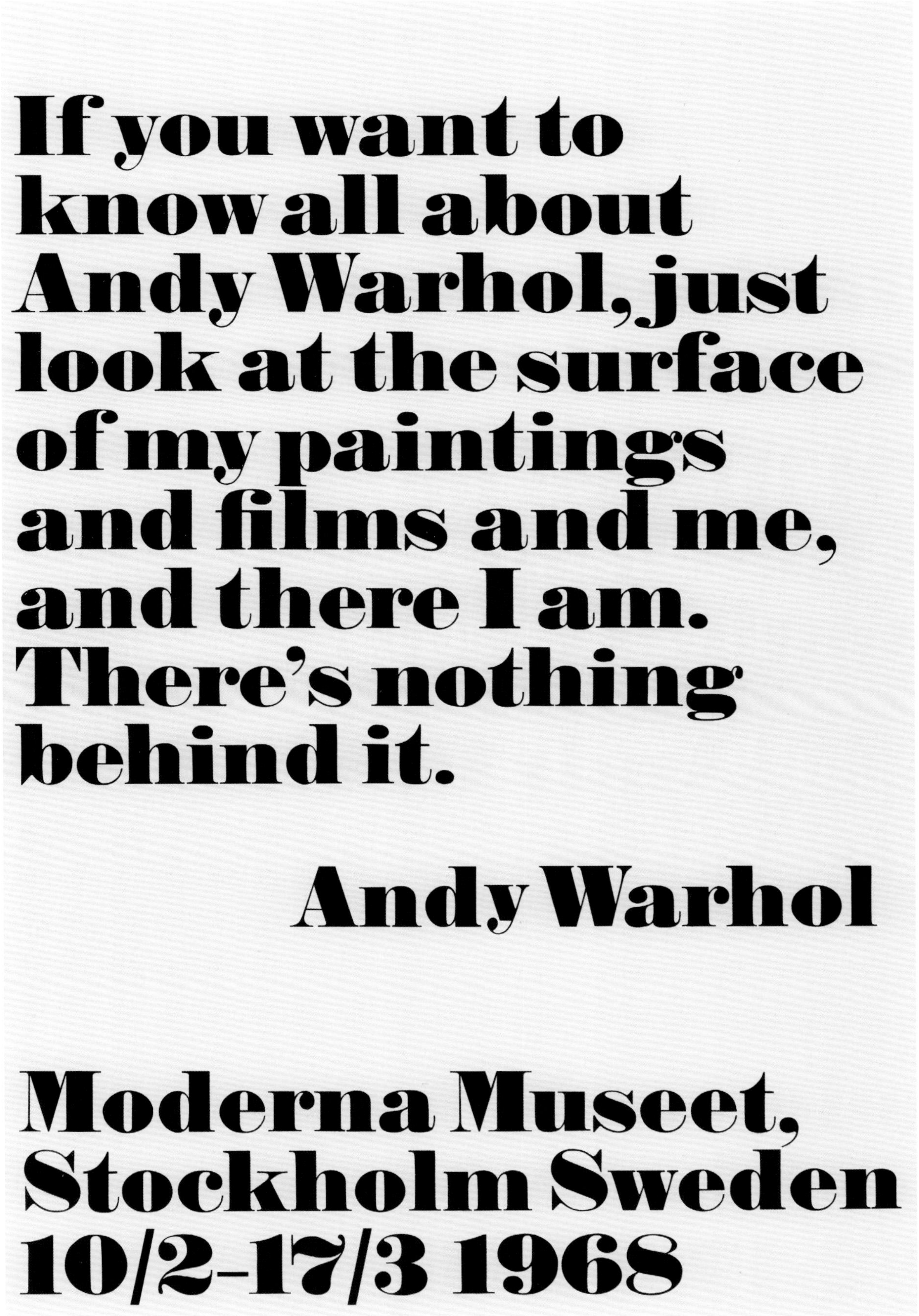

If you want to know all about Andy Warhol, just look at the surface of my paintings and films and me, and there I am. There's nothing behind it.

Andy Warhol

Moderna Museet, Stockholm Sweden 10/2-17/3 1968

Plate LXXX White Paper Black Type; Number of prints: 2; Collection number:
AWTP.1968.006, AWTP.1968.013 **(illustrated)**.

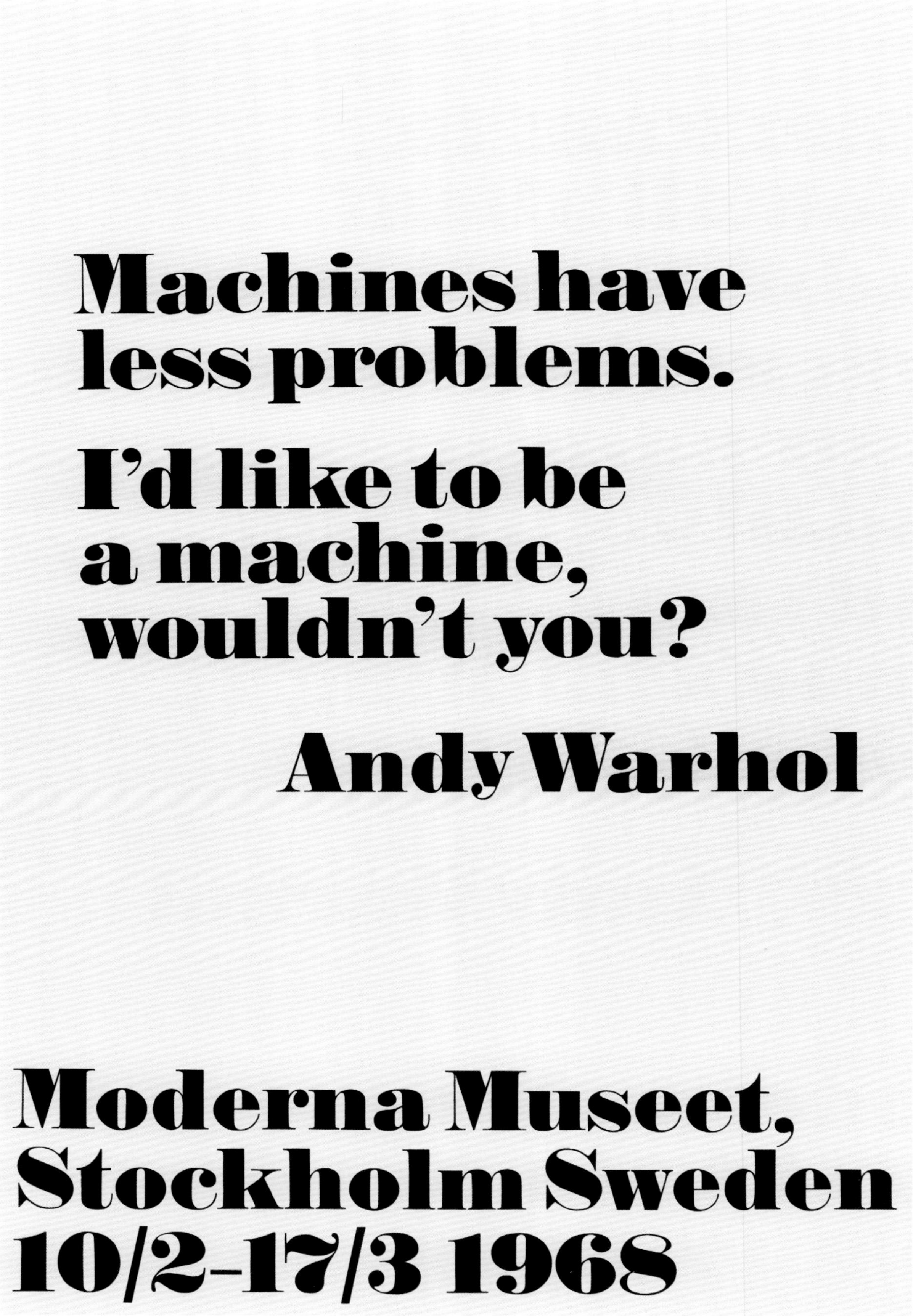

Machines have less problems.

I'd like to be a machine, wouldn't you?

Andy Warhol

Moderna Museet, Stockholm Sweden 10/2-17/3 1968

Plate LXXXI   White Paper Black Type; Number of prints: 2; Collection numbers: AWTP.1968.007, AWTP.1968.014 **(illustrated)**.

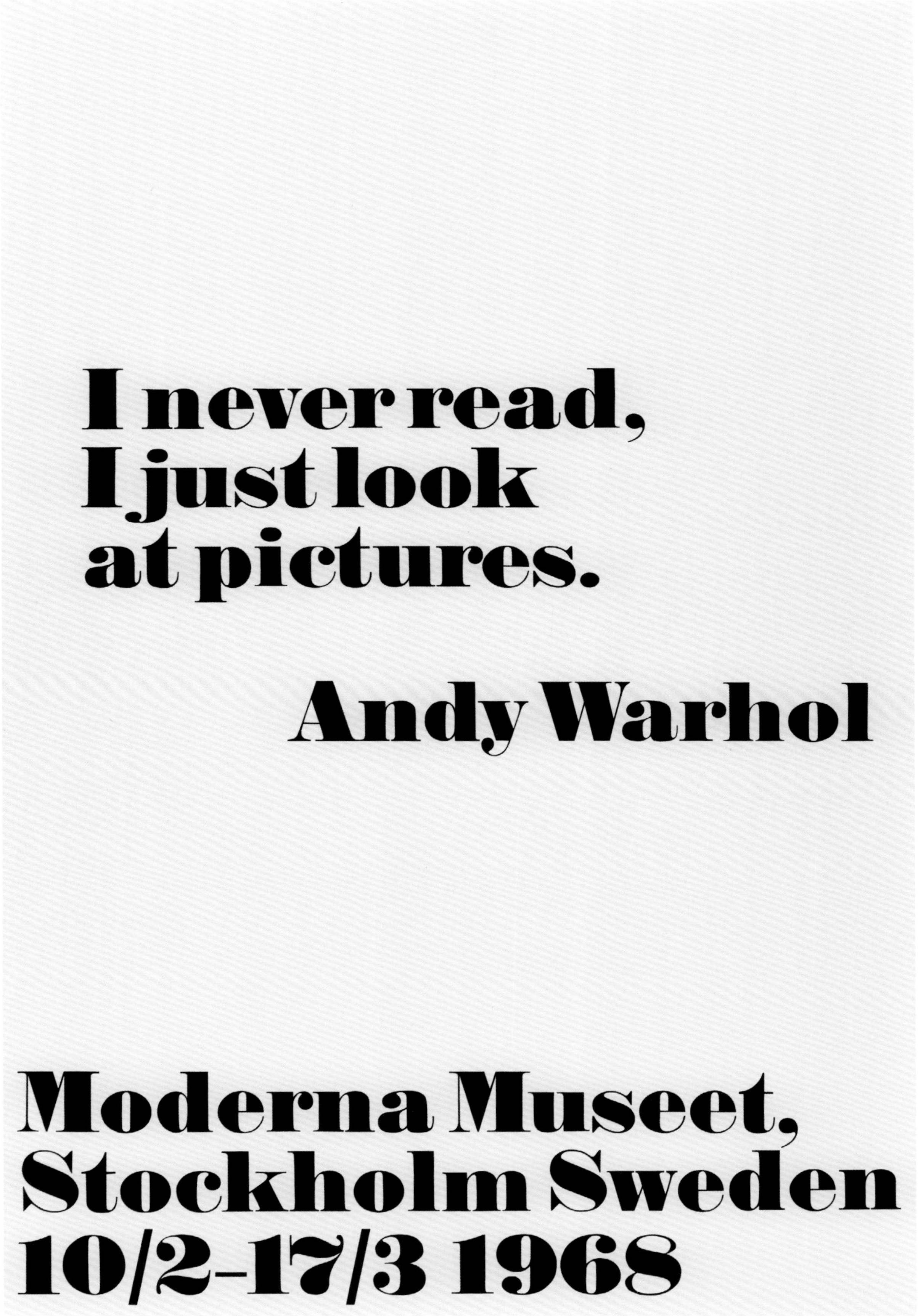

I never read, I just look at pictures.

Andy Warhol

Moderna Museet, Stockholm Sweden 10/2-17/3 1968

Plate LXXXII   White Paper Black Type; Number of prints: 1; Collection number: AWTP.1968.010.

Appendices

Appendix A
Acquisition History and Provenance of the McCoy *Marilyns*

PURCHASE DATE	QUANTITY	PREVIOUS OWNER	COLLECTION NUMBER
30-Nov-09	3	Swinge	AWMM.1968.001–003
4-Jan-10	1	Swinge	AWMM.1968.004
11-Feb-10	3	Swinge	AWMM.1968.005–007
13-Apr-11	1	Swinge	AWMM.1968.008
15-May-11	3	Swinge	AWMM.1968.009–011
6-Dec-11	2	Swinge	AWMM.1968.012–013
16-Dec-11	1	Swinge	AWMM.1968.014
9-Jan-12	1	Swinge	AWMM.1968.015
8-Jan-13	1	Garpenhus	AWMM.1968.016
31-Jan-13	25	Larsson	AWMM.1968.017–041
5-Apr-13	1	Garpenhus	AWMM.1968.042
5-Apr-13	1	Swinge	AWMM.1968.043
9-May-13	5	Garpenhus	AWMM.1968.044–048
11-Jul-13	6	Balcke	AWMM.1968.049–054
18-Sep-13	6	Arbman 1	AWMM.1968.055–060
27-Dec-13	30	Arbman/Reklamteknik	AWMM.1968.061–090
8-Jan-14	56	Arbman 2	AWMM.1968.091–146
14-Feb-14	1	Garpenhus	AWMM.1968.147
13-Mar-14	1	Garpenhus	AWMM.1968.148
28-Mar-14	1	Balcke	AWMM.1968.149
19-Jun-14	12	Larsson	AWMM.1968.150–161
27-Apr-15	47	Andersson 1	AWMM.1968.162–205; AWTP.1968.008–009
29-Jun-15	1	Garpenhus	AWMM.1968.206
11-Aug-16	59	Schultz 1	AWMM.1968.207–266
10-Oct-16	7	Schultz 1	AWTP.1968.001–007
11-Oct-16	14	Schultz 1	AWMM.1968.267–280
1-Dec-17	6	Arcana	AWTP.1968.010–015
25-Mar-17	11	Schultz 3	AWMM.1968.281–291
18-Jan-18	12	Schultz 2	AWMM.1968.292–303
2-Nov-18	1	Andersson 2	AWMM.1968.304
25-Mar-19	1	Stockholm	AWMM.1968.305
30-Oct-19	1	Freeman's	AWSAS.1968.001
13-Jan-20	1	London	AWMM.1968.306
28-Jul-20	6	London	AWMM.1968.307–312
13-Jan-21	5	Andersson 2	AWMM.1968.313–317
1-Mar-21	5	Andersson 3	AWMM.1968.318–322
5-Jan-22	1	Andersson 2	AWMM.1968.323

Figure A.1   McCoy purchases of 323 *Marilyn* screenprints from various between 2009 to 2022, sorted by date.

Arcana	Irving Blum Gallery (Los Angeles, CA, USA); Arcana: Books on the Arts (Culver City, CA, USA); Gregory McCoy (Moorestown, NJ, USA)
Andersson 1	Reklamteknik Screenprinting Company (Malmö, Sweden); Bengt Andersson (Malmö, Sweden); Bengtsson Fine Art (Lanskrona, Sweden); Gregory McCoy (Moorestown, NJ, USA)[1]
Andersson 2	Bengt Andersson (see footnote); Heir of Bengt Andersson, by descent; Bengtsson Fine Art (Lanskrona, Sweden); Gregory McCoy (Moorestown, NJ, USA)
Andersson 3	Bengt Andersson (see footnote); Heir of Bengt Andersson, by descent; Bengtsson Fine Art (Lanskrona, Sweden); Gregory McCoy (Moorestown, NJ, USA)
Arbman 1	Private Seller, Former Partner, Arbman Advertising Agency (Malmö, Sweden); Bengtsson Fine Art (Lanskrona, Sweden); Gregory McCoy (Moorestown, NJ, USA)
Arbman 2	Private Seller, Widow of a Former Partner, Arbman Advertising Agency (Malmö, Sweden) or Reklamteknik Screenprinting Company (Malmö, Sweden); Bengtsson Fine Art (Lanskrona, Sweden); Gregory McCoy (Moorestown, NJ, USA)
Arbman/Reklamteknik	Group of Five Private Sellers, Former Partners or Employees of the Arbman Advertising Agency (Malmö, Sweden) or Reklamteknik Screenprinting Company (Malmö, Sweden); McCoy (Moorestown, NJ, USA)
Balcke	Nils Balcke, Partner, Arbman Advertising Agency (Malmö, Sweden); Bengtsson Fine Art (Lanskrona, Sweden); Gregory McCoy (Moorestown, NJ, USA)
Freeman's	The Robert J. Morrison Collection (Philadelphia, PA); Freeman's (Philadelphia, PA); Gregory McCoy (Moorestown, NJ, USA)
Garpenhus	Private Seller; Jan Garpenhus, Director, Garpenhus, Konst & Auktion (Malmö, Sweden); Bengtsson Fine Art (Lanskrona, Sweden); Gregory McCoy (Moorestown, NJ, USA)
Larsson	Pontus Hultén, Director of the Moderna Museet; Gift in lieu of payment to a then employee; Georg Larsson, by descent (Lanskrona, Sweden); Bengtsson Fine Art (Lanskrona, Sweden); Gregory McCoy (Moorestown, NJ, USA)
London	Private Seller (London, UK); Bengtsson Fine Art (Lanskrona, Sweden); Gregory McCoy (Moorestown, NJ, USA)
Stockholm	Private Seller, Spouse of a Former Employee of the Moderna Museet (Stockholm, Sweden); Bengtsson Fine Art (Lanskrona, Sweden); Gregory McCoy (Moorestown, NJ, USA)
Schultz 1	Eva Schultz, Former Assistant to Arne Wahlqvist, Founder of Reklamteknik Screenprinting Company (Malmö, Sweden); Bengtsson Fine Art (Lanskrona, Sweden); Gregory McCoy (Moorestown, NJ, USA)
Schultz 2	Eva Schultz; Private Seller, family of Eva Schultz, by gift of Schultz; Bengtsson Fine Art (Lanskrona, Sweden); Gregory McCoy (Moorestown, NJ, USA)
Schultz 3	Eva Schultz; Friends and Family of Eva Schultz, by gift of Schultz; Bengtsson Fine Art (Lanskrona, Sweden); Gregory McCoy (Moorestown, NJ, USA)
Swinge	John Melin, Graphic Designer and Partner, Arbman Advertising Agency (Malmö, Sweden); Mattias Swinge, Representative, Estate of John Melin; Bengtsson Fine Art (Lanskrona, Sweden); Gregory McCoy (Moorestown, NJ, USA)

Figure A.2 Key to owners.

1. Reklamteknik was founded by Arne Wahlqvist in 1953. Bengt Andersson joined the company as a printer in 1973. In 1980, Wahlqvist retired, and Andersson purchased the company and assumed its leadership. In 1991, Reklamteknik merged with another printing company in Malmö and the name changed to (2)Screen Tryck AB. In 2001, leadership of the company was assumed by Andersson's son, Mikael Lönnströn, and the company now operates as (3)Screen Tryck AB (https://www.3screen.nu/). Bengt Andersson remained owner and on staff of the company until his death in 2018. The prints acquired through Bengt Andersson were found among skids of printed material printed when Reklamteknik was owned and operated by Arne Wahlqvist. Title passed to Andersson through the purchase of the company.

Andy Warhol Art Authentication Board, Inc.

Date: July 25, 2011

Description of Work: *Marilyn Monroe*
Seven reproductions on paper,
39 ¼ x 27 ½ inches (each)

The Andy Warhol Art Authentication Board, Inc. (the "Authentication Board") has caused the above-described works to be examined by its representatives. It is the opinion of the Authentication Board that said works are posters with the following printed information: "Andy Warhol Marilyn Monroe in Black and White Marilyn Monroe i svart och vitt 1962 Detalj. Akryl och silkscreen pä duk 208 x 140 cm Moderna Museet, Stockholm". The Board has not been able to determine whether said posters were produced by the Moderna Museet, Stockholm.

THE FOREGOING IS MERELY AN OPINION BASED UPON AN INSPECTION OF THE WORK AND CIRCUMSTANCES KNOWN TO THE AUTHENTICATION BOARD AT THIS TIME, AND IS NOT A WARRANTY OF ANY KIND. NEITHER THE AUTHENTICATION BOARD, THE ANDY WARHOL FOUNDATION FOR THE VISUAL ARTS, INC., THE ESTATE OF ANDY WARHOL, NOR ANY OF THEIR RESPECTIVE MEMBERS, OFFICERS, DIRECTORS, EMPLOYEES, AGENTS OR REPRESENTATIVES, OR OTHERS ACTING FOR ANY OF THEM, OR THEIR SUCCESSORS, SHALL HAVE ANY LIABILITY WHATSOEVER TO ANYONE BY REASON OF THE FOREGOING OPINION.

The foregoing opinion may change by reason of circumstances arising or discovered by the Authentication Board after the date hereof, or by reason of new scholarship or additional information coming to its attention. The Authentication Board will endeavor to respond to inquiries by individuals or entities having, in the Authentication Board's absolute discretion, sufficient basis for making inquiries as to whether such a change has occurred. This letter is subject to the terms and conditions of the letter agreement pursuant to which it has been issued.

ANDY WARHOL ART
AUTHENTICATION BOARD, INC.

By: _____
Authorized Representative

525 West 20 Street, 7th floor   Gary Garrels
New York NY 10011   Judith Goldman
Telephone: 212.727.1735   Christoph Heinrich
Facsimile: 212.242.2836   Sally King-Nero
   Neil Printz

Figure A.3   Andy Warhol Authentication Board Letter, 2011.

Andy Warhol Art Authentication Board, Inc.

Date: April 30, 2012

Description of Work: *Marilyn Monroe*
Four posters,
39 ¼ x 27 ½ inches (each)

The Andy Warhol Art Authentication Board, Inc. (the "Authentication Board") has caused the above-described works to be examined by its representatives. It is the opinion of the Authentication Board that said works are posters, three of which have the following printed information: "Andy Warhol Marilyn Monroe in Black and White Marilyn Monroe i svart och vitt 1962 Detalj. Akryl och silkscreen pä duk 208 x 140 cm Moderna Museet, Stockholm". The fourth poster does not have any printed information. Said works may or may not have been produced by the Moderna Museet, Stockholm.

THE FOREGOING IS MERELY AN OPINION BASED UPON AN INSPECTION OF THE WORK AND CIRCUMSTANCES KNOWN TO THE AUTHENTICATION BOARD AT THIS TIME, AND IS NOT A WARRANTY OF ANY KIND. NEITHER THE AUTHENTICATION BOARD, THE ANDY WARHOL FOUNDATION FOR THE VISUAL ARTS, INC., THE ESTATE OF ANDY WARHOL, NOR ANY OF THEIR RESPECTIVE MEMBERS, OFFICERS, DIRECTORS, EMPLOYEES, AGENTS OR REPRESENTATIVES, OR OTHERS ACTING FOR ANY OF THEM, OR THEIR SUCCESSORS, SHALL HAVE ANY LIABILITY WHATSOEVER TO ANYONE BY REASON OF THE FOREGOING OPINION.

The foregoing opinion may change by reason of circumstances arising or discovered by the Authentication Board after the date hereof, or by reason of new scholarship or additional information coming to its attention. The Authentication Board will endeavor to respond to inquiries by individuals or entities having, in the Authentication Board's absolute discretion, sufficient basis for making inquiries as to whether such a change has occurred. This letter is subject to the terms and conditions of the letter agreement pursuant to which it has been issued.

ANDY WARHOL ART
AUTHENTICATION BOARD, INC.

By: _____
Authorized Representative

525 West 20 Street, 7th floor   Gary Garrels
New York NY 10011   Judith Goldman
Telephone: 212.727.1735   Christoph Heinrich
Facsimile: 212.242.2836   Sally King-Nero
                        Neil Printz

Figure A.4   Andy Warhol Authentication Board Letter, 2012.

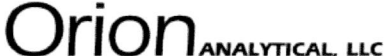

A Materials Analysis and Consulting Firm

Post Office Box 550, Williamstown, MA 01267 USA   (413)458-0233   info@orionanalytical.com   www.orionanalytical.com

March 27, 2012

Mr. Gregory McCoy

Re: Orion Project No. 1760

Dear Mr. McCoy,

This report describes examination and analysis of colored inks on three prints you described as "Andy Warhol Marilyn Monroe" (each 39 1/4 x 27 1/2 inches). You asked Orion to examine the inks to look for materials to help you date the prints.

Laboratory analyses

Orion examined three inks (fluorescent orange, orange, and green) using Fourier transform infrared microspectroscopy (FTIR) and dispersive confocal Raman microspectroscopy (Raman).

Following are the materials detected in resulting FTIR and Raman spectra (additional materials could be present but not detectable due to their chemical composition, abundance, or both).

Ink color	Detected materials
Fluorescent orange ink	Kaolin. FTIR spectra showed features that point to toluene-sulfonamide type resin, possibly with melamine formaldehyde. The fluorescent pigment was not identified.
Orange ink	Kaolin, titanium dioxide, Pigment Orange 34, cellulosic ether. Possible calcite.
Green ink	Kaolin and Pigment Green 7. FTIR spectra showed features that point to toluene-sulfonamide type resin, possibly with melamine formaldehyde.

Figure A.5   Orion Analytical LCC, Ink Analysis Report, 2012.

The fluorescent orange pigment was not identified. Generally speaking, manufacturers use very low levels of fluorescent pigments.

According to the literature and experts Orion consulted, the generic pigments and other materials detected in three inks were available as early as the 1960s (and also in subsequent decades, including the 1980s).

If you would like Orion to examine other prints in the set for possible anachronistic materials to help you date the prints, then Orion would recommend prints that contain red or yellow inks.

Please do not hesitate to contact me if you have questions about this report.

Very truly yours,

James Martin

Orion Analytical, LLC
By James Martin

Williamstown Art Conservation Center, Inc.
227 South Street, Williamstown, MA 01267
413-458-5741 tel • 413-458-2314 fax

Analytical Services Report

Date: 3/24/17
By: C. Puza

Purpose of Analysis:

Examine the red and yellow colored inks on four screenprints described as "Andy Warhol Marilyn Monroe" to look for materials that may be able to elucidate the date of manufacture.

Each print is 39 ¼" x 27 ½" inches and are designated as the following:
- AWMM.1968.109, yellow background, silver image
- AWMM.1968.119, yellow background, grey image
- AWMM.1968.019, red background, gold image
- AWMM.1968.065, red background, blue image

Analysis Performed:

- FT-IR
- Dispersive confocal Raman microspectroscopy (Raman)

Results:

The following materials were detected in the resulting FT-IR and Raman spectra. Additional materials could be present but are not detectable due to their chemical composition, relative abundance, or both.

Peaks for **kaolin**, **titanium dioxide**, **calcium carbonate,** and **cellulose** were detected in all samples. These materials likely represent the paper substrate and substances used in the calendaring process, and are consistent with those found in the previous analytical report performed in 2012 by Orion Analytical.

Both red prints have the same red pigment present: **Pigment Orange 34**, a disazopyrazolone pigment.

Both yellow prints also have the same pigment present: **Pigment Yellow 17**, a diarylide pigment.

Figure A.6   Williamstown Art Conservation Center, Inc., Paper Analysis Report, 2017.

Both diarylides and disazopyralones were patented in 1910 and 1911 but were not commercialized until the late 1930's and 1940's. According to Herbst and Hunger [Industrial Organic Pigments, 3rd ed.] "it was not until the early 1950s that PO34 gained recognition as a commercial product". According to an expert at the National Gallery of Art, both of these pigments are still being manufactured at the present time for use in printing inks and other applications. Therefore, the presence of these two pigments are not diagnostic for any particular time period between 1950 and the present.

Diketopyrollo pyrrole pigments, a class of red and yellow pigments also used in printing inks, which were first manufactured in the mid-1980's, were not detected.

Appendix I: Raman Spectra

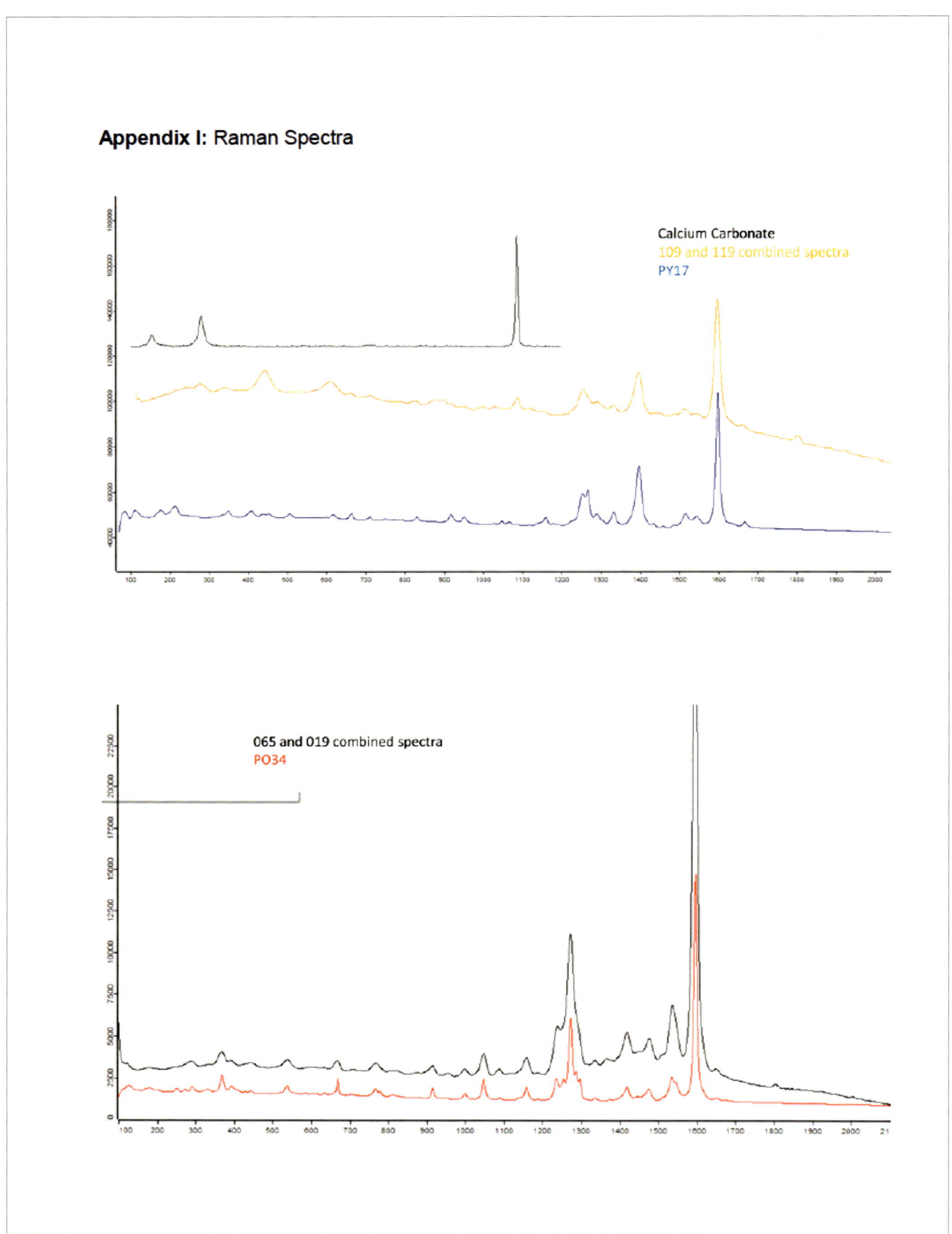

Figure A.7   Results of Raman Spectra Graph, Williamstown Art Conservation Center, 2017.

Appendix B
Stories of a Collector
Gregory McCoy

I would like to take this occasion to share with you some of the extraordinary experiences I have had as a collector over the past thirty years. Included will be some of my favorite anecdotes and descriptions of what was going through my mind as I was building my collection of Andy Warhol's art and signed ephemera.

My first major purchase was an Andy Warhol *Double Mona Lisa* print in the beginning of 1993. Although I had made a couple of smaller purchases before this, the acquisition of this *Double Mona Lisa* was in many ways the beginning of my forays into the art world. This unpublished, black and white print was by far the largest and most expensive piece I had acquired up until this point. It measured 35 × 45 inches. Initially, I had the *Double Mona Lisa* framed in a big, ornate gold frame. Then, after rethinking it, a couple years later I had it reframed in a contemporary straight-edged maple frame. I hung it in my parents' home for about ten years. My mother once told me that Mona Lisa's eyes followed her around as she vacuumed the floor *(Fig. B.1)*.

Then one day in say 2004 or 2005, I googled the title of the print and was shocked to find out that one almost exactly like mine had sold for six figures. I remember sitting in front of my computer and not reading the price that the piece had achieved at auction, but instead just counting the number of digits. One, two, three, four, five, six digits! When I started to collect, back in the 1990s, three artists were equally popular with young collectors: Peter Max, LeRoy Neiman, and Andy Warhol. For some reason, Andy's artwork just stood out to me.

At lunch time, I used to walk from gallery to gallery in SoHo visiting art dealers like Leo Castelli, Ivan Karp, and many of the new art dealers in the neighborhood. As time went on, I set my sights on purchasing a Warhol

Dollar Sign painting *(Fig. 3.2)*. I knew that the only way I was going to be able to do that was by selling something. At the time, *The Da Vinci Code* with the Mona Lisa on the front cover was all the rage. When I got on the subway, you could barely see anyone's head; it seemed like almost everyone was holding up a copy of the book in front of their faces. Then a few years later when they announced they were going to make a movie based on the book, I decided it might be a good time to sell the print.

I did what I considered, given my background in the field of advertising, to be almost like a product placement. I called one of the major auction houses and they offered to put it in an evening sale if I was willing to sell the print in the Middle East. The *Double Mona Lisa* achieved $192,000—about fifty times what I paid for it after deducting the auction house's commission. At that time, you could buy a house for that amount of money, but instead I remained in my one-bedroom apartment and reached out to a collector I had read about who owned three small paintings by Andy Warhol.

It was my dream to purchase one of them, a red *Dollar Sign (Fig. 3.2)*. Along with the *Dollar Sign*, the collector also owned a yellow *Hamburger* painting and a gold *Be Somebody with a Body* painting. Thinking that I wouldn't have enough money to purchase all three of these original paintings, I decided to make an offer on only the *Dollar Sign*. When I met with the owner, they expressed an interest in keeping the paintings together and made me an offer that I couldn't refuse. I am proud to say that all three paintings remain together in my collection today.

In 2011, I appeared on the TV show *Buried Treasure*, starring the celebrity antique appraiser twins, Leslie and

Leigh Keno, popularly known as the Keno brothers. Like the exhibition at the University of Pennsylvania, I still can't believe I was given the opportunity to do it! I remember driving up to the taping of the show and realizing at one point that I wasn't going to get home in time to watch *Antiques Roadshow* on PBS that evening and then I said to myself, "You idiot, you are going to meet the *Antiques Roadshow* hosts!" When I got to the set, the Keno brothers said, "You're the Warhol Guy." That made me laugh. It made me think of the Nantucket Nectars "Juice Guys." Suddenly, I realized that I had some "juice" too. The Keno brothers treated me like gold, or, better yet, like a Warhol! I say that because the last question they asked me was something like, "What do you think is the future of the Warhol market?" I remember thinking of something that Merv Griffin once said when he was interviewing Zsa Zsa Gabor on his daily talk show: "If you are not sure what to say, don't say anything. People won't notice the silence, but they will notice if you say something stupid."

The first thing that came to my mind to say was, "Andy Warhol's artwork has a strong trajectory." Then I thought to myself, "That will not sound right coming from me. I had better leave the 'auction speak' for the auction house experts." Next I thought of something I heard on the radio driving into the studio that day. A financial advisor said something about gold being a non-traditional asset. So, I told the Keno brothers that Warhol's art was going to become a non-traditional asset, like gold. They nodded in agreement with me. In the clip that was chosen for use on the show, the Keno brothers asked me how much I had paid for a big pad of drawing paper from the 1960s with a Campbell's Soup can reproduced on the cover that Andy had signed. I told the Keno brothers that I had paid $299 for it on eBay. As soon as they heard that, one of them yelled out something like, "Stop the filming, this is the introduction to the show!" Then one of the Keno brothers asked me the same question again, "Gregory, how much did you pay for the Andy Warhol Soup Can?" I again said, "$299 on eBay." The two of them then quickly walked over to me and shook my hand and patted me on the back. If you watch the show online, you will see me standing in front of the two Keno brothers who are holding the signed soup can, and one of them saying, "This is a classic!" *(Fig. B.2)*.

News of my collection began to circulate, and I was asked to share it with a wider audience. My first

exhibition took place in my hometown at the Moorestown Community House in 2006. Moorestown, New Jersey, had just been designated "America's Best Place to Live" by *Money* magazine, so I titled the exhibition "Moorestown's 15 Minutes of Fame." The three paintings that I mentioned earlier had not yet been framed, so my sister and a friend of hers stood in front of them to make sure that no one knocked them off their easels.

My next exhibition took place at the Arts Council of Princeton in 2009. That was the first time I showed my pieces of signed ephemera. The Princeton University Art Museum was kind enough to loan the Arts Council some of their vitrines. Consequently, my collection was secure, and my sister and her friend didn't have to stand guard. They could instead enjoy opening night and eat one of the dollar-sign-shaped cookies served that evening.

In 2011, The Lawrenceville School, which is located down the road from Princeton, offered to do an exhibition focused on the story of how I built my collection. The title of it was *Andy Warhol: Property from the Collection of Gregory McCoy*. Wanting something unique for the front of the invitation, I bought a signed dinner roll to appear on the front of it. The day I delivered the dinner roll to the gallery, the assistant to the curator met me at the front door and commented about how small the dinner roll was. She said something like, "I thought it was going to be more like a Portuguese roll" *(Fig. 3.6)*. Honestly, I didn't even know what a Portuguese roll was.

As I walked towards the main gallery, I noticed a sign that read, "No Food or Drink in the Gallery." I respectfully asked if I could bring the dinner roll into the gallery, and the curator said with a big smile on her face, "Yes, Gregory, you can bring that roll into the gallery." The signed Warhol roll has been a godsend. Up until now, it has been the piece in my collection that I have been best known for owning. In an interview I did for that exhibition, I made the comment that "Sometimes I find the art and sometimes it finds me." The *Marilyns* in this exhibition and catalogue are another example of something that I think found me, every bit as much as I found them.

My next exhibition took place at the new Moorestown Public Library in 2014. The title of that exhibition was

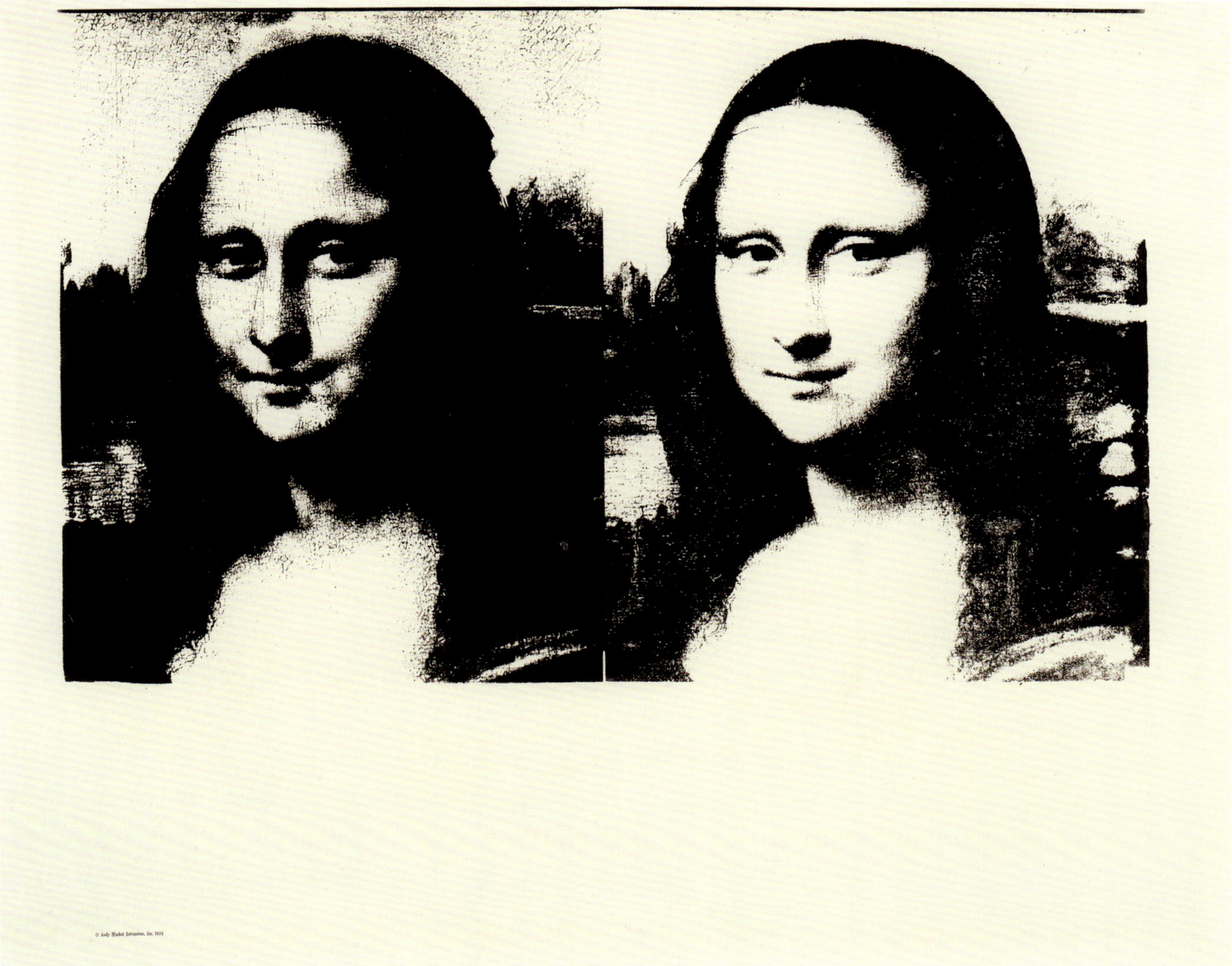

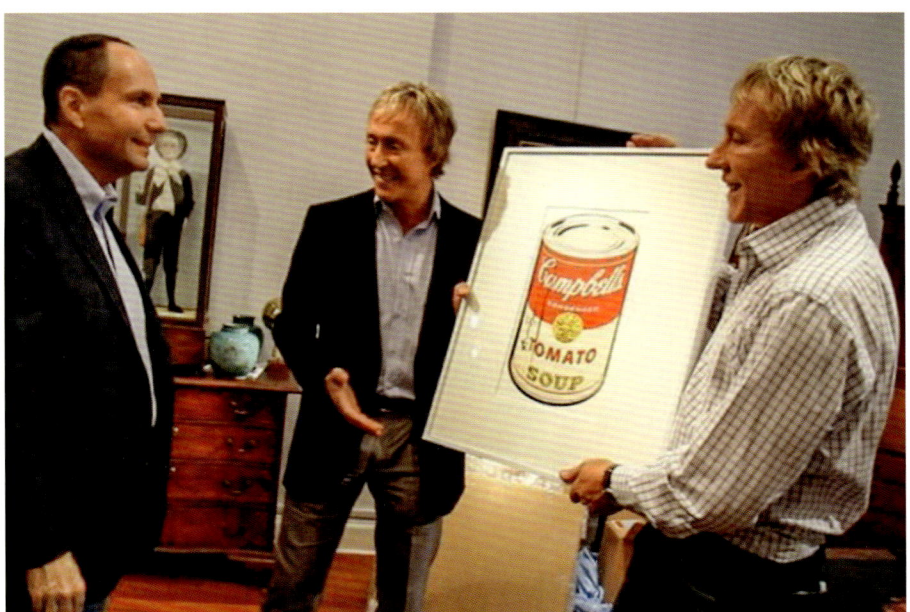

Figure B.1   Andy Warhol, *Double Mona Lisa*, 1978, screenprint, 34 ¼ x 45 ⅜ in.
Image used with permission.

Figure B.2   Gregory McCoy on the set of *Buried Treasures* (2011). Gregory
McCoy on the left, Leslie Keno in the middle, Leigh Keno on the right.

Warhol, Andy, in keeping with how an author's name appears on library catalogue cards. The special guest at the opening was James Warhola, Andy's nephew and acclaimed children's book illustrator. James was kind enough to do a book signing on the afternoon of the opening. He quickly drew either one of his uncle's cats or soup cans in each of the books. The line to get one of the books was so long that the director of the library had to keep the library open for an extra hour and a half. While people waited in line, they were served dollar-sign-shaped pretzels, but without the usual serving of mustard on the side. I did not want to risk getting any on the art!

At the same time these exhibitions were taking place, I was busy collecting the *Marilyn Monroe* screenprints. I kept them a secret from pretty much everyone. There were a couple of people who I trusted and wanted to tell about my discovery, but I decided not to ruin the surprise. I knew my friends were aware that I was up to *something*. I would like to take this opportunity to let them know how much I appreciate their respect for my privacy and to thank them here for not asking me any questions. I showed the *Marilyns* to the Andy Warhol Art Authentication Board in 2011 and 2012, plus a handful of trusted museum personnel and a senior specialist at a major auction house. The specialist at the auction house told me that I may have discovered Andy Warhol's first reversal piece and that the image of Marilyn used for my screenprints was the most desirable of all the images of Marilyn that Andy Warhol used. The first time I showed this specialist one of the fluorescent *Marilyn* prints, I asked them what they thought of it. Before they gave me their opinion, they asked me what I thought of it. I said that, in my opinion, one day people would stand in line to see it. We are about to see if I was right.

This catalogue documents my discovery of the *Marilyn Monroe* screenprints, which are exhibited in public for the first time at the same institution where, in 1965, Andy Warhol had his first solo museum exhibition in the United States *(Fig. 2.3)*. Based on recorded conversations with people who worked for the Moderna Museet in Stockholm and the advertising agency used by the museum at the time, the *Marilyn Monroe* screenprints were produced by the Moderna Museet for Andy Warhol's first one-person public museum exhibition in Europe, which took place at the Moderna Museet in 1968, from February 10 to March 17. Why the

screenprints were not exhibited remains a mystery. I have theorized that it was either because of copyright problems or the prints themselves were a Plan B of sorts. In other words, had the paintings and prints that Andy Warhol produced in the United States not arrived in time for the opening of the exhibition, these *Marilyn Monroe* prints that were printed in Sweden would have been pressed into service. Instead, the prints sat practically unknown for nearly fifty years. Some were framed. One was tacked to a wall with pushpins. Most of the *Marilyn* prints were simply tucked away for safekeeping. I would like to give credit to all the previous owners for maintaining them in such excellent condition. The prints came from approximately nineteen different sources. Most were individuals, some of whom have asked to remain anonymous. The first cache of prints that surfaced was accidentally discovered by a friend of the John Melin family who was cleaning out a storage locker. (Reva Wolf notes elsewhere in this volume that Melin was the designer of the 1968 Moderna Museet Warhol exhibition catalogue and the seven type posters printed to promote the exhibition, including one with a line for which Warhol is famous: "In the future everyone will be world famous for fifteen minutes.")

That is where I came into the picture. Börje Bengtsson *(Fig. B.3)*, an art dealer based in Landskrona, Sweden, from whom I had been buying art and signed ephemera for years, sent me a list of items that he had for sale. On this list was a description of one of these prints. The moment I read the description, my curiosity was piqued, and I sent him an email asking for a photo and more information about it. In his reply, Börje described the circumstances under which it was found. The story sounded like the Da Vinci Code or, should I say, the "Warhol Code."

Are the *Marilyns* masterpieces or, more specifically, masterpieces by a group of masters? Based on the evidence, I believe the *Marilyns* are a collaboration between Andy Warhol, Pontus Hultén, John Melin, Arne Wahlqvist, and perhaps other individuals whose involvement has been lost to time.

Speaking of collaborations, the act of collecting these 323 screenprints was also a collaboration. In the beginning of this adventure neither Börje nor I had any idea that there were approximately 300 more *Marilyns* waiting to be brought back together. We spent the next twelve years hunting them down as I recognized that this was a once in a lifetime opportunity. I am very proud of the fact that we were able to reunite the *Marilyns*. I must say that without the loyalty and support of both Börje Bengtsson and Bengt Andersson, this reunion would never have happened.

Additionally, the collaboration with the University of Pennsylvania has been extremely rewarding and enjoyable. Everyone at Penn recognized the significance of the collection and treated it and me with the utmost respect. After offering to host the exhibition and symposium, Penn went on to assemble a team of experts to write this catalogue and to invite a group of world-renowned experts to participate in the symposium. Along with designing the layout of the galleries with David McKnight and Brittany Merriam, one of my favorite parts was writing the titles of the overall project and the exhibition with Reva, Ruth Sutton, and Mary Ellen Burd. My experience working for an advertising agency in New York City for over twenty years came in handy here. I was very pleased with the title of the overall project, *Andy Warhol @ Penn Again*, and the title of the Marilyn exhibition, *Out of Sight: An Art Collector, A Discovery, and Andy Warhol*. Not having a master's degree or a Ph.D. like many of the people with whom I worked, I would like to think that my DNA allowed me to hold my own with all these very accomplished academics and administrators.

In closing, I would like to take this opportunity to thank the people who recognized the importance of my collection. First, I would to thank everyone at Penn, past and present: Amy Gutmann, Sean Quimby, Will Noel, David McKnight, Eric Dillalogue, Hannah Muckle, Matthew E. Pilecki, Mary Ellen Burd, Sarah Reidell, Elizabeth McDermott, Katherine Aid, Elizabeth T. Bates, Hannah Bennett, Ruth Sutton, Matt Neff, Brittany Merriam, Libby Saylor, and Lynn Smith Dolby. They had the foresight and courage to exhibit a previously unknown collection brought to them by a practically unknown collector. Me. Where do I start when it comes to thanking Reva Wolf for all her brilliant observations and hard work. I would like to let her know that I still cannot believe that I had the opportunity to be interviewed by a Warhol scholar of her stature. I would also like to thank Maureen McCormick of Atelier Fine Art Services (former Chief Registrar of the Princeton University Art Museum) for being my registrar and

making me look so good; her checklists were masterpieces unto themselves. Thank you again for putting up with my umpteen questions and silly jokes. Finally, I would like to thank Andy Warhol, Edie Sedgwick, and Marilyn Monroe whose superstardom allowed me to have my fifteen minutes of fame. Thank you again everyone.

The last thing I would like to share is my vision of how I think the *Marilyns* should one day be put on permanent display. In my opinion, they should either be exhibited in a museum built specifically for them or they should be housed in the wing of a major museum. The experience of seeing all of them displayed together would be truly "out of sight!"

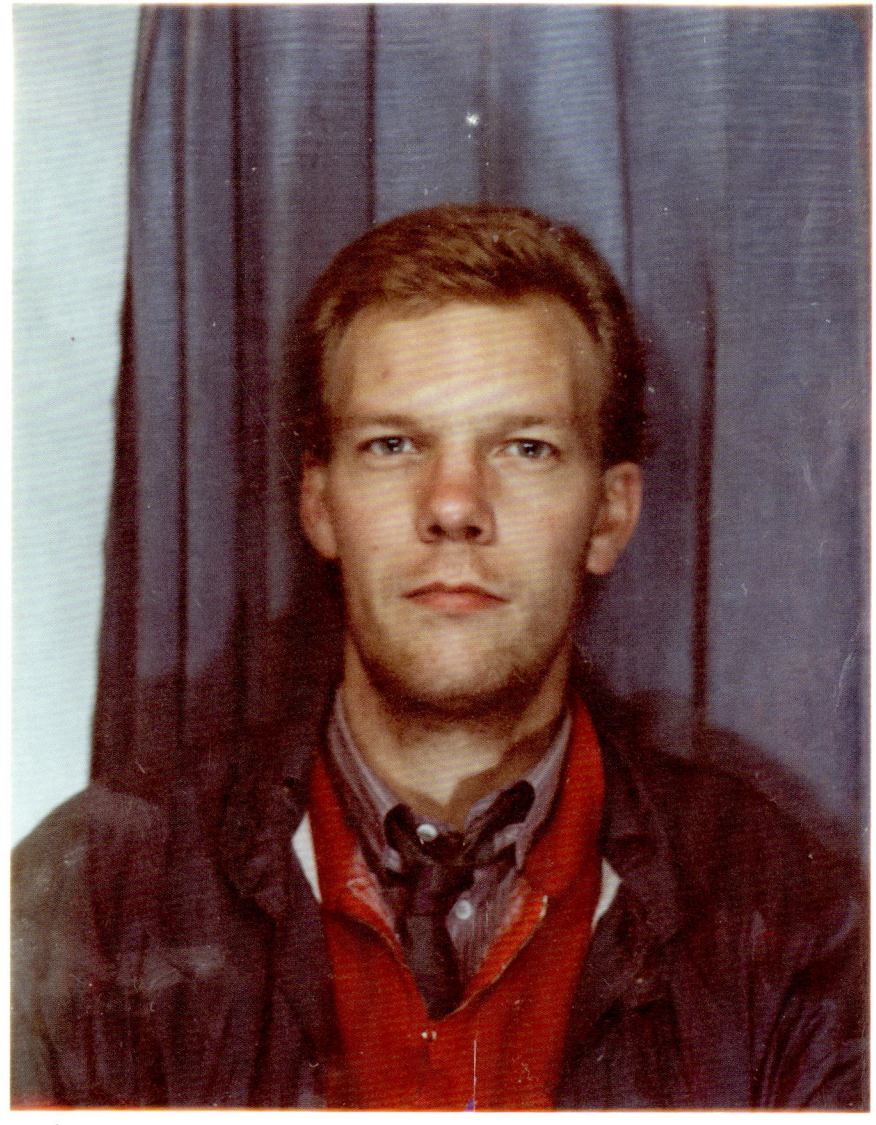

Figure B.3   Börge Bengtsson. Photograph by Andy Warhol. 4 ½ x 3 ½ in.
Image used with permission.

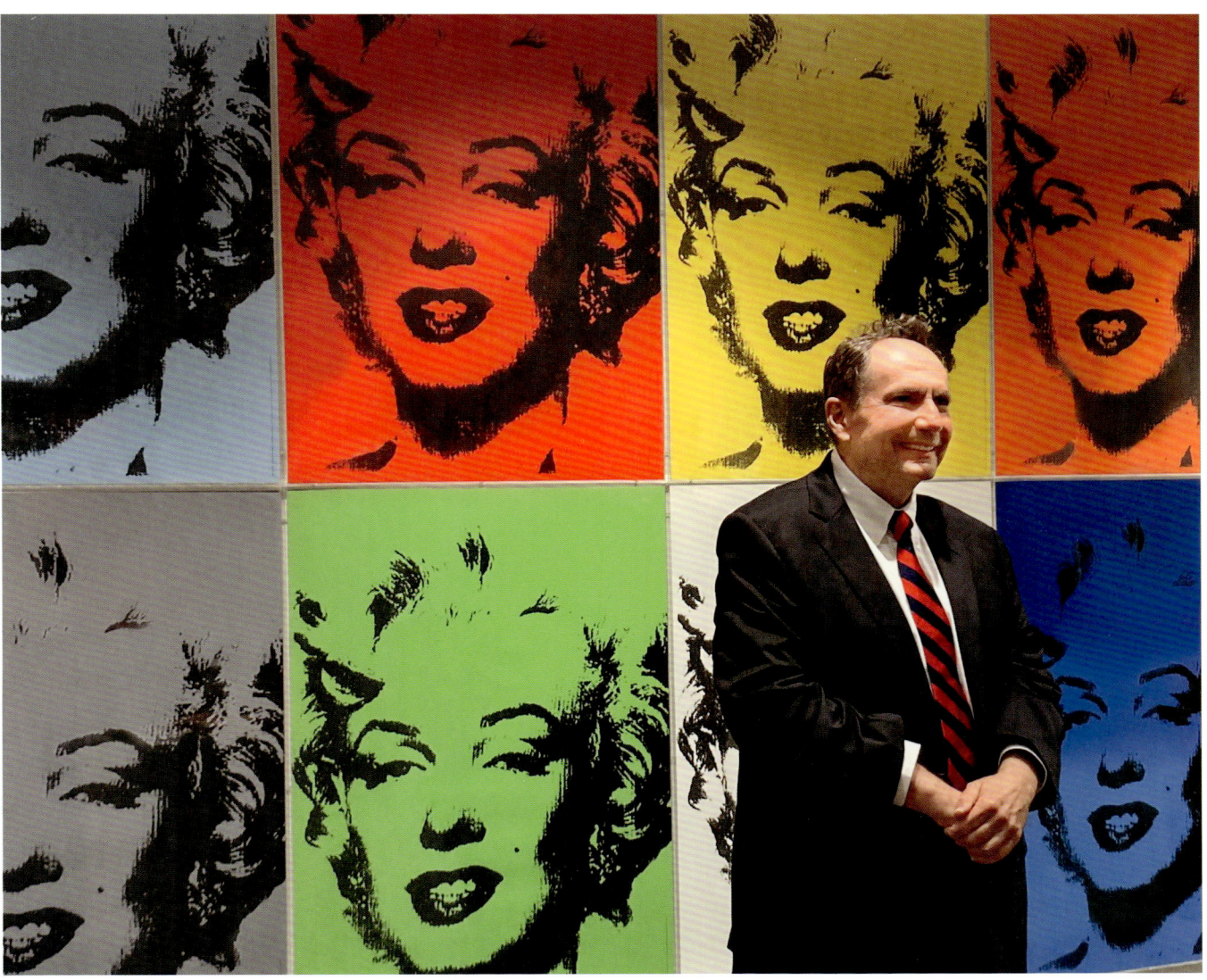

Figure B.4   Collector Gregory McCoy standing in front of a grid of his *Marilyn* screenprints at the opening of the *Out of Sight* exhibition, May 19, 2022. Photograph © Lynn Smith Dolby.

Contributor Biographies

Hannah Bennett is currently the Director of Columbia University's Avery Architectural and Art Library. Prior to Columbia, Bennett served for more than four years at the University of Pennsylvania Libraries where she oversaw three divisions–the Fisher Fine Arts Library, the Penn Museum Library, and the Music Library–as well as the Materials Library and Common Press Letterpress Studies. Prior to Penn, Bennett served as the Librarian for Princeton University's School of Architecture Library, which was preceded by appointments as Assistant Director for Collections & Research at Yale University's Haas Family Arts Library and, earlier, as Research Librarian at the Ryerson & Burnham Libraries at the Art Institute of Chicago. Bennett received her Master of Library Science from the University of Illinois at Champaign-Urbana and a Master of Arts in Medieval Studies at University of York in England.

Kenneth Goldsmith is an American poet and critic. He is the founding editor of UbuWeb and since 2020 is the ongoing artist-in-residence at the Center for Programs in Contemporary Writing (CPCW) at the University of Pennsylvania, where he teaches. He is also a senior editor of *PennSound* at the University of Pennsylvania. He hosted a weekly radio show at WFMU from 1995 until June 2010. He has published ten books of poetry, notably *Fidget* (2000), *Soliloquy* (2001), *Day* (2003), and his American trilogy, *The Weather* (2005), *Traffic* (2007), and *Sports* (2008). He is the author of three books of essays, *Uncreative Writing: Managing Language in the Digital Age* (2011), *Wasting Time on the Internet* (2016), and *Duchamp Is My Lawyer: The Polemics, Pragmatics, and Poetics of UbuWeb* (2020). In 2013, he was appointed the Museum of Modern Art's first poet laureate.

Maureen McCormick is Director of Registration at Atelier Fine Art Services, Philadelphia. McCormick joined Atelier after more than twenty-five years at the Princeton University Art Museum, Princeton, New Jersey, as Chief Registrar and Manager of Collections Services. For the past six years she has worked closely with Gregory McCoy as collection manager and cataloguer of his collection of Marilyn Monroe screenprints and related works. McCormick received her Master of Fine Arts from the Tyler School of Art of Temple University, Philadelphia, where she studied printmaking and photography. She remains a working artist but now paints icons in the manner of medieval Russia and is an Affiliate Instructor for the Prosopon School of Iconology, and is Trinity Church, Princeton's Iconographer in Residence.

Gregory McCoy worked for twenty years at an advertising agency in New York City where he won multiple gold awards for his writing and art direction. Starting as an art director, he was ultimately made the VP of Print Production and Senior Art Buyer. Gregory's art education includes the School of Visual Arts and The Barnes Foundation. He has been collecting Andy Warhol's artwork and signed ephemera for thirty years. Gregory has held Warhol exhibitions at the Arts Council of Princeton, The Lawrenceville School, and the Moorestown Library. He appeared on the television show *Buried Treasure* hosted by the Keno brothers from *Antiques Roadshow*.

David McKnight is the Director of the Annenberg Rare Book and Manuscript Library at the University of Pennsylvania Libraries. Mr. McKnight possesses a BA in Classics and History (McGill University, Montreal, 1985), an MLIS (McGill University, Montreal, 1992), and an MA in English Literature (Concordia University, Montreal, 1993). Prior to Penn, McKnight worked for McGill University Libraries for fifteen years. Recently he curated two major exhibitions, *Experiment: Printing the Canadian*

Imagination (Bruce Peel Centre, University of Alberta, 2018) and *Wise Men Fished Here: A Centenary Exhibition in Honor of the Gotham Book Mart: 1920 – 2020* (Kislak Center for Special Collections, 2019). In 2021, McKnight co-edited *Cross-Cultural Pound* (Clemson University Press, 2021) with John G. Gery and Walter Baumann.

Reva Wolf is Professor of Art History at the State University of New York at New Paltz. She teaches and writes about art of the eighteenth century to the present. She is the author of *Goya and the Satirical Print* (Godine, 1991) and *Andy Warhol, Poetry, and Gossip in the 1960s* (Chicago, 1997), and is co-editor of *Freemasonry and the Visual Arts from the Eighteenth Century Forward* (Bloomsbury, 2020). Her recent work focuses on methodology, the reception of art, Freemasonry and art, and other aspects of the social history of art. She has held fellowships at the Metropolitan Museum of Art, Harvard University, the Institute for Advanced Study, Princeton, and the Center for Advanced Study in the Visual Arts (CASVA), National Gallery of Art, Washington, DC. She was a 2010–11 recipient of the State University of New York Chancellor's Award for Excellence in Teaching.

List of Figures and Tables

Figure 1.1   *Andy Warhol*, Exhibition catalogue page opening | p. 14
Figure 1.2   Photograph, Andy Warhol and Pontus Hultén | p. 17
Figure 1.3   Photograph of exterior of the Moderna Museet, 1968 | p. 17
Figure 2.1   *Daily Pennsylvanian* | p. 25
Figure 2.2   Photograph, Interior of Fisher Fine Arts Library | p. 27
Figure 2.3   Photograph of Lallie Lloyd | p. 27
Figure 2.4   Photograph of Andy Warhol and Edie Sedgwick | p. 28
Figure 2.5   *Daily Pennsylvanian* | p. 29
Figure 2.6   *Penn Comment* | p. 31
Figure 3.1   Andy Warhol, *Dollar Sign*, 1981 | p. 34
Figure 3.2   Andy Warhol, *Dollar Sign*, 1982 | p. 35
Figure 3.3   Leo Castelli Andy Warhol Gallery poster | p. 36
Figure 3.4   Leo Castelli Gallery Andy Warhol exhibition announcement | p. 37
Figure 3.5   Leo Castelli Andy Warhol exhibition announcement | p. 37
Figure 3.6   Invitation to The Lawrenceville School exhibition: dinner roll signed by Andy Warhol, ca. 1971 | p. 37
Figure 3.7   Image from *Penn Comment* article | p. 40
Figure 3.8   Marilyn Monroe poster | p. 41
Figure 3.9   Damien Hirst, *Untitled* [skull balloon] | p. 42
Figure 3.10   *Campbell's Soup Can* mug | p. 42
Figure 3.11   Irving Blum advertisement | p. 45
Figure 3.12   Andy Warhol, Moderna Museet exhibition catalogue, 1968 | p. 45
Figure 3.13   Andy Warhol, *SAS Passenger Ticket* | p. 46
Figure 3.14   The Poster Center | p. 46
Figure 3.15   Photograph of Gregory McCoy | p. 47
Figure 3.16   Andy Warhol, *Mao Wallpaper*, 1974 | p. 50
Figure 3.17   Photograph of Gregory McCoy | p. 50
Figure 3.18   Installation view of the 1965 Andy Warhol ICA exhibition | p. 50
Figure 3.19   Photograph depicting the crowd scene at the ICA preview in October 1965 | p. 51
Figure 3.20   Photograph of Andy Warhol | p. 51
Figure 4.1   Photograph of the exterior of the Moderna Museet | p. 56
Figure 4.2   Andy Warhol, *Ten-Foot Flowers*, 1967 | p. 56
Figure 4.3   Photograph interior view of Moderna Museet exhibition gallery | p. 57
Figure 4.4   Andy Warhol, *Electric Chair*, 1967 | p. 57
Figure 4.5   Photograph interior view of Moderna Museet gallery | p. 58
Figure 4.6   Photograph interior view of Moderna Museet gallery | p. 58
Figure 4.7   Letter from John H. Loeb, Brillo Company, to Kasper König, July 7, 1967 | p. 61
Figure 4.8   *Marilyn*, Lac print | p. 64
Figure 4.9   Poster designed by John Melin and Anders Österlin | p. 65
Figure 4.10   Photograph by Gene Korman | p. 67
Figure 4.11   Andy Warhol, *Marilyn Monroe in Black and White (Twenty-Five Marilyns)*, 1962 | p. 68
Figure 4.12   Details of inscriptions on three *Marilyn* prints | p. 68

Figure 4.13   Andy Warhol, *Marilyn Monroe*, 1962 | p. 69
Figure 4.14   Andy Warhol, *Marilyn Monroe*, 1964 | p. 70
Figure 4.15   Andy Warhol, *Marilyn Monroe*, 1964 | p. 70
Figure 4.16   Andy Warhol, *Marilyn Monroe*, 1964 | p. 71
Figure 4.17   Photograph of Andy Warhol exhibition catalogue cover | p. 74
Figure 4.18   *Andy Warhol: Screens, Films, Boxes and a Book, 1968*, exhibition invitation | p. 75
Figure 4.19   Statements by Andy Warhol in *Andy Warhol*, 1968 | p. 75
Figure 4.20   Andy Warhol, *Dollar Bills* | p. 78
Figure 4.21   Andy Warhol, *Dollar Bills* | p. 78
Figure 4.22   Andy Warhol, *Dollar Bills* | p. 79
Figure 4.23   Photograph of the cover of *Blanderen* (1954) | p. 80
Figure 4.24   Marcel Duchamp, *Rotorelief*, 1935/1959 | p. 80
Figure 5.1   Photograph, *Marilyn Acetate 1*, 1964 | p. 92
Table 1   Paper or Support Type by Color | p. 95
Table 2   Ink Color Prints with Inscription | p. 95
Table 3   Ink Colors | p. 95
Table 4   Ink Color Prints, No Inscription | p. 95
Figure 5.2   John Melin, poster for Moderna Museet exhibition, 1970 | p. 97
Figure 5.3   John Melin, poster for Boda Nova exhibition, 1972 | p. 97
Figure 5.4   AWMM.1968.298 | p. 98
Figure 5.5   AWMM.1968.189 | p. 99
Figure 5.6   Three proposed images used as base image for the McCoy *Marilyns* | p. 101
Figure 5.7   Photograph, Eugene Korman, *Marilyn Monroe*, 1952 | p. 101
Figure 5.8   Detail of Andy Warhol, *Twenty-Five Marilyns in Black and White*, 1962 | p. 101
Figure 5.9   *Andy Warhol* (Stockholm: Moderna Museet, 1968) | p. 102
Figure 5.10   Invitation to opening of Andy Warhol exhibition, Moderna Museet, 1968, recto | p. 102
Figure 5.11   Invitation to opening of Andy Warhol exhibition, Moderna Museet, 1968, verso | p. 102
Figure 5.12   AWMM.1968.242 | p. 103
Figure 5.13   AWMM.1968.242 | p. 103
Figure A.1   McCoy purchases of his *Marilyn* screenprints | p. 192
Figure A.2   Key to owners | p. 193
Figure A.3   Andy Warhol Authentication Board Letter, 2011 | p. 194
Figure A.4   Andy Warhol Authentication Board Letter, 2012 | p. 195
Figure A.5   Orion Analytical LCC, Ink Analysis Report, 2012 | p. 196-197
Figure A.6   Williamstown Art Conservation Center, Inc., Paper Analysis Report, 2017 | p. 198-199
Figure A.7   Results of Raman Spectra Graph, Williamstown Art Conservation Center, 2017 | p. 200
Figure B.1   Andy Warhol, *Double Mona Lisa*, 1978. Image used with permission | p. 203
Figure B.2   Gregory McCoy on the set of *Buried Treasures*, 2011 | p. 203
Figure B.3   Börge Bengtsson | p. 206
Figure B.4   Collector Gregory McCoy at the opening of the *Out of Sight* exhibition | p. 207

Permissions

I would like to thank the following individuals for granting permission to use images in this catalogue. Every effort has been made to identify the copyright holder.

Broc Blegen, Castelli Gallery, for the use of images on pages 36 and 37.

James Duffin, University Archives, University of Pennsylvania, for use of images on pages 31 and 40.

Christine Knooren, *Daily Pennsylvanian*, for the use of images on page 25 and 29.

Christopher Lippa, Penn Libraries, for the use of images on pages 87–90.

Gregory McCoy for the use of images on pages 34, 35, 37, 41, 42, 45–47, 50, 64, 68, 75, 97–99, 102, and 103.

Joanna Smith for the use of the image on page 203.

Lynn Smith Dolby for the use of the image on page 207.

Stefan Ståhle, Moderna Museet, for the use of images on pages 14, 17, 45, 56–58, 61, 68–71, 74, 75, 78–80, 101, and 102.

Kim Tischler Rosen, Artists Rights Society, for the use of images on pages 42 and 80.

Paloma Torres, The Lawrenceville School, for the use of the image on page 47.

William Whitaker, Architectural Archives, University of Pennsylvania, for the use of images on pages 27 and 28.

Images in the public domain or under license appear on pages 45, 46, 67, 100, and 203.

Acknowledgments

David McKnight

I would like to thank the following for their contributions to the *Andy Warhol @ Penn* exhibition: Katherine Aide; Patrik Lars Andersson; Atelier Art Services; Elizabeth Bates; Börje Bengtsson; Hannah Bennett; Erik Beranek; Walter Biggins; Brilliant Graphics; Constantia Constantinou; Eric Dillalogue; Lynn Smith Dolby; Suzanne Donohue; Sam Duplessis; Lynne Farrington; Janice Fisher; Drummond Framing; Mary Francis; Leo Gearin; Kenneth Goldsmith; Andrea Gottschalk; David Hales; Bart Johnson; Claire Kincaide; Zoe Kovacs; Chris Lippa, Maureen McCormick; Gregory McCoy; Elizabeth McDermott; Brittany Merriam; Hannah Muckle; David Nerenberg; William G. Noel; Gitte Ørskou; Mick Overgard; Peter Philbin; Matt Pilecki; John Pollack; Sean Quimby; Sarah Reidell; H. Carton Rogers, III; SCETI; Joanna Smith; Claire Squires; Stefan Ståhle; Ruth Sutton; Bob Tursack; Dustin Tursack; William Whitaker; Reva Wolf; and Kenneth Zeferes. Special thanks to Libby Saylor, who arrived on the scene at the right moment. And as always, Lillian Eyre.

Maureen McCormick

I am grateful to Julia Bunn, Associate Registrar at Atelier Fine Art Services, who assisted me throughout the cataloguing process, offered insights, and acted as chief sounding board, and to Derek Jones and all my AFAS colleagues for their support and friendship. I am of course especially indebted to Gregory McCoy for entrusting me with the care and feeding of this remarkable collection, and to David McKnight for inviting my participation in this catalogue.